The Music of
Brahms

Michael Musgrave

CLARENDON PRESS · OXFORD

1994

Oxford University Press, Walton Street, Oxford OX2 6DP

Oxford New York Toronto
Delhi Bombay Calcutta Madras Karachi
Kuala Lumpur Singapore Hong Kong Tokyo
Nairobi Dar es Salaam Cape Town
Melbourne Auckland Madrid
and associated companies in
Berlin Ibadan

Oxford is a trade mark of Oxford University Press

Published in the United States
by Oxford University Press Inc., New York

British Library Cataloguing in Publication Data
Data available

ISBN 0–19–816401–7

Library of Congress Cataloging in Publication Data
Musgrave, Michael, 1942–
The music of Brahms / Michael Musgrave.
Originally published: London; Boston; Routledge & Kegan Paul,
1985, in series: Companions to the great composers.
Includes bibliographical references (p.   ) and index.
1. Brahms, Johannes, 1833–1897—Criticism and interpretation.
I. Title.
ML410.B8M87   1994   780'.92—dc20   93–37235
ISBN 0–19–816401–7

10 9 8 7 6 5 4 3 2 1

Printed in Great Britain
on acid-free paper by
Bookcraft Ltd.,
Midsomer Norton, Avon

f11-95

The Music of

Brahms

To the memory of my father

Contents

List of Plates

List of Figures

Acknowledgements

To the Archiv of the Gesellschaft der Musikfreunde in Wien for kind permission to reproduce the illustrations Nos. 1–5 and those at pages 28 and 77 and on the cover, and to its Director, Dr Otto Biba, and his staff for their great assistance in my dealing with its unique Brahms holdings.

To Dr Anthea Baird and the staff of the Music Library of the University of London, Senate House, for their helpful assistance with many and varied queries.

To Goldsmiths' College, University of London, for financial assistance in the course of my research.

To the Music Library of the Staats- und Universitätsbibliothek, Hamburg, for reproduction of illustration No. 7.

To Ludwig Doblinger (B. Hermansky) K.G., Wien, for kind permission to reproduce Ex. 21.

To Universal Edition (Alfred A. Kalmus Ltd) for kind permission to reproduce Exx. 53 and 78.

To the Allgemeine Musikgesellschaft, Zurich, and Zentralbibliothek, Zurich, for kind permission to reproduce illustration No. 6.

To Dr F. W. Sternfeld of the University of Oxford, for his time and his guidance of my early work on Brahms.

To Dr Imogen Fellinger of the Preussischer Kultur-Besitz, Berlin, for identifying the photograph which appears as illustration No. 8, and for obtaining Dr Wolfgang Fellinger's kind permission to reproduce it.

To Tabitha Collingbourne, for preparing the music examples.

Finally, to my fellow Brahmsian, Dr Robert Pascall of the University of Nottingham, for access to the above photograph and for his selfless encouragement, help and friendship over many years. I can only hope that he does not find that this volume offers too inadequate an approach to the great subject which he knows so well.

Michael Musgrave

Part One

1

An Introduction to Brahms and his Early Music

Unlike the observer of the centenary of Brahms's birth in 1933, the witness of the sesquicentenary year of 1983 might well have been familiar with different views of the composer's significance. The first – long-established and still the most familiar in the English-speaking world – portrays him as the great classic figure of nineteenth-century German music, a retrospective master of traditional forms in a period when they seemed increasingly outmoded by new aesthetic attitudes: a figure of the past. Thus Gerald Abraham summed him up as follows just before the Second World War: 'So . . . great a figure as he is, Brahms contributed little to the historical development of music [and he] stands practically alone. [Those] who came under his influence all seem to have been nonentities. Only the young Reger and the Hungarian Dohnányi really owe much to him.'[1] The years after the war have seen, however, a rather contrasted attitude: that of Brahms as a 'progressive', a pioneering individualist who, behind a conventional aesthetic surface, actually made a profound contribution to the very essence of musical language.

The first view was already very well established in Brahms's lifetime when the dialectics of nineteenth-century musical politics placed him squarely as the opponent of Wagner, albeit in a situation to which he had in some way contributed through his opposition to Liszt. This view was reinforced with the radical changes of taste which occurred at the turn of the century, when Brahms's very greatness as a craftsman became the object of scorn for the threat it posed to the advancement of art in the eyes of the more partisan 'progressives'. To the growing cleavage between the proponents of a 'progressive' philosophy of the relation of the arts and those who resisted the devaluation of traditional forms already focused on the Leipzig school before his appearance, Brahms came to be the inevitable symbol for the conservative camp; deeply interested in the past, suspicious of verbalizations on music, and gifted to a degree which was never questioned, even by his worst enemies. In his own words, he unwillingly became an 'anti-pope',[2] though he made no later attempt to influence developments through any means other than the power of his music. With his death in 1897, the ever-simplifying perspective solidified into the view of his position to which Abraham gave expression for later generations.

With the inevitable reaction which led a younger generation receptive to both Brahms and Wagner to seek to reassert his importance, an equally extreme view was posited. Writing in 1947, the radical Schoenberg sought to 'prove that Brahms, the classicist, the academician, was a great innovator in the realm of musical language, that, in fact, he was a great progressive'.[3] With the dissemination of Schoenberg's writings in English since the war, this view has gained increasing currency, so that what must have appeared a very conjectural aside in 1938 – Abraham's 'a good case might be made out for Schoenberg as the reconciler of Brahms and Wagner' – [4] would today be accepted as a natural relationship of musical history.

Like all historical generalizations, however, the reasoning behind these once-binding attitudes rings strangely hollow to later generations. The whole notion of 'progressiveness' so central to nineteenth-century thinking seems outmoded in a culture which has increasingly sought renewal through reference to its past and the pasts of other cultures. Indeed, the 'progressiveness' of which Schoenberg speaks seems to point much more to his own compositional predilections than to the facets which more broadly reveal Brahms's as a prophetic figure, someone arguing through his art for values – or only the restoration of values – which, castigated in his time, have become part of the modern musical world. For surely the most striking feature of music since the end of the Romantic era has been the rapidly spreading knowledge of, and desire to make creative relation with, the music of the past. So natural is this assumption to the modern musician that it is difficult to grasp the concept of originality which led Wagner so to criticize Brahms for its presence in his music. Brahms seems a much less reactionary figure today than he seemed to the nineteenth century: indeed his vast knowledge of earlier music presents him rather as a figure of continuity, a renewer of traditions which have remained vital to the present day. As is often acknowledged, Brahms literally made music out of the past and this relationship accounts for some of his music's greatest poignancy of effect. Yet, as Schoenberg was at pains to stress, 'he did not live on inherited fortune; he made one of his own'.[5] It is against this background – that of a language which richly relates to the past yet also looks to the future – that this book is written.

Some of the stimulus towards the view of Brahms as a conservative undoubtedly comes from the outward image of his life. Despite his prominence, Brahms kept apart from the aesthetic battles of the day to a remarkable degree. Only in his contribution to the Manifesto, directed against the New Germans in 1860, did he enter the public debate – and with unfortunate results. Whatever his part in this venture, the background to which is still unclear, it served as a focus for the developing rift in attitudes and created a situation which the older composer came to regret. Brahms's silence, not least in relation to Wagner's increasing aggression towards him, led those outside to imagine that he supported the views of his circle, notably Hanslick and Kalbeck, who kept up stiff resistance to the acceptance of Wagner in Vienna. In fact Brahms was more frequently at odds with them in matters aesthetic than with Wagner, whom he admired and respected as a musician. Yet Wagner's life-style and endless verbalizing were anathema to Brahms, and in his very simple tastes and desired pattern of life is to be found an image at odds with that of the romantic artist.

Born in Hamburg, Brahms desired from his early years a secure professional position in his native city, and it was with some bitterness that he finally left for Vienna in the autumn of 1862 to make a new life. Many years later, in 1894 when he was offered the directorship of the Hamburg Philharmonic Concerts, his reply made his feelings clear: 'There is not much that I have desired so long and so ardently in its time – that is, however, at the right time. It has taken a long time for me to get used to the idea of having to go along other paths. If things had gone according to my wishes, I would perhaps celebrate an anniversary with you today.'[6] The other paths were to involve professional appointments – first with the Wiener Singakademie, though only for a season, 1863–4, later the coveted position of director of the concerts of the Musikverein, for the seasons of 1872–1875. His only other 'permanent' positions were as piano teacher and choral conductor at the little ducal court of Lippe-Detmold, before the move to Vienna, from 1857 to 1859 and conductor of his Hamburg Frauenchor from 1859 to 1862. There seems little doubt that marriage and children were part of Brahms's own image of himself as a successful composer. He loved women, he loved children and he loved to be part of the domestic life of his friends at holiday times. In later years he admitted to Widmann, 'I missed my chance. When I still had the urge, I was unable to offer a woman what would have been the right thing . . . at the time that I was still willing to get married, my compositions were received with hisses or icy silence.'[7]

Yet the continuation of this letter suggests another aspect, perhaps a more realistic view of Brahms's nature:

> Now I was perfectly able to put up with this because I knew exactly what they were worth and that the picture would eventually change. And when I returned to my lonely lodgings after such failures, I was by no means discouraged. On the contrary! But if at such moments I had had to face a wife's anxiously questioning eyes . . . And if she had tried to console me – a wife's commiseration for her husband's failure – bah, I can't think what a hell on earth that would have been.

The price was too high. For there existed another side to Brahms: the desire for escape, for freedom, for complete creative independence with no responsibility save to himself and his muse. Infatuation was frequent with him, yet he never became inextricably involved, not even with Agathe von

Siebold, the daughter of a Göttingen professor to whom he became engaged briefly and whose name he enshrined in the String Sextet in G, where the notes A G A H E ring out at bars 162–8. 'Here is where I tore myself free of my last love,' he said to Gänsbacher.[8] Yet, this passage hardly seems to ring with disappointment: on the contrary, the reiterated phrase seems liberated in its effect. Undoubtedly, however, a major factor in inhibiting any permanent relationships was Brahms's feelings towards Clara Schumann. It seems clear that he was strongly drawn towards her well before Schumann's death as well as after. Although he sought to ensure that his letters did not survive – they agreed to exchange in 1887 and he threw many into the Rhine (though Clara, fortunately, was not as ruthless) – one passage of a surviving letter to Joachim (suppressed in the original published correspondence because of its nature) makes his feelings clear. He wrote in June 1854,

> I believe I do not respect and admire her so much as I love her and am under her spell. Often I must forcibly restrain myself from just quietly putting my arms around her and even – I don't know, it seems to me so natural that she would not take it ill. I think I can no longer love a young girl. At least I have quite forgotten about them. They but promise heaven while Clara reveals it to us.[9]

Brahms was then just twenty-one, Clara, almost thirty-five.

His feelings never changed, despite misunderstandings and tensions on both sides. He admired Clara as a woman and as an artist, and recognized in her the same qualities of idealism, nobility and humanity which were so strong in his own nature. That they never married must have been due, among many other factors, to their essential independence as individuals. They needed each other in one sense, but they had to keep their distance in another. Yet Clara was always there for Brahms, chiding him for his frequent infatuations with younger women – he even wanted to propose to her daughter Julie, whom she promptly married off – or being markedly cool towards the one woman whose artistic sensitivity created an additional bond in his affections: Elizabeth von Herzogenberg. This highly cultured daughter of a Leipzig professor who died aged forty-four, met Brahms in 1876 and thereafter maintained, with her husband, a regular correspondence in which she revealed an insight into his music comparable with that of Clara – indeed, she was more progressive, less pedantic in taste, and her husband, though an uninspired composer, was deeply knowledgeable about church music, especially Bach. Her early death shook Brahms, but not as much as that of Clara four years later in 1896, from which his own rapid decline cannot perhaps be disassociated. Brahms had always enjoyed the best of health, and his energy and vigour, not least on his walking tours, was the envy of friends who anticipated for him a much fuller span than his sixty three years from May 1833 to April 1897.

Loneliness and stoic reflectiveness have long been part of the Brahmsian picture. That he thought deeply and needed his solitude is true: but that was a part of his nature with which he came to terms. There were many other sides, reflected in a host of friendships and a very busy creative life which involved performing, editing, studying, travel – indeed, a life so full that it is difficult to see how he could easily have harmonized it with family life. For if its outward pattern was uneventful, Brahms's private life was rich in cultural interests and in the world of ideas. Although his regular education had ceased by the age of fourteen, and he came from humbler circumstances than any great musical contemporary, Brahms gained by the end of his life an enviable reputation for his culture and a firm place in the most educated circles of Vienna.[10] Much has naturally been made of the relationship between the virtual poverty of the background – Brahms's father was a very lowly orchestral player – and the rigour of his self-education. His irascible public manner was seen as defensiveness and his bachelorhood attributed to misogyny inspired by a comment to Billroth on his youthful impressions as a dance-pianist in dockland bars. Yet Brahms also spoke warmly of his family background and retained a close relationship with family, seeming to hold his experience in a mature perspective. Of his later life-style, the relationship with Billroth – the pioneering Viennese surgeon – might be taken as indicative. Billroth was obsessed with music and was a dedicated amateur player, his home becoming the focus for the first performances of many Brahms chamber works. But their correspondence reveals the remarkable range of their interests, naturally scientific as well as artistic. Brahms's library gives a fuller view of this world, with 850 titles of non-musical works – German literature and drama and foreign works in translation being central – quite apart from over 2000 volumes of music or studies of music;[11] and this is without the facilities of public libraries, which he used lavishly. Although Brahms was never associated with the organized church, he had an especially keen knowledge of scripture and maintained an interest in matters religious, as, for example, through his connection with J. V. Widmann, a prominent Swiss literary figure, who was also a pastor. Brahms's knowledge of the Luther Bible was intimate. Moreover, he reveals a remarkably scholarly bent in the volumes of his library. Many are carefully marked, errors seeded out and variant readings noted with cross references. Prominent are books on art and travel – he was a keen walker and sightseer, subjects which found particular accord in his many visits to Italy.

But the interests were not only scholarly. Brahms was a keen observer of the current scene, political as well as cultural. His patriotism is well known, though it was ultimately rooted in a cultural sense. He took particular interest in the contemporary theatre and, according to Widmann, 'never missed the first performance of anything significant', apparently possessing a keen dramatic sense and capacity to understand a plot and its potential.[12] Nor was he averse to new music, following events closely, not least in the Wagnerian sphere. Wagner was the subject of endless debate in his circle, and he knew the music dramas well, claiming with every reason to be 'the best of Wagnerians' and criticizing his circle for their lack of understanding. Even with the music of Bruckner and Wolf, to which he was particularly averse, he became acquainted, possessing scores of the Seventh and Eighth Symphonies, the Te Deum and the cantata *Heligoland*, as well as the *Mörike Lieder*. Where he approved, he could be unstinting in praise, as of Verdi's *Requièm*, which he knew only in score and on this basis stood in opposition to Bülow, or, particularly, Bizet's *Carmen*, undoubtedly his favourite modern work.

However, isolated examples aside, he stood temperamentally apart from most of what went on in his latter years, especially the consequences of what he described as the 'misunderstood' Wagner. His world was centrally that of the Viennese classics, and anything which might enrich it as a foundation for original work. He seems to have had a sober understanding of his own abilities – and a very positive one in the earlier years. Like many contemporaries, Goldmark recalls his sharpness in the belief in his own abilities, though seeing them in the broader context of his historical allegiances. In difficult rehearsals of one of the orchestral Serenades under Dessoff, he once exclaimed: 'Gentlemen, I know I'm not Beethoven, but I am Johannes Brahms.'[13] He compared his abilities with those of Cherubini, whom he greatly admired and whose fate as a neglected master he predicted of himself. It was to classical ideals of clarity and balance that he aspired, especially to Mozart: 'We can write no more with such beauty as Mozart did; so let us try to write with as much purity,' he is credited with saying in his last years.[14]

Yet, if there was one aspect of modern musical life which engaged Brahms continuously, it was the growing body of research into earlier music, especially German music of the Baroque and Renaissance, the fruits of which reached crucial stages during the span of his life, with the first complete editions of J. S. Bach, Handel, Palestrina, Lassus, Schütz, Couperin, as well as Mozart, Schubert, Beethoven and Schumann. Brahms came to know the leading scholars and played an important part in some of the work. For example, he edited, with Chrysander, the Couperin edition, wrote continuo realizations for the Italian duets and trios of the same editor's Handel edition, and made available his keen stylistic sense in the judgment of important issues; his views on the nature of Süssmayr's additions to the Mozart *Requièm* were included in the complete edition, and he even set himself in opposition to the leading Bach scholar Philipp Spitta in disputing the authenticity of the *St Luke Passion*, which is indeed today regarded as spurious[15]. From his earliest years he made manuscript copies from rare or obscure printed editions of old music, first in public libraries, later from the collections of friends in his growing circle. The Schumanns, for example, were keen students of 'early music' such as Bach and Palestrina, and encouraged Brahms, who had the run of Schumann's library from early 1854. By the end of his life Brahms had assembled a remarkable collection of manuscripts and printed editions of earlier music; some of the greatest treasures of the Vienna Musikverein library, among them the autographs of Mozart's late G minor Symphony and of the *Sun* quartets of Haydn, came from Brahms. But although there was an antiquarian aspect to his collecting, the chief thrust was creative. He studied to discover – and what he discovered he seems to have found much more fruitful than the musical developments of his own day. Something of the excitement with which he greeted new discoveries can be sensed in his response to the recent Schütz edition and the new *Denkmäler der Tonkunst* editions. 'What a luxuriant summer. A new volume of Schütz lies here; a [new one] of Bach is expected,' he wrote to Mandyczewski in 1892, and likewise declared of the first volume of the *Denkmäler der Tonkunst* series (Scheidt's *Tabulatura nova*): 'Do you not revel in contemplation of him and of his links to Bach. . .?'[16]

The creative stimulus was in turn directed to audiences and to his own work. In his first choral appointment at the court of Detmold from 1857–1859, he performed two Bach cantatas, *Christ lag in Todesbanden*, no. 4, and *Ich hatte viel Bekümmernis*, no. 21, from volumes 1 and 3 of the then new Bach Gesellschaft edition to which he soon became a subscriber, as well as the much more familiar *Messiah*. With the move to Vienna, however, he expressed his philosophy even more powerfully, performing from Winterfeld's pioneering *Johannes Gabrieli und sein Zeitalter* Schütz's *Saul Saul* and a Gabrieli *Benedictus* in twelve parts. Such works were much more obscure than the major choral works of Handel – even the Bach Passions – which had been reintroduced to Germany from 1829, notably by Mendelssohn. They proved too much for the Viennese audiences, though Brahms gained a respect which, together with his growing fame, supported the invitation to direct the Gesellschaft concerts from 1872 to 1875. The fruits of this work, together with the broader re-expression of the more direct tradition of the Viennese classics, were vital ingredients in the enrichment of language which we observe throughout Brahms's life. They also point very clearly to the modern world of historical study and creative response.

The depth of this integration poses the writer with considerable difficulties in approaching Brahms's complete output. For in his work there are no sudden changes of manner, no phases dominated by specific genres. The process is one of continuous integration and re-absorption of principles to new ends, and it is characterized by long consideration, endless revision and ruthless self-criticism. Experiments are there in plenty, but they have to be unearthed. Thus he wrote to Henschel of his attitude to a work: 'Let it rest, let it rest and keep going back to it and working it over and over again until it is completed as a finished work of art, until there is not a note too much or too little, not a bar you could improve upon. Whether it is beautiful also is another matter, but perfect it *must* be. You see, I am rather lazy, but I never cool down over a work until it is perfected, unassailable.'[17] His work must therefore be approached rather through the creative development which lies behind the continuity: the inner pattern. Viewed in this way an outline is clear: two major phases divided by the completion of the First Symphony in the significant year of 1876, which also witnessed the first complete performance of Wagner's *Ring*. The first phase shows the creation of an individual style capable of essaying a symphony worthy of Beethoven, the second the exploration of a wealth of possibilities in forms large and small – the composer's 'high summer'. The beginning of the first is marked by the year of Brahms's first concentrated formal studies towards a much wider mastery than he had needed at first, 1855; the end of the second by his intended retirement in 1890. These are flanked by two short periods, the first from 1851, the year of the earliest compositions, though published later, the second until 1896, the year of the Chorale Preludes for organ, posthumously published in 1902.

The richness of Brahms's musical achievement justifies study at the deepest levels, and his attraction for analysts of music who proceed from the norms of the instrumental tradition is particularly obvious: Brahms is certainly due for much more specialist work. The purpose of the present study, however, is rather to give a more general picture, pursuing certain prominent characteristics and preoccupations across the entire output with closer focus only on certain strategic works in his development, detailed descriptions existing elsewhere; and if I dwell little on the content of the many songs, it is because they raise specific aesthetic questions which require individual treatment. In taking such a view, the nature of the first, 'instinctive' genres of piano writing and solo song provide the starting point from which to explore the expansion of means to the largest-scale compositions.

The concluding calendar elaborates the foregoing sketch of Brahms's life, paying particular attention to his role as professional performer and exponent of his own works and adding other details complementary to the study.

The early music

It is a measure of the tenacity of the view of Brahms the conservative, the late developer who took years to perfect a symphony worthy of Beethoven, that the sheer originality and command of his early music can be so easily overlooked – and this despite the advocacy of Schumann, who never spoke of any contemporary as of Brahms: 'Many new and significant talents have arisen . . . [and] it seemed . . . there inevitably must appear a musician called to give expression to his times in ideal fashion; a musician who would reveal his mastery not in a gradual evolution, but like Athene would spring fully armed from Zeus's head. And such a one has appeared . . . his name is Johannes Brahms.'[18] Rigorous as Brahms was certainly to feel his preparation had to be in order for him to fulfil Schumann's prophecies of his later achievements, his natural gifts were already prodigious when he met the Schumanns. There can be few other composers whose musical identities were so evident – or possessed such confidence in their expression – by the age of twenty or so. Of the prominent figures in Brahms's background, only Mendelssohn was more advanced, while his great contemporaries in the aesthetic battles of the day, Wagner, Liszt and Bruckner, took much longer to reveal their own languages. And nor is this point undermined by the presence of borrowed material in Brahms's work. On the contrary; such undisguised references as to the 'Hammerklavier' Sonata, or, less baldly, to the finale of Mendelssohn's Piano Trio in C minor, merely serve to illuminate the energy and originality with which he builds newly upon them.

The early works presage virtually all the elements characteristic of the mature style, and show their extremes. The fundamental love of song, especially the very simplest kind of self-sufficient melody, yet also the attraction to the largest and most demanding forms. The feeling for variation, for the radical transformation of surface, yet retention of basic elements whether in formal or free contexts; the bold use of harmony, as adventurous in its way as that of Wagner, not least in the capacity for generating rich variety over a pedal; the intense rhythmic vitality and the instinct for asymmetry and continuity in thematic processes; the attraction to rhythmic characters drawn from the dance, especially the 'gipsy' idioms of his day; and behind it all, the fundamental sense of contrapuntal thought and instinct for the structural whole.

Indeed, the confidence with which Brahms writes songs and piano music reveals an ease which he was to find difficult to regain in exploring the concerted media of the next decade. Even the most virtuoso of the early works, the Piano Sonata in F sharp minor of 1852, is far from the rambling structure sometimes suggested, as witness, for example, the economy of its recapitulation; tension between form and content in the slow variation movement may be great, but the structure is still clear.

Nor were these features merely ones of general style. Clear Brahmsian archetypes are already present, especially in spheres rhythmic and thematic. The Scherzo in E flat minor, written in November 1851 when Brahms was only eighteen, stands at the head of a sequence of powerful movements of the scherzo type which express his rhythmic sense with particular focus: three in the piano sonatas, one in the composite 'F A E' Violin Sonata for Joachim, one in the piano ballades and one in the Piano Trio in B. Moreover, the 'F A E' movement associates the rhythm with C minor, to establish a model for the more expansive workings of the scherzos of the Piano Quintet, Piano Quartet in C minor and eventually the scherzo-influenced first movement of the First Symphony. A comparison of the products of 1853 and 1862 shows a type which was still to retain its pull into Brahms's maturity:

Ex. 1 (i) Scherzo from 'F A E' Sonata, bars 1–9
        (ii) First Symphony: first movement, bars 157–65

Of the thematic elements, the recurrent type 5 – 1 – 2 – 3 – 2 – 1 (especially in the minor) is immediately suggested in the variation theme of the Sonata op. 1, to which he was to return in the last of the folksong collection of 1894 with the remark 'So the snake bites its own tail':[19]

Ex. 2 (i) Second movement of Sonata op. 1 (1853)
   (ii) Scherzo from Piano Trio in B major, op. 8 (1854)

And in addition to such characteristic types, his new world of artistic contact also brought him personal mottos which were to remain deeply significant, most notably those associated with Joachim and the Schumanns.

The scope of Brahms's language is the more remarkable in view of the relative conservatism of his pianistic background under Cossel and later Marxsen, with whom he studied in Hamburg from 1840 to 1845 and 1843 to 1851 respectively. He went to Marxsen as a pianist, his composition lessons only beginning when the teacher realized his pupil's gifts, and the essential grounding was in the keyboard classics. The primary stress was on Beethoven, though Marxsen's knowledge of Bach, gained through his own teacher Seyfried, and still unusual at the time, was just as important to Brahms. Of the other figures central to Marxsen's keyboard method were Czerny, Cramer, Hummel and Clementi; the last name is of particular interest in the development of Brahms's strong formal sense, an affinity which he shared with Beethoven himself. Brahms was later to declare to Clara his admiration for Clementi's 'large, free employment of form';[20] his library contains the complete sonatas and his extensive revision of the datings on the thematic index indicate his scholarly as well as compositional interest in the composer.[21] But the most interesting link in the Marxsen background was probably to Schubert, specifically to the 'Wanderer' Fantasy, since Marxsen had studied with Schubert's friend von Bocklet, who gave the work's first performance. Various links will suggest the possibility of Brahms's knowledge of this very significant structure, though we have no conclusive evidence. Of interesting figures nearer Brahms's time, however, Marxsen seems to have offered few indications. His strongest influence was probably to the composition of facile variations and pots-pourris of popular songs and operatic excerpts, such as he dedicated to Brahms years later, in 1883, in his 100 Variations on a Waltz, op. 100. These lay behind the various compositions Brahms apparently produced under the name of 'G. W. Marks'.[22] The pianistic advances of Liszt, Chopin and Schumann had to be Brahms's own discoveries, though again evidence will suggest his explorations here. His knowledge of Schumann is of particular interest in view of the nature of his own pianism. Although his aversion is recorded in 1851 in response to the enthusiasms of his Hamburg friend Louise Japha, a change of attitude is discernible even before the sudden impact of personal association in 1853.

Like Schumann himself, however, Brahms's musical expression existed within a broader world. Even before their meeting, Brahms's deep feeling for German literature had already emerged: indeed, it is again necessary to set aside an image, that of the mature, bearded philosopher, for another, as tangibly projected in the drawing by Laurens dated 1853, which shows a dreamy, romantic youth, whose appearance and profile were a little later to inspire Berlioz to liken him to Schiller and find parallels in his art.[23] Like Schumann, Brahms also lived in an imaginary world, relating himself to ETA Hoffmann's famous Kapellmeister Kreisler in the novel *Kater Murr*, and signing his compositions 'Johannes Kreisler Junior'. This world of ideas is vividly recorded in the notebook he kept for quotations, *Des Jungen Kreislers Schatzkästlein*, (The Treasure Chest of the Young Kreisler). Here, up to 1854, he copied down 645 quotations ranging from the Greeks to the latest remark of of his friend Joachim, but chiefly from German poets, Goethe and Schiller being balanced by Jean Paul and Novalis in his strongest preferences, though a wide range of interest is revealed, especially in the Romantics. Quotes from composers are few, Beethoven's letters being the main source, though he also quotes Weber and, in one case, Wagner. A second, unpublished collection shows a particular interest in Goethe's artistic philosophy, especially as revealed in letters to Schiller.[24] Although the collection contains only one folksong passage, Brahms's knowledge of this aspect of the Romantic attitude to the past was already strong when he completed the *Schatzkästlein*. He was familiar with the sources which would stimulate his later settings, notably *Des Knaben Wunderhorn*, Herder's *Stimmen der Völker*, Scherer's *Deutsche Volkslieder* and most significantly, the Kretzschmer-Zuccalmaglio *Deutsche Volkslieder mit ihren Original-Weisen* and Arnold's *Deutsche Volkslieder*. His personal contact with Arnold was intensified after the meeting with Schumann, who had strong links with the Rhenish folklorists.

Songs

The twin worlds of modern, Romantic literature and anonymous, or supposedly anonymous, folksong are most obviously reflected in the early songs which Brahms completed between 1851 and 1853. He released them in three groups, though not reflective of chronology, comprising eighteen songs as op. 3, 6 and 7 in 1853, 1853 and 1854 respectively. Folksong furnishes the texts of three, two from German collections and one Spanish,

1. The Elizabeth-Brucke, Vienna, by Franz Alt, 1872, with the Gesellschaft der Musikfreunde, distant left, and the Karlskirche, right (Gesellschaft der Musikfreunde).

2. Clara and Robert Schumann (Gesellschaft der Musikfreunde).

3. A photograph of Brahms inscribed to Frau Ida Flatz 'zur freundlichen Erinnerun[g]' in 1864. The notation is of the canon 'Göttlicher Morpheus', op. 113/1, in an early version (Gesellschaft der Musikfreunde).

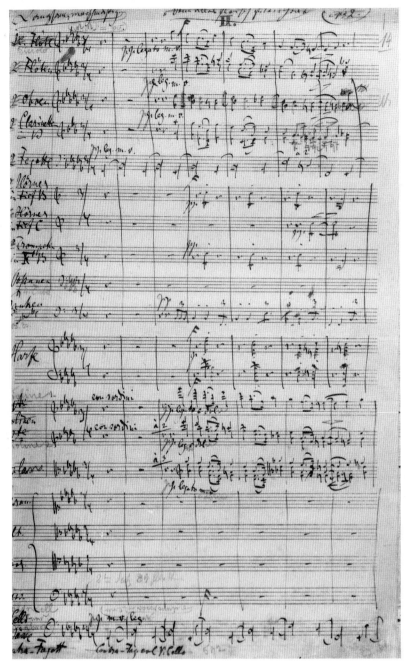

4. The opening page of the full autograph score of the second movement of *Ein deutsches Requiem*, 'Denn alles Fleisch es ist wie Gras' (Gesellschaft der Musikfreunde).

5. Brahms and Joachim, Klagenfurt, 1867 (Gesellschaft der Musikfreunde).

6. The opening page of the first movement of the Fourth Symphony in Brahms's autograph score (Zentralbibliothek, Zurich).

SCHICKSALSLIED

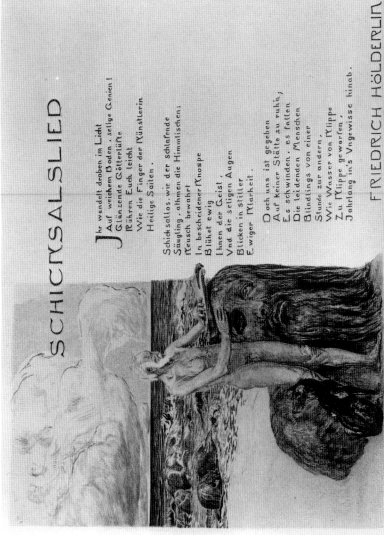

Jhr wandelt droben im Licht
Auf weichem Boden, selige Genien!
Glänzende Götterlüfte
Rühren Euch leicht
Wie die Finger der Künstlerin
Heilige Saiten.

Schicksallos, wie der schlafende
Säugling, athmen die Himmlischen;
Keusch bewahrt
In bescheidener Knospe
Blühet ewig
Ihnen der Geist,
Vnd die seligen Augen
Blicken in stiller
Ewiger Klarheit.

Doch uns ist gegeben
Auf keiner Stätte zu ruh'n,
Es schwinden, es fallen
Die leidenden Menschen
Blindlings von einer
Stunde zur andern,
Wie Wasser von Klippe
Zu Klippe geworfen,
Jahrlang in's Vngewisse hinab.

FRIEDRICH HÖLDERLIN

7. Max Klinger's 'Schicksalslied' from *Brahms-Phantasie* (1894) (Staats- und Universitätsbibliothek, Hamburg).

8. Brahms in later life with Marie Soldat-Roger
(photograph by Maria Fellinger).

in Heyse's translation. His modern texts focus most distinctly on the work of Hoffmann von Fallersleben, all being drawn from his *Gedichte* of 1843. Schumann had also drawn on this source for settings, as on other volumes by the same poet: eleven poems in all. More familiar Schumann associations are found in three settings by Eichendorff and two by Reinick. Of Brahms's other poets, Meissner, J. B. Rousseau, Ferrand and Uhland, only the last was to attract him later, and significantly. He grew increasingly conscious of the quality of his texts and the aesthetics of text setting.

The two settings of German folksongs, both written in August 1852, offer a fascinating insight into his earliest treatment of such material, both drawn from Scherer's *Deutsche Volkslieder*. The first, 'Die Trauernde', ('The Griever') sets its stylized text concerning a forlorn girl with the simplest melody and piano support, merely admitting a repeated cadence bar in echo in the piano. Its greatest feature is its harmony, a 'modal' effect being suggested by the unusual progression of chords which avoid the dominant and therefore the leading note, except at cadences, and make a feature of the 'prolongation' of A minor through chords of G (6/3) and F to create a far-away effect which captures the mood of a girl who longs to escape into death. In the similarly texted type of the previous piece, merely named 'Volkslied' ('Folksong'), the independent role of the piano is expanded, with a four-bar introduction, three-bar interlude and seven-bar postlude, though of the simplest kind, merely articulating the tonic chord. Here the echo is drawn into the vocal line to create a structure very subtle for its simple means (4 – 9 – 3 – 8 – 7):

The 'Spanisches Lied' ('In dem Schatten meiner Locken' in Heyse's translation of Geibel) explores a different response to folk poetry, one in the tradition of Schumann – compare the 'bolero tempo' of no. 5 of his *Spanisches Liederspiel*. Yet, again, harmonic effect is very memorable, with the same lowered seventh, in A minor, to create the effect of an A minor – C major juxtaposition. Though the song is quite different from Wolf's later setting, the prominent use of the augmented triad F – A – C sharp offers a rare point of contact between them. The same modal effect also characterizes another song in A minor, the Eichendorff poem 'Anklänge' ('Hoch über stillen Höhen'), though in a much quieter and less pointed context. This text was not set by Schumann, but in two other Eichendorff settings Brahms draws directly on Schumann's settings in the *Liederkreis* op. 39, since he retains Schumann's text modifications. 'Mondnacht', published posthumously, and 'In der Ferne' op. 3 no. 5 both retain essential elements from the Schumann settings while revealing Brahms's distinctive approach to text. Thus 'Mondnacht' keeps the 3/8 metre, the essential accentuation and the formal outline, verses 1 and 2 having the same material, verse 3 varying it, though Brahms does diverge in recalling his opening at the close. Even the gentle semiquaver support of the accompaniment to the vocal part is similar. Yet Brahms extends his musical setting not by repetition or the interpolation of the piano, but by augmentation of the vocal line to create

(i)

Mei Mue - ter mag mi net, und kei Schatz han i net,
Ge - stern isch Kirchweih g'wä, mi hot mer g'wis net g'seh,

ei wa - rum sterb i net, was tu i do?
denn mir ischs gar so weh, i tanz ja net.

twenty-two bars against Schumann's sixteen. A similar method functions in 'In der Fremde', where, from a common four-bar phrase, Brahms builds a seven-bar response through augmentation with comparable extension in the latter part.

Augmentation, together with inversion and imitation, appears more formally in other songs. In the two related settings of Fallersleben's 'Liebe und Frühling', op. 3 nos. 2a and 2b, the first phrase of the song is quite plainly given in augmentation towards the close, and Brahms plays with the ascending and descending versions of the original, at one point in obvious imitation. The setting of Reinick's 'Liebestreu' features imitation between bass and voice, the piano's right hand stabilizing the harmony. Such examples stand in considerable relief to the much less individual recollections of operatic recitative, as in the earliest song, Uhland's 'Heimkehr', or the various Mendelssohnian settings with regular phrasing and compound metres.

(ii)

Ex. 3 (i) 'Die Trauernde', op. 7 no. 5
       (ii) 'Volkslied', op. 7 no. 4

Piano music: E flat minor Scherzo and sonatas

Powerful as is the contrast between the extremes of song types favoured by Brahms, the larger canvas of the extended piano works shows his range even more clearly. For here he brings into association immensely challenging pianism and simple melody – in one case of the simplest, one of the folksongs he was later to include in the 1894 collection, 'Verstohlen steht der Mond auf', from Kretzschmer-Zuccalmaglio, which serves as the subject of the variation-form slow movement of the C major Sonata. A folk poem, 'Mir ist leide dass der Winter beide', also matches the melody of the slow movement of the F sharp minor Sonata, though the melody appears to be Brahms's own: indeed it relates closely to the previous example. Although Brahms suppressed this reference in the published score, the slow movement of the F minor Sonata retains its textual basis, another piece of romantic moon imagery, from Sternau, which fits the melody. Moreover, it has been shown that the following poem in the source also fits Brahms's second idea. Against this background it is predictable that one of the ballades should also reveal an essential dependence on words, explaining its title of 'Edward'. In addition to the generation of instrumental melody from imagined song, Brahms was also free with his use of borrowed ideas. The subtlety of the quotation of Zerlina's aria from Mozart's *Don Giovanni* in 'Liebe und Frühling' is outstripped by a quotation from Marschner's *Hans Heiling* overture in the Scherzo in E flat minor, while the finale of the C major Sonata draws on the Scottish song 'My heart's in the Highlands'. Finally, the last movement of the F minor Sonata uses Joachim's F A E motto (for 'Frei aber einsam') as the source of its second theme (bars 39–40) in a form much plainer than that of the 'FAE' Scherzo itself.

The contrasting world of heroic pianism which characterizes the outer movements and scherzos of the sonatas, the Scherzo in E flat minor and the Ballade in B minor is often termed 'symphonic' in order to distinguish Brahms's language from the more figurative devices of the modern school. Yet his links here are strong. The Scherzo in E flat minor seems obviously dependent on the Chopin scherzos generically, as an independent and expansive composition for piano, while its distinctive opening rhythm and its sequel at bars 17–20 recall the Chopin Scherzos in B flat minor and C sharp minor (from bar 25) respectively.

Yet Brahms claimed that he had never heard any of Chopin's music when the relation was pointed out by Raff on the occasion of the famous meeting with Liszt, when Brahms allegedly fell asleep during Liszt's as yet unpublished B minor Sonata.[25] While he might easily be forgiven for denying any such model for so powerful a youthful work, it is, however, equally possible to see the piece as relating to a broader tradition. The marking 'rasch und feurig' is distinctly Schumannesque, as are the two trios; and the Marschner quote finds a parallel in Schumann's *Etudes Symphonique*, whose finale quotes from *Der Templer und die Jüdin*. Moreover, Brahms's formal clarity and working processes are entirely characteristic of him. Though the young composer's structure is very square, the subtlety of the retransition from the second trio is already masterly. Moreover, the way in which the first theme is developed and the new material generated by counterpoint is prophetic of later methods. The movement falls into the pattern A – B (Trio 1) – A – C (Trio 2) – A – Coda, with extensive inner sections. The progression from the opening motive through the first paragraph to bar 32 is continuous, the powerful scalic descent at bars 17–20 clearly emerging from bars 4–7 and generating the prominent motive of the next paragraph as a counterpoint, which then serves, slightly modified, to accompany the Marschner quote at bar 46. The scalic descent serves to link to Trio 1 in its turn and its inverted workings can be seen to prompt the distinctive bass line of Trio 2. The skill of the re-transition, and the motivic emphasis in the 'piu mosso' coda (an emphatic treatment of a diminished variant of the Marschner theme, then inverted in augmentation) clearly reveal the organic nature of Brahms's thought.

The distinctive rhythmic character of the Scherzo in E flat minor provides a clear link to that of the Sonata in F sharp minor, completed in November of the following year, 1852. Although the Sonata's Scherzo transforms the 3/4 metre into a slightly broader 6/8 (now merely marked 'allegro'), and lacks a second trio, the thematic process is strikingly similar at the outset, again based on an urgent motive, though here repeated in varied form and built into a more symmetrical period (eight bars instead of ten). But the movement now appears in a quite different context – that of a very broadly planned four-movement sonata whose ideas seem more determined by factors of pianistic virtuosity than in any other of Brahms's piano works. Like its predecessor, this work can easily suggest an immediate influence, here the Liszt B minor Sonata (bars 105–11), which seems to offer a striking parallel to the un-Brahmsian texture of strident octaves and reiterated quaver accompaniment from bar 41 of his first movement; against this background one naturally views the overt thematic relationship between the inner movements – the scherzo a direct variation of the slow movement in its first section, the finale theme anticipated likewise in the slow introduction – with special interest. Yet in this case we can be sure that Brahms did not know the work, for he only heard it on the occasion aforementioned, in the following year, the year before its publication in 1854. Again, the parallels must be placed in a broader perspective, including Schumann and Beethoven.

Whether or not Brahms shared Liszt's fascination for the 'Wanderer' Fantasy, there is no stylistic aspect which supports the view of this powerful model of thematic integration as the stimulus to Brahms's methods. Rather than the Schubert-Liszt tradition, he seems to reflect his own deep love of variation, stimulated by the sonata style of Schumann and rhetorical manner of Beethoven, with its crucial thematic consequence. Schumann is there in the pianism – note especially the three-stave writing in the slow movement

Ex. 4 Scherzo in E flat minor, op. 4: thematic evolution

– while rhythmic links to Beethoven's C minor Symphony seem to underlie the aural connection between the quote of the rhythmic motive eight bars before the end of the first movement and the variation theme which follows. What does link Brahms to Liszt, however, is the desire to regard such powerful relations as proper to a sonata, rather than as a special feature appropriate to the title 'Fantasia': even Schumann had termed his thematically experimental D minor Symphony a 'Fantasy-Symphony'. The parallels between the Brahms and Liszt sonatas illuminate in turn their essential differences, for while Liszt anticipates later developments in bringing sonata

elements into a continuous structure, Brahms retains his separate movements, thus intensifying the effect of contrast. Indeed, in this context,
the finale-oriented structure lays an early emphasis in its expansive finale
introduction. However, its closing return to make a strangely ambivalent
conclusion belongs to a much less structurally directed phase: indeed its
almost expressionistic quality, to which may be compared the extraordinary
harmonic juxtaposition in the retransition to the scherzo, shows how poten-
tially different a composer Brahms might have appeared to observers at this
stage.

Ex. 5   (i) Piano Sonata in C, op. 1, bars 1–4
       (ii) Beethoven: 'Hammerklavier' Sonata, op. 106, bars 1–4
      (iii) Schubert: 'Wanderer' Fantasy, bars 1–6

It seems clear that Brahms's instincts towards formal integration and concentration of working were conditional upon the nature of his ideas, and in the next sonata, in C major, he presents a much tighter organization, the pianism pruned almost entirely of any rhapsodic character – features symbolized in the familiar parallels observed between its opening and those of the 'Hammerklavier' and 'Waldstein' sonatas. Yet the Beethoven links must be kept in perspective. Brahms certainly seems to take the Beethoven rhythm for his opening, but the position on the keyboard, in the middle register, taken with the key, bring its realization as close to the 'Wanderer' Fantasy, and Brahms's inspiration can well be seen to conflate both backgrounds.

The subsequent progress of the movement, however, shows the 'Hammerklavier' as the more essential stimulus in the use of imitation in thirds between the hands (compare bars 17–36 of the Brahms with bars 137–200 of the Beethoven), though Brahms never attempts to match the dramatic risks and idiosyncrasies of Beethoven's later manner. He soon checks the allusions to bring in a characteristic second subject over a pedal which recalls Mendelssohn, and his development, though drawing on imitation, leans heavily on predictable sequence with no reference to the fugal obsession which emerges in Beethoven's movement. Most striking of all is the individuality of Brahms's handling of the recapitulation, which he makes tonally ambiguous by adding the flat seventh to the C triad and intensifying the movement through F major, producing a further modification of the original passage to move boldly through C minor, D flat and D to C minor for the second subject. His tonal virtuosity also serves to sharpen the relation with the 'Waldstein' Sonata. Beethoven merely passes through the degree of B flat on his way to the dominant, G. In contrast, Brahms establishes B flat as a new centre on which he repeats his subject, returning to the tonic in a very adventurous fashion through the sudden reintroduction of B natural in the upper part of the progression from E to C minor. His thematic process is equally striking when set beside its precursor. Brahms's opening may echo the 'Hammerklavier's rhythm, but the way he builds his theme is entirely personal – and very prophetic of his characteristic methods. Thus, where Beethoven constructs by immediate repetition of the phrase, answered by a new consequent, Brahms develops his idea creating successive variation of a kind that obviously relates to the process elsewhere identified by Schoenberg as 'developing variation'.[26]

In the third and final piano sonata, in F minor, Brahms draws together the main features of the preceding works, returning to the expansive layout of the F sharp minor while developing the working processes generated in the C major. The pianism is prodigious, anticipating the use of two pianos in the planned D minor Sonata, whose characteristics we can only surmise from the surviving parts of the *Requiem* and D minor Piano Concerto. Thus, the fourth movement transforms the second through the addition of timpani effects; the second itself builds to a sustained climax whose cross rhythms

Ex. 6 Brahms, op. 1, bars 1–8

demand orchestral treatment; the broad 3/4 metre of the first movement clearly foretells the funeral march of the *Requiem*, with its comparable timpani beat. If contained in the C major Sonata, Beethoven's strain on the medium certainly finds parallels here. But the structural scope is that of the F sharp minor Sonata rather than the C major, to which, indeed, it throws clear figurative links in the first movement (compare bars 71–75 with the main subject of the earlier work). Although the first movement is more tightly organized, the finale lacks an introduction or balancing slow coda; the very extensive coda 'piu mosso' serves to balance the weighty contents of the inner movements. The slow movement may be more intimate than any of the previous movements, its textual background stimulating musical links to the song 'Mondnacht', but the movement is built to contain contrast in the scheme A – B – A – C, the final section rising to a climax as powerful as that of the first movement. The recall of the main idea in simplified and varied 'orchestral' form after a very powerful scherzo (which transforms the model of the finale of Mendelssohn's Piano Trio in C minor) posed a problem of finale structure, which Brahms solves not merely through his coda but through contriving to give the unusual rondo structure an introductory quality by internal contrasts and the tonal movement to the dominant by bar 6, recalling the layout of the work's very opening. The scheme A – B – A (variation) – A – C – C (variation) – A coda (A) is so constructed as to give the coda the role of stabilization and resolution. Indeed, in its contrapuntal combination of two versions of the same idea (the second rondo theme) it suggests the coda of Schumann's Piano Quintet in E flat, which might be related to the rest of the finale as an important structural precedent.

The sense of an overall structure is mirrored in the internal workings of the movements, especially their thematic processes and tonal relationships. The first movement can fairly be described as monothematic, everything deriving progressively from the transformations of the first, assertive figure.

Even the seemingly lyrical second theme grows from it through an augmentation previously established, the whole taking the clear tendencies of the
Scherzo in E flat minor to all-pervading use through a now greatly
developed transformational capacity:

Ex. 7 Piano Sonata in F minor, op. 5, thematic evolution of the first movement

In the tonal structure of the work, Brahms shows his familiarity with the
tradition of powerful F minor works in Beethoven through the use of the
submediant rather than mediant relation for contrast. Thus, the Trio

contrasts F minor with D flat, while the 'Rückblick' is also in D flat, likewise the key of the central episode of the finale. Most strikingly, D flat offers the tonal goal of the second movement, achieved through A flat, also the key of the second subject.

Piano music: Ballades

No work so well fits Schumann's description of 'veiled symphonies' as the F minor Sonata. Further exploration of the solo field had obviously to lie elsewhere and, although the second section of the first ballade still reflects its manner in triplet-duplet juxtaposition and orchestral inner parts, Brahms's approach elsewhere in these pieces is more idiomatic and much more restricted in scope. The term 'Ballade' had two clear meanings for him: first, a vocal setting of a declamatory or narrative poem stemming from the tradition of Schumann and Loewe, to which he would later contribute himself, and secondly a purely pianistic composition, to which he returned in the fourth piece of op. 118. That the vocal link, rather than that of the Chopin ballades, was primary seems clear from the known background to the first, D minor Ballade of 1854, which Brahms inscribed 'after the old Scottish ballad "Edward", in Herder's *Stimmen der Völker*'. Following the hint, Paul Mies[27] has shown that the opening eight-bar theme serves to set the first line of text, in which Edward is questioned by his mother: 'Dein Schwert, wie ist's von Blut so rot, Edward', while its sequel, 'poco piu mosso' in the major submediant, B flat, serves as his reply 'O, ich hab' geschlagen meinen Geier tot':

Ex. 8 Ballade 'Edward', op. 10 no. 1 in D minor, bars 1–13 with added text

The pattern of question and answer can be traced throughout, culminating in Edward's final statement 'The curse of heaven shall ye for me bear'. However, Brahms contrives to produce a rounded A B A form from the successive stanzas by evolving a central, development section from the figure of the second reply, its growing intensity reflecting the mother's anguished questioning, the tragic revelation of the true victim, the father, reflected in the quiet closing reprise of the opening.

No such textual background has been identified for the other ballades, though their vocal qualities suggest the possibility in some passages. The second, for example, suggests a seven-bar vocal line, preceded by a two-bar introduction, which merely articulates the pedal on which it is built in the manner of a lullaby. A dramatic background might well lie behind the contrast of this initial idea and the percussive sections which follow before the varied reprise of the opening, a possibility also for the lyrical fourth piece, which is essentially a song without words, though its range precludes vocal performance. Only the third piece, a driving scherzo in B minor akin to op. 4 in its use of a reiterated figure and thematic relation of its consequent, could not be vocal in stimulus. However, the seemingly contradictory title 'Intermezzo' is not contradictory of its function, since Schumann provides a precedent in many such forceful movements of this title: the fourth of the *Novelleten*, for example, marked 'rasch und wild' in 6/8, shows a similar character functioning as a link between outer sections of a lighter and contrasted nature.

Brahms's ballades provide in little an excellent focus on some of his most characteristic features, not least the individuality of his pianism. His idiom here has been unfavourably compared with Liszt's in his works of the same title for ignoring the innovations of the modern school. Yet Brahms's was a very individual and powerful keyboard sense which he developed through an immense output of piano music, including the two concertos and the *Paganini* Variations, which were of great influence on later generations, perhaps most fruitfully on Rachmaninov. Two features stand out, both concerned with richness of sonority. First the breadth of spacing, frequently involving octaves in one or both hands in which a third is placed within the extremes – a feature anticipated in Schubert, as shown, but especially intensified by Brahms. Secondly, the placing of the melody in the middle parts surrounded by full, and not merely decorative writing in the outer parts, as in the second section of the D minor Ballade. The spacing which opens this piece is recurrent in his style, either in a reflective milieu, such as that of the A minor Intermezzo of op. 118, or in a rhetorical context, such as that of the weighty Rhapsody in E flat op. 119 no. 4. It even appears in the popular vein of the waltz, the Waltz in C sharp minor op. 39 no. 7 even reproducing the thematic outline from the ballade. The love of the apportioning of melody to a middle voice, reflected in the central section of this ballade still recurs, even when Brahms had mastered the orchestral idiom to which this particular example aspires. The late piano works again richly illustrate the tendency.

The individuality of the ballades is equally determined by purely compositional features. Brahms's later obsession with the relationship of 3/4 to 6/8 is already apparent in the cadence pattern of bars 20–21 of the 'molto staccato e leggiero' section of no. 2; but it is the harmony that is especially striking here. Much of the stark quality of the music arises from the constant presence of contrary motion between the outer parts. The passage from bar 9 'poco piu moto' of no. 1 (the reply) cannot reasonably be regarded as employing 'inversion' or even 'free inversion' of the bass, with the implication of conscious planning; it is an instinctive relationship which is to be found throughout the set and is deeply to permeate Brahms's music, whether 'unconsciously' as a stylistic feature, especially in his technical exploration of the keyboard (see, for example the *Paganini* Variations, Fifty-One Exercises and piano arrangements), or 'consciously' in the field of counterpoint. So powerful is it a feature, that one senses harmonies arising as a consequence. Brahms produces some remarkable effects combining contrary motion with the juxtaposition of root position triads. The '*pp* sempre legato' middle section of no. 3 is a case in point, at once romantic in its twilight atmosphere through high positioning on the keyboard, yet also 'archaic' in the avoidance of the conventional mixtures of diatonic progressions:

Ex. 9 Ballade, op. 10 no. 3, bars 46–50

In other passages, the effect arises through linear movement, as in the forementioned cadence of no. 2 or the passage nine bars later which recalls the assertive second section, the lowering of the third of the 'dominant' (A sharp) being especially characteristic. Thus, when Brahms came later to study modal harmony in the choral music of the Renaissance, it was to intensify already clear inclinations.

Piano music: Schumann *Variations op. 9*

The world of the ballades is intensely personal to Brahms: only one passage could conceivably be by another composer, the Schumannesque first and second sections of the final piece. In contrast, the Variations on a Theme of Schumann explore a world which, through known in part in earlier years, only burst upon Brahms fully when he met with the Schumanns in the summer of 1853. Unlike the first Clara dedication, the F sharp minor

Sonata, this work completely inhabits the world of Schumann and Clara, realizing the potentiality of the model in terms grounded in their pianism and expression, and pointing the homage through many specific references, the range of which is much wider than has generally been noted. Freely acknowledged is the fact that the ninth variation is a paraphrase of the second of Schumann's *Albumblätter* and that the last four bars of the tenth quote the 'theme of Clara Wieck' from the sixth of his Impromptus op. 5. Further recent suggestions have included the obvious parallel between the bass of the final variation and that of the aforementioned Clara theme, between the eighth and fifteenth variations and nos. 7 and 14 of the *Davids-bundlertänze*, the obvious lyricism of the former (though Brahms's canon is his own) and the opening progression of the latter, and between the quicker part of 'Fabel' from the *Phantasiestücke* and the figuration of Brahms's 'poco scherzando' twelfth variation.[28] Yet one can go even further and suggest the inspiration for the opening figure of variation 11 in the first of Schumann's *Concert-Etuden* op. 10 and of the figuration of variation 13 in his Toccata. Furthermore, Clara's own variations on this theme played a part.[29] Brahms surely responds to the intensification she provides at bar 14 of her final variation in his own work; compare, for example, bar 14 of his variation 15. Indeed, parallels seem almost endless and vividly portray Brahms's sudden absorption into this new environment.

Keyboard idiom finds a parallel in variation method. Setting aside the rigid repetitions of the Variations on a Hungarian Song of the previous year – so characteristic of virtuoso variations on popular tunes at this time – the two variations movements in the sonatas in C and F sharp minor are essentially based on the retention of the theme with its phrasing and harmony, though the very atmospheric character of both inspires many licences of harmony, repetitions and interpolations, especially in the accommodation of the latter to ternary form. The *Schumann* Variations move very much further away from the identity of the model in several cases and clearly reflect Schumann's distinctive and free approach to the form rather than the more conventional models with which Brahms would have been well familiar by this time, for example Mendelssohn's *Variations sérieuses* or the large-scale Beethoven variations before the *Diabelli* Variations. Schumann's most distinguishing feature is the dependence upon bass and melody as starting points in a process which may disturb phrase structure and harmonic progression, as in the *Etudes symphoniques*, whose alternating variations and studies show the importance of pianism in his concept of the form. But though indebted to them, Brahms's work is no way dependent on Schumann's examples, and he exceeds him in the resource and complexity of his working. He really exhausts all the possibilities of an approach based on the theme and its bass and the free transformation of the model under their influence, even suggesting at one point the much more radical method of thematic compression which seems to find its source in variation 14 of Beethoven's *Diabelli* set.

His basic methods might be seen in three stages of complexity. First, there is the retention of the original phrase structure with distinct elements of theme, bass, and, where the two are combined, harmony. Second, there is the obvious disturbance of these relationships through repetition or canonic treatment, the identity of the elements still remaining clear. Finally, the most radical method arises through the interaction of many devices and the very free treatment of phrasing and derived elements.

Exemplifying the simplest methods, variations 1 and 3 place the theme in the bass, though admitting some licence in its latter part and treating harmony freely, as, for example, at the opening which is harmonized in the dominant key. No. 2, though clearly retaining the bass, is slightly more complex in transforming the metre to 9/8 (two bars into one) and repeating the entire progression. To this slightly expanded form belongs also no. 10, which employs sectional repetition in order to reveal the simultaneous combination of bass and inversion of the opening as a canon by inversion. Obvious extensions are also determined by the length of a canonic entry, as by two bars in variations 8, 14 and 15. The desire to stress the ternary structure also accounts for some simple variants of the original proportions. Hence variation 6 extends the cadence to the middle section by two bars and also transforms the natural repetitions by transposition while variation 12 defines the structure even more radically by differentiating the material within each part and building to the main cadences. Of the most radical kind is No. 5, of forty-three bars' length, combining these methods with a very free treatment of the given material in the style of a study (compare for example No. 9 of the *Etudes Symphoniques*) and No. 7, which not only compresses the whole progression to a mere eleven bars, but varies the internal progressions, the metre and the harmonic plan.

Brahms's command of canon is perhaps symbolic of his technical advance over Schumann. But despite the classical grounding he already possessed, however, Brahms must have received very great stimulus from Schumann, who was himself deeply interested in counterpoint, especially in Bach, as witness his various studies for pedal piano and organ; it should first be to his example that the exploration of canon within the context of very romantic pianism must be attributed. Indeed, the finest instance of the idiom was yet to come – the delicately obscured canon by contrary motion of Var. 4 of the Variations on an Original Theme, which Brahms could not resist identifying through a Latin tag in the score: the closest that Schumann comes to this is perhaps variation 2 of the *Etudes symphoniques*. But the ground is very clearly prepared in the Brahms's *Schumann* Variations, all of whose canons are strict – at the octave in Variation 8 (a clear precursor and link to Schumann), at the second in Variation 14 (with supporting figuration which relates to these examples), at the sixth below, between outer parts in variation 15, and, supremely, as shown, by inversion at the tenth below and simultaneously in Variation 10.

Fascinating as variation technique and keyboard idiom appear, in this

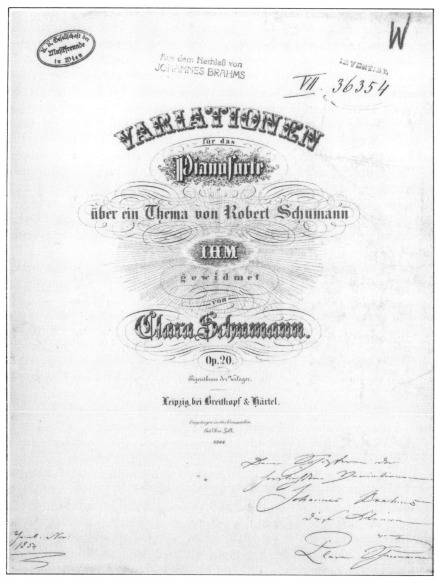

Fig. 1 Brahms's copy of the *Variations on a Theme of Schumann*, op. 20 by Clara Schumann with her inscription to Brahms. 'Dem Schöpfer der herrlichsten Variationen Johannes Brahms, diese kleinen' (To Johannes Brahms, the creator of the finest variations, these little ones) (Nov. 1854, Düsseldorf)

work, however, it is in the choice of theme that Brahms's intimacy with the Schumanns is most clearly revealed and establishes a musical symbol for Brahms's relationship with Clara – a relationship of immense importance musically, whatever the nature of their emotional attachment and its expression. The theme, taken from the first of the *Albumblätter* which appear in the *Bunte Blätter* op. 99, had been used by Clara and dedicated to Robert in the previous summer. But in November 1854 she inscribed a copy to Brahms: 'Dem Schöpfer der herrlichsten Variationen Johannes Brahms, diese kleinen' – 'For the creator of the finest variations, these little ones'.[30] He also retained the manuscript, which she inscribed 'Dem verehrten Johannes Brahms, auf freundliches Verlangen' – 'For the esteemed Johannes Brahms, on friendly request'. Her reaction to Brahms's variations, written earlier in the year during Schumann's illness, makes their personal significance absolutely clear; in her diary she recorded, 'he sought to comfort me, he composed variations on that wonderfully heartfelt theme that means so much to me, just as last year when I composed variations for my beloved Robert, and moved me deeply through his sweet concern', a response which was obvious in Schumann as well.[31] Had he lived, however Schumann would have seen an even more fruitful and individual expression of this symbolic idea:

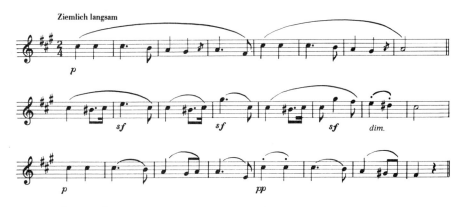

Ex. 10 Theme of the Variations on a Theme of Schumann, op. 9

Chamber music

The surviving early works for piano, as presumably the songs, are but a part of the instrumental music which Brahms produced, for the C major Sonata is marked as 'fourth' and Schumann's article mentions string quartets and violin sonatas that did not appear. The only survivor of such works is the C minor scherzo for violin and piano which Brahms contributed to the composite sonata for Joachim's birthday in October 1853, whose other movements were composed by Schumann and Dietrich, all incorporating Joachim's motto 'F A E'. That Brahms did not publish the work at the time is perhaps explained by its context, since no attempt was made to publish the work as a whole, and its varied stylistic content would have precluded its use other than as a curiosity. There can be no musical reason, since this is a fine example of the genre he had so convincingly employed in the piano sonatas. It is planned very broadly, its momentum generating a clear second theme, the closest that Brahms came to citing Joachim's motto, by drawing on the opening of the Sonata's first movement, a subtle variant devised by Dietrich, in complete contrast with the overt statement in the finale of Brahms's F minor Sonata.

Although Brahms broke new ground in his treatment of the combination of violin and piano, it was not one which he was to continue, for the later violin sonatas are most careful to differentiate roles and achieve subtle balances, avoiding such an intense expression. Indeed, there is already a remarkable change in approach in the scherzo of the B major Trio of the following year. Influenced by the characteristic idiom of Mendelssohn rather than Beethoven, it is a delicate and evocative moment based on his basic shape and throwing a further link to his late music in the easy triple motion of its trio, another Brahmsian archetype. The careful balance of piano and strings, in which the composer explores all the possibilities of combination, beginning with cello solo, is reflected in the work as a whole and stands in considerable contrast to the piano-conditioned textures of the trios of Mendelssohn and Schumann, reflecting rather the knowledge of a more distant tradition, that of the trios of Mozart, Beethoven and, possibly, Schubert. Indeed, the immense breadth of Brahms's conception – if, indeed, the individual movements were planned as a unity – relates to Beethoven's grandest work for the medium, the *Archduke* Trio, a link which is particularly suggested by the piano opening to which cello is added. But Brahms at twenty-one was not Beethoven of the middle period, and the first version of the B major Trio is most interesting – uniquely so in the period – for the light it throws on the scope of his ambitions, the depth of his romantic background and the gap which separated his happily completed works from their earlier stages of evolution. Although Brahms allowed the first version to be published in 1854, and was content to regard the later version as merely an alternative, not a replacement, there is a vast difference in the success of the two versions. The radical nature of Brahms's structural changes is better discussed in the context of the mature trios. Suffice it here to say with the completion of this work with its lavish material and reflection of a remarkably wide range of background elements (too wide a range to make effective for the medium), Brahms had reached a position where he needed to take stock of his achievements and his future. It was to be in the following years that the rigour of his self-discipline turned him from a richly endowed artist into a master craftsman as well.

Part Two

The Second Period

2

Songs and Piano Music

Just how Brahms's creative life might have developed without the impact of the meeting with the Schumanns and the equally traumatic effect of Schumann's attempted suicide and decline is a matter for conjecture. Even before Schumann's death, however, Brahms was taking stock of his position and looking to the future. He had reached a point at which his ambitions towards extended chamber and orchestral composition lay beyond his immediate powers of realization, as the problems of medium and form in the Piano Quartet in C sharp minor and the Sonata/Symphony in D minor clearly demonstrate; even the Piano Trio in B was subsequently to be radically revised. Thus a notable break in large-scale composition and a change in direction are discernible around the summer of 1854, in which a new emphasis on the study of counterpoint – already reflected in the trio – becomes apparent. Beginning with the keyboard, Brahms applied himself rigorously to contrapuntal study, involving his friends as well, and subsequently producing many small choral works reflective of a deep absorption in a wide range of early models. Not until 1860 did another chamber work appear, drawing on this as well as many other influences. Although orchestral music came before this, the main weight of Brahms's original orchestral language arrived long after the first and very full period of chamber works from 1860 to 1865, the *St Antoni* Variations and First Symphony only appearing in the early to middle 1870s. The systematic unfolding of Brahms's mastery offers a natural pattern for discussion. From the continuing and essential base of song and keyboard composition, his choral works may be traced through the small works of 1855 to 1860 and the later, large-scale works, and his chamber works from 1860 to 1866 and 1873 to 1875. Finally, the orchestral works may be viewed against this background, spanning the entire period from 1855 to 1876.

Song and folksong

Both the extremes to be observed in Brahms's earliest songs – the preference for simple, self-sufficient melody, and equally the inclination towards the dramatic and declamatory – provided the foundation for the growth of his

song style after 1854. Yet the continuation was not to be direct: quite apart
from the gap in song composition which followed, not until the appearance
of op. 43 in 1868 did Brahms again include such a range of types in his
song groupings. In the intervening years from 1858 he explores now one,
now another aspect of this background, first the simplest, then the most
elaborate, extremes which helped him further to define the formal norms
possible within his preferences in the lied. 1858 saw the publication as op.
14 of eight songs entitled *Lieder und Romanzen*, whose texts and music betray
a susceptibility to a romantic image of folk simplicity and medieval archaism.
Six of the poems are titled 'Volkslied' and drawn from his earlier collections
– Kretzschmer-Zuccalmaglio, Arnold, Herder, as well as from Simrock's
Deutsche Volkslieder – while two others are better authenticated: a thirteenth-
century text and a Scottish text, both from Herder's *Stimmen der Völker*. The
following set, the *Fünf Gedichte* op. 19, preserve in their texts the folksong
spirit in three poems by Uhland and one by Ludwig Hölty, the first of an
even more significant relationship of composer and poet, the texts matched
by Brahms's folk-like settings. Only one of the group differs in style –
and that markedly so: the very evocative setting of Mörike's symbolically
Romantic image of the Aeolian harp, no. 5 of the set. The folksong links
reflect a deep preoccupation of the time. This is the period of the Twenty-
Eight German Folksongs and the *Volkskinderlieder*, both completed in 1858,
though the former was never published until it appeared in the complete
edition in 1926. The latter was written for Clara's children and published
in the year of completion, both sets reflecting the same preferences in
sources. The importance of the folksong as a model for song composition
and Brahms's commitment to it emerges quite clearly from a letter to Clara
of 1860: 'Song composition is currently sailing on so false a course that one
cannot sufficiently remind oneself of an ideal – and that to me is folksong.'[1]
This focus was not, of course, new. The model of the popular 'folk-like'
melody is clear in Schubert, Schumann and Franz and was deeply significant in German Romanticism: it offered both a symbol of idealized folk
quality and also, in contrast, a means of identity in a rapidly expanding
expressive world – as Einstein has termed it 'a cure for isolation'.[2] But with
Brahms the focus became intense. The prominence of the folksong as the
subject of variations in the early sonatas predicts an obsession which lasted
with increasing refinement and subtlety until the completion of the Forty-
Nine German Folksongs (forty-two for solo voice and piano, seven with the
addition of chorus), which he published in 1894, his favourite work whose
completion seemed to him to round out his career symbolically. It is
important to stress the Romantic nature of Brahms's interest, for he applied
none of his scholarship to his folksong choices. He loved these melodies
because they identified with the deepest character of his own style.
Throughout his life scholarly research was to reveal that many of his
favourite melodies were fake: much of the work of Zuccalmaglio was shown
to be invented or freely adapted, many of his regional attributions mani-

festly false. Brahms's reaction shows his unconcern. 'Not really folk music? Oh well, so we have one good composer the more, and for him I do not need to apologise, as for myself.'[3] It is interesting to note the interpretation of Brahms's attitude given by Morik, who classes him in the 'almost exclusively creative group (Herder, Buerger, Goethe, Arnim, Brentano, Zuccalmaglio) who assumed a constructive, hermeneutic stance as did later Bartók', in contrast to the 'more rationalist, positivist standpoint, of Nicolai, Voss and Fallersleben'.[4] In musical terms this implied the application of an aesthetic criterion to the melodies, which for Brahms determined the collections of Zuccalmaglio and Arnold as his prime sources, the former providing over 80 per cent of his material.

However, Brahms's ideal concerned not merely the quality of the melody. The musical and textual character of the folksong related to deeply held views on the proper relation of text and music, which set Brahms in a special position in the history of the Romantic lied. It has long been the fashion to relegate his achievements in this field to the second class, despite his output and the popularity of his settings on musical grounds, on account of his avoidance of the great lyrics set by Schubert, Schumann and Wolf and his apparent carelessness in the declamation of his texts. Such evidence is taken to confirm the view of him as an 'absolute' composer whose abilities declined as he moved into the sphere of words, and especially drama. Such a notion is mistaken. Brahms held very clear views of the proper relation of music and words, and his output and its characteristics reflect this. As he later informed Jenner, he held the structure of the poem to be a major consideration, censuring mistakes in its realization especially strongly as 'defects in musical understanding'. His teaching was known in Vienna. Thus Schoenberg could observe later: 'It is well known that Brahms's aesthetic canon demanded that the melody of a song must reflect, one way or another, the number of metrical feet in the poem'.[5] This attitude even brought Brahms to challenge the approach of earlier masters – and he tended strongly to avoid re-setting poems that had already been treated. Hence, Mendelssohn's and Schubert's settings of Goethe's 'Die Liebende schreibt' are challenged for not observing the sonnet form, and his own setting is much truer to the model than theirs.

This attitude also affected his choice of text. Not only did he tend increasingly to avoid texts already set, but he was strict in his attitude to the possible range of texts for setting. As Henschel recalls, it seemed to him pointless to set texts which seemed complete in themselves, as in his comment to Henschel concerning Schubert, one of several indicating his admiration for Schubert, who provided his most consistent model in song composition: 'Schubert's *Suleika* songs are to me the only instances where the power and beauty of Goethe's words have been enhanced by the music. All other of Goethe's poems seem to me so perfect in themselves that no music can improve them.'[6] Such a view certainly explains the pattern of Brahms's settings, where the great lyrics are so conspicuously absent.

Given, in addition, Brahms's natural lyric gift, his love of self-sufficient and rounded melody, and his concern for a complementary bass line (he used to cover the middle parts in examining any songs shown to him), the appeal of the folksong model becomes apparent. It offered him the simplest structures and opportunity for folk-like melodic invention around texts which, though exploring all the images of Romantic poetry, pose no conflicting challenges of sophistication, and most of his preferred poets for setting worked very skilfully within this frame – for example Hölty, to say nothing of the rich field of folksong translation. This 'ideal' was, of course, profoundly limiting, and Brahms's later songs explore many metres and achieve great subtlety of formal means. But he never lost his love for such types, which remain a backcloth to his mature songs, every now and again emerging in some new guise.

In the songs op. 14 and 19, published in 1861 and 1862, this background is still clearly apparent and he develops the types and treatments already explored in the earliest settings. Thus, the textual affinities between op. 14 nos. 2 and 8 and op. 7 no. 5 stimulate similar archaic effects through harmonic means. In the latter, an E minor chord is constantly associated with a G chord to support the lowered D of the melody, with striking avoidance of seventh chords. Likewise the role of the piano is minimal, with only a two-bar tonic chord as prelude. Op. 14 no. 2, 'Vom verwund-eten Knaben', though much closer to actual models in its opening melodic line and more straightforward harmonically, also creates a modal effect in the interpolation of a chord of C before the expected dominant – another echo effect. 'Gang zur Liebsten', op. 14 no. 6 illustrates that Brahms did not always seek to imitate favoured models in borrowing texts. Thus he ignores the minor structure and characteristic shape of the melody set as no. 38 of the 1894 collection in favour of an independent melody in the major in a different metre, 6/8 for 2/4. The opening call of 'Trennung' op. 14 no. 5 – 'Wach auf' – recalls the parallel passage in 'Wach auf, mein Hort' (no. 12 of the 1894 collection) though producing a much fuller accompani-ment and a freer form, with verse 4 set to contrasting music. Similarly, 'Vor dem Fenster' op. 14 no. 1 absorbs a characteristic pattern and metre into a freer structure (compare nos. 8 and 32, of 1894) where interludes and preludes serve to break up the poem's regularity, as does tonal contrast between verses. In 'Ständchen' op. 14 no. 7 Brahms establishes the kind of wider ranging rhythmic melody drawn from folksong which is so character-istically expressed in the setting of Uhland's 'Der Schmied' op. 19 no. 4, with its similarly lengthy postlude. Only two of the op. 14 settings are not relatable to folk models of some kind, 'Murrays Ermordung', another bloody Scottish tale drawn like *Edward* from Herder, and 'Ein Sonnett'. The former draws on a Schumannesque folk idiom (compare, for example 'Des Knaben Berglied' from Schumann's op. 79) while the latter creates a more flowing 'langsam' to capture its thirteenth-century Romanticism. The first four songs of op. 19 develop these ideas. The three Uhland settings – two of the same

text, 'Scheiden und Meiden', and 'Der Schmied' – adapt the extended range
established in 'Ständchen' to very personal ends. 'Der Schmied' is perhaps
the best known of the group, with its characteristic omission of the tonic
in the opening of the melody and its long postlude, comparable with the
earlier song. In 'In der Ferne' the feeling is even more personal, with a
more broadly inspired melody, again omitting a note of the triad. In Hölty's
'Der Kuss' the manner of 'Vor dem Fenster' recurs with greater variation
and yet more freedom.

Ex. 11 'Der Schmied', op. 19 no. 4

Magelone *Romances*

Despite its great influence, the folksong ideal represented only one side of
Brahms's inclinations as a song composer. Throughout his life there existed
another, though the mature Brahmsian lied achieves some notable inte-

grations of the two. The declamatory idiom already shown in the earliest songs was to achieve very characteristic expression in the 1860s, during which Brahms's interest in opera and oratorio was particularly strong. The contrast with the folk idiom is starkly demonstrated in the last song of op. 19. This highly evocative setting of Mörike's 'An eine Aeolsharfe' begins with the marking 'recit' as the poet describes this very Romantic symbol of the harp, resting on an ancient wall, whose strings are intoned by the wind. Its quality of mystery, bearing messages from a dead lover, is evoked by softly repeated triplet chords in the piano; the return of the 'recit' draws directly on the 'poet's music' from Schumann's *Kinderszenen* (compare bars 74–7 of the song with the last piece, bar 12) before the music of this uncharacteristically through-composed and evocative setting returns. With the Fifteen Romances to Tieck's *Die schöne Magelone* these operatic tendencies appear within a much larger context. Begun in 1861, this work contains no simple songs at all, but rather long and almost undisciplined structures which Brahms found difficulty in completing, the first set appearing in 1865, the rest in 1869. In the meantime he had completed the much more contained songs op. 32 to texts by Daumer and Platen, which have much clearer consequence for his later style, though they also relate to these settings.

In conception, the *Magelone* Romances are unique – and very interesting in relation to the Romantic world of Brahms's youth and his sensitivity to text. Although Tieck's lines all come from the same source, the work is not a cycle in the traditional sense of related and self-sufficient poems. The poems, not termed romances by Tieck, were written to accompany a story which is intended to be read with them – an interesting form which is in accord with Brahms's views on the function of music in dramatic or related contexts. Yet Brahms does not respond to the evocation of medieval chivalry with any archaism or folk-style such as is found in the previous Romance of op. 14. He draws in many modern lyric expressions, in which the piano plays a large part, frequently suggesting Schubert and Schumann lieder, yet also operatic scenas.

The story concerns the romantic adventures of Count Peter of Provence, who longs to travel from his ancient castle to distant lands. During his travels he falls in love with the beautiful Magelone, daughter of the King of Navarre, who is promised to another. They elope and, after his infatuation with the beautiful Sulima, are reunited and live happily ever after. The function of the music is to mirror the emotions and reactions of Count Peter – and in one case, Magelone – and Brahms produces his largest and most open structure in the process. Thus, very uncharacteristically for him, even the five strophic poems beget expanding sectional structures, while the continuous poems are treated even more freely. The treatment of the three settings whose opening ideas bear a relation to the preceding songs shows the scope of the change. 'Liebe kam aus fernen Landen' (no. 4) could almost be a developed 'Volkskinderlied' at the outset. But Brahms builds his ten-bar theme into a total structure of 37 (12 – 12 – 13), 34 bars (10, 11, 13) and 15 bars in the pattern A (a b a) – B (a b a) – A (a, coda). 'Traun! Bogen und Pfeil' (no. 2) might well seem to be a Romantic adaptation of 'Der Schmied' with its heavy triple beat, yet this single strophe of eight lines reflects a sonata structure in the tonal contrast of its second idea and its tonic restoration on repetition to later text.

In some cases the prominence of the very instrumental piano writing seems to influence the form. The only two titled pieces of the series 'Verzweiflung' (no. 10) and 'Sulima' (no. 13) both have piano parts of extreme difficulty. The first might almost be a Schumann fantasy piece, complementing an instrumental melody in depicting the raging storms which symbolize Peter's despair, while the characterization of Sulima draws a capriccio-like piano part unusual in the set and demands a contrast within the continuity, the opening ideas recurring in the final part. The variety of non-strophic designs offers great opportunity for sectional structure in the music, which Brahms exploits to the full, as in the six unequal sections of no. 1, the minstrel's prologue, whose opening bars immediately evoke the special world of Wunderhorn Romanticism so strong in the music of this fascinating work:

Ex. 12 Romances from Tieck's *Magelone*, op. 33, opening bars

Daumer and Platen songs

The nine Daumer and Platen settings, published in 1865, can well be seen as relating to the *Magelone* group as does the *Requiem* to *Rinaldo* in terms of its greater concentration and maturity of utterance. For, if in the *Magelone* Romances Brahms's personal preoccupations appear in the context of his youthful Romanticism, with its familiar Wunderhorn symbols and evocations of medieval romance, these settings are much more personal: his feelings come direct, as in the baritone writing of the *Requiem*, though here the subject is not that of the great background mysteries of life and death, but the intense and immediate human emotion of sexual rejection. The poet is enthralled, but his love is refused and the texts reflect on the frustration of wasted time and the futility of life as well as the rationalizations and recriminations which characterize the inability to accept reality. The final text is an unconditional avowal of love for the unattainable object of desire. These texts, selected from Daumer's *Hafis* and Platen's *Romanzen und Jugendlieder* drew from Brahms some of his most powerful expressions – indeed some of the most powerful songs of the kind since Schubert's *Winterreise* and late songs, to which some links exist. They are especially notable for their declamatory quality, which in turn throws links to the *Requiem*: compare for example, the closing bars of no. 1 with the close of the first solo passage in 'Herr, lehre doch mich'. Like the *Magelone* Romances, the folk text settings are far away, though Brahms does include one strophic setting which might be considered in relation: the simple rhyming couplets of no. 3 beget a response very similar to that of 'Scheiden und Meiden' op. 19 no. 2, but with the marked difference that Brahms suspends the expected cadence which resolves the question 'How could I be woebegone' with great effort prior to its completion. In nos 6, 7 and 8 relatively simple melodic lines are built into ABA structures, with varied conclusions and a more important role for the piano. But most powerfully indicative of the new manner are the first and second songs. The first, depicting endless wandering, recalls *Die Winterreise* in its steady step, powers of expansion, and telling variation of the basic ABA, though the harmonic ambiguity between F minor and D flat through which the text is reflected is Brahms's own. The second is a much simpler and starker piece, poised between the character of no. 1 and operatic recitative, to open up, in Friedländer's words 'an entirely new field to the musical lyric'.[7] Much of the effect rests in turn on the remarkable economy of motivic means, even the contrast of the major central section deriving by simple inversion.

In no. 4 another prophetic type employs augmentation of cadence bars to give a metrical contrast between common time and 3/2 within the ABA structure, creating a dramatic effect without distorting the poem's structure. In the final and best-known setting of the group, 'Wie bist du meine Königin', the ABA structure draws many of these features into a much warmer and more radiant context, establishing another very Brahmsian type.

Ex. 13 'Nicht mehr zu dir zu gehen', op. 32 no. 2, bars 1–5 and 11–12

Other songs

A year before the publication of the third set of *Magelone* Romances in 1869, Brahms released no less than five sets, op. 43 and 46–9, comprising twenty-five songs which reflect a composition period of at least ten years. The remaining sets appeared in the early 1870s: op. 57 and 58 in 1871, op. 59 and 63 in 1873 and 1874 respectively. Only one group, the Seven *Daumer* Songs op. 57, continues the focus on a single poet. Elsewhere Brahms groups more loosely, though sub-groups of poets or subjects are frequent. Established textual preferences remain, though they are significantly extended. Thus only four German folk texts appear – in fact only two, since two were first apparently set for chorus. In contrast, Brahms draws on three translations from Bohemian folk poetry by Wenzig, prophetic of his interests in this source, and two from Italian sources by Heyse. However, the preference for the folk-like in poetry continued, with further settings from Uhland as well as Wenzig. Of his earlier poets – Eichendorff, Reinick Meissner, Rousseau, Ferrand, Fallersleben, Uhland, Mörike, Hölty and Daumer – the last two were of greatest significance in his maturity. The interest in Daumer particularly reflects his search for a wide range of metres and types. Though not a first-rate poet – indeed he was hardly noticed before Brahms's interest – Daumer was a very fine translator and sought to make a wide range of material available to German readers, offering Brahms much of interest. Even his less original poems appealed to Brahms as they provided the ideal possibility for 'fanning the hidden spark of genius into a bright flame' as Friedländer sees it.[8] Hölty, a fellow North German, set frequently by Schubert, was Brahms's other favourite.

The poets new to Brahms are Schenkendorf (four songs), Goethe (three), Hebbel, Felix Schumann, von Schack and Candidus (two each) and Flemming (one). The Goethe settings arouse special interest in showing how Brahms relaxed his ideals in the avoidance of texts previously set or in the choice of fine lyrics. Both 'Trost in Tränen' op. 48 no. 5 and 'Die Liebende schreibt' op. 47 no. 5 had already been set, the former numerous times, the latter by Mendelssohn and Schubert. Friedlander[9] points out the notable parallel between Brahms's setting of the former and that of J. F. Reichardt, whose music Brahms valued, notably in the rhythm of the setting and the persistent use of repeated chords. The sensitivity of his approach to 'Die Liebende schreibt' has earlier been noted in connection with his predecessors. The third setting, 'Dämmerung senkte sich von oben' op. 59 no. 1, was also created in the spirit of improvement, here on a setting by Levi, four bars of which Brahms reworked in his very atmospheric setting with its effective variation of basic idea and modal contrast in response to text.

While the texts of Brahms's songs continue with his basic preoccupations – longing, lost love, despair, as well as the conventions of folk types – one notes an increasing tendency towards reflection which is to become so powerful later, as well as, and perhaps related to it, a yet more overt expression of sexual emotion. The Daumer settings of op. 57 caused considerable comment in Brahms's circle for the little-disguised sensuality of the texts which drew from Brahms some very direct musical expression. In contrast, the moods of brooding reflection on passing time were a common experience for both Brahms and another north German, Klaus Groth, finding particularly strong expression in the second of the three poems he entitled 'Heimweh', which Brahms set as op. 63 nos 7–9. The character of the harmonic progressions and broad cross rhythms of 'O wüsst ich doch den Weg zurück', with the intensification of the middle strophe, are pointers to the maturing Brahmsian style, which finds a contrasting expression in the widely roving harmony of the second of the *Junge Lieder* by Clara's son Felix Schumann: his 'Meine Liebe ist grün' delays the confirmation of its tonic until the close, actually beginning with a modulation *into* its tonic.

Although the connection between folk texts and folk-like settings is not absolute in Brahms's work – the very powerful and declamatory 'Von ewiger Liebe' op. 43 no. 1 is, for example, a Wenzig translation (from the Wendish) and 'Magyarisch' op. 46 no. 2 has no Hungarian effects – Brahms continued to explore the creative potential of this background. Thus Uhland's 'Sonntag', a stylized love song with refrain, is set in op. 47 no. 3 to a new Brahms folksong melody, whose transformation of favoured patterns seems clear; a comparison of the genuine folksong 'Soll sich der Mond nicht heller scheinen' (no. 35 of 1894) seems particularly revealing, with the original rhythm retained closely, the melodic shape transformed to major and completed to match the new text, with an especially folkish refrain. This makes an interesting coupling with the more familiar case of the 'Wiegenlied' op. 49 no. 4, whose derivation from a popular song is well known, the borrowed material here in the piano introduction to which the vocal melody appears as a response, perhaps even a counterpoint. Comparison of these very natural Brahms folk types with the earlier settings of folk texts, as well as the 'archaic' types, shows a clear process of absorption.

Of the more ambitious settings of the period, the declamatory idiom strong in op. 32 is not marked; only in the later songs does it return as a central feature of the mature Brahms. The often quoted 'Von ewiger Liebe' is very unusual for the period, both in the nature of its declamatory style and its through-composition, with a separate final section drawn from an earlier source. Likewise the central section of Schack's 'Herbstgefühl', set in op. 48 no. 7, is a particularly powerful passage. Much more characteristic is the emergence of an instrumental style of song writing, in which a wide-ranging lyric melody and richly figurative piano part come close to the instrumental idiom of the violin sonatas. The focal examples here are the Groth settings 'Regenlied' op. 59 no. 3 and its sequel 'Nachklang' op. 59 no. 4. The text relates the poet's association of dropping rain with childhood memories, and the extensive vocal line and very distinctive piano accompaniment, both significantly varied in the sequel, provide more than

(i) Gehend und mit herzlichem Ausdruck

Voice

Soll sich der Mond nicht hel - ler schei - nen, soll sich die
Sonn nicht früh auf - gahn, so will ich die - se Nacht gehn
frei - en, wie ich zu - vor auch hab ge - tan.

(ii) Nicht zu langsam

Voice

So hab ich doch die gan - ze Wo - che mein fei - nes
Lieb-chen nicht ge - sehn, ich sah es an ei - nem Sonn - tag wohl
vor der Tü - re stehn:

sufficient material to sustain yet another and much longer movement in the G major Violin Sonata of 1879.

In between the extremes of the folk ideal and the instrumental and declamatory types lie songs which represent perhaps Brahms's most characteristic contribution to the German tradition in song composition: the tendency is towards varied strophic setting in which the core idea of the first strophe is subtly varied to create a contrasted but related second strophe or central group, prior to the varied reprise of the first. His setting of Hölty's 'Die Mainacht' in op. 43 no. 2 offers an ideal focus. The text, like its author, was deeply reflective of Brahms's moods in evoking the poet's loneliness as against the idyllic relationships of nature, symbolized in a pair of cooing doves. The musical response draws yet again on a folk archetype which Brahms extends in his first stanza into a closely folk-related melody, though one whose harmonic context raises it to the level of a personal art song. Furthermore, it was this song that Brahms used to illustrate to Henschel his attitude to composition, in contrast to those song composers 'who sit at the piano with a poem before them, putting music to it from A–Z until it is done [and] write themselves into a state of enthusiasm which makes them see something finished, something important in every bar'. Rather, 'when I, for instance, have found the first phrase of a song . . . I might shut the book there and then, go for a walk, do some other work, and perhaps not think of it again for months. Nothing, however, is lost. If I afterwards approach the subject again, it is sure to have taken shape; I can

Ex. 14   (i) 'Soll sich der Mond nicht heller scheinen' (*Deutsche Volkslieder*, no. 35)
     (ii) 'Sonntag', op. 47 no. 3
     (iii) 'Wiegenlied', op. 49 no. 4

now begin really to work at it.'[10] Yet the working process is here at some variance with the 'ideal' mentioned earlier, for Brahms considerably transforms his starting points, both musical and textual.

The process begins with the poem itself, Brahms dispensing with the second of Hölty's four stanzas, in which the life of the 'flötende Nachtigall' is also praised, leaving a three-stanza poem of strophic design.[11]

The musical response to the first stanza retains the accentual patterns, except in the final line, where the necessities of musical cadence require the augmentation of Hölty's shorter, and cadential, final line. The second stanza, however, draws the regular structure away, through a variant of the opening now placed in the submediant, notated as B major (the key of the song is E flat), the retained rhythm being gradually loosened through the interpolation of the piano and the augmentation of the now declamatory vocal line, which extends the strophe length from eleven bars to seventeen, concluding with a greatly extended cadence on 'Träne'. In the third stanza, this phrase is incorporated into the original material at its point of thematic derivation and newly extended through yet another submediant move, from A flat minor to F flat, to conclude the song in a deeply moving way.

This variant arises directly from the text, a verbal pattern linking 'Und die Nachtigall flötet' in the first stanza with 'Und die einsame Träne rinnt' in the second and more powerfully in the third with, 'Und die einsame Träne/ Bebt mir heisser die Wang herab', the latter including some text repetition to round out the melismatic extension to a strophe of sixteen bars, a four-bar postlude balancing the two bars of the prelude.

Duets and quartets

In addition to writing solo songs with piano, Brahms also continued the traditions of the lied with a number of duets and quartets, many of which date from this period: they appeared in the sets of Three Duets op. 20, (1862), Four Duets op. 28 (1863), Four Duets op. 61 (1874), Five Duets op. 66 (1875), Three Ballads and Romances op. 75 (1878), Three Quartets op. 31 (1864) and Three Quartets op. 64 (1874). All the quartets are for SATB while the sets of duets alternate between SA and A Bar until the op. 75 set, which also introduces tenor and second soprano into the groupings. The texts relate directly to those of the solo songs. Of the nineteen duet texts, nine are from folksong sources: three from Herder, two from *Des Knaben Wunderhorn*, one 'Altdeutsch', two Bohemian translations from Wenzig and one from the Italian. Brahms's modern poets are again Goethe (two duets), Groth (two), and Eichendorff, Hölty, Candidus, Fallersleben and Mörike (one each); Kerner is the only new name. Of the six texts set for quartet, only two are folk texts: one is the Bohemian text 'Der Gang zum Liebchen' also used in the solo song op. 48 no. 1, the other is his only setting from the Moravian (these are op. 31 nos. 3 and 2 respectively). The remainder are from Goethe, Sternau, Schiller and Daumer.

Consistent with the genre, there are no duets as directly related to the folksong as are to be found in the settings of folk texts for solo voice. Rather it is the dominant influence of Mendelssohn in this sphere that is immediately apparent. The familiar text of op. 20 no. 1, Herder's version of the text familiar in England as 'Love will find out the way', is given a buoyant 6/8 setting whose directness recalls earlier examples, although the harmonic turn of the final cadence recalls the contemporary solo songs. In the second song, which uses the continuation of the text, Brahms transforms the background more characteristically through harmonic means. Another feature of the tradition, the prominence of thirds and sixths in the vocal harmonization is clear in the two Groth settings op. 66 nos 1 and 2. Where folk-type melodies do appear they are in the freer forms noted in the solo songs, with wider-ranging vocal parts and repetitions, as in the triadic associations employed for Fallersleben's, 'Der Jäger und sein Liebchen' in op. 28 no. 4 or Mörike's 'Die Schwestern' in op. 61 no. 1.

A relationship of particular interest is that between the setting of the Scottish Ballad 'Edward' in op. 75 no. 1 and the earlier piano piece inspired by this text. The duet is much the more direct in manner, the text declaimed very much in the tradition of Loewe's famed setting, Brahms simply employing common time, where Loewe sets in compound time, though the Brahms version starts with his familiar melodic outline 5 – 1 – 2 – 3 – 2 – 1 in the minor. Unlike the piano piece, which creates a developing ABA structure, the duet is a continuous alternation between mother and son, the parts growing in intensity and range with the mother's repeated questioning; only at the opening of the boy's first response is there the faintest suggestion of the parallel part of the piano setting.

The far greater scope of the settings for four voices and piano encourages Brahms to explore different moods and more varied textures, particularly employing imitation between the voices or writing homophonically with particular effect in relation to the piano, creating a texture which reflects the choral works with orchestra. A notable example of the former approach appears in the first of the op. 31 set, in which Goethe's 'Wechsellied zum Tanze' is depicted vividly, the first, indifferent, pair (alto and bass) inviting the amorous pair (soprano and tenor) through the contrast of imitation against simultaneous statement, both against the tempo di minuetto of the accompaniment, with complete contrast of material, all finally coming together, though retaining their musical identities, in the final section. Dance associations become even stronger in the third of this set, the familiar 'Der Gang zum Liebchen', where Brahms draws on the piano waltz op. 39 no. 5, here in E flat rather than E major, for the opening of his material. In the later set he is much more atmospheric in effect, especially in nos 1 and 2.

Second-period keyboard music: an introduction

The received view of history, that Brahms does not belong to the front rank of song composers, might well be seen as affirmed in the songs produced from his earliest years until the middle 1870s. At a time of life when the song composers to whom he was closest were exploring the finest lyrics of the German language, Brahms's taste was remarkably limited. The strictness of his aesthetic view prevented him from attempting the spontaneous fusion of words and tone which marks the greatest songs of his predecessors. And where he is spontaneous, moving far away from the folk model, he attempts in the *Magelone* Romances an experiment the scope of which he cannot contain with the success of earlier song cycles. As with other aspects of his art, it was to be only in full maturity that he produced consistently his most characteristic lyrical expressions, and the finest of these certainly belong to the canon.

This gradual development was not a feature of the piano writing, for in the second period, Brahms's innate mastery of piano writing made immense achievements possible. Of the three interests manifest in the earliest piano works, the sonata, the character piece and the variation set, it was the last to which he devoted most of his energy, using the piano at his most fluent and technically competent stage to realize one of the most central aspects of his musical mind and reach perhaps a greater technical pre-eminence than in any other sphere. With the exception of the various dances for four hands which appeared in the middle and later 1860s, all the piano works of this period are in variation form, drawing on a remarkable range of historical reference to create a synthesis which was quite unique in its historical context. Four phases may be discerned. First, that of the early years 1855–8, in which Brahms produced a number of keyboard studies for piano and organ, some ultimately released, and the Variations on an Original Theme, subsequently published as op. 21 no. 1 in 1862: the variations may be considered first since they effect an obvious transition from the Romantic world of the first period into the specific variation techniques of the second. The two great sets of virtuoso works for solo piano appeared between 1862 and 1866, the first published quickly: they were the Variations and Fugue on a Theme of Handel op. 24 and the Variations (Studies) on a Theme of Paganini op. 35, to which may be added the Variations on a Theme of Schumann for piano duet op. 23 of 1863. The various dances appeared between 1866 and 1869, the second set of Hungarian Dances not until 1880, though they may be considered here. Finally, the Variations on a Theme of Haydn for two pianos op. 56b (1873) seem to sum up the achievements of the era in their technique and stylistic nature. Although more familiar in their orchestral version, the Haydn Variations seem to have been conceived in both forms simultaneously, and the two-piano version may rightly be taken as a culmination in relation to its keyboard predecessors.

Variations on an Original Theme

The association of the key of D major with pastoral and reflective qualities unites the Variations on an Original Theme with the second of the ballades which had been written two years previously – and suggests the possibility of an earlier date of conception. For the themes of both possess the same improvisatory and self-absorbed quality in which pedal, which features in fully half of the variation model, plays a conspicuous part, along with irregularity of phrasing through internal repetition and characteristically extended spacings for the right hand against broken chords in the left, both with the capacity to generate strong percussive contrast in the minor key (compare variations 7 and 8 with the second section of the ballade). As earlier shown, the very Romantic quality of Brahms's canon by contrary motion also looks to Schumann's variation methods, and the nature of Brahms's beautiful coda on a pedal clearly reflects such an example as that which concludes Schumann's *Fantasiestücke* op. 12, already echoed in the coda to the variation movement of Brahms's C major Sonata composed three years before. Yet, this atmospheric mood now appears at the service of a quite different technical end: the creation of a series of variations subject to much more precise conditions than hitherto. Chief of these is the striking lessening of the role of the theme, though at the same time, the retention of its phrase structure and cadential skeleton – only the basic elements of its identity – giving the maximum opportunity for new invention, in which, however, the elements of the model still play a crucial part, though in a new context. Exceptions to these new principles were to be so rare as to prove the rule with which Brahms began the second phase of his variation writing.

The spirit in which he approached these variations is clear from the often-quoted remark to Joachim in the year of their composition:

> I occasionally reflect on variation form and find that it must be kept stricter, purer. The old composers retained the bass of the theme, the actual theme, strongly throughout. In Beethoven, Melody, Harmony and Rhythm are so beautifully varied. But I sometimes have to admit that the newer composers (ourselves included) rather (I don't know how to put it) rummage around the theme . . . we keep anxiously to the melody, we do not treat it freely, do not actually create anything new from it, but only load it down. Yet the melody is thus barely recognizable.[12]

His meaning gains further perspective from later remarks to Elizabeth von Herzogenberg:

> I wish that people would distinguish variations from fantasy variations, or whatever we may choose to call the greater number of modern writings in this form. I have a particular affection for the variation form and consider that it offers great scope for our talents and energies. Beethoven treats it with extraordinary severity and rightly calls his variations 'alterations' [Veränderungen]. All the later ones by Schumann, Herzogenberg, Nottebohm . . . are very different. I am of course objecting neither to the form nor the music. I only wish for some distinction in the name to denote the specific character of each.[13]

Brahms's commitment to the former principle, though defined in his own special terms, has often been linked to a remark to his pupil Jenner to the effect that 'the bass carrying the harmony must be clearly present in each variation',[14] as, for example, by Geiringer.[15] That this was specific advice for a pupil, rather than a rule of composition seems abundantly clear from his own practice. The 'severity' which he shared with Beethoven was not a commitment to technical restriction, save in the very broadest sense, but surely to the potential of the model in sustaining a whole movement through the response of the creative imagination, in which regard Brahms had as much resource as Beethoven himself. The remarkable fertility of the *Schumann* Variations yields, therefore, not to more, but to less restriction here.

However, the process by which Brahms attained his mature mastery of the form was not to be simple, and despite many pointers to the future, the Variations on an Original Theme do not yet achieve the freedom he sought, despite their many and insufficiently appreciated qualities. The melody as such may be removed – only hinted at in passing – but the 'bass' (by which differentiated term Brahms presumably implied 'harmonic model') is still present, indeed with much greater clarity than in later works. This arises from the nature of the model's structure – notably its use of pedal, which functions in the first and last four bars, leaving the composer the extreme options either of retention, with the consequence of repetitiousness, or of realizing the inherent harmony, in which case a new bass pattern emerges which loosens its relation to the model. Brahms responds to both possibilities, as the progress of the variations shows. Hence, variation 1 ignores the pedal and realizes the harmony behind it working the outline of the melody into broken chording in the left hand. Variation 2 begins identically in in the left hand but adapts the idea to yet a new harmonic frame. Variation 3 and 4 both return to the pedal with even greater emphasis, variation 3 to the last bar of the first part, and with only an intermediate cadence in the second part, variation 4 virtually likewise. Variation 6 unites the pedal with the cadential progression of variation 1, as does variation 7. Even the minor variations 9 and 10 retain the pedal's role. Only variation 8 uses the minor tonality to create a new progression, drawing on variation 1 in the process, although it is left to the canonic variation to create an entirely new harmonic pattern. Despite Brahms's skill within his framework, the effect is one of similarity, arising from the structural nature of the model, or of great contrast; the pedal is part of an insufficiently differentiated harmonic scheme which requires more intermediate goals, leaving the intervening progressions to be more freely handled. A comparison with the harmonic models he chose for the later variations illuminates both the differences and their consequences.

Although the relation of the harmonic patterns of the variations seems much less subtly organized than in later works, certain aspects of Brahms's search for freedom do point forward, as indeed they also relate to the past. For example, the boldness of the progression in the second part of variation 9, where he substitutes the minor mediant of his original tonality, D major, for the expected submediant, B flat, major or minor, established in the previous, minor variation, focuses on a point of frequent change in later works, and the fluidity of the passage after the double bar is also prophetic, as in variations 2, 7 and 10. The controlling aspect of structure is most clearly evident in the grouping of the variations and the role of the coda. As earlier implied, the groupings are very obvious: namely 1–2, 3–4, (5), 6–7, 8–9, (10), 11–coda. Indeed, the coda offers the most striking evidence of Brahms's desire to complete the work organically. Variation 11 complements the model in its retention of the pedal (the only variation with written out varied repetition), and then proceeds to recall the figuration of variation 1, though here restricted by pedal, the further movement reveals

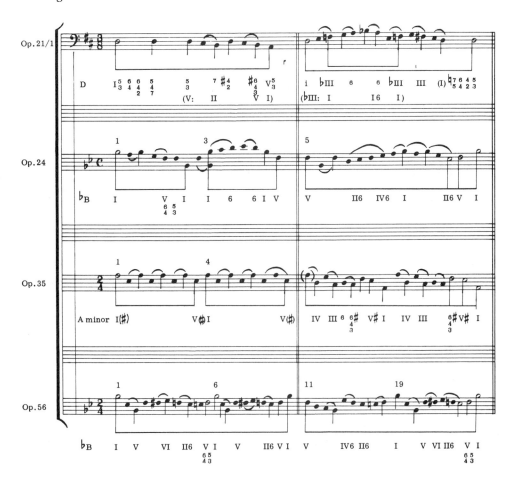

Ex. 15 Harmonic models of the Variations op. 21 no. 1, op. 24, op. 35 and op. 56
  (i) Op. 21 no. 1
  (ii) Op. 24
  (iii) Op. 35
  (iv) Op. 56

the fresh possibilities of the figurations of variations 1, 2 and 6. The gentle imitations of the final page, and the return to the earlier pedal figuration create one of Brahms's most beautiful passages. In this work of transition, therefore, Brahms explores procedures which had the potential to sustain works of infinitely greater scope and stylistic variety than he here attempted. In five years the Variations on a Theme of Handel were to show just how fruitful their realization was to be.

Baroque movements

The remarkable transition in style between these two variation sets was not, however, to be achieved without considerable preparation. As early as 1855 Brahms had been emulating Baroque models: indeed, the fugue of the B major Trio indicates even earlier such working. Important as Schumann's stimulus was to Brahms in matters contrapuntal, he sought more rigorous, complex and historical models. Extensive material which emerged after Brahms's death, some of it only very recently, has shown just how deep was the interest. It covered not merely the conventional forms of the prelude and fugue and the canon, but what were at that time obscure dance movements of the Baroque. The tonal pattern of the pairs of sarabandes, gavottes and gigues written in 1854–5 strongly suggest the intention to complete Suites in the keys of A minor A major and B minor, with the Bach English Suites as the obvious models. Brahms has clearly absorbed both the figuration and the techniques (note, especially the inversion of the subject after the double bar) of the Bach gigues in G minor and B minor in his own pieces in A minor and B minor. However, his characteristic pianism – his chains of thirds and sixths and rigorous contrary motion which produce harsh and unstylistic dissonances – suggest that the imitation served a personal and not a scholarly purpose, well symbolized in the character of the A minor Sarabande, which served with little modification, transposed into C sharp minor, to provide the slow movement of the String Quintet in F op. 88 of 1882. The two Preludes and Fugues for organ in A minor and G minor have similar status, the latter suggesting Bach's 'Great' organ fugue in A minor, as well as the figuration of the Chromatic Fantasia and Fugue, both betraying Brahms's pianism throughout. Indeed, it is the style of the piano transcription, not of the models, which he seems to have applied to his own organ music; we know that, as well as the Chromatic Fantasia and Fugue, his youthful programmes included the great organ works of Bach in transcription.

The only organ works he permitted to be published, and this only considerably later, were the Chorale Prelude and Fugue on 'O Traurigkeit, O Herzeleid' and the Fugue in A flat minor, of 1858 and 1856. They complement his piano variations in showing the fascination for the creation of the maximum variety from the simplest of material. The chorale melody appears in four different forms: slightly decorated in the upper part in the Prelude, as a *cantus firmus* in the pedals in the Fugue, reduced to its simplest thematic and rhythmic form, and in two derivations which provide the subject and its inverted answer. Inversion serves in the Fugue to intensify these relationships. The absence of the constraint of a chorale leaves Brahms free in the single Fugue in A flat minor to explore these principles more fully. Not only is the subject, but also the countersubject inverted, the latter serving to accompany an episode derived from the subject, this generating a second subject, again treated in inversion. The combination of these elements together with the change of temporal relationships through stretto, with the use of augmentation and diminution in varied combinations, reveals not only a remarkable contrapuntal mind, but predicts the thematicism which was to pervade 'free' works with increasing force. It is instructive to compare this subject with that of the idea which Brahms makes the subject of the fugal working in the B major Trio, which shares its abstract quality, directly referable to the *Art of Fugue* that was its most likely stimulus, a manuscript copy of which he possessed at the time, not in his hand, but with his markings (that is, before its appearance in the Complete Edition). But in the later work, Brahms has created an individual, stylistically integrated movement which already breathes the air of the *Requiem*, just as in the contemporary works for chorus.

Handel *Variations*

In the sphere of keyboard writing, as in that of choral composition, Brahms's deep absorption in the past led him to produce a major culminatory work within the next half-decade. In seeking an adequate model for a large-scale set of variations reflecting his new and continually refining ideas on the form, it was to the past, not to his own pianistic imagination, that he now turned. As with the 'St Antoni' Variations of ten years later, the obscure source reflected the depth of his interests. Thus, the Handel theme had only just appeared in a modern edition (vol. 2 of Chrysander's Handel Gesellschaft Edition, which had begun in 1858) – though we have it from Kalbeck through Nottebohm that Brahms knew it through the first edition (published by Walsh in London in 1733),[16] with its French title, 'Suite de pieces'. The theme is the Air from this 'Lesson in B flat', taken from the second volume of Suites. Brahms's choice was symbolic of the depth of his historical commitment. To audiences without a knowledge of his interests, an extensive set of variations (twenty-five) and a lengthy concluding fugue which drew on such distant stimuli came as a challenge. Although Hanslick records that Brahms's performance of his variations at his first Viennese concert in 1862 drew the most applause, he also indicates the inherent difficulty of the richness of his language for an uninitiated audience. For his part, Wagner, though warmly acknowledging 'what could still be done in the old forms'[17] must have sensed the challenge to his 'progressive' aesthetic. Brahms here juxtaposes keyboard styles far removed from his earlier style with those more common in the time, though achieving through his own natural feeling for them a mediation with his natural pianism. Thus he honours not only Handel, but also the French school of Couperin, whose music he edited, in the 'Siciliano' variation no. 19 or the 'Music Box' variation no. 22. But a comparison with such a modern idiom as the 'Hungarian' style of no. 13 brings home the force of the stylistic range. In the field of counterpoint, the rigour of Bach is reflected, though in the culminating fugue it is Bach through the mediation of Beethoven: the challenge that Brahms declined to meet within the context of his Piano Sonata in C major, that of emulating Beethoven's pervasive use of fugue within the sonata context, he here accepts on his own terms, for this keyboard writing could not have occurred without the 'Hammer-klavier' Sonata. But Brahms reflects the inspiration through a self-contained fugue, whose structure is entirely his own, though its function obviously relates to the other Beethoven tradition embodied in the climactic fugues of the *Eroica* Variations and, above all, the *Diabelli* Variations.

Remarkable as it is, however, the great enrichment of keyboard idiom is only one aspect of the *Handel* Variations. In the treatment of theme and harmony, Brahms makes immense strides towards a method which, if inspired by Beethoven, is highly individual in its detail. For the structural clarity of the model, its clear cadence framework, thematic simplicity and degree of repetition, offered him the strength of form which left the maximum freedom to invent, an opportunity which he explored to the full, transcending the relatively intuitive approach of op. 21. The transition from Handel through Beethoven to Brahms is not undisguised as the work unfolds. The gesture to Handel as starting point is obvious in the first variation. Both composers simply fill out the chordal space with figuration, though Brahms retains the original bass more accurately: Handel uses broken chords, Brahms, with greater span, likewise, but with a recurrent decorative motive in the upper part, likewise outlining the melody quite clearly.

But whereas Handel continues the process through five variations, Brahms is quickly drawn to more radical treatments, and the source of his freedom is the principle contained in the decorative motive. Schoenberg draws particular attention to this principle, pioneered by Beethoven, which he terms the 'motive of the variation':[18] that is, a figure taken from the theme which will then provide the entire thematic material of a variation, supplanting the theme itself as the means of unity. He draws important parallels between the *Handel* and *Diabelli* Variations in revealing the vast potential of the method. While outlining a melody, it has a limited role, whether as in variation 1 or in variation 3, where an appoggiatura functions to decorate the melody notes. Once freed from this function, however, the motive can transform the surface of the model. Two stages are elaborated as the *Handel* Variations unfold: the obscuring of the model by octave transposition of the motive, or the provision of free material not so obviously derived, as, for example, through the further variation of a derivative. Variation 4 shows the octave transposition of a thematic motive, even more clearly demonstrated in variation 10 and more distant derivatives are shown in variations 15–18. But the fuller transformational consequences only appear when the motive generates longer phrases. From variation 5 Brahms begins to evolve two-bar phrases, through the transformation of previous material, which then demand repetition, removing the original pattern, a principle which functions through variations 6, 9, 11, 13, 14, 19 and 20–22. Many of these larger phrases contain within them their own motivic repetition, little developments reflecting the principle.

Such larger-scale repetition has a profound effect on harmony, since both harmony and theme are interdependent. In cases where the melodic outline and phrasing are retained, the harmonic identity of the model is also likely to be retained; but when the outline is disturbed by repetition, harmonic modification is likely to result. In variation 11, repetition can be accommodated to the harmonic model, but in many other cases it cannot, producing in turn much more radical harmonic results. Most notable in this work, and attributable to the influence of the rise of a third so prominent in the theme, is the transposition of bars 1 – 2 up a third, the original cadential goal only being restored at the end of bar 4. Brahms makes this shift in fully ten of the twenty-five variations. In extreme cases, the repetition has further consequences in the second part, as in variation 9, which repeats a semitone higher than expected, on F sharp. More fundamental variants involve the modification of an important cadence degree. As early as variation 2, Brahms substitutes the dominant for the tonic as cadence goal in bar 2; in variation 3 the tonic chord in bar 7 is given a seventh to serve as dominant to E flat, rather than the tonic original, whereas in variation 17, this subdominant is established as a main structural degree. Into such radically altered patterns, Brahms can incorporate the kind of local reorderings and surprise shifts apparent in the D major Variations, as for example the Neapolitan stress in variations 15 and 16.

As is clear from the unfolding of thematic and harmonic possibilities, Brahms's structure is very systematic and therefore very different in concept from that of the *Diabelli* Variations: where Beethoven's aim is so often to surprise by fragmentation and aphoristic presentation, Brahms erects a more steady structure in which Beethoven's radical methods achieve a new identity. The principle of grouping plays an important role in this effect, not only by the traditional method of 'variation of variation', as clearly in variations 15–16, 17–18 and 23–24, but through affinities of mood, material and key as in variations 1–3, 5–6, 7–8 and 11–12. The more individual characters of the remaining, single, variations serve to show how Brahms intensified the effect of growth and relationship by local contrast, and these variations contain some of the most striking of his inventions. Counterpoint also provides an important resource in securing unity and variety, just as in the Beethoven variations. The canon at the octave in variation 16, for example, seems very close in spirit to that of variation 19 of the *Diabelli* set, though the octave canon in the minor of variation 6 is more Brahmsian (compare the final variation of the *St Antoni*). Again, however, Brahms's method is distinctive, as in the creation of new counterpoints to the theme when placed in the tenor voice; variations 17 and 18 provide an illustration, as well as showing the force of grouping, since the latter derives from the

Ex. 16 (i) Handel: 'Air in B flat' with variation 1
        (ii) Brahms: Variations and Fugue on a Theme of Handel, variation 1

former, while variation 12 offers an earlier and less ambitious version of the same approach. The greatest evidence of contrapuntal design naturally appears in the concluding fugue. It has often been observed that this fugue is more Bachian than Handelian in its exhaustive wealth of contrapuntal device which brings all the devices of the Fugue in A flat minor into the context of a virtuoso piano work. Thus Brahms brings his subject, derived, like that of the *Diabelli* fugue, from the theme, into contrapuntal relationships involving diminution, augmentation, stretto, building to the final peroration through a long dominant pedal with two distinct ideas above.

But the pianism is an equal part of the conception, and in this, the most complex example of Brahms's virtuoso style, the characteristic spacings in thirds, sixths, and the wide spans between the hands are employed as never before. Indeed, the pianistic factor serves to create the great contrasts within the fugue, which transcends a conventional fugal movement to create a further set of variations, in which many of the previous textures are recalled in the context of the equally transformed fugal theme.

Schumann *Variations* (op. 23)

Brahms completed only one other keyboard work before leaving Hamburg to settle in Vienna for good, a work which looks both forward and backwards in terms of his creative and personal life: forward to the medium which was to be associated with his most popular works in Vienna, backwards to the continuing memory of his mentor Schumann in a work based on a theme of his. The Variations on a Theme of Schumann written in November 1861 give the first evidence of that mastery of the duet medium that was to penetrate right through the Hungarian Dances and Waltzes into the keyboard realizations of his symphonic music into which Brahms put such artistry. They also show the continuing depth of his feeling for Schumann, this in the adoption of his manner in variations, in strong contrast to the rigorous methods apparent in the *Handel* set.

Brahms's reasons for the composition have never been fully explained, but it represented a bold step at the time, since the theme possessed, and was to retain, a symbolic significance in the Schumann circle. Known traditionally as 'Schumann's last thought', which he believed to have been dictated to him by the spirits of Schubert and Mendelssohn, just before his death, it was in fact a recollection of the theme of the slow movement of his Violin Concerto, written in 1853, whose publication Joachim later forbade in deference to Schumann's reputation. Finally published in 1937, it was to retain its spiritual associations, since its discoverer, Jelly d'Arányi, believed it to have come to her through the spirits of Joachim – her great-uncle – and Schumann himself. Brahms did not include Schumann's piano variations in the complete edition which appeared from 1893 (they finally appeared in 1939) and his contribution of a set of his own variations on a then unknown theme, concluding with a funeral march, was an obviously personal gesture to the memory of his departed friend.

He even builds on Schumann's first variation, which simply adds a voice to the retained theme in the middle parts in a manner comparable with variation 10 of the *Handel* Variations and there is an improvisatory freedom that Brahms shared with Schumann but rarely permitted in his later variations. He modulates much more frequently than normal, through E flat major to minor, B major, E flat, G minor, C minor, E flat, though he never disturbs the length of the model as in the earlier Schumann set, only extending one variation, no. 2, by a single bar in an elaborated cadential progression. In his range of mood he reflects current interest, however, by including hints of the 'Hungarian style' (variation 8), of the waltz (variation 5) and even a reference to the 'learned' contrapuntal opening of the introduction to the finale of the Piano Quintet. Once again, the close is related to the opening, the theme being reintroduced into the funeral march in the most touching manner.

Paganini *Variations*

Consistent with the character of its model, hints of a popular style permeate even more strongly the two sets of Variations on the Theme of Paganini, the waltz variation (No. 4/2) being especially conspicuous. Indeed, they combine with other variational features to relate to the more serious model of the *Handel* Variations in illustrating Brahms's developing methods and to contradict the traditional view of the works as merely providing a vehicle for virtuoso display. That the latter quality is of central importance is undeniable: Brahms called the sets 'Studien für Pianoforte' and they relate directly to the Fifty-One Exercises and the various arrangements which he made for technical purposes. The extent of the virtuosity belies the view of him as a highly expressive and powerfully symphonic pianist, yet no virtuoso in the modern, Lisztian sense. This virtuosity actually exceeds that of both Liszt and Schumann in their responses to the Paganini caprice and draws all the elements already noted in the ballades and the variations into a challenge as great in pianistic terms as that posed musically by the *Handel* Variations. Thus Brahms offers examples of contrary motion (vol. 2 nos 8 and 11), hands in sixths and thirds (vol. 1 nos. 1 and 3), alternating hands (vol. 1 no. 3), wide-spaced upper figurations (vol. 2 no. 7), octave work (vol. 1 no. 7), taxing cross rhythms with octaves and so forth. Something of Brahms's style is, of course, attributable to Tausig's example (since they were written for him) as shown, for instance, in his *Tägliche Studien* of which Brahms possessed a copy; but Brahms's technique itself extended into the future in its influence. There are clear parallels to the methods of Rachmaninov in his own variations on this theme in the Brahms variations vol. 1 no. 3 and vol. 2 no. 6.

Hungarian Dances

Brahms's growing interest in popular dance elements, first clear in the Variations on a Hungarian Song op. 21 no. 2, prominently displayed in the 'Gipsy Rondo' of the G minor Piano Quartet op. 25 and hinted at in the variations just completed, comes into fuller focus in the extensive collections of Hungarian Dances and Waltzes for piano duo, which he completed in the later 1860s, later sets following. The Hungarian Dances have a special connection with Brahms's youth, for the first set contained material dating from his tour with the violinist Reményi of 1853, which Reményi regarded Brahms as having no authority to use. Accordingly, Brahms designated the second set as being written 'in the Hungarian manner'. As will be shown more fully in connection with his interest in German folksong, Brahms's scholarship did not extend to the sources of the melodies which captivated his musical imagination. Like Liszt and others, the interest was not in genuine Hungarian peasant music, as, for example, later to be explored by such a figure as Bartók, but in popular composed music of recent provenance played by gipsies as café entertainment. In this sense, the dances stand in considerable contrast to the 'Hungarian song' of the earlier variations, with its alternation of 2/4 and 3/4 metres, a feature never explored in these works or the later *Zigeunerlieder*.

It is quite possible that Brahms never saw his melodies notated, since he apparently accompanied Reményi by ear. The melodies which he used, nearly all of which have been identified, fall into several broad types. Most common is the czardas, synonymous with Hungarian music in the popular imagination, though only, in fact, evolved from the courtship dance 'Verbunkos' earlier in the century; it is a fast 2/4 movement generally in the minor key. Brahms made four settings, exploring varieties of the type. Nos 1 and 8, 'Isteni Czàrdás' (Sárközy) and 'Luiza Czàrdás' (Frank), employ a very similar pattern of rhythm and melody, both generating parallel second sections with a common decorative figure.

Ex. 17 Hungarian Dances
    (i) No. 1
    (ii) No. 8
    (iii) No. 2
    (iv) No. 9

No. 2, 'Emma Czàrdás' (Windt), is more forceful, intensifying the offbeat accompaniment with a quicker middle section, 'vivo'. No. 9, 'Makóc Czàrdás' (Travnik), takes this pattern a stage further, with heavy downbeats and a more strident melody, though now with a quieter middle section. These examples are complemented by three other types: nos 3 and 10 (from *Tolnai Lakadalmas* by Rimer), and no. 7 (not identified) represent a more playful kind, the first especially, both generating more strident middle sections in the major key. Nos 4 and 5, 'Kalocsai Emlek' (Merty) and 'Bartfai Emlek' (Kéler-Bela), are of a more intense nature, in the minor key, the first improvisatory, conditioned by a very strong upbeat pattern and suggesting the cimbalom in its tremolo accompaniment, the second more direct, both generating 'vivace' middle sections in the major key. No. 6, 'Rózsa Bokor' (Nittinger), is the most singular in its constant tempo changes and initial, preludial use of the pauses within the first theme.

It is the most popular pieces of the first set that represent Brahms's Hungarian music in the public imagination. Yet, in the context of his output, it is the second set which is the more interesting, both in musical content, and in the much more direct evidence it furnishes of what Brahms regarded as Hungarian in his own music (whatever the degree of invention in the first set, his ideas must have been largely conditioned by the borrowed material). His comment that the second set was better because of the finer piano duet writing could be applied much more generally, since the greater equality of writing between the two players creates greater subtlety of compositional balance, especially as regards possibilities for contrapuntal relations and the role of variation. Many of the dances present a clear and prominent counterpoint to the main theme, and in two instances (nos 14 and 17), the two are of equal weight, no. 14 actually presenting two forms of the same basic idea. Indeed, Brahms leans very little on the popular melodic idioms of the first set, offering, for example, no further variations on the czardas type illustrated in nos 1 and 8. He merely retains the 2/4 metre and the various sectional possibilities established in the first set. Rather, he draws on his own rich vein of 'gipsy' feeling, drawing various of the characteristic surface idioms into a seemingly instinctive expression. One notes especially the role of what might be termed the 'gipsy cadence' and the omnipresent improvisatory turning figures of the style as demonstrated in the first set. The characteristic minor cadence of no. 9 is taken up and intensified in no. 14, its bold manner reflecting the very strong use Brahms makes of it in the central section of the 'Gipsy Rondo' of the op. 25 Quartet. But it is the endless potential of the turning figure that is the most absorbing. At one point, the arresting 'ritenuto sempre' just before the end of no. 15, Brahms seems to present *to* the listener the idea from which he creates so much.

These features also come into association with more obviously Brahmsian elements to achieve a synthesis which is symbolic of the growing absorption of elements in his maturing style. The second section of no. 11 is, for example, both idiomatic in these terms and Brahmsian in showing the growing interest in figures which turn on the manipulation of a simple scalic shape, whose repetition may create asymmetry. A comparison of this example with no. 16 and, more distantly, the opening of the late Intermezzo in E flat minor is very illuminating.

Of equal interest is the role of the harmonic effects associated with the style on Brahms's receptive ear. Only one of the first set is really interesting in harmonic terms, no. 9, whose modal inflections Brahms seizes on to create a special effect. No. 14 explores the harmonic device in conventional D minor, extending the relation to create an unusual progression, whose improvisatory quality is stressed by the imitation of the cimbalom, in parallel with no. 4, as mentioned. Its associated accompaniment pattern seems clearly inspirational of Brahms's first dance, no. 11, though he goes further and places it in the Dorian mode, permitting a first main cadence with a major rather than minor chord on the fourth degree.

Waltzes

If the Hungarian Dances reflect an early and continuing passion, the waltz represents a seemingly new attraction in the early 1860s. Although a pronounced ländler movement may be seen penetrating the broad triple time of the opening of the B flat Sextet in 1860, Brahms's early triple-time movements are all very dour and march-like, as in the first movement of the F minor Sonata and the funeral march of the *Requiem*. The waltz variation of the *Paganini* Variations heralds a new feeling, seemingly reflective of the move to Vienna, and to prove almost as pervasive as the gipsy idiom. From now on waltz rhythm will often be sensed even in the sphere of chamber and orchestral music, and the immediate and immense popularity of the op. 39 four-handed waltzes published in 1866 led quickly to the publication of the solo version and even the issue of four arranged for two pianos. Moreover the piano waltzes were to lead to the composition of waltzes for four hands at one piano with vocal participation to texts by Brahms's favourite Daumer, which he called *Liebeslieder-walzer*. As with the Hungarian Dances, the demand stimulated a later set, *Neue Liebeslieder*, which are similarly more complex and artistically rewarding. Attention is often drawn to the fact that the latter set were composed to be performed as vocal pieces whereas the first set are only for performance with voices 'ad lib'. However, the intimate relation between words and music indicates that they cannot have been composed as purely keyboard works. Just as in earlier examples, therefore, one may suggest the possibility that the keyboard waltzes which preceded them may also have had a vocal or textual stimulus.

As with his later interest in the appearance of minstrelsy[19] in Vienna, Brahms responded eagerly to rhythmically distinctive popular music. Of the various waltz backgrounds which Vienna provided at the time the strongest is that of Schubert's four-handed waltzes and ländler. Brahms seems to have been unaffected by the more capricious and idiosyncratic inspirations of Schumann, themselves rooted in Schubert's style. He seems to have found more than sufficient stimulus in the wide range of Schubert's pieces which explored both the bold upbeat idiom of the German dance or the gentle swaying style of the ländler, to say nothing of the wide harmonic range which Schubert employs within such a narrow binary context, with its regular first part of eight bars or multiples. Like Schubert, Brahms brings into his waltzes other aspects of his style with the greatest ease. Thus there is a strong gipsy element in no. 4, while cross rhythms dominate no. 6. Of numerous examples, nos 8 and 9 show harmonic digression in the second part, and no. 14 demonstrates the motivic preoccupation which displaces the accent, the 3/4 metre admitting 2/4 phrasing.

St Antoni *Variations*

The decade which separated the *St Antoni* Variations from the *Schumann, Handel* and *Paganini* sets reflects a remarkable maturing and refining in Brahms's command of the medium. Even allowing the different characters of these works, one senses here a much greater originality and effortless exploration of methods already fully instinctive. The work stands in succession to the *Handel* Variations rather than the others in the nature of its model and the comparable subtlety of its treatment. It is both freer in effect yet more 'severe' in Brahms's Beethovenian sense, no longer an unfolding series of variations which move further from the model but a mere eight variations of totally distinct characters. Even the structurally freer duo variations of op. 23 do not rival them in this regard. Brahms seems to draw on the more relaxed character of much of his music of the middle 1860s, not least the dances, yet at the same time looks much further back to the past in his use of a more obscure theme and in his concluding passacaglia. For if the Handel theme was esoteric, it was at least available. Brahms only came to know the 'Chorale St Antoni' three years before he completed the work: it was a theme in a wind partita discovered by the Haydn scholar C. F. Pohl, though now Haydn's authorship is disputed and the general view is that the melody is by Pleyel or is an anonymous Burgen-land pilgrim's chant.[20] In relation to the Beethoven tradition of a concluding fugue, the use of a passacaglia was also a pointer to the historical orientation of Brahms's thought, for the form was considered archaic. Yet his primary interest was creative. Already deeply influenced by the ground-bass principle in the evolution of his variation methods, he found the form offered great freedom as well as pervading unity. In terms of his creative development, the work clearly relates to the keyboard background and may best be seen in this context, orchestral features being considered at a later stage.

Viewed overall, Brahms's achievement in this work rests on three factors:

first, the subtlety with which he treats the model; second, arising from this, the originality of his derivation of thematic material; third, the crucial role of counterpoint now permitted by the more ample medium of two pianos. As in the *Handel* Variations, the harmonic model is treated in three basic ways, though the first – the retention of the original progression intact – only appears in one variation (no. 6), where it is quickly overcome by radical structural alteration which substitutes the upper and lower mediants, D and G, for the first two cadence points of the first half, the second working freely. Elsewhere the harmonic movement is either reduced by the use of pedal or elaborated by the insertion of passing harmonies. These methods may occur together. Thus, variation 5 freezes the harmony in its first and last four bars over pedal, but recalls the original progression of the opening of the second part with surprising interpolations throughout. By contrast with the systematic treatment in the *Handel* Variations, each of these character variations contains some special but different harmonic turn which contributes to its special personality. Such an example as the stress on the bass F sharp at bar 3 of the 'Siciliano' variation (no. 7), a diminished chord substituting for the expected dominant, is typical of the passing detail which can help to stamp character.

Ex. 18 *St Antoni* Variations, bass of model and of variation 7, bars 1–5

The freedom of such working, taken with the special nature of the model, which admits repetition within the first part and recalls this material at the close, offered Brahms great opportunities for varied repetition exploiting the resources of two pianos and of the orchestra. It is rather through this means than by mere 'learned' device that the contrapuntal ingenuities come into play. Thus after the simple process of contrapuntal inversion in variation 1. Brahms produces double counterpoint at the twelfth in variation 4, bar 11, at the same by inversion in variation 8, bar 6, and in mirror at the same in the second part of this variation. Diminution provides another method of varied repetition in variation 3.

As emerges from the comparison of successive variations, Brahms does not grow steadily away from his model but rather establishes an initial and immediate contrast with entirely new surface material, only restoring the original shape at the midpoint, in variation 6, where this is counterbalanced by the greatest tonal modification of the set, as indicated. However, the more straightforward plan is restored in the concluding passacaglia, which builds successively upon the recurring five-bar bass, derived, like that of the *Diabelli* fugue, from the model, here by conflation of theme and bass.

Since harmony and theme are complementary aspects of the same unity in such a work, all these features are also reflected in thematic aspects of the individual variations. Again, three methods are clear: the decoration of the original theme, the abstraction of parts of its contour to form a new surface and the creation of an entirely new surface in which derived material is more apparent to the eye than to the ear. Again the simplest method is related to the simplest harmonic form, variation 5 complementing its initial harmonic retention with an obvious decoration of the theme, by analogy with variation 7 of the *Handel* set. Harmonic change is naturally reflected in the thematic contour, the progression from F to G flat minor being mirrored in the upper line's, C – D flat.

However, the process of decoration is not as overt elsewhere. Indeed Brahms's motives cannot be termed 'decorative' since they make new and logical developments of their own. Thus he creates a new surface with its own continuity matching the harmonic variants of the model. Indeed, in one example, the power of the evolution is such that it radically affects the phrase structure of the model, normally inviolate in Brahms's variations. In variation 3, motivic variation can be seen to penetrate the more confined world of the formal variation, extending the first phrase from four bars to five – a process which makes interesting comparison with the thematic extension associated with the transposed models of op. 24. Finally, completely new contours are evolved in three variations, nos 1, 7, 8, which can be compared with parallel cases in the earlier work.

Ex. 19 *St Antoni* Variations, theme and variation 3, bars 1–7

3

Choral Music

The remarkable scope of historical reference achieved in the keyboard works of the second period would have represented adequate evidence of a vital new attitude to the past by itself, and one quite sufficient to enrich greatly an extensive output of chamber and orchestral music. Yet the relationship seems very immediate when compared with the much more distant world he evokes in his output of choral music. For here the link between historical exploration, performance and composition is at its clearest, especially in the works written between the beginning of his period of intense study, from 1855, and the appearance of his first mature chamber and piano works from 1862. The numerous compositions reflect the practical circumstances of his life, as conductor of the choir at the court of Detmold from 1857 to 1859 and of the Hamburg Frauenchor from 1857 to 1861. Even in recent years, material from the latter source has continued to surface to show the importance of the compositions for female voices in the emergence of his choral style.[1] Of earlier published works so inspired we have the Three Sacred Choruses op. 37 and the Twelve Songs and Romances op. 44, both SSAA (published in 1865 and 1866 respectively). The tradition of the male chorus is represented in the Five Choruses op. 41, while mixed settings range from four parts (the two sets of German Folksongs published in 1864 and some of the Secular Songs op. 62), five parts (the Motets op. 29) to six parts in the remainder of op. 62 and the Three Songs op. 42. The preference for unaccompanied female voices is also apparent in the accompanied sphere, in the Ave Maria op. 12 and Psalm 13 op. 27, both with organ, and the Four Songs with two horns and harp op. 17. Two works combine four-part mixed voices with instruments, the *Geistliches Lied* op. 30 (with organ) and the *Funeral Hymn* op. 13 (with windband), both of which have been seen as preparations for the mood of the *Requiem*. The known composition period of the *Requiem* (though almost certainly not its real period) covers 1865–9 and is preceded by that of *Rinaldo* (begun in 1863 but not completed until 1868) and followed by the Alto Rhapsody (completed in 1869), the *Song of Triumph* (1870–1) and *Song of Destiny* (1868–71).

Smaller choral works

Almost all the smaller choral works of this period reflect traditional elements in some obvious way, even the settings of secular romantic texts. They may be surveyed from the two broad standpoints of melodic idiom – its nature and origin – and treatment, specifically with regard to counterpoint and harmony. The complete absorption in German folksong shown in the solo songs and, before them, the piano works, appears with even greater scope in the choral settings. The two sets of German Folksongs, to which can be added the unpublished folksongs of the same period, draw again on his favourite source, Kretzschmer-Zuccalmaglio, as well as on Corner, Meister, Arnold and Becker. In addition to these sources, however, a closely related element appears very strongly, and one destined to play a comparably pervasive role in Brahms's work: the chorale melody. Both the unaccompanied works which crown the first phase are chorale based: the first, *Est ist das Heil uns kommen her* uses the melody set several times by Bach, once in the same key in his cantata of the same name, while the less familiar *O Heiland reiss die Himmel auf* op. 74 no. 2 draws on the German version of the plainsong *Rorate Coeli desuper*. Yet neither element represented merely a historical symbol, to challenge the composer's ingenuity in setting. As shown, the idioms were intimately associated with Brahms's own.

The *Marienlieder* op. 22, to folk texts from the above sources as well as Uhland, provide the ideal illustration of the interaction, for Brahms described them as having been composed 'somewhat in the manner of German folksong and chorale'.[2] A comparison with sources is possible in view of the texts, which were already associated with melodies, and which Brahms had himself arranged in the solo as well as mixed folksong settings. Thus, in 'Marias Wallfahrt' (no. 3). Brahms can be seen to retain something of the outline of his favoured source melody (see no. 14 of the 1894 collection) whilst creating a new 'folk melody'. However the preceding two pieces 'Der Englische Gruss' (no. 1), and 'Marias Kirchgang,' (no. 2) both draw on the folk source, the first replacing the associated melody set in the German Folksongs (no. 14) with a melody in the major which begins with the familiar initial phrase, in the alto, the second offering an obvious variant of the material in the minor mode. This basic idea also recurs in 'Magdalena', no. 6 of these Marian songs.

The very personal nature of Brahms's 'traditional' idiom becomes clearer if these settings are compared with the ancient Marian composition which he performed several times, Eccard's *Übers Gebirg Maria geht*, which in fact appears more 'Romantic' through the richness of its harmony than the Brahms work. So natural was the interaction of borrowed and invented material that Brahms could write to Grimm of the opening of the *Funeral Hymn*, seemingly ironically: 'I don't need to tell you that I have not used any folksong or chorale material.'[3] In fact the opening is strikingly like the

(i)

(ii)

(iii)

Ex. 20   (i) 'Maria ging aus wandern' (*Deutsche Volkslieder* no. 14)
         (ii) 'Marias Wallfahrt' (*Marienlieder*, op. 22 no. 3)
         (iii) *Marienlieder*, op. 22
              'Der englische Gruss' (no. 1)
              'Marias Kirchgang' (no. 2)
              'Magdalena' (no. 6)

chorale – Nun lasst uns den Leib begraben', as Reimann notes, and Kalbeck in the same spirit identifies other much less obvious chorale links.[4]

If Brahms's feeling for the past is apparent in the nature of his melodic idiom and preferences, it is equally so in the treatments he accords his material, specifically the very extensive and ingenious use of counterpoint and the frequent suggestion of archaic harmonic devices. Contemporary with the contrapuntal keyboard works of 1855–6 are movements of a 'Mass' planned throughout in canonic form and illustrative of the aspiration which led him to declare to Clara in 1856: 'I can now write canons in all possible artistic forms.'[5] Canons were the first preoccupations in the growth of his choral language, some of the op. 113 canons known to derive from the period. The recent publication of most movements, previously known only from the correspondence and from the surviving 'Benedictus', also used in the third section of the Motet op. 74 no. 1 to new text, helps to illustrate the attitude which led him to remark to Joachim: 'quite apart from the ingenuity, is it good music.'[6] Joachim shared the concern; of a Kyrie movement (not part of the 'Mass'), he writes: 'Your Kyrie is in spirit much more than a study – the word can only refer to the great range of the voice movement, not to the work's character, which is without any dryness or pedantry.'[7] Reference to the long-published Three Sacred Choruses op. 37 confirms the essentially – if not effortlessly – Brahmsian character of the pieces. The Latin explanation of device, used for the canon in contrary motion in the Variations on an Original Theme, was applied to each of op. 37 in the manuscript: 'O Bone Jesu' is a double canon by contrary motion, 'Adoramus Te' a canon with answers at the fourth and fifth below and octave. 'Regina Coeli' stands a little apart in idiom, essentially built on canon by inversion, though with homophonic support. It has been related to Mozart's setting of the same text.[8]

Other examples of canon appear in the last of the female settings op. 44, of Uhland's 'Märznacht', a canon at the fifth and octave below, as well as in 'Morgengesang' and 'Der englische Gruss' in the German Folksongs, both using pre-imitation before the appearance of the melody in the top voice, the latter at the fifth and octave, the former by contrary motion through modulating intervals. The device is subtly incorporated into the *Marienlieder*, as mentioned.

In the two chorale motets, *Es ist das Heil uns kommen her* and *O Heiland, reiss die Himmel auf*, of 1860 and (begun) 1863 respectively, Brahms draws many of the devices of the smaller works together with an assurance and a vigour which points to a new emphasis in the relationship with the past, far exceeding the efforts of Schumann or even Mendelssohn in restoring such links. The first is comprised of a harmonised chorale followed by an extensive chorale fugue in which the melody is presented as a cantus firmus in the first bass part, its successive phrases anticipated in the pre-imitation of the other parts. The latter is a chorale motet in strict variation form, like the traditional motet 'per omnes versus', in which the melody is successively varied in each verse. The most obvious stimulus for the latter setting was the work of J. S. Bach, especially the cantata *Christ lag in Todesbanden* and the motet *Jesu, meine Freude*. Brahms would have known both works especially the cantata, which he performed in Detmold in 1857 and later with the Gesellschaft in 1876. However, Brahms used neither work as a model, rather reflecting in the basic principle of chorale variation many other personal devices evolved in response to the past.

The background to *Es ist das Heil* is less clear. Although the chorale harmonization clearly suggests Bach in function and in general, though certainly not detailed, style, Bach's own cantata on this text is in no way connected to Brahms's extensive cantus firmus fugue, which again draws many elements in its very Brahmsian expression. Hints of *Christ lag in Todesbanden* have again been pointed out in the work.[9] Yet Brahms effects a remarkable synthesis of devices and in his strict working we can see the technical background from which he drew so fruitfully into the 'free' works, as in the combinations of diminutions, augmentations and inversions on the chorale's first phrase.

In seeking a closer background model for the movement it is possible

Ex. 21 *Es ist das Heil uns kommen her*, op. 29 no. 1, bars 19–22

that a nearer influence was significant: that of Mendelssohn. His chorale setting 'Aus tiefer Noth', from the *Drei Kirchenlieder* op. 23 for four-part mixed chorus, is not identical in form but offers important parallels. Its harmonized chorale is followed not by one but three movements, the first and last fugal, the middle an arioso; however the fugues contain many of Brahms's prominent elements, the first based on the chorale, the last introducing it as a cantus firmus. Yet the greater strictness and ingenuity of Brahms's writing points an essential difference between two very historically inclined composers of the Romantic era.

Although Brahms sought to display his brilliant contrapuntal gifts in all kinds of choral music, there exist examples where he seems to hide them, thus pointing to an essential aspect of his developing language, the structural rather than stylistic use of devices of strict counterpoint. The first and third sections of the four-part motet *Schaffe in mir, Gott, ein rein Herz* op. 29 no. 2 (1857–60) conceal respectively a canon by inversion between the outer parts and a canon at the seventh below, both adopting a lyrical and reflective manner in response to the text's 'create in me a clean heart, O God' and 'for in Thee do I put my trust', and giving no hint of their art. By contrast, the second and fourth parts rival the other motets in contrapuntal ingenuity, with double counterpoint, strettos, inversions and combinations of different types. In the *Geistliches Lied* of 1856, the accompanied medium which points in its mood directly to that of the *Requiem* also obscures a canon by inversion.

The contrapuntal is the most frequently stressed aspect of Brahms's technical response to the past. Yet his interest as a harmonist was equally profound. His love of the Romantic archaic effects of juxtaposed triads receives a particular emphasis in two settings of this period, both also included in the solo songs: 'Vergangen ist mir Glück und Heil' op. 62 no. 7 for mixed voices and 'Ich schwing mein Horn ins Jammertal' op. 41 no. 1 for male chorus. However, while both use root position triads throughout, the former achieves the more archaic effect through its simulation of harmonies associated with the Dorian mode. It is written in D minor, though with no sharps or flats, save for a C sharp for cadential purposes, as is acceptable in the modal tradition. Only in the first phrase does a B flat chord appear, where it can be seen as part of the tonicisation of F on its way to D minor. Elsewhere, the provision of a major chord on IV, incorporating what is often termed the 'Dorian sixth' gives the composition a very special flavour, though, as Schenker points out, it is not a modal composition as such; rather it suggests the mode through the resources of modern harmony, exactly as does Beethoven in the 'Lydian' movement of his A minor Quartet.

The Dorian mode, by far the most common and easy to evoke in the nineteenth-century musical language, is also a background to the chorale motet *O Heiland, reiss die Himmel auf*, where it appears in F with a key signature of three flats. Here the harmony is much more individual through the free working of parts, inversions enabling the 'Dorian sixth' (D in F minor) to be very naturally absorbed into the harmonic movement. In contrast, however, the harmonization of *Es ist das Heil uns kommen her* appears very modern in its incorporation of Brahmsian chromaticism within the context of a harmonization in the contrapuntal-homophonic tradition of Bach. Like Bach in his parallel E major setting (Riemenschneider no. 4), Brahms absorbs the modal origin of the melody (Mixolydian, with lowered seventh, in E major) within his functional harmony. A comparison of their methods is particularly illuminating, Bach harmonizing with the chord on the leading note to A, Brahms using the dominant seventh to A, though avoiding immediate resolution so as make a stress on F sharp (the submediant of A), which permits his chromatic bass movement E – E sharp – F sharp. Thus Brahms draws a Bachian progression (compare with bar 8) into a more advanced context (Example 22).

Although Brahms's whole emphasis was towards the reabsorption of more distant traditions of German choral music, there exists a number of works in which, as in the solo songs, more recent idioms are employed, notably the Mendelssohnian partsong, as well as works which bridge the gap in various ways with subtle fusions of the many elements in his choral language, especially reflecting folksong. These examples provide the core of the Twelve Songs and Romances for female voices op. 44 and the *Weltliche A Cappella Gesänge* for mixed voices op. 42 and 62. The four male choruses which follow 'Ich schwing mein Horn' in op. 41 are much more consistent in type, being essentially military songs to stylised texts by Lemcke which stand in the Schumann tradition, as well as reflecting the interest in the male chorus which led Brahms to couple it with solo voice in the large-scale settings of *Rinaldo* and the Harzreise fragment (the *Alto Rhapsody*). The settings for mixed voices offer some of the richest textures of the period, pointing directly to the autumnal beauty of the later op. 104 set. Brahms's textual choices parallel those of the solo settings including folksongs in translation as well as German (Italian and Slavonic in op. 44 nos 3 and 4, from *Des Knaben Wunderhorn* in op. 62 nos 1 and 2), as well as folk-like texts, for example by Uhland and Heyse. The enthusiasm for Heyse's texts *Aus dem Jungbrunnen* is even more marked in the choral sphere, providing words for nos 3–6 in op. 62 and nos 7–10 in op. 44.

Again, textual type is directly reflected in setting. The folk texts beget

extensions of the folk idiom: compare, for example, 'Rosmarin' op. 62 no.
1 with the Gungl piece Brahms draws into the 'Wiegenlied' op. 49 no. 4.
Yet Brahms is always ready to vary the pattern. Thus the second part of
each strophe of 'Rosmarin' substitutes the initial triple metre for common
metre to support the text. The Heyse settings reveal great interest in phrase
extension and harmonic subtlety within a narrow context, the opening
phrase being two and a half rather than the expected two bars through
augmentation of the final foot 'kühle', while the handling of the continuation, especially the cadence on 'dein rauschen süss' recalls the characteristic iv–I progression which opens 'In stiller Nacht'. Phrase interest is equally
strong in the more conventional settings and provides a means of
distinguishing Brahms from a Mendelssohnian background, whether
through textual choice – 'Vineta' op. 42 no. 2 reflects its five metrical feet
in five bars of 3/8 – or compositional choice, the four feet of 'Minnelied',
op. 44 no. 1 phrasing in three bars of 3/8.

In the pieces which flank 'Vineta' in op. 42 Brahms achieves his most
subtle fusions of the archaic and the Romantic. 'Abendständchen' draws
on the archaic associations of progressions of root triads and open-fifth
chords (G minor – D minor – F major – G minor – D minor open) as well
as on repeated chords in antiphony (compare the choral recitative of the

Ex. 22 (i) J. S. Bach: *Es ist das Heil uns kommen her*
        (ii) Brahms: *Es ist das Heil uns kommen her*

Gabrieli pieces he knew) to evoke the distant atmosphere of the Romantic text 'Hör, es klagt die Flöte wieder'. In 'Darthulas Grabgesang' the links are even more tangible. The phrase 'sie trauren um dich, den letzten Zweig' closely parallels the opening of 'Vergangen ist mir Glück und Heil', while the preceding (and opening) unison phrase has the effect of an intonation, its dominant opening actually proceeding D – F – G – E flat – D before the G minor response, which is, however, always coloured by these progressions subsequently. However, the call to awake in the middle section recalls the partsong idiom.

Songs with horns and harp

In the Four Songs for female voices with horns and harp op. 17 Brahms brings his preoccupation with female voices (here SSA) into contact with two of the instruments with which he was most intimately concerned at the time: as the Horn Trio and orchestral serenades show, Brahms probably possessed a more natural sense for the idiom of the horn than for any other instrument, while the harp, essential to the sound of the *Requiem*, is a recurrent symbol of Romantic mystery in the songs. In these settings,

Brahms's intimate sense of German Romanticism achieves perhaps its most vivid evocation in response to equally atmospheric texts. His interest in Scottish balladry, apparent in the 'Edward' ballade for piano, the song 'Murrays Ermordung', and the Ossian setting for double choir 'Darthulas Grabgesang' is further expressed in another Ossian setting, 'Gesang aus Fingal', likewise a lament with sea imagery. The other texts are from modern German Romantics, Ruperti and Eichendorff, as well as an English source regarded as Romantic by the Germans: Shakespeare ('Come away, death' from *Twelfth Night*).

The idioms employed, especially in the first and last pieces, draw quite uninhibitedly on Romantic compositional models. The wild call of the horn and improvisatory response of the harp at the opening draws on Schumann's *Concertstück* in G major for piano and orchestra, where the horn has the same motive and the piano similar figurations, a relationship also suggested at the close of the D minor Piano Concerto; (compare bars 1–4 of the song with bars 5–8 of the *Concertstück* in G major and bars 520–24 of the concerto). The final Ossian lament is in turn very like Schubert's song 'Death and the Maiden' in its chordal progression, vocal line with the melody in the inner part and bare octaves in the outer. Schubert also influenced Brahms's use of the horn, as will appear. It is interesting to note that he made an orchestral arrangement of Schubert's setting of Ellen's second song from Scott's *The Lady of the Lake*, for four horns and bassoon with SAA chorus and soprano solo, in which the horn writing is extremely atmospheric. The particular combination with harp, however, may reflect Brahms's interest in Méhul, who made a feature of this ensemble. There is some affinity between the overture to his opera *Uthal* (a great Brahms favourite, which he planned to perform)[10] and Brahms's orchestral style.

Rinaldo

The background to the songs with horns and harp relates to the special character of the first large-scale work for chorus and orchestra, the cantata *Rinaldo*, to bring into focus the very important but under-considered question of Brahms's attitude to opera. His failure to produce an opera has always provided a conspicuous piece of evidence in classifying him as an 'absolute' composer, and thus to oppose him to Wagner. The implications of this view are misleading. Brahms maintained great interest in opera throughout his life, not least in Wagner. Although his failure to produce an opera from the many libretti which he sought and considered must, ultimately, reflect an insufficient priority in this area, he for long considered operatic composition, the major works involving solo voice and orchestra, *Rinaldo*, the *Requiem* and the Alto Rhapsody, all benefit from being considered in relation to these background interests.

Brahms's attitude to dramatic music was entirely in accord with his general aesthetic outlook, already noted in connection with the songs: a respect for the identity and character of the allied genre. As with the sanctity of poetic texts, so he held the integrity of drama to be a prime consideration. His apparent feeling for dramatic schemes led him to become very conscious of the adverse influence of any extraneous element. He even criticised Goethe for weakening the effect of the fine text of *Tasso* through its 'long duets'. The role of music was equally clear to him. Widmann recalls that 'it seemed to him that to compose music for the whole drama was unnecessary, even harmful and inartistic: only the climax and those parts of the action where words alone cannot suffice, should be set to music. By this means, on the one hand, the librettist gains more space and freedom for the dramatic development of his subject, and, on the other, the composer is able to devote himself exclusively to the demands of his art, which can best be fulfilled when he has musically complete mastery of the situation (as for example, in an ensemble portraying a joyful climax). Besides, he held it to be a great presumption to expect music to accompany a purely dramatic dialogue all through several acts'.[11] This attitude inevitably influenced his own operatic preferences and his own approach to opera composition. From the late 1860s to the 1880s he toyed with opera, actually specifying plays, especially from the Calderón-Gozzi folk fables, from which one complete libretto, for *Das laute Geheimnis*, was produced.

He had a special interest in *Der Raube* and, especially, *König Hirsch*, whose realisation he long discussed with Widmann. However, if the musical nature of a Brahms opera is clear in essentials – that of a play with music, going back to the Singspiel tradition and ignoring the trends towards continuous setting in Schumann as well as Weber and Wagner – the character of the play he considered may well cause surprise, for *König Hirsch* was actually a comedy, though, as Brahms noted, 'with a continuous undercurrent of the serious'. However, Widmann had considerable reservations about providing a 'rational and poetical' libretto for such a 'grotesque and extravagant farce', fearing a second-rate *Magic Flute*, an undertaking quite inappropriate to Brahms. The play certainly confirms his fears posing problems of character transformation – the king into a stag and into an old man, the magician Durandarte back into his proper state from the guise of parrot in which he appears first – and of general plausibility which hardly seem amenable to Brahms's characteristic musical expression. Equally, however, Brahms had an interest in the genre: he took part in a performance of a Singspiel by Turgenev, and many of his shorter songs, folk-like and self-sufficient, could easily have functioned in a traditional play with music.[12]

Brahms's great interest in modern dramatic music, and the strictness of his aesthetic view in matters of text, inevitably places the cantata *Rinaldo* in a very interesting position in his development. Although in no sense an opera – this dramatic cantata was intended and has always been performed as a concert work – it is certainly the closest Brahms ever came to the genre, presenting a central character in a dramatic situation, and taking up a Tasso subject that had already served for operas by Lully, Gluck and others. The relation of the central character to the commenting chorus and the orchestra creates dramatic effects, if no sustained dramatic plot. In contrast to his views noted above, Brahms's attitude to the text was obviously very different in 1863 when most of this work was written. Here, with a brief scenic introduction in the score, Brahms sets the entire text, with some repetitions, and the merest break after the chorus 'Zurück, zurück' prior to the separate structure of the final chorus 'Segel swellen'. The essential independence of this chorus illuminates the problem lying behind the work, however. It was not completed until 1868, Brahms having doubted in the interim the nature and quality of the work, just as with the *Magelone* Romances, whose commencement and conclusion mark the same period. Many parallels link these works as twin manifestations of common preoccupations and problems. The texts are similar, essentially stressing a basic preoccupation with the relation between the path of duty and the attractions of profane love. In both cases nobility is the outcome, from which we may draw certain points concerning Brahms's own nature. Textual structures are also far from Brahms's previous norms. Here very few passages fall into the rhyming schemes which he normally treated. Thus he draws on passages such as 'Stelle her der gold'nen Tage' and 'Aber alles verkündet' to write his most lyrical, aria-like passages in relatively closed forms. The first is a continuous setting of the text, mirrored in a continuous musical development, the passage preceded by a recitative and arioso, the former so marked, the latter an ABA in text and music.

But *Rinaldo* is of course the much more ambitious undertaking, and one which lay outside Brahms's normal and natural sphere of lied composition. History has judged it a rather limited success, because it falls into that category of lyric-dramatic works which led so many Romantic composers into stylistic conflicts, to which the solutions of Wagner have traditionally been judged the right ones. Yet in the context of changing attitudes to dramatic composition this work demands attention, for it relates closely to contemporary attempts. Two areas are of interest: its stylistic relations to the world of opera, and its special structural qualities, especially concerning the role of soloist and chorus.

Much of *Rinaldo* is in fact very individual, and only the work's continuous structure prevents passages from being separately performed in the way that, for example, 'Wie lieblich sind deine Wohnungen' is from the *Requiem*. But stylistic links to other composers do exist. The most striking is undoubtedly the character of the work's climax: the recognition by Rinaldo of his state of degradation when he sees his image reflected in the diamond mirror. Here Brahms draws directly from Beethoven's music for the return of the Minister, the climactic moment of *Fidelio*, similarly building to an interrupted cadence on which the harmonic movement is frozen to announce repeated notes for brass, except that Brahms writes two trumpet parts rather than piercing trumpet solo. Much more subtle is the link to

Wagner in the arioso passage from bar 830 onwards, the orchestral introduction to Rinaldo's aria 'Zum zweitenmale seh' ich erscheinen und jammern', where he is tempted to look back again. Here, though the main theme is Brahmsian in shape (compare the coda to the first movement of the First Symphony), the whole feeling is of an operatic aria, the closest Brahms ever comes to Italian opera in its warmth of feeling; yet the way in which the line is carried in the orchestra, the solo voice as a counterpoint at bar 862, shows Brahms very close to Wagner. Indeed, the parallels can easily be related to Brahms's known favourite Wagner opera, *The Flying Dutchman*, these parallels extending to subject – the sea imagery, sailors' chorus and so forth – and to style and structure. It is likely that Wagner's growing fluidity in the handling of aria and recitative appealed to Brahms in his considerations of dramatic music, not least opera.

But opera did not provide the primary background to *Rinaldo*. This lay more in the genre of the dramatic cantata, employed regularly by Brahms's immediate predecessors Mendelssohn and Schumann. Those of Schumann were particularly familiar to him, notably *Paradise and the Peri*, and, especially, the *Scenes from Goethe's Faust*, with whose language he had strong affinities. However, none of these works achieves the subtlety of relationships between aria and recitative which characterises *Rinaldo*. For this one must go back to a work now virtually unknown, yet one which was of profound interest to Brahms: Schubert's *Lazarus*.[13] Brahms discovered

Fig. 2 The first page of Schubert's *Lazarus* as copied out by Brahms (*Gesellschaft der Musikfreunde*)

the work when he made his first, enthusiastic Schubert discoveries in Vienna in 1863, anticipating in glowing terms the more sober judgment of 1887 with regard to song though of broader significance, clearly: 'Schubert, not Mendelssohn or Schumann is Beethoven's true successor'.[14] To Schubring he wrote in 1863:

> My love for Schubert is of a very serious kind . . . Where else is there a genius like his, that soars with such boldness and certainty to the sky where we see the very greatest enthroned? He impresses me as a child of the Gods, who plays with Jove's thunder and occasionally handles it in an unusual manner. But he does play in a region and at a height to which the others can by no means attain.[15]

He took special interest in the aria of Simon in the second part ('You would not believe such loveliness' he wrote to Dietrich[16]) and also in Schubert's recitative, copying extensively. Although he makes no detailed comments, he may well have accorded with the view later expressed by Einstein:

> If we say that, from the point of view of the historical development of opera towards the music drama, Schubert's fragment far surpasses *Tannhäuser* and *Lohengrin*, we are not making too great a claim. Schubert was free of every consideration of operatic convention and here attempted something which he had only occasionally achieved in his operas: the blending of recitative and aria.[17]

Both in the recitative and aria features of *Rinaldo*, Brahms can well be seen to have reflected this enthusiasm, which coincided with his beginning of the work.

The flexibility of lyrical declamation which Brahms achieves in this period, already noted in the songs of op. 32 and their relation to the solo passages of the *Requiem*, seems very close to Schubert's achievements in *Lazarus*, and the solo writing of *Rinaldo*, though of a much less Brahmsian nature, may well provide the clue to much of its stimulus. In both cases the pervading lyricism of expression enables the distinction between aria and recitative to be blurred. Moreover, in the structure of a double aria-arioso Brahms may be seen to follow the formal outline of Simon's aria, though modifying it through the insertion of choral parts. Hence both the arias of Rinaldo follow this pattern, the first 'Stelle her der gold'nen Tage', a poco adagio in A flat leading to a choral section is in E after which it is resumed in E, the second section leading to the complementary 'Aber alles verkündet' in C, Allegro. The second aria 'Zum zweitenmale' is a lyrical andante in A minor, followed by 'Und umgewandelt seh' ich die Holde' in C minor. The mood of Simon's second-act aria 'O könnt ich, allgewaltiger im Staube nur einmal', followed by the allegro molto 'Wehe, wehe' in the minor mode is very similar to the latter, not least in the wide harmonic range, whilst the parallel treatments of the dramatic entries of Simon and Rinaldo, moving fluidly from dramatic recitative into the aria sections are also notable.

Alto Rhapsody

Like *Rinaldo*, the Alto Rhapsody is scored for solo voice and male chorus with orchestra. But the function of the chorus is now very different: it appears only in the final of the three clear sections as a support rather than protagonist, sharing the final hymn for the man's restoration. However, the work stands in obvious succession in its use of the recitative-aria/arioso pattern in its first two sections, though 'recit' is no longer marked as such. Indeed, Brahms never comes closer than here to indicating the possible character of an opera. Taken with the introduction to the last movement of the First Symphony with its rushing agitated string passages and clear horn calls, it suggests a lineage from the overture and Wolf's Glen scenes of Weber's *Der Freischütz*. Like that of *Rinaldo*, the text is also an extract from Goethe, here three stanzas from the poem *Harzreise im Winter*, which depicts a lonely and misanthropic young man wandering alone through the Harz mountains in winter: the first stanza shows him lost in the desolation of the scene, the second focusses on the state of mind of one 'whose balsam has turned to poison' and the third offers a prayer for him: 'Is there in your psaltery, O father of love, one sound acceptable to his ear – O refresh him with it'. The musical response is very direct and atmospheric. The introduction, which subsequently reveals itself as the accompaniment to the vocal recitative, quickly roves distantly from the initial key of C minor through B minor (VII – VI – II) before reapproaching the dominant for the solo entry. Tremolo muted strings, pointed horn chords and heavy syncopated dissonances, and a descending figure for flutes and clarinets in unison conjure the scene unmistakably. In the second stanza, the man's emotional ambivalence is mirrored in the cross rhythm of 6/4 and 3/2 – Brahms's most advanced and overt use of this device so far, proceeding initially in three-bar phrases.

Ein Deutsches Requiem

To a greater extent than any other of his works, even the First Symphony, Brahms's *Requiem* appears as a synthesis. For not only does it reflect the years of technical exploration in the sphere of unaccompanied choral music – the mastery of counterpoint, of unusual and historically oriented harmonic effects and of vocal groupings and colours – but, equally, the larger world of the cantata, oratorio and concert setting of liturgical texts. It thus spans a period from the Renaissance to Beethoven and to Brahms's immediate predecessors. From such a rich background Brahms produced a work which has become one of the most universal expressions of religious sentiment through its masterly combination of choral, solo and orchestral writing. Indeed, the orchestra has no merely supportive role: many aspects of Brahms's development as an orchestral composer are reflected in the

Requiem in a completely characteristic way. Yet of equal importance with the purely musical aspects is the text, and it is perhaps inevitable that the sources of Brahms's texts and their associations provide the best key into the special character of this unique work, which, though it stands in a clear musical tradition, is in its essence without precedent.

The nature of Brahms's text is of particular interest, not least in the context of the world through which it became established. For, despite its popularity, not least in solid Victorian Britain, the work does not include a single reference to the name of Christ, although the earlier English trans-lations duly set right the omission. That the New Testament context of a number of the texts implies the translation of 'Lord' as 'Christ' was a point immediately taken up with the composer by the conductor of the first performance in the Bremen Dom, the cathedral organist Karl Martin Rein-thaler, eager to establish Brahms as a conventional believer. Thus:

> You occupy not only religious but very definitely Christian ground. The second movement, for example, touches on the prophecy of the Lord's return and in the next to last movement the mystery of the resurrection of the dead 'we shall not all sleep' is treated in detail. But what is lacking, at least for the Christian consciousness, is the pivotal point: the salvation in the death of our Lord. 'If Christ is not raised, your faith is in vain'.

After this Reinthaler suggests such an inclusion near 'O death, where is thy sting' or in a new movement.[18] Brahms's response was telling:

> I confess that I would gladly omit even the word *German* and simply put *Human*; also with my full knowledge and will I would dispense with places like St John 3: 16 ('For God so loved the world that he gave his only begotten Son'). On the other hand I have chosen one thing or another because I am a musician, because I needed it and because with my venerable authors I cannot delete or dispute anything. But I had better stop before I say too much.[19]

In challenging Reinthaler's assumptions, therefore, Brahms clarifies important aspects of his outlook: that the work was essentially humanist in conception, that its texts had essentially musical significance, not only for him as a composer, but in their existing associations. He chose his texts because they had special significance for him in the culture in which he lived and that culture was, in its orthodoxy, Christian. But this did not hold Brahms to dogmatic associations in their use. The association was not theological but cultural. Just how strongly Brahms felt about this aspect of the text's sanctity can be deduced from his sharp reaction to Goldmark's setting of Luther's psalm text 'Wer sich die Musik erkiest', declaring that it was impossible for Goldmark, as a Jew, 'to adjust his mind to a world of poetry that must be utterly strange to him',[20] and that the result must necessarily be false. Though, as noted by Specht, this was an unfortunate exaggeration on Brahms's part, it clearly reveals his outlook. Brahms's text sources indicate the range of his interest. Not only are Old and New Testaments drawn upon, but also those 'unofficial' writings contained in the Apocrypha. His Old Testament preferences lay in the Psalms and Isaiah (Ps. 126: vv. 5–6; 39: vv. 4–8; 84: vv. 1,2,4 and Isaiah Ch. 35: v. 10; 66: v. 13). In the New Testament he went to St Matthew (Ch. 5: v. 4), St John (Ch. 16: v. 22), James (Ch. 5: v. 7), 1 Peter (Ch. 1: vv. 24, 25), Hebrews (Ch. 13: v. 14) and, especially, Revelation (Ch. 4: v. 11; Ch. 14: v. 13) and Corinthians (Ch. 15: vv. 51–5), the last providing his longest and most directly Christian reference in the passage beginning 'Behold I show you a mystery, we shall not all sleep' and concluding 'O grave, where is thy victory?' The Apocryphal sources from Wisdom (Ch.3: v.1) and Ecclesiasticus (Ch.51: v.27), simply serve to complement the authorised texts, the former with theistic connotations – 'The souls of the righteous are in the hand of God' – and the latter with broader wisdom: 'Behold with your eyes how I laboured but a little and found myself much rest'.

The first reference to the work as such is in Brahms's correspondence with Clara, where he quotes a fragment of the middle, imitative, section of 'Wie lieblich sind deine Wohnungen' with the remark: 'This is probably the least offensive part of the said *German Requiem*.'[21] Dietrich's much later *Reminiscences* confirm that the funeral march we know as the second movement originated in the Two-Piano Sonata of 1854, though he does not clarify its nature.[22] The full form of this movement must have been achieved by 1867, with nos 1 and 3, since Brahms gave a performance of three movements in the Musikverein in December 1867. The work was given in its first complete form in 1868 at Bremen, with the soprano movement added, as the fifth, in 1869. The traditional view that the work existed in a preliminary form as a cantata around 1861, comprising movements one to four, is pure conjecture, based on Kalbeck's interpretation of a sheet containing the entire text.[23] Here Kalbeck noted certain differences in ink and calligraphy as between the first four and the remaining texts; the reverse of the sheet contains the *Magelone* Romances written in 1861. In fact, all that can be drawn from the sheet is that, at some stage, movements one and two bore slightly different tempo markings: 'Andante' instead of the published 'Ziemlich langsam', and 'Andante' instead of 'Langsam, marschmässig' respectively.

If Kalbeck's interpretation seems fanciful, however, the general proposition that Brahms only reached the finished work through stages, even including a possible cantata stage, cannot easily be dismissed. In particular, the special textual character of passages drawn from Luther's Bible stressing the suffering of life and the comfort of the bereaved take the work closer to the Lutheran tradition, especially the cantatas of Bach, than to any other possible model. That Brahms was deeply involved in the study and performance of these works while in Hamburg and increasingly in Vienna gives the emphasis considerable strength. Through his subscription to the Bach Gesellschaft Edition he had access to them all and performed two with the Singverein: *Liebster Gott, wann werd' ich sterben* and *Ich hatte viel Bekümmernis*. He was a keen student of both Bach and Luther and their role in the clarification of a religious work cannot be ignored. Indeed, certain of Bach's cantatas may have provided crucial stimulus in the transformation of an instrumental funeral march into a choral movement, from which point broader factors of choral tradition became absorbed in the total conception of this mighty work.

The key to its development could well lie in a casual remark of Brahms to Siegfried Ochs, to the effect that the entire work rested on a chorale melody – one which we can easily identify as 'Wer nur den lieben Gott lässt walten' – which he found present in the march of the second movement and in the work's opening.[24] Thus, he drew on yet another form of his basic theme for a central and symbolic work. The chorale is quite unmistakable in the funeral march, despite its omission of the upbeat, and modal inflexion, through its powerful choral statement.

If this chorale was present in the original instrumental march – and the Kalbeck view that it was not seems to have no justification in Dietrich's remarks – then this passage represents the work's embryo and we must ask what led Brahms to take it up again later in choral form with his own selected text: 'Denn alles Fleisch, es ist wie Gras'.

(i)

(ii)

(iii)

Ex. 23   (i) Chorale melody
         (ii) *Ein deutsches Requiem*, second movement, bars 22–26
         (iii) first movement, bars 3–5

Here the association with Bach cantatas seems crucial, for they use both Brahms's chorale and texts which relate very closely to his own. He devoted particular attention to *Ich hatte viel Bekümmernis*, in which the chorale is used. Its association with texts of gloom and pessimism reflects a very long tradition, which is especially clear in the works of Mendelssohn; the chorale is used for the comment on the stoning of Stephen in *St Paul* and even more interestingly the thematic substance of the motet *Mitten wir im Leben*

Ex. 24 (i) J. S. Bach; Cantata no. 27, first chorus, bars 14–18
(ii) *Requiem*, bars 22–6

sind, of which Brahms possessed the autograph, is drawn from it. Still more suggestive is the cantata *Wer weiss wie nahe mir mein Ende*, because here, as in no other setting, Bach like Brahms employs the common time chorale in 3/4. Other aspects of the setting confirm the relationship, as comparison shows.

When we further note that Brahms's third movement employs the text of which Bach's text is a poetic paraphrase, 'Lord, let me know mine end and the measure of my days', then the relationships seem even harder to dismiss. In this context it is interesting to record that Brahms once referred to his funeral march as being in C minor: there is no evidence that it was ever planned in this key and, unless it be a printer's error, seems a possible example of a Freudian slip, for this is the key of the Bach movement.[25]

This movement apart, however, Brahms's reference to the chorale's overall significance is far from clear, not least in the first movement, where it appears in the major mode, without its upbeat, a relationship which could not be evinced aurally. More obvious is the thematic character of the march 'Denn es wird die Posaune schallen'. As has been observed, the thrice-repeated arioso entry may well be compared with the alternation of recitative and chorus in the cantata movement aforementioned.[26]

But these relationships are only a small part of the whole. Much more telling are basic tonal links, formal relationships, thematic recall at the close and a network of thematic motives in the main ideas. For the first time in an extended work, Brahms overtly recalls his opening material at the close, the appearance of the choral passage from bar 15 at bar 132 reinforcing the textual link between 'Selig sind die da Leid tragen' and 'Selig sind die Toten die in den Herren sterben', and thus completing the work's emotional circle. The modulatory passage which links the recall, in E flat, to the resolution in F is a master stroke in this process. A much less obvious but highly pervasive thematic linkage offers another pointer to Brahms's structural tendencies in the later music. Virtually all the themes not chorale-based make use of a rising 1 – 3 – 4 motive as shown:

And to complement this is a symmetrical tonal scheme of movements, including mediant relations, as in *Rinaldo*, thus:

F – B flat minor/(major) – D minor/(major) – E flat major – G major – C minor/(major) – F. Moreover, internal relations reflect the mediant connection as well: thus F – D flat in the first movement, B flat minor – G flat in the second, G – B flat in the fifth, F – A in the seventh.

In the work's actual musical character, there is also a remarkable blend of past and present elements, not least in harmonic language. At the very opening of the choral part Brahms presents a progression of juxtaposed triads which draw directly from the manner of the choruses to 'Altdeutsch' texts, though blending them with modern unprepared sevenths. Moreover, it is very difficult to divorce this passage from a parallel setting by Schütz. Although we have no absolutely direct evidence that Brahms knew the Schütz setting from the *Geistliche Chormusik* of 1648, it was available in print,

Requiem: first movement, bars 15 – 17

Second movement, bars 79 – 82   111 – 114

Third movement, bars 5 – 6   Third movement, Fugue subject, bar 173

Fourth movement, orchestral inversion   Soprano, original, bars 4 – 8

Fifth movement, oboe counterpoint, bar 4

Sixth movement, counterpoint to fugue subject, bar 208

Ex. 25 *Requiem*, occurrences of motive 1 – 3 – 4

and he may well have known it.[27] Thus emerges yet another stimulus, for Brahms's language, like his religious outlook, shared as much with Schütz as with Bach. Yet the infusion is not always as obvious. Brahms's natural harmonic sense fuses with his knowledge of the past to enable modal passages to sound entirely characteristic, as in the Dorian opening of the baritone passage 'Herr, lehre doch mich'. Though the key is ostensibly D minor, Brahms avoids any C sharp in a progression which rather stresses A minor, his favoured minor mode on the fifth degree, giving a clear anticipation of the ambivalent modal suggestion at the opening of the *Tragic Overture*, in the same key.

Yet a more recurrent link to tradition exists in the sphere of counterpoint, where Brahms proclaims his affinity with the choral background in the writing of three extensive fugues to complete the second, third and sixth movements. That of the third is particularly notable as the fullest expression of Brahms's, love of pedal: an entire passage of thirty-five bars over a D pedal. Yet the other movements are also technically interesting, in the incorporation of all the fugal devices used in the earlier works: inversion, retrogression, diminution, augmentation, stretto. The manner is not academic, though, as in the A flat minor organ fugue or the chorale fugues. These concluding fugues are above all dramatic – sections designed to balance and to conclude with great effect, thus relating much more directly to Beethoven and Handel than to Bach and Mendelssohn. Indeed, the fugue to the sixth movement, 'Herr, du bist würdig' is free in the manner of Handel, with the fugal exposition quickly yielding to homophonic writing. The process of modulation and dramatic contrast in the latter parts resembles that of the last movement and represents a considerable originality in the handling of the form. But counterpoint is not restricted to contrapuntal movements. On the contrary, the whole fabric of the score is rich in the elements of counterpoint, working together with the motivic process to create a work more intensely thematic than any precursor. Indeed, it is possible that counterpoint is the crucial structural link between the chorale material of the opening and the motivic cell which links the rest of the thematic outlines.

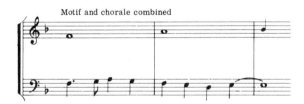

Ex. 26 *Requiem*

If the *Requiem* is the most powerful German religious work since Beethoven's *Missa solemnis* in structural design and sheer force of expression, the influence of the more recent Romantic past is not entirely absent, though conveyed not through Mendelssohn but rather Schumann. An interesting suggestion has been made of the role of Schumann's secular cantata/oratorio *Requiem für Mignon* to texts from Goethe's *Wilhelm Meister*.[28] The association of the title 'Requiem' with German texts expressing the idea of comfort rather than the traditional judgment is certainly important, not least since

Brahms performed this work in the period of the *Requiem*'s growth, in November 1863. Another even closer Schumann link seems, however, without support: Schumann's project book had contained the title 'German Requiem', though Brahms was completely surprised when he heard of it through Kalbeck years later. But although the *Requiem* drew on a very wide range of backgrounds, it is not only a work of synthesis. In its employment of the traditionally religious genre of the oratorio for the expression of essentially personal emotions, it is forward-looking, to twentieth-century tendencies of individual expression drawing to a greater or lesser extent on the associations of religious texts, a notable example being Britten's *War Requiem*.

Triumphlied *and* Song of Destiny

Two aspects of the musical background and character of the *Requiem* are further explored in the choral works which conclude the second period: the *Triumphlied* op. 55 (1870–71) and the *Song of Destiny* (1868–71). The tradition of grand, contrapuntal effect, especially associated with Handel, is especially clear in the former work, a *pièce d'occasion* which is Brahms's least performed large-scale composition. The *Song of Destiny*, the most widely known choral work after the *Requiem*, expresses much more personal moods drawing on both the contemplative atmosphere of the *Requiem*'s opening and the passionate expression of earthly transience of the choral section of the sixth movement. The Handelian background of the *Triumphlied* – the source of one of Wagner's increasing jibes against Brahms, whom he casti-gates for wearing 'the Halleluia perruque of a Handel'[29] – can be traced to his current preoccupations as scholar and performer. 'Take special note of the "Denkmäler der Tonkunst" ', he wrote to Joachim in acknowledgment of Chrysander's epoch-making collection, 'You will find the Te Deum by Urio remarkably interesting. Compare also *Saul* and Handel's *Te Deum*, very striking.'[30] The Urio work provides the source of Handel's composition, which Brahms placed in his first concert with the Gesellschaft in 1872. The interest inevitably influenced his own work in view of the close parallels in circumstances of composition – Handel's in celebration of the English victory over the French at Dettingen in 1743, Brahms's acknowledging the German victory over the French in 1870–1. In idiom Brahms draws quite openly on the initial 'maestoso' figures and following semiquaver move-ment, as on the trumpet fanfares, to say nothing of the concluding Halle-luias. His love of chorale variation finds a new expression in this work: the first movement begins with a theme based on the melody of 'God save the King' – the old German national anthem 'Heil Dir in Siegerkranz' – while the second movement includes 'Nun danket alle Gott', set in a much more reflective manner to a rocking triplet chorus, played by wind. The latter treatment points to the work's personal qualities, for it is by no means a pastiche. The 'tranquillo' close of the first movement is another example of Brahmsian expression, and the final, third movement introduces the baritone solo which recalls the individuality of Brahms's writing for this voice in the *Requiem* and the op. 32 songs.

Although musical characteristics of the *Requiem* are clear in the *Song of Destiny*, it stands apart in one crucial sense, in that it draws not on Christian sources but on the more detached and epic world of Greek mythology as expressed through the Romantic poet Hölderlin, thus revealing a world of associations which Brahms was to explore further in the later choral works. The text contrasts the bliss of the immortal Gods with the despair of suffering mankind, beginning with its evocative line which resists adequate English translation: 'Ihr wandelt droben im Licht, auf weichem Boden, selige Genien!'. As has often been noted, the text posed Brahms a problem in ending in despair, with mankind plunged 'headlong into the abyss', thus denying him the opportunity, always exploited in the texts of his own selection, for ending with consolation, with a hope of some kind. Yet Brahms was too attached to this wonderful poem to leave it on that account, and in treating it, he gives the orchestra – already more prominent in the introduction than in any parallel choral work – the last of the three broad sections to itself, its scoring made even more atmospheric by the transference of ideas first given by the strings to the wind, led by solo flute with gentle string support. Moreover, the reprise is now in C major, resolving the fatalism of the central section in C minor, and achieving, in the move from the initial E flat, an interesting example of progressive tonality. In the apportioning of the two sections of text Brahms creates a striking musical contrast, exactly reflecting the contrast of the poem. His scoring of the choral entry, altos alone presenting the melody with horn doubling and triplet counterpoints in the flute and oboe, recalls the reprise of the opening material of the *Requiem* in the last movement, though the pizzicato bass which supports the full entry is more characteristic of the middle period (compare the final section of the *Alto Rhapsody*). The mood of the central section, an allegro in triple time with a turbulent string figure and pervading cross rhythms, draws clearly on the triple-time choral passage of the sixth movement, though without its interposed solo passages.

Chamber Music

Important as was Brahms's *Requiem* in projecting his name to a wider public, it only placed him in a perspective of a certain kind, one relating directly to the inherently conservative world of the choral society and religious music. His instrumental compositions were still only known to a limited entourage focussing on the circles of Joachim and Hellmesberger in Vienna. The numerous performances of the *Requiem*, which quickly went the rounds of the choral societies after its first full performance in 1869, were in no way matched by the works which became central pillars of his reputation, the piano variations and chamber and orchestral works. Indeed, it was the popular piano and vocal works, the Waltzes and Hungarian Dances, which were best known after the *Requiem*, as Wagner's various barbed comments reflect.[1] Yet what Brahms was achieving in the serious instrumental genres was of immense significance, because it represented a revitalising of forms which had lost their dominance in Germany with the spread of Romanticism with its stress on the programme, on text and on the illustrative miniature. Only in chamber and orchestral music does the force of his achievement come into the fullest perspective. For he makes immense strides in uniting a natural feeling for the symbols and moods of German musical Romanticism with equally powerful instincts for formal clarity, direction and balance inherent in his nature and stimulated by his sense of the past and its resources. In his works we see the re-establishment of the Austro-German tradition with enrichments from a past never even comprehended by his Classical and Romantic predecessors. In turn, new emphases on counterpoint, harmonic experiment, thematic process and pervasive variation create new, characteristic processes which point to the individuality of the high maturity of the composer's style after 1876. But it is in the works of this period, especially the chamber works of the first decade after 1855, that the style was forged.

As in other fields, very clear phases can be identified. First, the entry into a world of Classicism and early Romanticism without the dominance of the piano through the medium of the string sextet. (Although the two works in this medium are four years apart, in 1860 and 1864–5, their shared characteristics group them together). Second, the return to the use of the piano in 1861 for the two Piano Quartets, works which lay the foundation for a most important successor in 1864, Piano Quintet in F minor, recast from a string quintet with two cellos through the intermediary medium of a two-piano sonata. With this weighty group completed, Brahms turned in 1864–5 to the completion of his first duo sonata, for cello, whose first two movements date from 1862, and to the unusual genre of Horn Trio, significant in both personal terms and in relation to his development as an orchestral composer. After these works, seven years elapse before the completion of the final group, the production of the *Requiem* being the most significant creative event in the interim. The phase is primarily concerned with the genre of the string quartet, for it shows Brahms's finally releasing two quartets in C minor and A minor which were long in preparation and which are but a fraction of the twenty or so he claimed to have discarded in the previous years. Only with this hurdle surmounted was he able to return to the ideas of the Piano Quartet in C minor, first essayed in C sharp minor in 1855 and to rework and resolve the strikingly powerful and original first inspirations.

It is clear therefore, that the pattern of the chamber works is very different from those of the genres already discussed, for during most of the period none of the works of whose existence we read from Schumann were to appear. Only in 1879 was the first violin sonata published; the string quartets were not to appear until 1873. Even the Piano Trio in B major had to wait until the 1880s for companions. The problem of matching an idiom rooted in his unique and natural pianism to his wider-ranging ideas was to preoccupy him for years and it was only after repeated attempts that he was satisfied. Yet, it is not to the later quartets that pride of place is generally given: that goes to the Piano Quintet, as later to the Clarinet Quintet in his fullest maturity. And although Brahms began his mature Chamber writing for strings alone, he chose the much fuller ensemble of the string sextet, a genre which, in accord with his own creative needs, he effectively inaugurated as a medium for the highest artistry.

String sextets

The B flat Sextet is invariably classified as Brahms's most accessible chamber work, the proximity to the composition of the orchestral Serenades noted as part of the stress on its 'Classical' quality. Yet the three years which separate it from the first and most derivative of the orchestral works give it much greater interest, for in no other work of the period is the scope of Brahms's background preoccupation so clearly displayed. Each movement seems to pose a different background. Brahms's intense interest in the style and methods of variations, reaching back to the Baroque, appears unmistakably in the slow movement, whose model preserves for some time the character of a chaconne, strictly keeping the bass and harmony of an idea of archaic character, and clearly drawing on the tradition of the division in its elaboration, a quality underlined in its reference to the traditional bass 'La Folia'. (Brahms's piano arrangement of this movement may perhaps have influenced Rachmaninov in his piano variations on the traditional model in the form given by Corelli.) Two particular Brahms favourites in variation form must also have contributed to the conception: Bach's Chaconne for unaccompanied violin and Beethoven's Thirty-Two Variations in C minor.

The rigour of the style may even suggest that, more than any other model, the chaconne type lay behind his new approach to variations, though the original realisation of the principle in the *St Antoni* Variations was to have only one, partial, parallel in this period, the slow movement of the Second Serenade op. 16. The pattern of the sextet's variations, three in the minor, two in the major, with a broad coda, establishes a pattern which is essentially respected throughout the variation movements of the later chamber works; but it also looks back to earlier achievements. Variations 1 and 4 may be directly compared with variation 1 and 11 of the Variations on an Original Theme for piano, allowing for the different mode in the first case.

The scherzo is in a completely different style, essentially a reworking of the theme of the Haydnesque scherzo of the First Serenade op. 11, while the trio, a faster section in the manner of a rustic dance, is obviously akin to the scherzo of Beethoven's 'Pastoral' Symphony. In the finale, the accents of German folksong are brought into the context of a classical rondo. The first movement appears the most modern in spirit, suggestive of the composer to whom Brahms was increasingly drawn as stimulus in this period: Schubert. The intense lyricism has, for example, been related to Schubert's late Piano Sonata in B flat major.[2] If the parallel is not exact in emotional terms, Brahms seems closer to this world than to any other here, and the sudden appearance of a ländler second theme at bar 61 tends to confirm this association. Indeed, the Schubertian spirit really goes much deeper. The very different style of the contrapuntal development passage of the finale also suggests Schubert's idiom, as revealed in such examples as the development section of the slow movement of his Second Symphony or of the first of the 'Unfinished'. Brahms was to return to this manner in the development of the slow movement of the Fourth Symphony in magnificent terms.

However, the stylistic differences between the movements are never really stark: rather is a Brahmsian sense of the past the strongest overall feature – as the contradictory stylistic attributions of commentators seem to suggest. Such an example as the transformation of the archaic opening of the variations through to a very Romantic and personal conclusion seems symbolic of his approach. Indeed, the clarity and ease of the expression of ideas served another and very obvious purpose in this, his first mature chamber work: that of enabling the creation of a texture which was self-sufficient, free of any sense of a sustaining pedal and facilitating a new richness of working. For, if the surface is 'Classical', the fullness of texture and extension of instrumental possibilities are new. Obviously inspired by the most challenging of the chamber works of Beethoven and, especially the 'orchestral' chamber works of Schubert, Brahms's language was becoming his own. Although he may well have found in Spohr's Sextet of 1850 a possible stimulus – he admired Spohr, and would have known much about him from Joachim and his acquaintances at Detmold – Spohr offers no model for this work. Texture and instrumental difficulty are particularly revealed in the changing role of counterpoint. The developments of the two outer movements show Brahms applying the 'learned' methods explored in the contrapuntal studies to new effect. Hence the first development, beginning with imitation on the first theme, gradually gains a stretto aspect, before the passage at bars 173–9 demonstrates sectional variation in which invertible counterpoint plays a significant role, intensifying its function in the closing group, bars 115–35. The role of counterpoint is equally strong in the development section of the finale, the passage from bar 209 inverting the parts from the statement at bar 180. Such methods contrast with the laboured use of fugue in the first version of the B major Trio. Here the devices of counterpoint permeate the texture. They function as a means of variation and development within a texture which has other facets and consequences; Brahms absorbs into his expanding language the principles, while leaving the manner.

Consistent with the new stress on counterpoint is a new challenge for the performers. The first cello and first viola especially are required to match the other four players in producing equality of tone, even when taken into high and exposed registers, and performance problems (the sextet still being an unusual combination) remain in the popularisation of this work. In the presentation of the themes themselves, however, associations to the past remain in Brahms's imagination. Chief of these is with the cello, by far the most prominent instrument in the B major Trio apart from the piano, as also in the Piano Quartet in C sharp minor. Brahms gives effectively all his main themes to this instrument; both of the first movement, that of the variations and all of the finale. Only the scherzo is free. In noting this new role for the cello, it is impossible to ignore the background of the Schubert Quintet in C; as a friend of Hellmesberger, Brahms must have known this work from the time of his first Viennese visits, and a copy of the first edition, published by Spina in 1853 remained in his library.[3] Although the works remain very different, there is no other model as significant for the singing role of the first cello.

The B flat Sextet has been compared to its successor, the G major, as a sketch to a finished work. Although this remark is misleading in denying the very distinct aesthetic quality of the earlier work, its point is undeniable in terms of the greater subtlety and compositional sophistication of the latter, which lives in another world: one of a much more intense and personal as well as vibrant Romanticism. It is surely the greatest successor to the Schubert String Quintet in the nineteenth century. Here the stylistic compass of the earlier work is entirely dissolved: the one link to the more distant past – the scherzo, derived from the Gavotte in A minor – is so handled that its Baroque source would never be suspected by the uninformed listener. Only one compositional stimulus appears to remain, and that so contemporary that it would not have been classed as historical by Brahms: Schubert. The tremolando writing of Brahms's finale, strikingly anticipated at the end of the first movement's development, immediately recalls the sound world of Schubert's String Quartet in G, a work which, with its superabundance of material and richness of sound represented just the model which the young composer needed, even if another side of him recognised the dangers it also exposed. Even more, the subtle harmonic colouring of the opening, semitonal inflections suggesting bitonality with E flat and endowing G major with new potential, seems strikingly akin to the opening of the C major Quintet, a work symbolic of Romanticism in the chamber sphere, yet never known by those who might also have drawn so much from it, Schumann and Mendelssohn. But the stimulus is no longer a burden to Brahms; rather it enables him to work with an assurance, a lyric intensity and spontaneity which reveal a new experience in composition. This is symbolised in the rhythmic characters of the outer movements, both of which now use triple metre, the first simple, the latter compound. In contrast with the staid rhythm of the first movement of op. 18, this is a subtle alternation of possibilities, showing the influence of his new enthusiasm for the dance: the source is surely the cross rhythms of the dances, piano duo and vocal, which so absorbed him in these years.

This new assurance enabled Brahms to transform many of the aspects of his earlier approach to the medium, for there are very strong parallels in basic approach to the sextet medium. That of counterpoint might be taken as symbolic. The parallel passage to the development of the first movement of op. 18, (b. 217–249) intensifies the methods of the earlier work, now offering imitation by inversion and stretto and creating a fertility of working which lasts Brahms throughout the development. Yet, despite the contrapuntal skill, it is perhaps the sense of colour which most strikes the listener, the mixture of pizzicato and arco writing creating a kind of colour counterpoint. In the finale, the imitation of the first subject in the development section is equally colouristic, whilst – most remarkable of all – the variations of the slow movement explore particular contrasts of smooth lines in the upper voices and pizzicato contrasts and pointing in the middle or lower voices, notably in variations 1 and 5 which are highly evocative. The resolution to arco phrasing gives even more effect to the pedal coda, whose rich interweaving of parts seems the very apotheosis of the pedal in early Brahms.

A comparison of the middle movements with their predecessors is particularly revealing of the freedom which Brahms achieves in relation to the same background preoccupations. Thus the variations – though their formal plan is almost identical in confirming a pattern of several variations in the tonic, with contrast of mode, and coda – inhabit a different world of feeling. The harmonic scheme and phrasing remain basic, yet Brahms only gradually unveils the identity of his harmonic model, to create from the outset a very atmospheric mood. The source of the theme is, however, surprisingly early: Brahms quotes the opening of this A B A form in a letter to Clara of February 1855, and it is also included in a surviving notebook of this year.[4] The obvious link between the fugal material of variation 3 and the finale of the Cello Sonata in E minor suggests that both passages may well have derived from the contemporary study of Bach's *Art of Fugue*, to which later reference will be made, whilst, in that connection, one also notes the clear relation between Brahms's variation theme and the first subject of the Sextet itself. In stark contrast to the model of the variations of op. 18, the bass appears only in a linear, decorative melodic role initially, employing inversions rather than roots of the harmony in its course, full harmony only appearing in variation 3. Moreover, the thematic handling is extremely subtle; not a cumulative process of diminution, as in op. 18, but a variation of relationships as well as of the model. Hence the model's counterpoint is reworked in the first variation, the upper part in diminution in the bass, the lower in diminution above. The subsequent thematic unfolding is difficult to trace, though a point of reference is provided in the short transition which prepares the major, 'adagio' variation 5, whose material furnishes the essence of the coda which recalls the theme in the lower parts at its close.

An even more inventive reference to traditional forms appears in the Scherzo, which, however, is not a movement of any traditional type, but rather a new, Brahmsian type in 2/4, in minor mode, marked 'allegro non troppo'. The true 'scherzo' function is absorbed into the finale, a fleet 'poco allegro' in 9/8 which surely draws the inspiration of the Scherzo of Schubert's Quartet in G major into the context of a sonata-rondo of individual design with another buoyant second subject for first cello; the continuity of development and recapitulation anticipates Brahms's experiments, with an omission of the recapitulation of the first theme, subtly introductory in character, at the expected recapitulation, serving rather as the launching point of a powerful coda, which gives extensive evidence of Brahms's awareness of the culminatory effect of phrase variation in repetitions. The stylistic source of the true Scherzo lies much earlier than Schubert, in the Baroque manner of the Gavotte. As has recently been shown, its opening quotes the beginning of Brahms's Gavotte in A minor[5]. But Brahms does nothing to confirm his stylistic starting point, as he does in the severe diminutions of the op. 18 variations. Here the origin is obscured by colouration – the pizzicato bass – and by the working – for the regular phrase structure characteristic of the dance is here avoided, Brahms giving further examples of his growing interest in phrase irregularities and motivically evolving themes. Though the surface phrasing is 17 bars in 4/4/4/5, it actually suggests 4/4/1½/2½/1½/3½.

Ex. 27 (i) Gavotte in A minor
        (ii) String Sextet in G major, op. 36, scherzo, bars 1–16

(Theme Ib of the finale is handled along similar lines, its motivic augmentations counterbalanced by overlapping of phrases, again to resolve on the
beginning of the bar following.) This intricacy predicts the expansive
working of the section, which is continued in the 'Presto giocoso' Trio, in
effect a fast rustic dance not unlike that of the *Pastoral* Symphony. The
subtle thematic retransition, at bar 227, which gradually works the shape

of the opening back into the Trio material, is further evidence of the preoccupation with transition and continuity.

Piano quartets in G minor and A major

Despite their richness of texture and the strain they impose on the medium as a result, the two string sextets remain chamber music; indeed, the exploration of string sound reveals a side of Brahms which is only regained in the later quintets for strings of his full maturity. But for the expression of his most powerful and characteristic moods, the participation of the piano remained indispensable, as the piano-quintet reworking of the String Quintet in F minor shows. It is, indeed, very difficult to imagine how this work could have been conceived for strings alone, and one almost senses that the two-piano version may have lain behind the string concept. A comparison of the opening with that of the finale of the F major String Quintet shows the juxtaposition of *ff* chords with a running figure, and the effect is much lighter than that which we know in the earlier work. In its final version, the Piano Quintet was to represent by 1864 a moment of clarification, an achievement of structural balance and direction with characteristic individuality of working down to the smallest details, laying the foundation for the even greater emotional outline of the First Symphony. Yet, in its texture and processes, it rested on two much less well-known works completed in the previous three years, the two Piano Quartets in G minor and A major, op. 25 and 26. In these exploration is much more comprehensive than in the string works, affecting not only form and mood very strongly. Thus, the G minor work brings together a dour sonata movement with a gipsy finale of vigour unparalleled so far; the scherzo movement is now a very individual fleeting 9/8 mood, with muted strings, forming the normal movement into a tone picture, which Brahms soon retitled 'intermezzo' on Clara's advice; the strident third movement also brings new elements of song and Romantic march together. Extremes are less powerful in the A major work, but here also the inner movements create personal atmospheres, the scherzo equally inappropriate in title in its gentle 3/4 movement and the slow movement another muted creation.

In all the outer movements, the balance shifts firmly from chamber music to symphonic thought. These two works are of symphonic scope, in terms both of sonority – especially their concerto quality in the matching of piano to strings – and the sheer extent of their ideas and handling. When Schoenberg arranged the G minor Quartet he was doing more than simply 'making the parts clear'.[6] He realized the symphonic potential of the work. Even the more lyrical A major Quartet offers parallels in material to the first movement of the First Symphony, first made known to Clara in this very period (compare bars 51–68 of the symphony with bars 37–45 of the quartet). Nor is the G minor work merely symphonic in utterance. The first movement represented the boldest structural experiment Brahms had attempted, one prophetic of later developments, yet posing great problems of its context and consequence for the whole. Indeed, it raises all the issues at the heart of the Romantics' problems with large-scale form, which Brahms shared as deeply as any: the love of self-contained elements, especially song periods, yet the desire to achieve evolving structures in sustained argument, already shown in the character of the previous large-scale works, the piano sonatas. In Brahmsian terms, this was expressed through the desire to integrate the extremes of expression represented by Beethovenian intensity and Schubertian expansiveness. He was to find many and varied solutions to the balance of these elements in his maturity. In 1860, however, such richness and flexibility was unimaginable. The path from the relative simplicity of form and ideas of the B flat Sextet to the complexity of the Piano Quintet, string quartets and eventually the First Symphony was to be arduous. In the first movement of the G minor Quartet he confronts the problems head on.

For if the lyricism of the sextets is still clear in the second subject – again a singing theme given by cello and taken up by first violin with elaborations – one such idea is no longer enough for the section. Brahms adds two more, the third gaining in forcefulness so much that Clara felt impelled to declare, perhaps not without some justification, of its being 'too commonplace for Johannes Brahms'.[7] Such second-group expansion – it takes no less than eighty bars in an exposition of 180 – was without parallel, even in the most protracted four-movement chamber work before Brahms, Schubert's late G major String Quartet. Yet it represents only one side of the exposition, for the first subject and closing groups are devoted to ideas of quite a different kind. The lyric character to be observed in the principal themes of all the chamber music so far disappears here in favour of a first group comprising two distinct ideas, both built from the overt repetition of one-bar units, and revealing the return of the motivic preoccupation so strong in the early piano sonatas. As in the F minor Sonata, the tonic statement is quickly contrasted with another idea in a new key. But here the second idea is in no sense a variation, nor is it placed on a complementary degree; the theme is new and is placed without transition on the relative major. Moreover, the basic motivic units are no longer gestural, rhetorical, but part of a continuous process of the connection of closely related shapes, in the first case over a descending bass to the dominant, in the second bar over a pedal B flat. Though the opening motive is certainly not without classical precedent (see for example its use in the original slow movement of Mozart's String Quartet in G major, K. 156) – and the spiritual background of Mozart's great piano quartet in this key cannot be discounted either – Brahms's thematic process is all his own: a new kind of motivically rooted lyricism.

In continuing the flexibility into the second idea he is able to obscure further the traditional transition section, the first idea only occurring in

Ex. 28 Piano Quartet in G minor, op. 25, bars 1–10

passing. Further variation serves to expand the ideas in the closing group.

Hereafter, this pervading motivic evolution appears even more comprehensively to signal Brahms's most radical treatment of the form so far: the re-ordering of the main thematic elements to create a continuity without expositional repetition, for the development begins not with the first subject in the closing key, but in the tonic. Thus the broad scheme.

			Exposition						/Development – Recap.				
Bar	1	11	50	79	101	130	161	171	237	249	259	281	304	332
Subject	1a –	1b –	2a –	2b –	2c	CG –	1a –	1b –	dev –	1b –	new –	tr –	2b –	2c – coda
Key	i	III	v	V	V	V	I	iv	I	i	i	VI	i	i

Symbols

Keys: Major and Minor Keys are indicated thus: I, i.
For example, in G minor: i – V – I – v = G minor – D major – G major – D minor

Subjects: Ia – Ib – Ic – tr – 2a – 2b – 2c – C.G – dev – retr. =
First subject, first theme, second theme, third theme – Transition – Second subject, first theme, second theme, third theme – Closing Group – Development, Retransition.
Brackets indicate an unclear key or subject.

This unusual reappearance is not, as the ear would immediately suppose, a repeat of the exposition, but an anticipation of the recapitulation, for the theme is not destined to reappear. Only with the reappearance of 2b in the tonic will the recapitulation continue as before: in presenting 1b in iv, C minor, Brahms launches a development which relentlessly pursues the first idea, through sequential modulation, imitation, varied repetition and stretto, moving through a wide tonal range. Such earnest concentration has no parallel in the earlier works, and nor has the close, not a subtle retransition nor a climax but simply a winding down. With the reappearance of 1b in the tonic, the recapitulation would seem to be restored, but the incursion of a new theme for cello predicts further changes, for the resumption of the transition is to lead straight to 2b, 2a having been elided and replaced by the new idea. A sequence of the basic motive confirms its role and the subsiding of the tone returns it to the mood of the opening, the mood also of the beginning of the exposition and the end of the development.

The extraordinary structure of this movement caused great comment in Brahms's circle.[8] Its aesthetic and formal quality is a matter of personal taste, and it is fascinating to compare it with other great movements in G minor, for example the Rhapsody op. 79 no. 2 or the Capriccio op. 116 no. 3. But its structural quality can only be ultimately judged by its place in the whole and here, judged by the standards Brahms was to achieve, it poses problems, for Brahms seems unable to find for it any natural continuation. Denied any structural model, he seems to respond to it simply by a process of balancing in adding three weighty movements. But the process also involves the degree of experiment to be found in the first movement. For

Brahms counterposes his most dour and concentrated sonata movement with his most uninhibited and sectional and popular: a full dress gipsy finale as symbolic of one side of his nature as the first is symbolic of the other.

Though the gipsy rondo was certainly a part of the chamber tradition – see for example that of Haydn's Trio in G major – this rondo is entirely characteristic of Brahms's own feeling for the idiom: it is not to the alternating metres of the Variations on a Hungarian Song that he turns, but to the idioms of the Hungarian Dances, soon to be published for piano duo. His capacity to evoke gipsy music-making is the same, and it is most striking in the middle section, where parallels to dance no. 9 are obvious. Less obvious are the links to his turning figure and to the phrase structure characteristic of some of the dances. Thus the rondo is constructed entirely of three-bar phrases, as no. 1 of the first set is of six bars, while the second section plays with the turning figure. But the larger context gives Brahms much more artistic scope, and he is able to play with the idiom by light-hearted reference to other features of the work. Thus he subjects the central section to a fugato, while in total contrast even more improvisatory writing is permitted before the return of the rondo, passages made brilliantly differentiated in Schoenberg's orchestration.

Brahms's desire for individuality of working, for exploring many aspects of his imagination, is equally clear in the middle movements. As in op. 36, his scherzo is a new concept, though more related to tradition: a compound movement, but in triple rather than the previous duple metre, and of a mood quite new and intimate, with muted strings. Its immense length, 116 bars, enables a relaxed and expansive presentation of the first idea and a full second theme before a redevelopment of both ideas. The transposition of the trio down a third to A flat gives it a development rather than contrast role, and a similar kind of elaboration ensues, to function briefly as coda after the reprise of the main section. These ethereal moods disappear in the main section of the third movement, a strident song-like melody which evolves very powerfully through several ideas until creating a middle section, 'Animato', effectively a very evocative march, recalling the earlier world of the piano pieces, Schumann's and Brahms's ballades, again subject to extensive working.

It is a measure of the resistance which Brahms experienced in Vienna that the second piano quartet, in A major, was regarded with little less disdain than the G minor, Hanslick finding its themes 'dry and prosaic',[9] reminiscent of Schumann's last period. Tradition has regarded it as posing less of a challenge to interpretation. Thus a conventionally outlined sonata movement leads to a gentle song-like Andante, a minuet-derived scherzo with trio, and a gipsy-inclined finale which seems to relate much better to the whole, gipsy elements being dominant in the central part of the slow movement. Yet in a sense Hanslick was right in implying parallels in the first movement, for the issues are the same, with comparable extremes between the 'motivic' and the 'lyric'. There is here only one first theme, though now with a more distinct transition, leading to another succession of strongly lyrical melodies all involving varied repetition, as in the G minor movement. However, the progression of the ideas and consequent effect is quite different, not least because the first subject contains contrast within itself, rather than through opposition. It comprises two distinct rhythms, triplets and even quavers, which are first balanced into a conventional sentence of eight bars (2 – 2 – 2 – 2), the consequent involving variation of the opening shape, which, however, evolves continuously by simple extension of the scalic material to a total response of nineteen bars; the procedure clearly anticipates the parallel passage of the opening of the Second Symphony, also in triple metre, major tonality and of comparable mood. This flexibility is equally apparent in the second subject's first idea: here a repeated one-bar phrase evolves in almost seamless continuity, which only cadences clearly after thirty bars, in which time the third idea of the group (from bar 106) has already been subtly exposed and variation worked into the process almost imperceptibly. As in the G minor movement, five-bar phrasing through cadential augmentation is present, though overlapping creates a greater sense of continuity. The motivic concentration of the passage at bars 82–96, finally resolving into a lyric idea, parallels that of the G minor movement (bars 130–160). The flexibility of motivic working is perhaps clearest in the development, where Brahms constructs a pattern of evolution not unlike that of the parallel part of the First Symphony. Bars 144–51 witness that motivic working could be lyrical as well as economical.

The greater subtlety of planning is also clear in the finale. Yet here the greater opportunities offered by a sonata, rather than a simple rondo, produce a structure which, though it shares the most vigorous qualities of the G minor Rondo, gives room for subtle asides and the element of surprise. Thus the transition is suddenly interrupted at bar 84 – a gesture which refuses to resolve as expected, through interrupted cadences, in a manner akin to the finale of Schubert's Grand Duo. This character is intensified in the second subject, thus establishing a sense of contrast on which Brahms plays, intensifying the first idea through overt contrapuntal working in the development. The same principle operates in the scherzo, which title Brahms retains although it bears less resemblance to the traditional type than does its companion. Here the planning is comparably broad, with two distinct subjects in tonic and dominant and a total length of 211 bars. The trio is in strong contrast. It is a weighty canon between piano and strings, and its second subject relates closely to the scherzo theme, thus contributing more to the sense of extended development (the basic inspiration may well relate to the famous canon in the 'Witches' Minuet' of Haydn's *Fifths* Quartet). The force of the closing pedals and the impressive quality of the harmony of the final cadence, I – IV minor – I, is entirely characteristic of the energy of Brahms's language in these works with piano. Comparable breadth is found in the slow movement, a broad

Ex. 29 Piano Quartet in A major, op. 26, bars 140–4̊6

ABA form which is made more complex by the alternation of material in the first part and the recall of the subsidiary idea in the Neapolitan, F minor, in the reprise. Stylistically it reflects the influences of gipsy music and of Schubert, the latter in the harmonic turns which connect the subsidiary with the main idea in the first part (compare the cadence at bars 22–3 from F minor to E 6/4 with the reprise in 'Pause' from *Die schöne Müllerin*). The gipsy idiom comes with the admixture of Bach: the figurations of the Chromatic Fantasia, which Brahms played.

Piano Quintet

As a work of synthesis as well as of culmination, the F minor Piano Quintet looks to the future as well as to the past. In its passionate spirit and sense of structural planning it obviously recalls its predecessor in both key and status – the F minor Piano Sonata, and its scherzo is a classic example of Brahms's youthful concept of this genre, set aside in the two piano quartets. Yet the character of the overall structure, the pacing of the whole and especially the character of the finale, look directly to the First Symphony, for which it establishes most of the formal outline. In more immediate terms, it provides a particular synthesis of the qualities of the preceding works for piano and strings – the earnestness of the G minor Quartet, yet the relative ease and sense of direction of the A major – and indeed of the string sextets, yet brought to a much more pointed and cogent shaping.

In broad terms, it might be seen as reflecting equally the two dominant inspirations so far observed: Beethoven in the intensity of the expression, especially the opening, and the sense of the whole, yet Schubert in the lyric character of the slow movement and much of the finale. Yet these were essentially spiritual backgrounds, rather than models, for Brahms's language and technique are by now very personal and of expanding range. The work's greatest fascination lies in how he further integrates the two tendencies of motivic, developmental melodic writing and expansive lyricism within a dramatically conceived whole which, if it reflects the greatest associations of this key in the works of Beethoven and Schubert, handles them in an entirely personal way. Thus, the axiomatic relation to the submediant, D flat, affects not just the second subject but also the coda of the finale, most unusually established as its starting point, in the form of C sharp minor. Moreover, this semitonal relationship to the dominant which emerges so powerfully in the course of the coda, is exploited elsewhere: the first movement recalls the second subject in F sharp minor before it slips to the tonic, and the many examples of this inflexion are perhaps symbolised in the grinding appoggiatura D flat – C at the close of the Scherzo, surely drawn from the Finale of the Schubert Quintet.

Finally, the work's texture achieves a new sensitivity in the union of piano and strings. As a string quintet it would have lacked the inherent concerto style which lies behind the quartets, especially the most forceful G minor work, and though concertante elements are obviously present – notably the consequent passage of the opening – the texture is very varied and resourceful, perhaps symbolised in the closing bars of the first movement, which must survive from the original.[10]

In common with other of Brahms's most powerful works, the opening idea embodies one of his thematic archetypes in a characteristic form. Here, the basic chorale/folksong outline, rising $1 - 2 - 3 - 2 - 1$ in the minor key, is given the distinctive stress on D flat prior to C which seems to have such consequence for the work as an organic whole. Moreover, its continuation also embodies that developed repetition so common in Brahms's thematic manner, as, for example, at the opening of the C major Piano Sonata. But the thematic transformation which follows as a consequent statement has no precedent, for Brahms is here uniting the principle of a contrasted subject at the outset of a work, demonstrated in both the F minor Piano Sonata and the G minor Piano Quartet, with the demands of a more sophisticated motivic process. Thus, the introductory character which all these antecedent statements possess is here intensified by the nature of the consequent.

Ex. 30 Piano Quintet in F minor, op. 34, bars 1–7

This sense of impetus and direction is to characterise the whole movement, for whereas the quartet obscures its traditional points of articulation in the expression of such rich and expansive ideas, relative to those of the piano sonata, this work creates an equally expansive sense in ideas while restoring a much clearer formal outline. Thus the two elements of the first subject group are united in a transition which leads clearly to the second group, the closing group rounding this off with an abrupt, cadential idea. A gradually unfolding development of the first subject leads inevitably to the sequential treatment of the second, whilst the recapitulation is approached through a retransition of remarkable skill, which gradually reintroduces the elements of the opening so as to intensify their introductory quality. Brahms plays further with this passage, constructing a reflective coda on the first theme which likewise builds back into the agitated idea to conclude the movement. Inherent in this very clear and dramatic outline is a more directed transition theme and a considerably more integrated second group, now only comprising two related themes, subject to immediate variation. Yet Brahms still retains fruitful features from the earlier works: the closing group again employs immediate variations, though these are subtly constructed to permit the displacement of the beat, a feature which Brahms extends into the development such that only as late as bar 122 is the downbeat restored, with the more animated sequential treatment of the first theme. Such finesse, taken with the myriad thematic links and fluidity of phrasing mark this movement as Brahms's most sophisticated sonata structure to date.

Remarkable as is the quality of this first movement, however, it is the structure of the whole which stamps the work's true greatness. For Brahms does not attempt to balance it simply by weight, as in the G minor Quartet. He constructs a broad finale, with introduction, whose most intensive writing is kept for its massive coda in which the main theme (in a varied inversion) is presented in traditional diminution, its weight underpinned by its tonal relationship to the tonic via the dominant. Within this outer framework, Brahms inserts two movements of traditional ternary design. Although the third, the Scherzo, might almost appear too powerful in its very extensive structure and accumulative growth, the introduction to the finale serves to effect a transition towards main ideas which are quite different in character from the scherzo and the first movement, comparable force only appearing with the abrupt transition to the second subject.

Indeed, the character of Brahms's main theme is of a very different type from that of the first movement and is really symbolic of Brahms's intense interest in Schubert at this time of his creative development. It was Tovey, reflecting his special knowledge, through Joachim, of Brahms's compositional backgrounds who first appears to have pointed out the movement's relation to the finale of the Grand Duo – a work intimately shared by the two artists.[11] The breadth and lyricism of Schubert's movement shares much with the Brahms, not least its establishment of a distinct key towards the end of the movement. But it is surely in a thematic character that Brahms relates most closely: a comparison of the fragmentary treatment of Brahms's theme at bar 162 with the opening of the Schubert theme shows a link which, though it may have been unconscious, reveals the source of his comparably folk-based inspiration, with its equal suggestion of a gipsy background. The sonic parallel of Joachim's orchestration of this passage – which he gives to strings – may also have prompted the link to Brahms's first conception for string quintet. If inspirational in spirit, however, the form of this movement offered Brahms no parallel. This is found in another and equally important work – the finale of the String Quintet in C. Here, Brahms's own preoccupation with the variation of sonata form meets Schubert's own predilections, most strikingly revealed in his string quintet in the context of a finale of rondo character. Schubert's pattern thus reads:

		EXPOSITION					/DEVELOPMENT – RECAP.				
Bar	1	45	107	141			169	197	267	334	370
Subject	1	2a –	2b –	C.G. –	retr. –		1a –	dev –	2a –	C.G. –	Coda
Key	i/I/	V	V	V			i/I		I	I	i/I

and Brahms's very similarly:

Bar	41	80	94	125	161		184	198	252	283	321	342
Subject	1	tr	2a –	2b –	C.G. –		1a –	dev –	2a –	2b –	C.G. –	Coda
Key	I		v	(v)	v		I		I	I		#v-i

If the movements enclosed by this dramatic scheme relate to the past, they also achieve a much greater individuality and sense of shape. The scherzo, though obviously relating to the C minor mood of the *Sonatensatz*, realises its percussive rhythmic character in a much more broadly planned context. The expansive tendencies of the scherzi of the preceding Piano Quartets here appear even more distinctly in a movement which combines three distinct ideas in an evolutionary succession quite without parallel in

Brahms's music to this time, and all the stronger in effect because the movement begins quietly with some harmonic ambivalence: the pedal C suggests not a tonic but the third of A flat at first. The opening idea is followed by a dotted figure notated in 2/4 and a broad chorale-like idea. The music evolves through varied repetition which also involves fugal textures until the onset of the powerful syncopated passage between piano and strings at bar 100, still 93 bars from the end, the final passage further intensifying the earlier ideas. The fugal manner is again suggested in the trio, built on one of Brahms's broad major themes. The Schubertian character of the final appoggiatura G flat – F also illuminates Schubertian links to the slow movement. Latham[12] has drawn a valid parallel between the structure and shape of the theme and that of 'Pause' from *Die schöne Müllerin*, and the alternation of major and minor also reflects this background. Yet Brahms's melody is still constructed from motivic units which can be extended for an entire section, though the movement never loses the sense of a song base. It shows a clear relationship to the slow movement of the A major Quartet in the subtlety of the formal handling, here an A B A form characterised by organic development of the transition and fluidity of the retransition, arising from the tonal contrast from A flat to E in the middle part. The broadening of the coda is particularly impressive, yet another Brahms slow movement ending with a masterly pedal.

Cello Sonata and Horn Trio

With the completion of these works, Brahms had fulfilled many of his earliest ambitions, in the creation of a self-sufficient string medium and the completion of one undisputed masterpiece in the combination of strings with piano. He had significantly related the influences of Beethoven and Schubert in a language increasingly his own both in its characteristic modes of expression and the richness of its means. The two works which he completed in 1864–5 are both, in their different ways, relaxations from the complexity of the textures of sextet, quintet and quartet, and, though less demanding, achieve a new stage of ease of expression and subtlety of means, especially the Cello Sonata.

It seems entirely fitting that the first duo sonata which Brahms released should have been for cello, since cello and piano is the most frequently heard combination in early Brahms. But if he loved its Romantic qualities – so clearly expressed for example, in the lyrical unfolding of the Piano Trio, as shown – he also appreciated its expressive potential in more distant contexts: for in this work Brahms's relation to the past and capacity to achieve a modern relation to it, is revealed even more directly than in the first String Sextet. As Altmann pointed out in 1912,[13] the main theme of the fugal finale is strikingly like Contrapunctus 13 from *The Art of Fugue*, and Brahms's thoroughgoing treatment of it reflects the knowledge we have observed in an earlier context. Moreover, Altmann argues for the link as also penetrating the singing main subject of the first movement, which he sees as leaning on the basic, generative theme of the Bach work.

(i)

Ex. 31 (i) Bach: Theme and Contrapunctus 13 from The Art of Fugue
(ii) Brahms: Cello Sonata in E minor, op. 38, first movement, bars 1–5; finale, bars 1–4

The second movement is an obvious recreation of the mood of a minuet, though with a romantic trio. Thus, Brahms has juxtaposed two markedly historical characters and built a first movement which mediates between them, establishing a mode of expression to which they can both relate.

In writing a fugal finale to a cello sonata Brahms offers yet another example of his reference to Beethoven in matters structural, for Beethoven's last, D major Sonata, ends with a fugue. However, Brahms's very assertive presentation of the Bach idea on the piano left hand and the way in which he plays the Baroque effects to the full makes a much stronger impression in terms of his stylistic development. Yet his treatment of the form of fugue with sonata form, established in Haydn and finding notable examples in the finales of Mozart's G major String Quartet (and *Jupiter* Symphony), as well as the finale of the C major *Rasoumovsky* Quartet, is very independent. Like his predecessors, he uses a fugal exposition in lieu of a first subject, building a transition to a second group in homophonic sonata style, leading to a development of both ideas involving stretto and inversion. However, his reprise radically disturbs the sonata-association, for it not only begins with a reverse of the tonal relations of the exposition – B minor – E minor (as a counterexposition), but it omits any reference to the second group, leading directly to a coda on the fugal idea. The second group is reprised partially thematically in the development, to which it makes only minor though telling, contributions, through the element of contrast to the prevailing contrapuntal working. This contrast element is extremely important, and the way in which Brahms creates his second subject in the exposition is a fine example of his integration of contrasts of style and period. For he draws from the original, forceful first subject an entirely characteristic melody, including motivic repositioning, the first phrase proper repeated in a different accentual position which is hardly noticeable to the ear, a phrase most subtly drawn from the 'neutral' figuration which liquidates the transition from the fugue subject. Moreover, the following, animated idea is a variant of the same phrase establishing a contrast – for this has a 'chiaroscuro' quality – with the main material.

Contrast of moods is a major quality of the second movement, the first recalling in Brahmsian terms the minuet character more traditionally expressed in the Serenade in D, and here contrasted with another very atmospheric Trio. All Brahms's love of harmonic effect, of the creation of a language with archaic qualities yet personal enrichments, is here drawn upon to characterise the minuet movement of the gentle 3/4, with its 'Phrygian Cadences' and disarming mobility of root-based progressions.

So natural are these effects that the sheer adventure of the harmony passes almost unnoticed. In the Trio, the harmonic treatment is much more direct, the same thematic contour being given 'romantic' arpeggiac treatment. In seeking to mediate between these movements, Brahms created a lyric first movement which explores yet another aspect of the cello's character – its lyricism. In the process, it establishes a type of subject which recurs in the Piano Trio in A minor, that of a lyric melody beginning over pedal and creating modal effects of harmony in the process, a very Brahmsian type which anticipates later examples, such as the Double Concerto in the same key or the development of the Violin Sonata in D minor. This long, evolving melody, initially divisible into an A B A structure, does not however lead to new transition material. Such is the power of the idea that the transition simply moves it to C and the rhetorical second subject grows naturally from it with no formal division, the exposition concluding with another pedal device, here of much greater length, confirming the dominant, though minor contrast also appears. The close imitation in the second subject affords a contrasted element which links to the finale, and very powerful tonal links are also present in the relationship of E minor/C and the structural use of pedal, which is already emphasised in the goal of the development section of the first movement.

In the Horn Trio in E flat completed in 1865, Brahms opens up the clearest link to his current preoccupations with orchestral composition, in which the treatment of the horn is such a notable feature. As has been shown in relation to the Songs with Two Horns and Harp, his early acquaintance with the instrument stimulated the interest he shared with many romantic

Ex. 32 Cello Sonata in E minor, op. 38 'allegretto quasi menuetto', bars 16–29

composers in its use, to create early a very idiomatic horn style, of which this Trio gives the most extensive evidence. For here it is required not merely to play an idiomatic symbolic role in an orchestral texture, but to take an equal part in a chamber context. However the work's most notable quality – its sheer sound – is never heard in modern performance as Brahms intended it, since he insisted on the use of the natural, or Waldhorn, an instrument already growing obsolete by this time: not only Wagner but Schumann had long opted for the modern valve instrument which facilitated the use of the total chromatic. Brahms limits his 'natural' notes to those of the harmonic series; thus (E flat) – E flat[2] – B flat[3] – E flat[4] – G[5] –

B flat^6 – D flat^7 – E flat^8 – F^9 – G^{10}, etc. up to E flat^{16}. Performance, not only with the hand horn, but with a piano and violin of the period, would throw invaluable light on his sound world and the scope of his imagination in this unique work.[14] Such a limitation explains the unique use in four movements of a tonic E flat and the formal restriction of these, the normal tonal range being unavailable, most notably in the first – his only first movement not in sonata form in the instrumental compositions.

Thus, the Horn Trio stands in no tradition, since only the Beethoven Horn Sonata (which Brahms knew well, for he played it) could be regarded as a precursor and its character is very different. Brahms explores two characters of horn music: the hunting type employed in the two scherzi, which form the second movement and finale, and the intimate reflective, which he uses in the second movement and the main idea of the first. Indeed this slow movement recalls the early Ballades or the slow movement of the Piano Trio in B in its intensity of reflection: music of great sadness. Much has been made of the association of the movement with the death of Brahms's mother in 1865 and it could certainly reflect the deep feelings he experienced. In such a context, the transforming effect of the F major phrase which the violin presents at bar 63, with horn in counterpoint, is very striking – like a ray of light piercing the gloom – not least since it anticipates the finale's main theme. Whether Kalbeck is justified in seeing this Brahmsian melodic archetype as a specific quotation of 'Wer nur den lieben Gott lässt walten' is, however, doubtful.[15] The formal pattern of the first movement has been likened to the Piano Sonata in F op. 54 by Beethoven in its unusual first movement form, both adopting the alternating pattern A B A B A. Such a relation cannot be ignored, since the parallels are close in the retention of tonal identity and slight, yet intensifying variation of the returns of the two ideas, with particularly broad extension of the final statements of A. The plan could well have given Brahms the outline he needed. Yet his own treatment is very different since his B section involves a change of metre and key, to the relative minor, where Beethoven continues into a section built on the rhythmic contrast of semiquavers which anticipate the movement of his second and last movement, whereas Brahms employs the form characteristic of most of his chamber works. His idiom is deeply Romantic, the opening figure's evolution bringing it very close to the fourth of the Songs with Horns and Harp similarly in a moderate 2/4, major key (compare bars 17–20) of the first movement with bar 6 of *Fingals Gesang*. The scherzo offers another example of the expansive tendencies of the period. For although the scherzo type goes back to the Brahmsian archetypes, the treatment is akin to that of the Piano Quintet, with clear second subject, closing group and powerful transition. The linking bars to the trio are new, anticipating the parallel passage in the Piano Trio in C, whilst the singing melody looks both backwards – to the Piano Trio in B – and forwards – to this Trio as to the Clarinet Sonata in E flat. If the horn writing relates to the Songs, however, it also looks forward to the orchestral works, for the notable transition in the slow movement, following two first subjects and working to an impassioned middle section drawn from it uses just the quasi-fugal type of subject which Brahms uses in the comparable passage of the Second Symphony.

String Quartets in C minor and A minor

The eight years which separate the completion of the works of 1865 from the string quartets of 1873 witnessed a considerable development in compositional sophistication towards the works of full maturity, to which the A minor Quartet throws especially strong links. As is well established, Brahms claimed to have discarded over twenty quartets before releasing his first, C minor work.

Precisely where these two fit the pattern has never been established, though various references from 1865 seem to confirm the natural assumption that the ideas of the C minor were the earlier by mention of a quartet in this key. The intensity of the opening theme and its use of tremolando suggest the orchestra, offering a parallel case to the opening of the late G major Quintet, and the finale similarly stretches the medium to its limit. The A minor work is of a very different stamp, a more approachable and lyrical composition closer to the E minor Cello Sonata in opening manner than to the orchestra. Whatever the period of conception of these ideas, however, the finished structures suggest a period close to their publication in finesse and economy. For the rich profusion of ideas in the earlier works is here reduced to classic proportions, yet, through the suppleness of phrasing and degree of contrast, creates comparable effect of richness. Though fully half the length of the Piano Quartets and Piano Quintet, the structure appears more of a whole, with much more overt means of unification and a scaling of the inner movements which strongly suggest overall conception rather than the uniting of discrete movements.

Tonal and thematic relationships are a particularly conspicuous part of this achievement, which is without precedent in Brahms's work so far. The very unusual first subject group provides the means of the work's large-scale shaping. The first subject stands in direct succession to that of the G minor Piano Quartet in giving two distinct ideas at the outset. But here the contrast is much more dramatic. The first idea is another example of the harmonic descent to the dominant which gives the impression of an introduction. But here the dominant is immediately re-interpreted as the first stage of a Neapolitan progression which establishes the distant chord of F major (through chromatic lowering) subsequently suggesting, though never quite confirming, F minor, the true dominant chord never being entirely banished. Whether or not one goes on to see the unharmonised F sharp at the close as representing, in Schoenberg's view, the dominant of B, minor, is a matter of hearing.[16]

The basic relationship of I with IV dominates the work's tonal processes. Thus, at the recapitulation, the original progression is modified to lead not to G, but to C. However, this C only serves to act as dominant of F minor, from which point the recapitulation of the transition proceeds, adjustment occurring later. The relationship is even more overt in the finale, where an introductory gesture drawn from the work's opening is placed in F minor, the subject proper roving from this key and only establishing the tonic at the first main cadence at bar 20. The idea is even more pervasive than in the first movement, for it forms the second subject through variation. In broader tonal terms, F minor is the unusual pairing with A flat in the third movement, though here again in an ambivalent tonal context. The effect of the opening of this movement is to recall the Neapolitan progression of the first subject – here IIb – V in C minor. Yet, the relationship does not exist in the tonality of C minor, but F minor, and Brahms obscures this goal until the close of the entire passage: the first main dividing cadence at bar 25 is only to the implied goal, C minor. As well as such tangible links, the outer movements also possess a basic relationship of contrast between the assertive mood of the openings, and the reflective, freely evolving and improvisatory themes which conclude the second group of the first subject and comprise that of the finale, giving not second subject impression but rather closing group shaping.

The force of Brahms's tonal and thematic planning is matched by the finesse and individuality of his thematic working. In this, his long-considered first quartet he reveals motivic and contrapuntal mastery already so clear in the developments of the string sextets, yet now in his most intense C minor mood and in the context of exposition rather than development. Thus, for example, the second subject (bars 41–53) offers invertible counterpoint, stretto and various motivic combinations which are handled even more boldly in the development, which deals alternately with the first and second subjects combining augmentations and motivic variants. The emotional pattern of the transition into the development may draw from the past – the background is the parallel passage of the Piano Quintet, whose rising, displaced phrase is virtually identical (compare bar 80 of the Quartet and bar 91 of the Quintet) but the contrapuntal concentration is new, symbolic of the new compositional intensity of Brahms's working around the time he completed the First Symphony. Thus he fulfils the classical obligations of the genre as he was to do with the symphony, yet in a very personal way, deeply reflecting his own background and path to maturity. A particularly notable feature of Brahms's interpretation of inherited principles is his treatment of the transition process, whereby the characteristics of one section are gradually displaced by those of another, a process which Schoenberg was later to identify as characterised through the term 'liquidation', and which was one of many very powerful links between his own thought and that of Brahms. The passage which follows the counterpoint just noted offers a fine example, the features of the preceding passage clearly reduced to permit the shapes of the improvisatory close of the exposition to appear gradually, and in such a way that Brahms can extend the close with remarkable fluidity, creating a complete contrast of mood with the assertive character of the opening.

Remarkable as the first movement appears, however, it is matched in structural ingenuity by the finale. For this explores another aspect of the prophetic first movement of the G minor Piano Quartet: the conflation of development and recapitulation. Here the use of an introductory gesture drawn from the work's very opening (1a) facilitates easier separation in the subsequent course of a much tighter and more sharply directed structure than the earlier movement:

			EXPOSITION					/DEVELOPMENT – RECAP.					
Bar	1	3	33	50	71	81	94		124	141	162	205	225
Subject	1a –	1b –	tr. –	2a –	CG –	retr –	1a –	dev –	tr –	2a –	CG –	retr –	1a –	1a (var)
Key	(i)	–		III	–		(i/iv)		i	i		i	

The development of the finale begins with this element leading directly to a continuation in A flat rather than the previously implied C minor. After due working of the first idea, the transition material reappears in A minor, followed by the second subject and material as before, thus preserving the original tonal pattern in the recapitulatory mode – that is, A minor to G major as dominant of C minor, for C minor to B flat major as dominant of E flat. A harmonised version of Ia now leads to a remarkable intensification of Ib, from which the original material of Ib in simple variation resumes to lead, in turn, to further, chordal variation of Ib to create one large coda passage. The conclusion is especially notable in using a relentless tonic pedal to build tension which is only resolved when the original opening, Ib, is, for the first time in the work, predictably resolved to great and culminatory effect.

Much of the tightness of the overall effect arises from the nature of the middle movements, which are much simpler in design than those of the parallel movements of the earlier chamber works and of a nature which clearly reflects Brahms's growing individuality in the exploration of new moods and characters, in two movements of comparable ternary design. The 'allegretto molto moderato e comodo' is especially interesting in representing the first substitute for the traditional scherzo which does not reflect triple dance metre. Here the movement is that of a little march in 4/8 which relates rather to such types in the music of Schubert, for example that of the Piano Trio in E flat or the 'Great' C major Symphony. But the mood is entirely Brahms's, a wistful inspiration which balances the main theme in the violin with an animated counter-theme by the viola, perhaps another stimulus from the viola theme of Schubert's G major Quartet. Its remarkable tonal character shows that the growing fluidity of his language was not restricted to the thematic sphere, for it begins by stressing the II in F minor (as dominant of the dominant), from which the composer then plays with the listener's expectations, only making his first cadence on E flat, still far distant from the tonic. The first stage of tonal clarification at the end of the first section, bar 24, is only to establish the dominant. The tonic is only finally confirmed at the final cadence of the reprise, the entire second section after the double bar moving far away. In contrast, the trio function ('un poco piu animato') contains the harmonic movement, making much use of pedal and complementing the tonic major with stresses on the upper and lower mediants A minor and D minor, which point to the growing emphasis on this relationship, not only in broad tonal planning, but in local progressions. The effect is given special character by the contrast of open and stopped notes in the accompanying figure. Whilst the 'Romanze' seems at first to relate more closely to tradition, especially the lyric slow movements of Mendelssohn, it soon moves with greater breath to more individual continuation. The passage from bar 25 has been compared to that from bar 42 of the 'Cavatina' of Beethoven's String Quartet in B flat in its gentle syncopation,[17] but the Brahms passage is much more elusive in rhythm – a very characteristic example of his advanced rhythmic sense, the felt beat gradually dissolved in a freely moving sequel which suggests once again the background of folk improvisation, almost the fluidity best known through jazz vocalists. The 'Minuet' of the quartet in A minor shows a similar preoccupation in the triplet variation of the theme at bar 33.

As with the relationship of the two earlier Piano Quartets, the companion work explores quite different surface characters whilst retaining strong links in terms of structural and working procedures. Although the view that

the works are based on common material seems extreme,[18] some obvious thematic links within each work, most notably between the first and last movements symbolise important parallels: in the subtlety of sonata structure (compare, for example, the two retransitions), the role of variation and counterpoint in ensuring concentration and coherence, the flexibility of phrase structure, the fluidity of harmonic language, the desire to link movements – here the third to the fourth and thus to the first.

But Brahms now relegates the dominant feature of the C minor work, its driving rhetoric, to a minor role. It is the lyrical and improvisatory quality which now claims his attention, and both the main themes of the first movement and that of the second demonstrate his growing interest in the generation of flexible and evolving themes. Schoenberg's emphasis on the 'advanced' nature of the theme of the slow movement is well known,[19] and it applies also to the other themes noted, the first being especially interesting in the fluidity of its harmony. Thus, a four-bar consequent evolves by varied repetition and extension to build to a climax followed by an extended cadence, a passage of 20 bars in all. Moreover, the harmony is centred on the subdominant – a necessary base for the theme is another example of the harmonisation of Joachim's F A E. The same principle underpins a second subject of 13 bars, directly comparable with the theme of the slow movement. Elsewhere, the connections and closings of ideas never reach the complexity of the comparable work. The transition is very direct, stressing an improvisatory quality in leading the second subject which is taken up in the closing group. This quality predicts the later evolution of

(ii)   Allegro

Allegro

Poco Adagio

Ex. 33   (i) String Quartet, op. 51 no. 2, thematic links between movements
         (ii) String Quartet, op. 51 no. 1, thematic links between movements

the work, where, in total contrast to the C minor Quartet, Brahms explores the dance qualities which also permeate the A major Piano Quartet, as well as the more distant qualities of the 'Minuet' of the Cello Sonata. For the slow movement of the quartet explores in its middle section the evocative world of the gipsy dance, through its rapid figures over tremolo strings. But the effect is much more integrated and intense – two short passages set into the calm unfolding of the main theme, whose only structural point of note is the reprise on the submediant, F major. This retrospective quality comes even more powerfully in the finale, a dance, phrased, like that of the gipsy finale of op. 25, in three-bar groups. Its shape and character recall directly the *Neue Liebeslieder*-waltz no. 14 'Flammen Auge, dunkles Haar' and suggest its possible background (publication dates are close). But its context is again different – another stage of integration, for it is now subjected to variation through extension, diminution and changing character to play a role in a complete sonata rondo movement. The adaptation goes even further in the third movement where Brahms again uses the manner of the Classical minuet, here in a complex alternating movement employing variation which provides the blueprint for the more familiar third movement of the Second Symphony. Here the minuet character, indicated in the title, is more individually treated, the inserted extension, prelude and coda of the original being replaced by a more individual continuation. The fast section which follows preserves something of this Classical quality of playful counterpoint, and the brief return of the minuet character is to new and improvisatory material which will return before the reprise of the first section, producing a sectional work in which two ideas develop in parallel, a principle clear in Stravinsky, as shown by Cone in terms of 'Stratification'.[20]

Piano Quartet in C minor

The chamber compositions of the period conclude with the work with which Brahms had been longest preoccupied, the Piano Quartet in C minor, which he took up again from its earliest ideas in 1873–4, releasing it in 1875. Despite the final maturity of much of the working, this quartet has never gained the popularity of the other chamber works of the period, though it is a fascinating document of creative revision and in the character of its ideas. As mentioned, the work was first conceived in C sharp minor rather than C minor. The traditional interpretation of its obscure chronology – that movements 1 and 3 (first and slow movements) were early, and movements 2 and 4 (scherzo and finale) late, has recently been revised by re-examination of existing information and provision of new, though many questions remain open still. Whilst the early origin of the first movement can be confirmed through the correspondence, as well as the reports of contemporaries, this does not, in fact, apply to the slow movement. It was rather

Kalbeck, taking the 'wonderful' Adagio in E major which Clara notes Brahms wrote for the Quartet in the Autumn of 1856 as the Andante in E major which we know, who made the connection. Yet Brahms's own register of works noted movements 1 and 2 as 'earlier' and 3 and 4 as '[18]73/4'. Seeking to interpret this evidence – especially to explain why, despite this indication, no mention is made of a scherzo in the early correspondence – Webster draws on telling details in Brahms's correspondence with Joachim to offer the very convincing hypothesis that the Scherzo did exist, but in the form of a finale, with an unusually taut structure and lack of a conventional trio.[21] Since only three movements were mentioned in the early correspondence, the slow movement would therefore have been discarded. This would date the scherzo in its original, finale form, in 1856. The first movement seems certain to have dated from the previous year, however. The questionnaire completed for Kalbeck by Dietrich proffers the recognition by him and Deiters in the opening of a 'very melancholy' movement with a 'melodic and expressive' second theme of 1855, the main ideas of the first movement we know:[22] '1855' is thus not merely Kalbeck's date. Yet Brahms's late dating of third and fourth movements does not necessarily preclude their also sharing a period of revision, though not, it would seem, for this work. General acceptance of the early origin of the slow movement rests partly on its singing cello melody, which seems much closer to the drawing room idiom of Mendelssohn (at least, at the outset) than to Brahms's later style; it could be part of a cello sonata or a character piece for the instrument. (It seems interesting that the lyrical opening of the slow movement of the C minor Symphony, in the same key, E major, is almost immediately bent to the work's broader structural needs.) And the finale, always taken as the last in order of composition, opens like a violin sonata movement, not unlike the finale of Schumann's D minor Sonata, though the texture is clearly related to that of Brahms's own first, G major, sonata, soon to appear in 1879. Its very unusual chorale-like second subject throws links back to youth, specifically the finale of a work already noted for its suggestion in Brahms, Mendelssohn's Piano Trio in C minor, with its similar response from the piano to each successive phrase. Thus we are presented with four separate movements of great individuality, though difficult to 'place' stylistically, and failing to function in the tightly integrated manner of other large-scale works of the 'Seventies, not least those in C minor: the first string quartet and the first symphony. When Brahms made his famous allusion to Goethe's Werther –' the man with a blue coat and yellow waistcoat' with pistol pointed towards his head,[23] the reference was of more than usual personal significance. As a composition, the work had cost him dear.

Though the correspondence reveals the extent of the reworking it seems clear that the main ideas of the first movement – and thus its essential contour – remained intact, and as such make fascinating comparison with other movements. Like the preceding F minor Sonata and later F minor

Quintet and C minor String Quartet, the first subject reveals an introductory quality through its immediate descent to the dominant – perhaps an early acquisition from the 'Waldstein' Sonata. Yet here the consequence is much bolder – a repetition on the lowered seventh degree, which can be seen as extending the adventure observed in the C major Piano Sonata through its much longer and more brooding quality posing more possibilities of continuation as it works its way gradually back to the dominant, the orchestral pizzicato-like bass creating a sense of expectation much like the slow introduction to the First Symphony. The transition follows, leading the first subject in an intense passage towards what might be anticipated as a passing subject and powerful closing group as employed in the Symphony or the Quartet. Yet Brahms's goal is here quite different – a self-contained lyric melody for piano to which the music winds down, reaching its Schubertian contrast with none of Schubert's sense of inevitability. The Schubertian model is, however, clear in the treatment of the subject, in which Brahms presents, as Tovey notes, no less than four variations the last deceiving to the ear despite its logical function (70–102). Like the other works, however E flat minor is the tonal goal of the exposition. With the development, Brahms treats the first subject with growing intensity, as he does the second, largely over pedal and in stretto, before it builds to a climax which mirrors that of the Symphony in the harmonic subtlety of its recall. Yet the movement has more structural experiment to reveal, for the original repetition on lowered VII and the transition are completely reworked so as to lead quietly to the second subject, though now in G major. Although the third variation recurs in this key, the intervening music is reworked and extended to give a completely new aspect to the section, from which Brahms builds an extensive coda culminating with recollections of the opening and ending very like the close of the first movement of the Symphony.

That Brahms could find no model for the continuation of a work beginning with such a powerful and individual movement may be reasonably deduced. The work which finally appeared follows Beethovenian precedent in placing a very powerful Scherzo second, another of the basic type of driving 6/8 in C minor. Yet as indicated, it is crucially different from that of the *Sonatensatz* and the F minor Quintet, despite its expansive working and many comparable rhythmic features: for it lacks a Trio. Brahms creates from the background model a continuous movement in which contrast appears, very surprisingly, at the first dominant cadence with a dance-like figure, which articulates a very simple triadic progression, this passage recurring in the recapitulation. If this music was drawn from the Finale, then its unusual scherzo-form is readily explicable – in principle at least. Scherzo-rhythm is not without parallel in Brahms's chamber finales; notably, that of the Violin Sonata in D minor op. 108 is a driving 6/8 of this class, though it establishes no such contrasts, either through a trio, or as here. There is certainly no evidence that Brahms was thinking in such radical terms of formal experiment in conventional scherzos in the middle 'Fifties. Just how close the scherzo we know is to the supposed finale is a matter for conjecture. At all events, accepting Webster's hypothesis, Brahms could not create an adequate finale from the movement. Although the finale which he eventually provided is of a very different kind – a flowing violin melody with quaver accompaniment – Brahms still achieves a sense of structural balance, if not of resolution, through it. This is not at first clear. After a relatively straightforward exposition, the development appears to run in very conventional sequential patterns, almost losing its direction and setting up the conditions which will eventually characterise the conclusion. Yet at bar 156, a powerful transformation of the second, chorale-like theme initiates a more intense treatment of the opening idea which stimulates in turn a transformed recapitulation, both themes appearing *ff*, the archaism of the chorale melody reinforced by harmonic emphasis. Although, despite the *ff* chords of the close, the music winds down, as does the close of the first movement, there is still sufficient weight and internal logic and interest to complement the preceding movements. Likewise, the Mendelssohnian promise of the slow movement is not fulfilled, but the later composer confirmed in the evolving character of the theme, the powerful manner of the middle section, the harmonic ambiguity of the retransition, which recalls the first theme with surprise, and the colouring of the original material through the use of pizzicato. The parallels in the closing of the slow movements of Quartet and Symphony in C minor may indicate similar working periods. Perhaps this work will always have a limited audience, since its deeper formal beauties and its outer emotional pattern are less easy of access than in other cases. Yet, at the end of the strivings of the second period, there could be no clearer example of Brahms's dedication to the working of valid ideas into an 'unassailable' whole, however difficult and problematic the task.

5

Orchestral Music

Piano Concerto in D minor

The status of the Piano Quartet in C minor in spanning an entire era and symbolising Brahms's struggle for mastery of the formal treatment of powerfully expressive ideas finds a striking parallel in the history, key and moods of the First Symphony. Although we cannot be sure that its earliest part, the first Allegro, was conceived at the same time as the Quartet – the familiar '1855' derives from Kalbeck's view only[1] – the overtly Beethovenian spirit does not contradict a possible date in the 1850s: and the final resolution likewise took until the 1870s. Further, it was not Brahms's first attempt in the genre. The Two-Piano Sonata in D minor on which Brahms worked in the earlier part of 1854 came in turn to be a symphonic project by the summer of that year, and plans for the Symphony in C minor quite possibly predated its final resolution into a Concerto. Thus the Piano Concerto is the first in a series of works including Piano Quartet in C minor and Piano Quintet whose final character reflects many changes and a central problem of medium, especially as regards the role of the piano. In contrast to the Concerto, it seems that the Symphony was conceived orchestrally from the first, its long period of gestation determined by other factors. The works which appeared in the intervening twenty years or so outline clear stages in the transitional process from pianistic to orchestral thinking. Although the first orchestral works in Brahms's newer manner actually predate the first comparable chamber works (the two Serenades occupying an analogous position to the Sextets), their role is the same – to enable through the use of relaxed, classically oriented idioms, the exploration of a much wider range of textures and colours. In turn, the marked individuality of Brahms's choral style in the large-scale works with orchestra, especially the *Requiem* and the *Alto Rhapsody*, further drew out his individual feeling for the orchestra and in the *St Antoni* Variations his expression reaches its first full maturity, not least through the special character of the variation technique, providing the foundation for the later concertos and symphonies.

Of the three great 'problem' works of Brahms's youth – the Piano Concerto in D minor, Piano Quartet in C minor and Piano Quintet in F minor, all offered immense challenge of resolution, the Quintet and

Concerto of change of medium, and the Concerto and Quartet of material, the original formal concepts modified through deletion of movements and probably material, and addition of new. In their final forms, the Concerto and Quintet join the Quartet in stressing a concerto character in the contrast of piano and a comparable instrumental body. For, as shown, Brahms's approach to the Piano Quartet, if less to the Quintet, stressed this feature, very fully exploited in the concerto reworking. If a total vision of the outcome of the original ideas of the Piano Quartet was denied to Brahms in the 1850s, however, he drove himself to complete the Concerto, though he seems never fully to have acknowledged his achievement and was obviously exhausted with its termination by the later stages. Even after he had determined the new form through reworking the first movement of the sonata/symphony and adding a new slow movement and rondo – the first movement was sent to Joachim in April 1856 and the other movements soon after – he continued to revise, and by December 1857 wrote to Clara of his 'frustration' at the 'amateurism' of the whole.[2] The disappointing first performances at Hanover and Leipzig in January 1859 did little to ease Brahms's problems, though the Hamburg performance in March was much better received. Publication, refused by Breitkopf and accepted by Rieter-Biedermann for a very modest fee, was as late as 1861; such was the lack of confidence that only the piano part was first published, the orchestral parts in 1862. The full score had to wait until 1874.

The extent of the reworking has often encouraged the work's disparagement as a hybrid – a symphony 'with piano obbligato', the most extreme example of Brahms's concertos as 'symphonies with soloist'.

Yet, although Brahms always acknowledged the special character of his 'Concerto', he worked assiduously to relate the work to the tradition he knew so well, that of the symphonic concerto as conceived by Mozart and Beethoven. In order better to approach its individual relation to tradition it is necessary to see it against its background, which falls into three phases: the original conception as a sonata/symphony, the reworking of the first movement, and the addition of the second and third.

In the first reference to the work, 9 March 1854, Grimm refers to Kreisler's having just completed 'three movements of a Sonata for Two Pianos'.[3] On 19 June, Brahms wrote to Joachim of his continuing preoccupation with 'the first three movements of my Sonata in D minor',[4] for which he felt he needed 'more than two pianos', apparently undertaking the instrumentation by the summer, seeking the advice of Grimm, Joachim, and Marxsen. He wrote to Schumann in 1855 of having 'started a Symphony' in the previous summer: 'The first movement is already orchestrated, the second and third already fully sketched out. (In D minor in 6/4 – slow)'.[5] Thus, like the funeral march of the *Requiem*, Brahms's original tempo conception was slower than the final version. Whether or not the original conception was directly affected by Schumann's attempted suicide in February 1854 has never been established, though the music which survives would certainly support such an interpretation. A tragic first movement of the utmost intensity – a massive funeral march bearing a chorale melody whose significance was profound, not least in relation to Schumann. Of the other movement we know nothing, but the total concept must have been vast. Moreover, there are obvious grounds for regarding it as carefully integrated thematically. There exist clear links between the chorale which underlies the slow movement as we know it from the *Requiem* and the second subject of the first movement – two examples of a Brahmsian basic shape. That the added finale also employs the shape strongly suggests its underlying role in the original conception.

(i)

(ii)

Ex. 34 (i) *Requiem*, second movement, 'Denn alles Fleisch'
      (ii) Piano Concerto in D minor, op. 15, first movement, bars 157–8; finale,
           bars 1–3

In seeking to uncover the symphonic outline of the first movement, the display element of the soloist offers an immediate guide. The development section, in particular, employs passages which could hardly have been part of the original, even in its sonata version: thus, the bravura octaves which link to the close of the exposition to the development, and the display passage from bar 287 to bar 297, the latter perhaps a little too contrasted in idiom, though reintegrated over the long-concluding dominant pedal with great effect. Elsewhere, however, it is difficult to distinguish between the natural elaboration of textures which could have formed part of the original, sonata conception, and passages which are additions. None the less, the work's symphonic quality still emerges in broad outline as the most powerful orchestral utterance in German music since Beethoven's Ninth Symphony in the same key, and one reflective of the most striking technical features of the composer at this stage, a quite remarkably original and personal work. The first movement is clearly cast along symphonic lines, with no anticipation of the second subject in the orchestral exposition which is only to appear in the solo treatment, with a great sense of continuity arising as a result. The very clear pattern of exposition, development, recapitulation, coda, taken with the lack of a solo cadenza and the culminatory power of the coda give an outline which is intensified in dramatic detail. Especially important is the role of the pedal at the outset in creating harmonic ambiguity at the outset and the brilliance of the harmonisation of the parallel point at the recapitulation, where Brahms places a chord of E over the bass D (rather than B flat), as dominant of the dominant, creating an effect of comparable drama with both the parallel points of the Sonata in C major and Piano Quartet in C minor. This power, taken with the comparable force of the Funeral March of the *Requiem* gives an indication of the scale of the original conception. Just how Brahms conceived the discarded third movement, and how he would have completed a four-movement scheme are matters for conjecture. Yet, the fact that he was able so effectively to re-cast the first movement as a concerto reflects not only his effort, but also the potential of much of it, inherent in the original version.

But there was more to the reworking than the incorporation of pianistic elements, or perhaps in some cases, reincorporation. The soloist's function is very distinctive, though not, in my view, in the way implied by Geiringer when he speaks of an affinity with 'Vivaldi Concerto Form', as employed by J. S. Bach wherein 'solo instrument and the orchestra elaborate different subjects'.[6] What is distinctive is that Brahms gives not only the second subject to a soloist for the first time, but also a new subject at its entry. However, this has obvious precedents – if not in Beethoven's concertos, certainly in Mozart's, whose two great minor key concertos in C minor and D minor begin this way. In their tradition, Brahms avoids the repetition of a symphonic idea which might appear inadequate on the piano in favour of a contrast, a soloistic idea which only builds gradually into the continuation of the first subject material, and acts as a structural foil to the recall of the expected theme, though not in the expected way, at the recapitulation. It can be no coincidence that Brahms played these concertos during the period of the reworking: much less apparent is the subtle link to a concerto he played even more frequently then – Beethoven's Concerto in G major, the outline of whose opening phrase is transposed into Brahms's minor mode, and whose phrasing is made almost Bachian by Brahms – a style feature often observed.

Infinitely more clear, however, is the lineage of the finale. Whatever the relation of its main idea to the original thematic plan of the sonata/symphony, its scheme and style are completely free of the conflict of genres inherent in the first movement. The soloist's relation to the orchestra is now entirely in accord with the tradition of the concerto rondo. Indeed, as Tovey hinted,[7] the obvious parallels in the writing of a fughetta on the main theme (or rather a variant of it) as a central episode with the finale of

Beethoven's Piano Concerto in C minor uncover much more detailed parallels. Although Brahms's movement is longer and becomes much more independent towards the end, he may well be seen as leaning thankfully on a proven model in the attempt to balance and therefore salvage the content of the magnificent first movement. The relations are based on fundamental parallels in the structures of the main subjects. That the parallels were themselves contrived by Brahms is, of course, not impossible either. Both main subjects fall into two sections of eight bars each, repeated by orchestra, the first ending on the dominant, the second closing with a short cadenza to link back to the repetition. The common metre, 2/4, and obvious parallels in keyboard texture and figuration further underpin the connection. The second subjects are slightly freer, Beethoven using three ideas, but both closing groups end with a solo cadenza to recall the rondo. The central episode occurs at an identical point, bars 181–2 in both, and the sectional proportions are very close, leading ultimately to the fughettas on the main subject, repetition of the first subject and short cadenza at comparable points. Whilst proceeding independently thereafter, both reach their major cadenza at analogous structural moments. Only then does Brahms expand his scheme, consistent with the greater scope of the first movement. The pianism of the major cadenza at bar 499 offers a rare example of purely improvisatory writing – 20 bars of figuration over dominant pedal to build powerfully back to the final tutti which, however, begins gently, retaining the dominant before the final peroration.

If the outer movements were both planned on models – the rondo specifically, the first movement much more generally – the middle movement seems quite free of tradition, and very personal in expression. The smaller scale of the Concerto relative to the Sonata/Symphony drew from him a movement of deep intimacy in total contrast to the inexorable drive of the original march. His characteristic pianism at its most reflective is revealed in relation to an orchestral fabric which suggests a background in religious choral music very strongly. Discussion of the background has focused almost invariably on the inscription which Brahms added to the lower staves of the score – 'Benedictus qui venit in Nomine Domini'. Kalbeck stressed not the religious but the personal significance of this quotation, pointing out, rather surprisingly, that Brahms was accustomed to call Schumann 'Mynheer Domini' and took it as a gesture of affection to the dead composer. Although he was aware that Brahms had written a polyphonic mass, he found no occasion to explore this possible inspiration.[8] Yet, whilst the material has no direct link to the material of the mass of which we know, composed at this very period, 1856, the orchestral opening has very much of the feel of vocal polyphony, and it seems difficult to dismiss from its background some link to his polyphonic activity in this period. One might note, for example, the relation between the opening shape with its rising fourth and descending scalic outline and the recurring figure of Palestrina's *Marcellus Mass* which Brahms copied as part of his studies, as shown. More broadly, the inscription might perhaps link to the moods of more recent choral music which affected him. The mood of the opening is, for example, not far removed from that of the Praeludium of Beethoven's *Missa solemnis*, similarly hushed, and scored predominantly for strings – though Brahms's prominent bassoons are very characteristic of his scoring in such passages in the period. Indeed, Beethoven's final cadence is very 'Brahmsian' and the shape of the flute solo which then introduces the 'Benedictus' is strikingly like Brahms's piano entry. Yet, from this solo entry the Brahmsian quality inherent in the orchestral spacing becomes greatly accentuated in completely idiomatic writing, first reflecting on the ideas, then building to a powerful central section through a passage from bar 29 which clearly provides a model for the parallel movement of the Second Piano Concerto (bar 25) in its stepwise upper part against widely spaced left-hand patterns, both to be traced to the parallel passage of the 'Emperor' Piano Concerto. The great sense of structure of the outer movements is again apparent in the handling of the recapitulation, where the first theme is recalled over F sharp minor harmony to resolve to D major, a memorable recall which parallels examples noted earlier. The quality of the variation, especially through the use of pedal, gives a masterly instance of the continuous integration of the principle into his 'free' movements. In the cadenza which he inserts before the orchestral coda, he seems to draw the experimental quality of the final page of the Sonata in F sharp minor into a larger and more effective context, for the improvisatory figuration and use of trills find their source here. Thus the earlier passage appears as a transition point between the pianistic worlds of Beethoven and Schumann, already mentioned, and the mature pianism which is already apparent in the Concerto.

Serenades

By the time Brahms had finished the First Piano Concerto in 1859, he had already been occupied for two years with orchestral composition of a different kind. Indeed, the mood in which the Concerto finishes, that of rustic association, with a bass drone and hunting horns above, followed by the assertive conclusion, parallels the close of the First Serenade, not only in mood but in actual material. In total contrast to the Concerto, and in parallel with the First Sextet, this work reflects Brahms's love of the creative relationship with the past. Yet, at this stage – three years before the appearance of the Sextet, the ease with which he draws on his favoured models is still relatively undiscriminating. Indeed, stylistic matters were clearly subservient to orchestral ones, for it is colour – the tone of instruments and their combination in the classical tradition – which dominates his mind and appears so much more effective than the piano-based textures which are still pervasive in the Concerto.

The stylistic debts of this work give a very clear picture of Brahms's preferences. Frequent observation has been made of the parallels between the bass of the second scherzo and the finale of Haydn's Symphony in D no. 104, but the links go much further. Beethoven is present repeatedly, for example in the motivic repetition of the development and the heroic style of the closing group of the first movement. Indeed, one passage provides a fascinating instance of Brahms's reinterpretation of the harmonic pattern of an earlier parallel passage (compare Brahms's first movement, bars 39–42, with Beethoven, Symphony No. 2 in D, first movement, bars 114–16). Schubert is frequently to be heard. For example, the second subject of the slow movement (bar 64) is virtually a recomposition of the second subject of the *Rosamunde* overture with the Great C major Symphony in the background. The passage for flute with clarinets and horns, bars 242–6, strongly recalls Schumann's orchestral colouring in slow or improvisatory passages in the symphonies; for example, the flute cadenza in the finale of the Symphony in B flat major and the closing bars of the slow movement of the Symphony in C major.

Brahms's early designation of No. 1 as a 'Symphony-Serenade' aptly suggests their characters. They are symphonic in their scope – the extent of the development and transition passages, the seriousness of the working processes and so forth, but Serenade-like in the degree of repetition presence of dance-movements and the great emphasis on wind in their scoring. Through this bias, especially the prominence of the horn and wind chorus, to which Brahms's studies in the Detmold Court library obviously contributed, Brahms was laying the foundations of his mature orchestral style. Indeed, in tracing this development, it is interesting to note May's assertion, from personal acquaintance with Bargheer, that the Serenade in D major was first conceived as an Octet for strings and wind; that is, not in the fully symphonic tradition of the Viennese classics, but that of semi-orchestral music – of such works as the Beethoven Septet and the Schubert Octet, whose scoring differs very little. The links to these chamber textures are not hard to uncover in the First Serenade, especially in the least demanding movements. The Minuetto I begins as a trio for two clarinets and bassoon, to which is added flute and cello, whilst the clarinets are also prominent in Minuetto II. The slow movement, beginning with two bassoons and strings soon reveals a texture for two clarinets and flute, with a later solo for the horn. The retransition is solely scored for two clarinets and bassoon, whilst the two clarinets and flute dominate the closing pages. Even in the fully scored movements, vestiges remain, most notably the prominence of the horn in the outer movements. It was a simple matter to recast for full orchestra and retain the distinctive colouring of the original. Indeed, the strongest link to a symphony – to the 'Scene by the Brook' from Beethoven's *Pastoral* Symphony – is to a movement which reflects similar qualities. Beethoven's murmuring semiquaver string figuration is clearly the source of bars 39–72 of the slow movement, as is his concluding writing for the flute.

That Brahms was a poor orchestrator is one of the more tenacious fallacies of nineteenth-century criticism, based on a separation of the arts of composition and orchestration, in which the use of the fullest instrumental possibilities was deemed essential irrespective of the compositional style involved. Unlike Schumann, whose monochrome textures in quick symphonic allegros (though not slow movements) reveal insensitivity to the colours and balances of the orchestra, Brahms knew exactly what he was doing. If his sound is rich and often dense in the lower registers, it is because this was his natural mode, and in few cases can it not be made effective through careful observation of his markings. But it is insufficiently stressed how rich and kaleidoscopic is Brahms's scoring for the wind and brass. At a time when the individual qualities of instruments, especially the brass, were being obscured by the use of self-sufficient choruses of wind and brass, as well as strings, in the developing orchestras of Liszt, Wagner and Bruckner, Brahms was returning to an independent, chamber-rooted texture in which the wind instruments played an expressive integral role quite apart from the need of any particular dramatic or symbolic function; as in the methods of operatic scoring. His insistence on the sonority of the natural horn is perhaps the most striking example of this interest, since it blended much more sensitively with the other wind instruments. In the fullness of time, Brahms's chamber scoring was to prove as significant as the Wagnerian tradition in providing resources for the vastly expanded orchestras of his successors, notably Mahler, Zemlinsky and Schoenberg.

Although the Second Serenade in A major dates from the same time, Brahms creates a much more subtle blend of elements within a much more concentrated work which reduces seven movements to five, with two scherzi flanking the slow movement. Although references to other composers are still apparent, most notably to Schubert and Schumann, the language is much more integrated and gives every impression of having been designed formally as well as sonically as a whole. Its most striking feature is its sound. Despite the adventurous writing for wind in the First Serenade, the pure wind chorus is heard but fleetingly. Here Brahms uses an ensemble which includes the classical complement of double wind, but a string orchestra which lacks violins, effecting a fundamental change in the apportioning of the upper melodies. Because of the changing colours Brahms requires between the lines, the wind are never doubled, whilst the viola achieves a new prominence in the texture – considerably more than the cellos. Though conceived for thirteen real instruments rather than nineteen, therefore, it actually creates a much richer sound, that of a wind serenade with string support, rather than a semi-orchestral work, a work with no parallel in terms of its sheer richness of sound since the divertimenti of the eighteenth century.

In formal terms, the work further characterises the various types drawn from the past. Thus, whilst he still employs a Minuet and Scherzo within the one work, their qualities are much more individual. The Minuet is much more characteristically turned, providing an anticipation of the gently archaic 'quasi minuetto' of the E minor Cello Sonata. Equally, the scherzo is now more individual, a driving 2/4 pattern which suggests a furiant – like a substitute for a scherzo. The ostinato of the Trio suggests the further influence of the slow movement of the *Schubert Quintet* in its use of pizzicato. Both outer movements are also much more interesting in formal terms. The first compensates for the lack of an expositional repeat by reintroducing the first subject in the tonic, thus creating the pattern:

		EXPOSITION			/DEVELOPMENT/RECAP.			
Bar	1		70	119		217	269	318
Subject	I	– tr –	2 –	1	– dev –	1 –	2 –	Coda
Key	I		V	I		I	I	I

whilst the development is much more concentrated, the repetition of the first subject leading to wide modulation, the section concluding with a very effective gradual retransition. Also striking is the nature of the first subject, with its natural association of triplet movement in the continuation, rather different from the bald recollection of Haydnesque hunting music which opens the D major work. The finale has similar qualities of integration between its classically inclined march-like main theme and lyrical second, to which he brings memorable contrapuntal refinement in its varied treatment. But it is again the slow movement which contains the work's heart. If Schubert's influence lurks in the D major work, it comes into clear focus here. The highly atmospheric bars 18–30 with reiterated bass and subito horns surely draw directly on the slow introduction to the finale of the Octet, which will also emerge later as a key work in Brahms's orchestral background.

The development of Brahms's orchestral language is also to be traced through the large-scale choral works, in which he shows a particular sensitivity to colour, the more restricted scope drawing from him his most characteristic sounds and associations. From the earliest choral work with orchestra – the *Funeral Hymn* – this inclination is apparent in a gravely scored piece which richly adapts the traditional use of wind with funeral motets to his sound.

In the *Requiem*, the scope is greatly enlarged for the expression of similar sentiments. He draws from the Second Serenade the effect of the omission of violins, though the focus on the wind which is such a strong feature of the work is here necessarily curbed by the text; rather it is the richness of divided cellos, reflecting the character of the first sextet which seems prominent. Wind is, however, prominent elsewhere. Brahms's favourite solo instruments, the oboe and the horn, are frequently present in the most expressive passages. Thus it is the oboe which so effectively accompanies the soprano solo, whilst it also leads, with rich wind support, against the baritone at the second section of the first passage 'Ach wie gar nichts'.

The horn is often paired very effectively with chorus, perhaps most notably at the moment of the return of the opening material in the last movement, where the altos lead against wind with horn in counterpoint.

Elsewhere, the Horn Trio is recalled in the accompaniment to the fourth movement 'Wie lieblich sind deine Wohnungen'. In dramatic passages, such as the call to the Last Judgement, the trombones are employed in a manner which anticipates the chorale of the First Symphony. These qualities are also strong in *Rinaldo*, except without their later subtlety – indeed, from the start *Rinaldo* is richer in wind colour, opening with wind and horn and, again, the expressive lead given to oboe. In addition to the operatic links to Beethoven mentioned earlier, the whole sound shows strong influence of Beethoven's overture *King Stephen*.

St Antoni *Variations*

By the late 1860s, Brahms's orchestral idiom had become clearly established, its characteristic colours and associations fixed, with certain textures for strings, favoured solo instruments and characteristic wind and brass spacings clear. Whatever the primary stimulus to the composition of the *St Antoni* Variations – if any – the work reveals the mature style in its most extended and refined form so far. Indeed, it is generally regarded as Brahms's finest score, free of the thickness which is often regarded as a defect, though it does yet comprehend the special qualities which were to emerge from the later symphonies. A tradition of criticism exists which sees this quality as residing largely in the use of Viennese 'broken work' (durchbrochene Arbeit) in which, to quote from Geiringer, 'the motives and themes rove continually from one instrument to another; long drawn-out melodies are divided among the various instruments, so that the lead is constantly changing from one section of the orchestra to another'.[10] But this view seems to me slightly misleading of an individual line, in the manner, for example, of Mozart in the second subject of the late Symphony in G minor, where wind are interrupted by strings in what could be regarded as a single line (bars 52–3). Such examples are approached in Brahms, such as in the effect of division between first and second violins at the second subject of the Academic Festival Overture (bar 130), but it is not as characteristic of the Variations. Rather they reflect the orchestral consequences of his contrapuntal thinking, for the invertible counterpoint already noted has its congruence in the scoring. Thus, for example, in variation 4 the inversion of parts given first to oboe/horn and violas effects a remarkable transformation of sound, though Brahms adjusts the balances, the upper part to flute/ clarinet, the lower adding violins to viola.

Yet, there is another sense in which this work is deeply characteristic of Brahms and interesting in the history of scoring: its sonic 'structure'. The work is structural not just in the sense of the relation of the variations to the model in terms of theme, harmony and tempo, but in the relationship of sound to the model through the work. It has been pointed out that Brahms preserved the quality of the model in his score, only substituting a double bassoon for the original serpent, and retaining the rustic quality of the bassoons, oboes and horns (although he seems, from the autograph of the full score, to have intended string support at some stage). The association of this sound with the model is a structural principle in the work, for the strings never take the varied form, only leading in the score when they have either a countersubject, as in variation 1 (the wind retaining the long notes), or a completely independent figure, as in the idiomatic writing of the last variation. In the intervening variations the sonic quality of the model is subtly explored through variations which treat the theme in remarkably different ways.

First Symphony

Whether or not the successful completion of the *St Antoni* Variations prompted Brahms to the final resolution of the First Symphony is not known. However, as comparison with the Second Symphony which appeared in the following year shows, he was more than ready to release it. Indeed, if one were to subject such a masterly work to any criticism at all, it might be that, at least in the main part of the finale, he is almost too efficient in articulating his structure – one gains the impression of almost ruthless pruning in the intense work which he undertook to see the project off between 1874 and 1875. In comparison with the Piano Quartet, the whole seems remarkably sure despite its rich content. Indeed, such is this quality that the scope of his achievement can be easily overlooked and the misleading nature of much received wisdom ignored. For the First Symphony has been the subject of more received views than any other Brahms work.

  That the First Symphony was the product of his reverence for Beethoven in the restoration of the symphonic structure after Beethoven is surely the best-known fact of its background, a view derived from several remarks selected to fit the picture in a world dominated by Beethoven criticism. Thus, Brahms's remark to Levi 'You don't know what it is like to be dogged by *his* footsteps';[11] the anonymous aside on the often noted thematic link in the finale 'Any ass can see as much';[12] Hanslick's famous review of the Viennese premiere and Von Bülow's reference to the 'Three Bs of Music – Bach, Beethoven and Brahms'. The danger with such repetition is that, whilst the remarks are significant in one sense, they serve to oversimplify the picture and to discourage the balancing of any other attitudes that Brahms might have had. Yet, as the background to so many other works of the period shows, no such simple historical background was conceivable by the time Brahms began to work on the final shape of the symphony: his language was too personal, his range of stimuli too deeply absorbed. That Brahms was so conscious of Beethoven does not imply that he felt obliged to imitate him in either idiom or structure. What engaged Brahms was the one quality in Beethoven which so marked him from his romantic successors: the capacity for a structural view in which every detail contributed to the completeness and direction of the whole. He had already established a pattern wherein Beethovenian qualities could be realised in a personal way in the Piano Quintet, and the Symphony builds on this model in an even more subtle and dramatic way, a true culmination of the evolution of ideas. As with the Piano Concerto, the work's nature can only be approached through reference to its background.

Relative to its significance in the development of the symphony after Beethoven, and the sheer span of its evolution, we know virtually nothing of the origins of the First Symphony. Brahms made only two references which give any indication of its content. The first was in the summer of 1862 when he sent an Allegro movement to Clara, the opening of which corresponds to that which we know. His letter does not survive, but Clara quoted the first four bars in piano score in a letter to Joachim of 1 July 1862.[13] The second indication was also to Clara. On 12 September 1868, her name day, he sent her a greeting, bearing the 'alphorn' theme and set to the text 'Hoch auf' m Berg, tief im Tal, grüss' ich dich, viel Tausendmal', simply prefaced with the words 'Thus blew the shepherd's horn today'.[14] The form of this melody is not identical with the familiar version: the rhythm shows slight differences and a fermata bar introduces the melody.

Ex. 35 'Alphorn' Theme – earlier version

Brahms's first letter started a wave of enquiries, first from Joachim and Levi, who wished to conduct the work they supposed to be near completion, subsequently from Bruch and again Levi. Yet in 1870 he was still far from confident of the work's successful outcome, making the aforementioned remark to Levi. Only in 1874, when he promised his publisher 'symphonies' is there evidence that the work was under way, and from that point effort must have been sustained. As to the pattern of the growth and its stages of clarification, we may only conjecture: whether, for example, the 'Alphorn' theme predated the finale, or was part of its composition when the slow introduction was added to the first movement; just how much changed was the first allegro from the form of 1862.[15] One reasonable assumption may, however, frame an approach, namely: that Brahms's central problem concerned the nature of the finale which should balance his first movement. Only with this established – not least the character of its dramatic introduction – could the proportions of the whole and the introduction to the first movement be clearly envisaged. Even the first movement's coda might well seem dependent on the overall scheme, since the tradition of a coda recalling introductory material at a slower pace as demonstrated in Schubert's Great C major Symphony and Mendelssohn's *Scottish* Symphony always involves a complementary introduction. Such was the scope of Brahms's development in the early 1860s that the implications of his movement were probably only dimly perceived in 1862.

That, however – like the first movement of the D minor Sonata/Symphony – Brahms's 'Allegro' sprang from the youthful experience of Beethoven as pianist and symphonist invites little challenge. No other movement is so fully imbued with the spirit of the Beethoven Allegro, with its rhythmic tension and drive, structural contour and dramatic handling of the main points of articulation. Models for certain passages are even suggested in actual material links. Thus, the closing of the exposition in the mediant minor, E flat, from which it plunges directly into development in the submediant of that key, B major, strongly recalls the rhythmic pattern of the parallel passage of the *Appassionata* Sonata. Another powerful precedent, the Sonata *Les Adieux*, can easily be seen as lying behind the dramatic motto-like introduction to the main allegro and its developmental pattern, returning to a similarly dramatic recall; the harmonic pattern of the openings is significantly similar and suggests, in turn, that Brahms's very bold original opening may earlier have occurred to him in the more predictable context it was finally to assume with the slow introduction.

Yet, if the structural background is clear, the character of Brahms's ideas is his own. Even acknowledging the rhythmic precedent for the unusual 6/8 metre of the first movement of Beethoven's Seventh Symphony, similarly provided with a slow introduction, the precise rhythmic mood and key belong to the world of early Brahms. Indeed, it is interesting that, having by the 1870s evolved scherzo substitutes, where other composers still retained them in the Beethoven/Schubert tradition, Brahms should employ the character in a symphonic first movement context. More individual still, however, is the character of the first subject itself, for no model in the symphonic tradition presented two ideas of equal status in contrapuntal combination as the basis of a main subject. The concept, and the ease with which the counterpoint is inverted, points to the more distant stimuli previously outlined, and signifies the infusion of principles already noted as fundamental in the keyboard and choral work into the context of the symphony, where they are to function in an even more pervasive and structural fashion than in the later works of Beethoven.

In the problem of matching first movement to finale, Brahms had, by 1864 at the least, provided himself with a satisfactory solution, demonstrated in the pattern of the Piano Quintet, reflecting in turn the more experimental Piano Sonata in F sharp minor. Although the dramatic content of the finale was very different from either, its introduction assuming vastly greater proportions and thematic importance, with its two symbolic ideas recalled dramatically in the main movement – the 'Alphorn' theme at the close of the development, the trombone chorale in the coda, – the relationships are strong and point to a parallel case of background: for the atmospheric quality of the introduction and the expansive character of the finale and its main theme point again to the synthesis of influences which lay behind the earlier work. The traditional view that the finale is a further example of Beethoven's dominance on Brahms's imagination seems to have derived from the respect accorded Hanslick's review.

> If I say that no composer has come so close to the style of the late Beethoven as Brahms in this finale, I don't mean it as a paradoxical pronouncement, but rather as a simple statement of indisputable fact . . . its simple, beautiful theme, reminiscent of the 'Ode to joy' in the Ninth Symphony, is over-powering as it rises onward and upward, right to the end . . . Brahms's quartets and the symphony . . . could not have been were it not for Beetho-ven's last period . . .'[16]

Yet this seems a very limited view in historical context, ignoring funda-mental differences in the themes and their contexts. As Mellers has pointed out, Brahms's theme is 'bourgeois', a comfortable folk-related theme of a much more accessible kind than the long accumulating theme which Beethoven introduces in such a hushed manner.[17] The only real parallel is in its context – a theme of comparable squareness following a dramatic introduction. Yet, nor is the theme as overtly Schubertian as that of the Quintet finale: it relates to a more Brahmsian background, of which the folksong 'Sandmännchen' (set for Clara's children in 1858) and the mood of the finale to the B flat Sextet offer the clues.

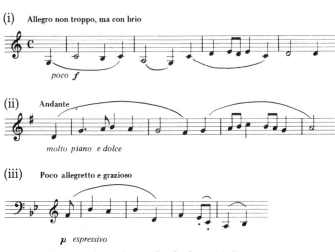

Ex. 36 (i) First Symphony, finale, bars 61–5
         (ii) 'Sandmännchen' (*Volkskinderlieder*, no. 4)
         (iii) String Sextet in B flat, op. 18, finale, bars 1–4

Different character determines in turn different function. The accumu-lating repetitions of Beethoven's theme imply variation treatment, either sectionally, or by the exploration of the different characters, as Beethoven so resourcefully demonstrates. The self-contained quality of Brahms's theme suggests either a rondo – as is the case in the even squarer finale of the Sextet, or a structure in which the theme is placed in contrast with other material. It is the latter which Brahms so brilliantly employs, drawing the weight of his development directly from the first movement within a formal contour which draws from his sonata experiments as most clearly paralleled in the finale of the Quintet. It seems not unlikely that Hanslick was encouraged, like others after him, to stress this relationship to Beethoven through one tangible thematic link – the repeated phrase which occurs in the second part of the two themes, and it was probably this incidental rather than essential relationship that Brahms observed 'any ass' could see, though it could still have been a conscious homage.

Ex. 37 (i) Brahms First Symphony, finale, bars 69–73
        (ii) Beethoven, Ninth Symphony, finale, bars 124–7

In emotional character and structural outline, Brahms's finale has no model – it derives from its composer's background in relation to the broad principles of symphonic planning in the nineteenth century to which Beethoven made the greatest contributions. But reference to the Schubertian side of its genealogy must include one reference which is to the present writer as tangible as that of the thematic links between the finale of the Quintet and the Grand Duo – and just as strong a part of its background through the sources of Brahms's orchestral language: the finale of Schubert's Octet, which similarly begins with a slow introduction followed by a main allegro. Material to be recalled in the body of the movement is likewise presented at the outset – and its shape, as that of the main theme which follows after 18 bars of introduction, is strikingly like the parallel passages of Brahms's finale.

And Schubert is not only recalled in the introduction. The reiterated bass figures which drive up to the recall of the chorale in the coda match those which close the String Quintet, and other Schubertian touches might also be noted.

An inevitable consequence of Brahms's architectural sense of the whole was the limitation of the scope of the inner movements. Even after the first

Ex. 38 (i) Brahms: First Symphony, finale, bars 1–6 and 60–64
        (ii) Schubert: Octet, finale, bars 1–5 and 17–19

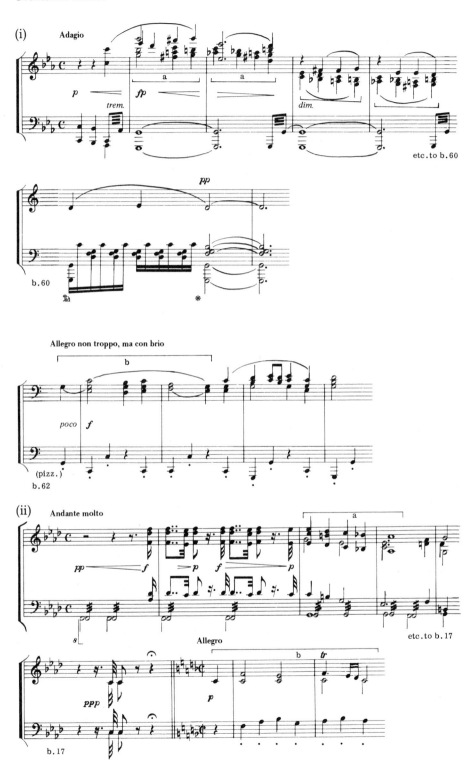

performance, Brahms was still pruning them, with the comment 'The Finale must be considered', while Levi responded that they seemed 'more suited to a Serenade than a Symphony'.[18] But Brahms realised that, whilst he might well include an expressive slow movement, a scherzo on the lines of that of the Quintet would have undermined the function and effect of the slow introduction to the finale. Thus he produced a third movement, 'allegretto ma non troppo' of a very individual type, though one which can be traced back generically. The common character of an 'allegretto ma non troppo' in 2/4 is underpinned by thematic links to show the relation to the second movement of the G major Sextet and thus back to the Gavotte.

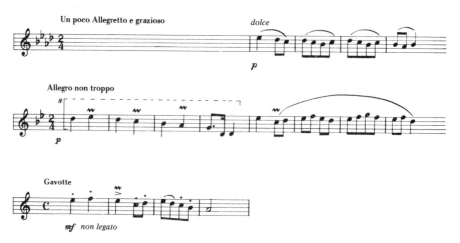

Ex. 39 First Symphony, third movement, theme and its background

But the later movement is broader, 'allegretto' rather than 'allegro', and no longer accorded the functional term scherzo. Moreover it is much more tightly structured, with antecedent-consequent relation by inversion of its five-bar subject and with a much more subtle transition into and from the trio. It is rather the slow movement which relates most closely to tradition – a lyric ternary design which can be traced back to Schumann's First and Second Symphonies. Yet even this movement is tightly controlled. We know that the version first performed was in a rondo structure, with a much more predictable antecedent-consequent relationship in its first theme. The remarkable turn to a freely developing reference to the first movement at bar 5 was, as might be assumed, a later interpolation, producing a final subject of remarkable fluidity, lasting for a total of 13 bars. However, Schubert again seems to figure in the background, for the duet between oboe and clarinet which constitutes the second subject is surely a homage to the slow movement of the Unfinished Symphony, which was only published in 1865, though Brahms may well have had access to it earlier.

Remarkable as was Brahms's sense of the structure of the whole – the function and shape of the finale, the nature of the middle movements – the sense of deep unity behind the surface variety accrues by more tangible factors, specifically its tonal organisation and pervasive network of thematic relations. All the tendencies toward tonal integration seem to come to a climax in this work which opens up the broadest tonal links in his music so far by the extent of the application of mediant relationships, the movements dividing the octave symmetrically in major thirds – C minor – E major – A flat major – C minor/C major. Although Schubert and Beethoven seem equally disposed to this relationship, Beethoven would seem the most direct source of the progression C minor – E major which he uses between the first two movements of the C minor Piano Concerto; Brahms's normal relationship is to the submediant in the key as in F minor/D flat, or C minor/ A flat, or to the mediant, as in C minor/E flat minor in the First String Quartet or the exposition of the first movement of this work. C minor – E, the raised mediant, serves to connect upwards as well as downwards to C minor, and furthermore, the inner relationships are also major-mediant based: thus, E – G sharp in the slow movement, A flat – E in the third, with E flat minor – B in the first movement, from closing group to development. Here Brahms gives a concentrated example of the tendency to be found throughout his later works to mediant relationships, one which had far-reaching consequences in the evolution of a symmetrical view of tonal relationships, significantly employed by Schoenberg in his early D major Quartet, which proceeds D – F sharp minor – B flat minor – D with inner mediant relationship as well.

These recurrent tonal patterns are complemented by a thematic network without parallel in the symphonic tradition. Drawing on the tendency to thematic integration to be noted increasingly through the period, he here achieves a degree of thematic variation of basic ideas which represents a new stage in symphonic thought. Thematic analysis has tended to focus on the role of the upper voice in the motto-like introduction, which clearly recurs in the main theme of the second movement (bar 5 onwards), and on the transformation of the slow opening of the finale in the main theme of the following 'allegro non troppo'. But this is only one aspect of the contrapuntal complex of this powerful introduction: for it also has a lower voice, a descending shape which can be shown to have a more far-reaching influence.

Thus, the exultant climax of the first movement's development, over dominant pedal, reiterates this motive in diminished form, which relates it quite clearly to the again harmonically varied reprise, where it appears in augmented form in the source-complex. Viewed overall the shape is pervasive. The finale's development is based not chiefly on its main themes – the broad first subject and the ostinato-based second – but on this shape, newly worked, which also furnishes material for the introduction and transition; the development is strikingly independent of the main themes, the first soon passing after its initial sequential treatment, a crucial aspect of the structural planning.

Ex. 40 First Symphony, first movement, bars 38–42

Ex. 41 First Symphony, finale, bars 106, 234, 246

From these connections appear yet broader ones to the third movement and introduction to the finale. For the finale is clearly anticipated in the reprise of the third movement where Brahms makes an anticipatory gesture towards its recall. In turn, this focusses attention on the movement's main theme, which can easily be seen as a variant through characteristic stepwise decoration. In turn, the shape now appears as the ostinato bass of the second subject of the finale, its original form now significantly simplified.

Yet, the shape is in itself also full of significance. That Brahms should one day have written a major work on Clara's motive – for this is surely

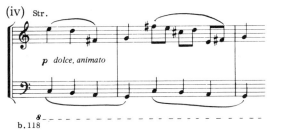

Ex. 42 First Symphony
   (i) Third movement, bars 109–14
   (ii) Finale, opening
   (iii) Third movement, bars 1–5
   (iv) Finale, second subject, bars 118–19

the same, transposed from F sharp minor to 'heroic' C minor – was perhaps to be anticipated. That it should have been the source of such a remarkable example of the unity of deep background ideas and a richly varied surface could not have been anticipated even by Clara herself.[19]

Thus the First Symphony presents a synthesis of the structural and the personal in Brahms's creative development. Just as a chorale melody of the

Ex. 43 Schumann's theme, and as it appears at the climax of the first movement from bar 321, transposed in C minor

deepest musical and textual significance underlay the growth of the *Requiem* as a symbol, so Clara's theme functions in the even more resourceful and far-reaching organisation of the Symphony. It gives the most comprehensive expression of an element active in various contexts after the early and unmistakable gesture of the early Variations on a Theme of Schumann op. 9. Thus the passionate Piano Quartet in C minor, inspired, as Brahms clearly acknowledged, by the hopeless love of young Werther for an older and married woman, opens with a clear elaboration of the idea, originally in C sharp minor,[20] whilst the Intermezzo of the G minor Piano Quartet retains it in C minor. Clara seems to have realised its significance in the latter case – 'You must have been thinking of me when you wrote the Scherzo', as perhaps in the case of the slow movement of the Second Serenade – 'My dear Johannes, you must know that I can feel it better than express it in words.'[21] But the most interesting light that these examples throw is surely on the background of the slow movement of the First Piano Concerto. Whatever the meaning of the inscription 'Benedictus qui venit in Nomine Domini'[22] the source of the 'gentle portrait of you'[23] which Brahms was painting seems unmistakable in the piano's first meditative commentary on the orchestral material, through its link to the Symphony:

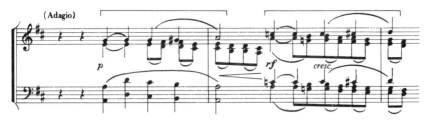

Ex. 44 Piano Concerto in D minor, second movement, bars 21–3

Yet, if Clara was ever in Brahms's thoughts and enshrined in his great Symphony, she was not alone. As Kalbeck implies, the character of the theme which furnishes the first subject of the original Allegro can well be seen as Brahms himself[24] – an assertive statement of a very characteristic shape. And to complete the personal circle of his youth, the Finale quotes not merely a Clara symbol in the 'Alphorn' theme but also the symbol of Joachim in its companion – the solemn chorale F A E in its most common form, cast in a suitably archaic romantic harmony which also evokes that whole romantic world of youth:

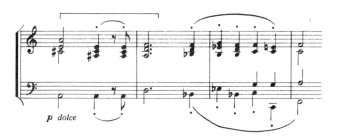

Ex. 45 First Symphony, finale, bars 47–50

Viewed in a broader perspective, Brahms's First Symphony can therefore be seen not only as the culmination of his early development, but also as the natural successor to the most significant symphonic expression of the previous generation, Schumann's D minor Symphony. For not only does the earlier work offer a clearer structural outline for the Brahms than any other precursor – with slow introductions to both the outer movements and thematic integration of a kind unparalleled in 1841 – justifying the subsequent designation 'Fantasy Symphony', but the source of the unity is the same. It is well established that this was Schumann's *Clara* Symphony, personal influences inspiring the symphonic experiment, just as they had served to integrate Brahms's symphonic aspirations over twenty years or so. Yet the striking parallels also serve to reveal Brahms's significance in the work. For Schumann's 'unity' is everywhere apparent – the surface of his music is obsessed with the theme. The work's immense power resides not in this – which threatens its musical integrity – but in deeper factors of tonal movement and rhythmic impetus. How different the effect of the Brahms work, even allowing for its greater length. For, even if he was deeply influenced by Schumann's radically motivic tendencies – not merely in the symphony, which builds on a pianistic background of such thought, in the earlier piano works – Brahms ensures spans of thought and a deep unity of thematic, tonal and contrapuntal relationships, whilst yet leaving a surface on which he can explore the most varied characters and push the individuality of the separate movements to a limit only achieved by the greatest of his predecessors.

Part Three

The Third Period

6

Songs and Piano Music

With the completion of the First Symphony, Brahms had established himself without question as the leading composer not only of choral, but also of instrumental, music in Germany and was increasingly regarded as the symbolic figure of the opposition to the aesthetic outlook of the New Germans. For not only had he demonstrated remarkable command of the forms of keyboard, chamber and orchestral composition but he had done so through a scope of historical absorption and synthesis with few parallels, drawing from it very individual modes of working capable of application to many different contexts. One major consequence of this richness was the complexity of his textures. The fullness of Brahms's inner parts, taken with the increasingly powerful contrapuntal relation of the outer parts – of which the First Symphony offers striking examples – produce a weight and heaviness which require great care in performance. Indeed, the sense of strength and balance in linear relationships which was so important to Brahms (he would cover the middle parts of songs, as shown, just for the outer voices) has been a source of irritation to those who are not sufficiently inspired by the power of his ideas. Related to this compositional emphasis is a lack of the dramatic instrumental character that we find so strongly in Haydn and Beethoven: even the 'lyrical' Schubert is only one aspect of a musical personality that can reveal violent contrast. Dramatic contrast is rare in Brahms's music – the appearance of the 'Alphorn' theme in the finale of the First Symphony is quite exceptional: rather the drama lies in the abstract play of form, the 'surface' of the music giving a very strong sense of continuity and 'security'. A consequence of the richness was the opportunity for ambiguity, for the simultaneous existence of several meanings, especially in the spheres of harmony and rhythm, a factor related to the subtlety of connections arising through permeative variation. In the third period, these qualities are developed very markedly. If the second period has been concerned with the creation of a style, the third was dedicated to its exploration and the re-integration of its elements; Brahms's language may not undergo any radical changes, but from the First Symphony onwards there is an ever-deepening instinct for an identity of form and content, capacity for formal individuality and harmonic freedom, growing subtlety of variation methods and sense of rhythmic fluidity. The

First Symphony had revealed the kind of organic thinking that seems to relate to what Schoenberg later associated with the term 'Grundgestalt'[1] and from now on such thinking becomes increasingly pervasive, achieving synthesis with other 'freer' elements, for example the harmonic fluidity especially stimulated by the experience of Schubert. In the rhythmic sphere, the Capriccio in C sharp minor op. 76 no. 5 offers a classic example of a rhythmic sense in which now one, now another, interpretation of metre – 3/4 or 6/8 – may be drawn from a group of six quavers. Further, the varied repetition of the second subject of the Third Symphony shows an instinct for transformation which is quite beyond the conventional modes with which he was so conversant in earlier years.

These tendencies find their fullest expression in the chamber and orchestral works, for which Brahms keeps his most challenging ideas and most personal symbols. Indeed, in contrast to the years of development, he can now draw a sharp distinction between the function of his media; thus, chamber music returns to an earlier concept of its role, usurped in Brahms's development towards the symphony, whilst solo piano music no longer strives to be symphonic. Brahms's genres have found their natural place in relation to his expression. But there is one area in which cross-fertilisation intensifies and becomes a major characteristic: the permeation of the lyric character into the instrumental sphere. Not merely subsidiary themes acquire the lyric feeling in Brahms's maturity; even his main ideas grow closer to his songs. This is most clearly displayed in the links from songs to the first two Violin Sonatas, but it goes beyond this naturally lyrical medium into the symphony and concerto, and many very tangible parallels

Ex. 46 (i) Capriccio in C sharp minor, op. 76 no. 5

can be drawn from the material of large-scale works to the simplest sources. In this integration and individuality of expression, the powerful impulse of the past is not lost. On the contrary, it grows deeper and more far-reaching, reflecting the continuing fascination for the discovery of the past which is so evident in Brahms's responses to the increasing fruits of musicology in his later years. Once again, his large output of songs provides the natural starting point for discussion, though relatively few piano pieces belong to this period.

Songs

In the fourteen years which separate the beginning of the third period from the publication of its final song opus, the Five Songs op. 107, in 1888, Brahms extended the possibilities of the types stabilised in the groups published between 1868 and 1874 through a total of 15 sets comprising 70 songs, which appeared regularly over the period. Although the focus on the work of a particular poet disappears, other forms of grouping appear. Thus, for example, there is a strong folk element in op. 69 and 84, Eastern European in the former, German in the latter, whilst 'Mädchenlieder' are prominent in op. 95 and 107. Voice type is also a determinant – op. 86, 94 and 105 being 'for low voice', a feature not observed in the earlier groups and reflective of the growing focus on the alto, bass and baritone voices in Brahms's late expression. In addition to folk texts, which draw again on his earlier interest in the translations of Spanish poems by Geibel, as well as

(ii) Third symphony, first movement, bars 36–7 and 47–49

Italian by Heyse and Kopisch, Brahms retained his deep affection for Daumer, Groth and Hölty in many settings, as well as drawing more texts from Eichendorff and Candidus. A significant development is the new interest in Rückert and especially Heine, on whom, though ignored in Brahms's earlier Schumann-influenced phase, he now draws for six of his most atmospheric settings. Other new poets are Keller, Reinhold, Lemcke, Storm, as well as the little-known Hermann Allmers and his friend Max Kalbeck.

The continuing hold of German folksong on Brahms's musical imagination is very clear in the songs of his full maturity. Indeed, some go beyond the general recreation of an archaic or folk-like idiom to reinterpret the models which he included in his own collection published in 1894, with his own accompaniments, in two cases building directly on them. They are 'Dort in den Weiden', op. 97 no. 4 (no. 31), 'Da unten im Tale' (called 'Trennung') in op. 97 no. 6 (no. 6) and 'Guten Abend mein tausiger Schatz' (called 'Spannung') in op. 84 no. 5 (no. 4). They can be seen as representing three stages of growth away from the models as represented by his arrangements, with clear relations in the first two, and marked independence in the third.

'Dort in den Weiden' retains the rhythmic and melodic pattern of the original in its opening phrase and likewise its accompaniment style. However, he uses it to a completely new end, radically changing the treatment of text. The folk setting contains its own internal repetitions; thus:

> Dort in den Weiden steht ein Haus, steht ein Haus, steht ein Haus,
> da schaut die Magd zum Fenster 'naus, zum Fenster 'naus,
> Sie schaut strom auf, sie schaut strom ab, ist noch nicht da mein Herzens
>   Knab?
> der schönste Bursch am ganzen Rhein, denn nenn ich mein!

In his own setting, Brahms ignores the repetitions of the first two lines to reduce the first part from eight bars of 2/4 to four, though creating interest through the extension of the final cadence to a bar of 3/4. In contrast, he extends the second part by repetition and cadential augmentation to replace the final four bars of the arrangement with six, followed by a five-bar (dovetailed) postlude which matches the other setting in function, concluding on the dominant. Variation in the accompaniment is present in both third verses. In 'Da unten im Tale', the musical material is even closer, the accompaniments so similar that Brahms can use the same postlude for both. The close relation of the melody is implicit in this link. In textual response, Brahms recalls the repetitions of the folk melody of 'Dort in den Weiden', also frequent in his folk-like songs, to extend the eight bars of the original to twelve. Verses 3 and 4 employ variation, as in the preceding setting. However, the provision of a prelude places the setting more distant in its effect. Unlike these settings, that of 'Guten Abend, guten Abend mein tausiger Schatz' retains text exactly, as well as metre, to produce an identical length of seventeen bars, to which Brahms adds a prelude. However, the new melody and accompaniment are completely independent and, with the provision of an alternative melody for verse 3 and a major version of the original in verse 6, the setting represents a considerable development from the folk pattern, beginning as follows:

Ex. 47 'Spannung', op. 84 no. 5

The favoured source Kretzschmer-Zuccalmaglio provides two more texts whose associated melodies Brahms did not include in his collections: 'Klage' ('Feinsliebchen trau' du nicht') and 'Vergebliches Ständchen' ('Guten Abend mein Kind, guten Abend mein Schatz'), both described as from the 'Lower Rhine'. They represent two extremes of treatment. 'Klage' matches its text with a very simple melody and postlude directly recalling folksong settings. In contrast, 'Vergebliches Ständchen' employs text repetition after the manner of 'Dort in den Weiden' to enable considerable musical expansion.

The original text is extremely simple, four strophes of four lines beginning as follows:

> Guten Abend mein Schatz, guten Abend mein Kind
> Ich komm' aus Lieb' zu dir, ach, mach' mir auf die Tür.

which could be set to eight bars from the opening phrase. However, repetition of the first two lines, partly by the piano, and of the concluding phrase 'mach' mir auf die Tür – mach' mir auf – mach' mir auf, mach' mir auf die Tür' create a structure of eighteen bars in which harmonic diversion in the latter is especially characteristic, with the prelude using the vocal opening. After the girl's response in verse 2, the persuasive male is presented in the minor mode, the clinching effect of the last verse arising partly from the abrupt treatment of the prelude/interlude and the cross-rhythms of the accompaniment.

The folk idioms employed in these various settings can be traced to more independent settings of folk-like texts. For example, Halm's 'Der Jäger' (op. 95 no. 4) reflects the prelude to 'Vergebliches Ständchen' whilst considerably extending the mobility of the vocal part.

The other famous Brahms Serenade, the setting of Kugler's 'Ständchen' ('Der Mond steht über dem Berge') op. 106 no. 1, draws on the manner even more radically to suggest an instrumental movement, with its clear modulation to the dominant and apparent second subject at 'neben der Mauer im Schatten'; indeed, the material of the following piano passage which effects a retransition to the return of the opening material for the third verse, draws directly on the *Academic Festival* Overture a relation also stimulated by the parallel background of student association; this text depicting the students serenading ·'with flute and fiddle and zither'. A parallel to the more restrained folk models is provided in the setting of Heyse's *Mädchenlied* op. 107 no. 5 whose stylised text is matched by a melody which seems to take such examples as 'Guten Abend' (no. 4) and 'Da unten im Tale' (no. 6) as its folk-background.

However, Brahms again avoids the models by the subtlest means, here the delay of the resolution of the cadence, facilitating a dovetailing of the piano postlude which has no parallel in the settings, to say nothing of the extended and varied last verse. As in the second period, popular Viennese song also permeated Brahms's language. As in the *Wiegenlied*, the *Minnelied* op. 71 no. 5, Hölty's 'Holder klingt der Vogelsang', draws directly on a current song. Yet here the connection is even closer, Kalbeck[2] pointing out the direct quotation of the 'Styrian Waltz' by Joseph Gungl. The setting is in the style of a Viennese concert song for tenor, an unusual idiom for Brahms.

Although Brahms's settings of Eastern European folksongs in translation are not as consistently reflective of folk idioms, his love of recreation and absorption of folk stimuli is equally apparent here. The rhythmic character of two Serbian settings to texts by Kapper is immediately notable – one notated in 5/4 throughout, the other in 3/4 alternating with 4/4, 'Mädchen-lied' op. 85 no. 3 and 'Das Mädchen' op. 95 no. 1. Friedländer quotes Brahms's friend, the Slavonic authority Georg Schünemann of Berlin, for the evidence of parallels: in the first setting,

> Brahms wished to give the song a national Serbian character. He limited the true melodic development to a minimum. Throughout there is an alternation between rhythmic form and a short final section (Abgesang). In contrast to this homely theme, so impressive in its repetition, he places rhythmic alter-nations of three and two crotchet groups in 5/4 time which are only lengthened at the end. The whole song closely resembles Serbian folksong, and above all the heroic songs, in the simplicity and uniformity of its melodic and harmonic line.

'Das Mädchen' reflects very similar features at the outset. However, as it develops, the composer works much more freely, developing earlier ideas with the change of mode and moving to a much more generalised style at the 'animato grazioso' before the opening rhythm recurs in the major key. Friedländer also points to the less obvious parallels with the other Serbian setting, 'Vorschneller Schwur'. ('The Rash Oath') op. 95 no. 5, where Brahms preserves the traditional contrast between the Schwur and the Reue, as well as including characteristic coloraturas and cadenzas.[3]

Parallel observations can be made of the Wenzig Bohemian settings op. 69 nos 1 and 2, both entitled 'Klage', both seen as very slavonic in rhythm and melody.

Against the background of Brahms's interest in slavonic music, it is inter-esting to note just how late was the first vocal expression of his lifelong passion for the gipsy idiom. The Eight *Zigeunerlieder* op. 103 which he published in 1889 were themselves rearrangements from the eleven vocal quartets which he composed in 1887 as *Zigeunerlieder* for Four Voices. His source was a collection of twenty-five Hungarian folksongs with piano accompaniment, by Zoltán Nagy which he knew in the German translation by Hugo Conrat, who actually made them known to Brahms himself. As in previous examples, they had a fertilising influence on Brahms's imagin-ation. Friedländer has pointed out the relationships between some. Most striking is that between the two settings of 'Röslein dreie', whose opening rhythm is identical. In 'Kommt dir manchmal', however, the relation is rather to the latter part, where it is close. As in the earlier *Marienlieder*, the relationship is not always direct. Thus, the original setting of 'Wisst ihr wann mein Kindchen' is much closer to Brahms's 'Lieber Gott, du weisst' than to his own setting, which is independent. In addition to these links, the broader element of Brahms's established gipsy idiom is also strong. Thus the first song, 'He, Zigeuner', recalls the czardas rhythm of the G minor Hungarian dance or its later sequels.

At the other extreme of form and expression represented by the 'instru-mental' and 'declamatory' types of song, comparable expansion of imagin-

Ex. 48   (i) Hungarian Dance in G minor, no. 1
         (ii) *Zigeunerlieder*, no. 1
         (iii) *Zigeunerlieder*, no. 8

ation and absorption is apparent. The 'instrumental' norm ideally
represented in the second period by the two 'Regenlied' settings finds
important successors, though with the important proviso that Brahms now
inclines to the range represented by the viola rather than the violin, as in
the Candidus setting 'Alte Liebe' op. 72 no. 1 and the Lemcke setting
'Verzagen', op. 72 no. 4, alto songs whose implicit relation to the viola
idiom is realised in the two songs for alto and viola op. 91 to texts by
Rückert and, in Geibel's translation, Lope de Vega.

In 'Alte Liebe' Brahms complements his very simple text – six four-line
verses of the pattern 7/6/7/6 – with a much freer musical form, a broad A
B A which gives opportunity for central development to reflect the text
which describes how the return of spring awakes old memories of increasing
bitterness. In the first verse the four natural phrases are extended to five
by the repetition of the closing words 'neues Glück' in augmentation, thus
extending to ten bars a section which could be projected as eight from the
opening. This opening does not recur as clearly until the sixth verse where
its varied continuation reflects the extensive development to which it is
subject in the intervening verses, the roving harmony, first to E flat, then
gradually back to the dominant, for an augmented cadence at 'ein Auge
sieht mich an' defining two sections, comprising respectively the second
verse and verses 3–5, which run continuously, losing the cadence repetition
characteristic of verses 1 and 2. The treatment of 'Verzagen' is much more
strict, the three verses set in an A A B pattern. However, repetition through
augmentation plays a more important role in varying the predictable structure. Thus, the two-bar phrase of the first of the four lines of the verse
leads to a total of fifteen through cadential augmentation of the second
close of the second and fourth lines. The triplet division of these extending
melismas recalls the compound movement of 'Alte Liebe'. Unlike the other
songs of this type, the piano establishes an equal role through its powerful

introduction, suggesting the underlying dashing waves of the poem, whilst the vocal part, which describes them, captures the poet's own identity.

These extremes of expression find an interesting balance in the two Songs for Viola, Alto and Piano op. 91. Although both reflect the text structure clearly, they do so with a considerable freedom, arising from the instrumental possibilities. The setting of Rückert's 'Gestillte Sehnsucht' offers the most notable example of an approach which is recalled by piano alone in the intense setting of Heine's 'Meerfahrt' op. 96 no. 4 and, anticipated in the earlier setting of Groth's 'Dein blaues Auge' op. 59 no. 8 – that of a lengthy instrumental introduction, to which the vocal part appears as a response, perhaps even a counterpoint. The viola introduction establishes an expressively moving 'adagio' line against triplet figuration in the piano, the much simpler vocal opening combining in counterpoint for six bars before working freely and subsequently taking over the viola idea to complete the first verse. The setting assumes an A B A pattern through the contrast of the middle section, which reflects the 'restless voices that stir without ceasing' through roving harmony and intensification of figuration, finely mirroring the question 'when shall I sleep again?' before the return of the opening. As with the earlier and more famous 'Wiegenlied' (op. 49 no. 4), Brahms drew on popular material to give a personal token to a close friend, though here the material is of much more antiquity – the old carol 'Resonet in laudibus', known in Germany as 'Lieber Joseph, Joseph mein', which provides the viola's introduction, from which the vocal part is derived by a process involving imitation and diminution. The central contrast is here in verses 2 and 3, the carol acting as a rondo idea between the growing animation of verse 2 and, with modal and metrical contrast, verse 3, the whole faithfully depicting Mary's lullaby with its fears of what is to come for the infant Jesus. In contrast, the instrumental ideas of the other settings mentioned sustain continuous thought, the former particularly pervasive in this rare example of a through-composed setting of a strophic poem. The character of the piano finds a different expression in the Goethe setting 'Unüberwindlich' op. 72 no. 5, where Brahms draws on a favourite Scarlatti sonata whose identity he reveals in the score, characteristically deriving the vocal part by augmentation of the close.[5] Again, this stands in a tradition, for the earlier setting of 'Blinde Kuh', op. 58 no. 1, draws directly on a distinctly Baroque keyboard style over which the folk text (Italian, tr. Kopisch) is given a folk-like opening, destined for more elaborate treatment.

The other direct source of song inspiration for an instrumental composition, the setting of Groth's 'Wie melodien zieht es mir' op. 105 no. 1 – whose opening shape is used in the Second Violin Sonata – represents a much simpler model than the expansive 'Regenlied'. Parallel links exist in the songs 'Immer leiser wird mein Schlummer' (to the slow movement of the B flat Piano Concerto) and the 'Sapphic Ode' op. 94 no. 4, (to that of the Violin Concerto) revealing these all as especially characteristic Brahmsian ideas. 'Wie melodien' attracts special attention for its subject, the poem dealing with the very essence of song aesthetic – the power of the various media of sound, absolute music, speech and lyric poetry, to arouse feeling. As Clarkson has put it,

> Of the three, pure tone (Melodien) arouses mood but fleetingly; it fades like spring flowers and the clouds of their fragrance. The spoken word (Wort) tries to grasp emotion and even to display it to the eye in script, but mood eludes speech too, fades like a mist and disappears like a breath of air. Of the three, it is only the lyric (Reime) that fully arouses emotion. Hidden within the lyric's blend of tone and word lies the power to bring tears to the eye. The strongest appeal to emotion is made by a combination of the explicit meanings of language with the evocative power of absolute music.[6]

Thus, the lyrical gesture which opens the song might have been either a response to the text, or, alternatively, applied from an instrumental idea – whether or not in its form for violin. Either way, it represents the most interesting feature of the setting, for, as Clarkson indicates, it is the only example of this metrical structure, which recurs in many other songs, in which the weak initial syllable is not treated as an upbeat to the strong beat of the second. Here the anacrusis is of three syllables which determine a five- rather than four-beat phrase, which the composer then complements with the expected four plus three, through repetition and harmonic reinforcement of the closing two bars 'und schwebt wie Duft dahin'. This thirteen-bar strophe, with the piano interlude, is then repeated in two variations to complete the setting. In the second, the parallel cadential pattern is more forceful, moving now to D rather than E major, and clinching in F sharp minor to confirm the sense of unfulfilment. The resolution of the last verse is expressed by even further modulation, to F major, with greater repetition leading to the close. There can be no finer or subtler reconciliation of formal and expressive demands than this fusion.

The following song of the opus, Lingg's 'Immer leiser wird mein Schlummer', shows an equal skill in strophic variation, though the poem is much more complex in structure, revealing a syllabic pattern of 8/8/5/ 7/ 7/7/9, varied in the second verse to conclude with only a five-syllable line. As Schoenberg points out,[7] Brahms loosens his aesthetic framework by augmenting the last word of the first line 'Schlummer', thus establishing initial three-bar phrasing. With the augmented repetition of the close of the third line 'über mir', the first part of the strophe covers ten bars where six might be regarded as sufficient to set the words. The extension is even greater in the remaining part which runs to fourteen bars, through the expansive treatment of the voice/piano relationship and the further augmentation of the cadence, which ends with bars of 3/2. In the second strophe, reflecting the poet's growing anxiety for the coming of the loved one, instrumental music takes more precedence, the original melodic line appearing in the piano, the voice from the second phrase, and thus inaugurating a recomposition of the first strophe, extending by three bars and concluding in the major. The interest lies in the first part, which generates new material over the old. Thus the whole again reflects the structure and the expressive content of the poem with little variation of the strict basis. Finally, the setting of the text described by its poet Hans Schmidt as a Sapphic Ode[8] matches the very irregular syllabic pattern of 11/11/16 with a musical structure which accommodates its accentual properties whilst also being varied in the interests of rounded form. Thus, the first two lines are reflected in the music through three-bar phrases, whilst the third achieves its accentual pattern through the use of 3/2 metre with 4/4, the alternation giving the opportunity for further cadential augmentation. Minor variants in the second strophe are very telling, giving a distinctive text/music relationship.

If the 'instrumental' types are prominent vocal expressions in the 1870s and early 1880s, the declamatory style returns with particular individuality in the later phases of composition in the 1880s, which draw on and develop the very personal types first apparent in the op. 32 set of 1865. In turn, they prophesy the quintessential expression of late Brahms in the Four Serious Songs op. 121 of the last period, all employing the bass or baritone voice. The link is strongest in the first song of op. 94, published in 1884, a mature setting of a text which might well have been set with Groth's *Heimweh* songs in the early 1870s: Rückert's deeply reflective 'Mit vierzig Jahren ist der Berg erstiegen' recalls in a sterner, more philosophical 'Langsam' the melodic type employed in op. 32 to express a similar mood through the imagery of the rushing stream, 'Der Strom der neben mir verrauschte, wo ist er nun?', symbolising the poet's loss of an earlier identity. The setting of Lemcke's 'Verrat' is of a similar mood, though here rising to a more animated expression which is intensified in the central section marked 'lebhafter' (op. 105/5).

The second op. 94 setting, of Halm's 'Steig auf, geliebter Schatten', employs an even more arresting declamatory opening to which the diminution of the piano part contributes significantly. Here again the repetition of the last phrase of a four-line strophe in augmentation serves to satisfy musical demands. The setting of Liliencron's 'Auf dem Kirchhofe' may be seen as presenting a synthesis of elements, its powerful opening employing pedal before the appearance of the voice, the changing metre giving a further sense of recitative-like freedom, the latter part moving rather towards expressive arioso, a later and even more personal expression of the mood which opens the Alto Rhapsody. Yet it also has a textual source, for the accentuations of the third and fourth lines of the strophe differ significantly from lines 1 and 2. In another sense, however, this song is a synthesis, for it unites – as a parallel example to the 'Geistliches Wiegenlied' of op. 91 – the extremes of Brahms's language: the declamatory and the folk-like. We have Brahms's authority[9] that the chorale-like melody which replaces the arioso music in the second strophe quotes the chorale melody most familiar from its setting to the text 'O Haupt von Blut und Wunden',

Ex. 49 'Sapphic Ode', op. 94 no. 4

the best known of the 'Passion Chorales'. Thus it represents a striking example of creative extension, for Brahms makes from the opening a new melody. Moreover, the climax of the melody provides the source of the final cadence of the Four Serious Songs, an association underpinned by text; for just as the Biblical text speaks of peace and release, so does this:

upon the gravestones of the windswept churchyard is written 'Genesen' – 'released'.

It is interesting to compare such a ripe expression of Brahms's lyric/ declamatory style with another powerful setting of an evocative text, through one which points to another influence occasionally to surface in the 1880s. Heine's 'Der Tod, das ist die kühle Nacht' op. 96 no. 1 is a much more Wagnerian than Brahmsian text, with its contrast of 'sultry day' with 'cool night', the day sapping strength, night bringing slumber, to which Brahms responds with a musical idea which is strikingly akin to 'O sink' hernieder Nacht der Liebe' from Act 2 of *Tristan*, though the song's development grows more characteristic of its composer. The rising figure over the gentle syncopations of the piano and the extent of the following chromatic progressions throws links to this model, just as the Brentano setting 'O kühle Nacht' connects these with Brahms's earlier 'An eine Aeolsharfe', whose Wagnerian links have been suggested.

Ex. 50 'Auf dem Kirchhofe', op. 105, no. 4, final bars

These various distinctive types of song style provide a framework to which many other songs can be more broadly related, the earlier backgrounds – especially to the songs of Schumann – never being entirely obscured. One might well refer to two of his Heine settings in praise of spring – 'Es schauen die Blumen alle' and 'Es liebt sich so lieblich im Lenze' op. 96. no. 3 and op. 71 no. 1 – as personal recreations of a Schumannesque mood. In conclusion, Brahms's final settings for vocal quartet, op. 92 and op. 112, rework familiar types in response to some favourite poets. Daumer's 'O schöne Nacht' op. 92 no. 1 recalls the *Liebeslieder* in broader treatment, as does no. 2, a setting of Allmers's 'Spätherbst'. Two settings of Franz Kugler (the author of 'Ständchen' op. 106 no. 1) are very contrasted in idiom, the first an evenly flowing setting of 'Sehnsucht' which, in its simple exterior reveals Brahms's skill in economy and equality of part writing, the second, of 'Nächtens', a very evocative setting 'unruhig bewegt', with tremolo piano writing which is set in 5/4 (2/4 + 3/4), thus absorbing a metre normally associated with folk-types into a very personal expression. The remaining pieces of op. 112 are four more *Zigeunerlieder* written for the medium of which the solo settings op. 103 are arrangements, in the same idiom, and in response to their great popularity.

Piano music

The Eight Piano Pieces op. 76 and Two Rhapsodies op. 79 appeared in 1879 and 1880 respectively. They stand, especially op. 76, stylistically, as chronologically, between the character pieces of Brahms's youth and the rich flowering of the later period, the four sets published in 1892 and 1893. Yet, though they offer strong contrast to the large-scale variation works which preceded them, in the second period, they actually draw much from them. Variation becomes an integral part of their exploration of characters and moods. Even the larger scale Rhapsodies reflect this in their broader designs – expanded ternary form in the B minor, sonata form in the G minor. In character these pieces stand a long way from the often austere and orchestral manner of the early *Ballades*, although the influence of song is still basic, despite rich pianism. In the intimacy of their moods, as in the dance-like quality of some, they show Brahms reflecting many years of exploration of musical character and the links to the moods and pianistic methods of the Piano Concerto in B flat published in 1882 are, predictably, legion.

The personal titles which Brahms employs in the op. 76 set establish a pattern for the later groups, as well as reflecting the earlier pieces. It is still possible to see the term Intermezzo as functional – a means of linking the powerful Capriccios together. However, the special character of the pieces is quite unlike the Intermezzo of op. 10; these intimate and reflective types point directly to the late pieces as particularly characteristic expressions of their composer's nature. The Capriccios can be traced more directly to the past, to Mendelssohn or even to Bach, though Brahms's types are, again, entirely his own. To what extent these titles were significant it is difficult to establish. Brahms sent the two Rhapsodies to Elizabeth von Herzogenberg with the request for better titles, obviously not entirely happy with the associations of the terms, which implied works of a display or popular character, as those of Liszt. To what extent he agreed with her reply to the effect that such pieces could never be effectively titled is not known.

In any examination of Brahms's music, matters of structure attract attention and one naturally looks to eight pieces for piano for an internal pattern of organisation. Though, like so many of the song sets which they effectively parallel as expanded songs without words, no obvious tonal or thematic pattern exists, Brahms compensates for the lack of any textual linking through creating a framework of powerful Capriccios; nos 1, 5, and 8 frame pieces of a much more lightweight or reflective nature, nos 3, 4 and 7, 8 functioning as Intermezzos within this group, no. 2 as a much more dance-like Capriccio. The pattern and moods of the outer pieces bear a significant relationship, both masking simple progressions and essentially stepwise melodic motion behind rich and wide-ranging figuration and following a parallel pattern of A B development A B (coda), in which the basic material is clearly disclosed. In the first, this structure is most apparent, the opening section moving steadily from I down to V in the manner of an introduction. The second section draws the scalic outlines into a regular melodic shape which recalls the fourth of the op. 10 Ballades, and thus Schumann. The development of this idea, with its syncopated treatment of the upper part recalling the B flat Concerto, leads to a restatement in which the theme is inverted in the middle part with new surrounding figuration. A shortened and varied reprise of the opening leads to the chordal reduction of B, its opening four notes – another archetype – now treated sequentially and subjected to further figuration, drawn now from the first idea. In contrast, the last piece handles the outline more fluidly, a tendency predicted by the freedom of the harmony of the first, repeated, part. The key is destined to be C major by the close, but the opening leads its dominant rather to the dominant of F major, and resolves to F, avoiding any suggestion of C by the close of the first section. The second section, proceeding after three bars from the dominant of F, is built on the inversion of a contour touched upon in the first part and wide-ranging modulation brings a disguised and abbreviated first theme. The stark chordal presentation of the idea serves further to confirm its background importance through the piece, here finally placed on the true dominant to cadence forcefully in the tonic.

Variation comes into much clearer focus in the remarkable C sharp minor Capriccio no. 5. Here the alternating form A B A B^1 A^1 A^2 (coda) indicates the successive application of variation to two basic sections, the first a prime example of Brahmsian cross-rhythm, 3/4 and 6/8 existing simultaneously as shown. The two ideas are themselves rhythmically differentiated, the second building to very expansive pianism and modulating more widely. The repetition of A retains its original pattern for 10 bars, after which it broadens to a lyrical cross-rhythmic passage 'poco tranquillo' not unlike the second idea of no. 1. Although the cadence is to D sharp minor (as dominant of the dominant), the reprise of B moves surprisingly to C sharp minor, although the immediate resolution is ambiguous, the notes E, G sharp suggesting either E or C sharp minor momentarily. The variation is now rhythmic, A transformed into 2/4, alternating with a background 6/8 from the opening, a radical variation which recalls the third movement of the Second Symphony. Rhythmic variation of A then follows including change of mode to major 'espress', the piece ending with a further rhythmic trans-formation – phrases of five quavers which completely obscure the metre – to a powerful climax.

The emotional pattern created by these powerful Capriccios is filled out by pieces of much more varied character, in which the one other Capriccio, no. 2 in B minor, is by far the most direct and classically oriented in manner. Here the link is clearly to Schubert's F minor *Moment Musical*, not only in its steady left-hand quavers but the thirds of the right after the double bar. Indeed the passage serves to link Schubert to Brahms's Concerto Finale, for the finale of the B flat Concerto is strongly suggested here. Yet Brahms's planning is much broader, for he develops his opening character into a large ternary design, with two subjects, though treated symmetrically to create the pattern A B (A), development, B A coda. The subtlety with which the first subject semiquavers generate the middle section, and the way in which the subject is finally recalled in the middle voice against 'leggiero', wrist staccato semiquavers reiterating chords over pedal with descending upper voice, are models of Brahms's art and pianism in this period.

In terms of the deepening pianistic individuality which comes to fullest expression in the short pieces of the final period, it is the remaining four Intermezzos which appear the more prophetic. Formal outline places them in two groups, nos 3 and 4 sharing a pattern A B A^1 B^2, in which B^2 serves as a coda, nos 6 and 7 observing a clear A B A shape, with a distinct middle section. Nos 3 and 4 are the least related to the final works. The Intermezzo in A flat reveals its unusual quality in the marking – 'Grazioso', yet 'anmutig, ausdrücksvoll', to which Brahms even adds 'espressivo'. It offers yet another example of Brahms's resource in the simple progression I – V with a prolonged tonic pedal leading to a quick descent, the repetition leading to C minor, as submediant of E flat, the dominant. In contrast to the simplicity of the opening, the descending upper phrase is given additional character by the simply broken triads of the left; the second idea is improvis-atory, a turning figure in triplets gradually broadening to a cadence on the dominant, implied through the passage. The free quality is intensified at the return of B^1 through extension of the phrasing to conclude in bars of 3/2 rather than 4/4 in a deeply reflective manner which looks to the late pieces. In the Intermezzo in B flat, the focus is harmonic, with the opening built on the dominant chord which then moves away through A flat to close its first section in G minor, with no suggestion of the tonic, though its dominant is easily recalled through the lowered G which connects to the repetition. The middle section takes its singing 'allegretto grazioso' idea much further tonally, incorporating the thirds of the preceding codetta naturally in its course until it returns to restore the tonic, only in minor mode in accord with the closing material of the first part.

The character of the Intermezzo in A no. 6 points directly to that of the later Intermezzo in this key op. 118 no. 2, a parallel which grows even stronger in the middle sections in F sharp minor. The earlier work is the more contained, articulated in eight-bar periods, with the smallest extensions in the middle section, which reverses the triplet/duplet pattern between the hands in the first. The Intermezzo in A minor no. 7 creates a very strong sense of ternary design through the brevity of its opening and closing section, an eight-bar passage of chorale-like character.

Brahms's original designations for the Rhapsodies serve to explain their different characters and backgrounds. The B minor piece was originally titled Capriccio (presto agitato) and the G minor merely 'molto passionato'. As a Capriccio, the B minor piece can therefore be seen as extending the potential of the genre as shown in the preceding pieces. In contrast, the G minor movement stands firmly in the sonata tradition, full-dress sonata form, though one of great individuality. Whilst the 'Capriccio' in B minor stands in a tradition of generally powerful movements, however, it has no precedent in its unusual form, a symmetrical A B A (the second A is literally repeated) and coda, with a completely contrasted middle section and outer sections with two distinct subjects, with transition and closing group. The middle section achieves its contrast in many ways – through the key, the tonic major, through its very slow harmonic progress, restrained by the prolonged use of pedal and inverted pedal, and above all by its melodic character, that of a lullaby 'molto dolce espressivo', Brahms's most extended treatment of this favourite kind of movement. Its effect is the more striking since this character transforms a theme already heard; its root is in the third bar of the second subject, where the accompanying figuration goes in the other direction, though it is never allowed to develop, creating a tension which the middle section resolves. In the treatment of the outer parts also the term Rhapsody is appropriate, for Brahms plays on a sonata background established by the first idea, to place the first subject surprisingly in D major as part of a clear transition to a more sustained movement for the second subject in D minor, which it dramatically interrupts, building to an immense climax before reprise, thus creating an A B A pattern for the outer parts. The virtuosic run which marks the climax, immediately repeated in the Neapolitan degree to gain the true dominant of B minor, is very uncharacteristic of Brahms's keyboard idiom and rather suggests Chopin, for example, passages in the Scherzos in B minor and C sharp minor.

It is against an even more strongly suggested sonata-form background that the G minor piece makes its effect, for here the first section follows a much more predictable path, arising from subjects more natural to the tradition in essence. However, Brahms's treatment of the first is harmonically very adventurous, a classic example of what Schoenberg designated 'roving harmony' through its mobility, in this case not even establishing the tonic. The opening offers a fine example of Brahms's special way with the 6/3 triad, here on the lowered second degree from the undefined chord on the fifth degree, enabling him to play with the possibilities of G minor or E flat as tonic. In fact he goes further by using the progression in sequence so that when G is reached, it is G major as basis for a repetition of the entire progression, from F sharp in accordance with the semitonal relationship, to cadence on B. G minor only appears as part of the transition from G major to D minor. Harmonic fluidity returns to characterise the development and intensify the tonal stabilisation of the recapitulation.

Ex. 51 Rhapsody in G minor, op. 79 no. 2

In conclusion, it is appropriate, in the period which saw the completion of the Second Piano Concerto, to outline the various studies, arrangements and cadenzas which further reflect Brahms's characteristic pianism: namely the 51 Exercises for Piano published in 1893, the Five Piano Studies (1869 and 1878), the transcription of a Gluck Gavotte, and cadenzas to concertos by Bach, Mozart and Beethoven. The 51 Exercises realise in strict pianistic terms many of the tendencies noted in the earliest compositions for piano. Thus, in addition to more conventional exercises for the perfection of various techniques – scales in thirds, broken chords in octaves, chromatic runs and so forth – one notes the mirror tendency of many studies, designed to create equality of phrasing and attack in both hands – a pianistic equivalent of the contrapuntal balance of texture so characteristic of his musical development and mature mastery. This tendency is strongly apparent in the various arrangements of earlier music, some of which he designated studies. The most notable example of the stress on the left hand is the arrangement of Bach's Chaconne for unaccompanied violin, his affinity with which has already emerged and will do so later in association with the passacaglia of the Fourth Symphony (Studies no. 5). The doubtful attribution of an arrangement of Schubert's Impromptu in E flat which inverts the parts to give the difficult right hand to the left and to apportion the second idea to the middle voice probably arose in recognition of this Brahmsian inclination. The Rondo after Weber places the emphasis with less force, whilst the two settings of a Presto after Bach apply the idiom of the early Gigues to more demanding technique, the first in contrary motion, inverting the shapes after the double bar as in the Bach models, the second simply inverting the whole texture with octave adjustment. The arrangement of the Gluck Gavotte reflects the fashion for free pianistic realisation which comes to its fullest expression in the arrangements of Rachmaninov. The cadenzas reflect both Brahms's deep affinity with historical styles which enabled him to deceive friends when improvising in familiar idioms and the interest in particular concertos, whose creative stimulus has already been outlined. Thus, all the concertos influential on his early works through his intimate understanding of them as student and performer, namely: the two great minor key concertos of Mozart, those in C minor and D minor, and Beethoven's concerto in G major as well as Bach's Concerto in D minor, the last of merely eleven bars prior to the final ritornello of the third movement. It is interesting to note the scale of Brahms's writing; although he was a pianist who wrote in as rhetorical a manner as any, he completely avoids the inflation which we find in, for example, the writing of Busoni, who in the last work mentioned provides octaves in contrary motion far less idiomatic than Brahms's accelerating scalic figurations, clearly drawing on his knowledge of the Chromatic Fantasia. Indeed, examination of Brahms's continuo realisations for Chrysander's edition of the Handel chamber duets and trios shows a very progressive historical sense of taste for his time.

7

Choral Music

By the third period, the technical and professional motives which had stimulated so much smaller-scale choral music in the second period had disappeared. With his retirement from the Gesellschaft concerts in 1875, Brahms undertook less choral conducting and the preoccupation with strict counterpoint was more for pleasure than necessity: 'When I don't feel like composing, I write some counterpoint,' he is quoted as stating. Thus, Brahms wrote very much less choral music. The depth of his commitment to the medium is, however, abundantly clear from its quality and individuality. The spiritual association with the past is again very strong, especially in the unaccompanied field, yet it is increasingly to a more distant past which reflects the vast scope of his historical explorations and of his capacity to integrate even more deeply with his own idiom. The works fall broadly into two phases. The first includes the two major choral works *Nänie* and the *Parzenlied*, completed in 1881 and 1882, and the first of the later motets, 'Warum?' op. 74 no. 1, written in 1877. The second includes the very late Motets, op. 110 and Festival and Commemoration Sentences op. 109 (Fest- und Gedenksprüche) with the two sets of secular partsongs op. 93a and op. 104, and the *Kleine Hochzeitskantata* and *Tafellied* op. 93b.

Nänie *and the* Parzenlied *(Gesang der Parzen)*

The two works for chorus and orchestra stand in direct succession to the *Song of Destiny* in their evocation of a Greek world of ideas rather than the Christian one of the *Requiem*, showing how deep was the fatalistic aspect of his nature. As in the earlier work, both texts are essentially concerned with the indifference of nature to man, set in strophes by Schiller and blank verse by Goethe respectively. *Nänie*[1] was inspired by the death of Brahms's friend, the neo-classical painter Anselm Feuerbach, whose noble realisations of stories from Greek myths Brahms greatly admired, though they were not well received in Vienna. The *Parzenlied* is taken from Goethe's *Iphigénie auf Tauris* where the weird sisters of ancient mythology intone a litany of man's helplessness before the Gods. Brahms responded to the classical background with what has rightly been described as his 'sublime style'[2] – a

choral and orchestral expression of immense power and beauty, though of a
lofty and detached kind, which undoubtedly permeated the orchestral
works of the period. That they are so infrequently performed, especially the
latter, is a reflection on changing taste, for they are among Brahms's most
moving and characteristic works.

The setting of *Nänie* was completed in the summer of 1881 and dedicated
to Feuerbach's stepmother in his memory, the painter having died in the

Ex. 52 *Nänie* for chorus and orchestra, op. 82, bars 1–4 and 25–32

January of the preceding year. Brahms imposed a musical form on the continuous text by recalling the music of the orchestral introduction for the last two lines and treating the preceding four as a central section, thus creating a ternary musical structure in which the bulk of the text is in the first part. Following the orchestral introduction, the first part begins with the text's essential message 'Even the beautiful must die' which is elaborated through many mythological references to the passage where Thetis arises from the sea to mourn her dead son Achilles, a loss so profound that 'the Gods and Godesses also weep'. The remaining text provides Brahms with a characteristic conclusion, however: 'And a song of lament from the heart of the loved is glorious'. The musical setting defines its form both tonally and thematically, the central lament being set in F sharp major in contrast to the D tonality of the outer sections. Despite its shorter length, the reprise is extremely effective through its dramatic treatment – restoration through an interrupted cadence which makes the greatest structural effect of the piece and recalls the importance of the prelude in expressing the underlying sentiment of the whole text. Indeed, it also reinforces the most notable feature of the opening – its harmonic interruption, from which Brahms develops twenty-four bars of continuously evolving music which shows his motivic art in a lyrical context and in association with very mobile roving harmony. Its effect is greatly enhanced by the scoring, which recalls the Violin Concerto (opening and second movement) in its rich wind writing and expressive role of the oboe. Brahms could scarcely have written a more effective prelude to such a text. The choral entry which follows draws on Brahms's contrapuntal art, seeming at first like a fugue on a long expressive soprano subject close in style to that of the motet 'Warum?', except that it is freely worked after the third entry. Each idea of the text has its own individual, though related idea and the pattern of the opening also serves in varied form for the third line of text. The central part offers marked rhythmic contrast which is gradually relaxed in the retransition. Geiringer's suggestion that Brahms was influenced by the earlier setting of this section in the version by Goetz[3] is entirely justified: there are marked parallels, not only in key – F sharp major – but in shape and feeling in the depiction of Thetis rising from the waters. Although there is no coda to balance the opening, the association of the closing material is quite sufficient to give the impression of balance.

In the *Parzenlied* Brahms achieves his form by recalling the first of the seven strophes after the fifth, with its music, though here the subsequent sections involve a considerable degree of variation, especially the last which is so handled to underscore its text 'thus chanted the sisters below among the shadows' and place their song into a different perspective. The impressive orchestral introduction was immediately noted by Billroth for its tonal ambiguity,[4] the chord of D minor serving as a point of departure rather than confirmation. Yet it is the ominous subject subsequently generated by bassoons and timpani which serves the more important role, given first to tenors and divided basses and then sopranos and divided altos: 'In fear of the Gods shall ye dwell, sons of men.' The first five strophes run continuously to music of great force before the return. The final strophe demands special attention both for its scoring – Brahms adds piccolo to muted strings and exposes the solo trumpet in a very uncharacteristic way in pursuit of effect – and for its harmonic treatment, which provided Webern with an

Ex. 53 *Parzenlied*, op. 89, for chorus and orchestra, closing bars, as noted by Webern

example of advanced harmony in his teaching: 'The cadences found here are astonishing, and so is the way its really remarkable harmonies already take it far away from tonality.'[5]

Sacred works

No one work better indicates the process of change in Brahms's choral language over the years than the motet *Warum*? Here are presented elements well familiar from the earlier motets – fugue, canon, chorale harmonisation – yet the effect is strikingly different and more personal. This is partly a result of its text, which is closely akin to the *Requiem* in reflecting on the travail of life and its ultimate purpose, and finding in God mercy and in death a release with no terror. Again, the texts are drawn widely to express Brahms's personal beliefs, essentially humanist ones though couched in the familiar terms of a Christian culture: 'Wherefore is light given to them that toil and life to them that are troubled . . .' (Job 3, 20–23), 'Let us raise our hearts and hands to God' (Lamentations 3, 41) 'See, blessed are they that have suffered' (James V, 11), concluding with Martin Luther's chorale text 'In peace and joy I take my leave.' As in the *Requiem*, the musical expression draws its earlier elements into a very convincing and characteristic fusion, though of quite a different character, for here the historical links are more clearly apparent. The chief stimulus has always been seen as Bach, partly through the text/melody association of the finale chorale setting, partly through the work's dedication to Philipp Spitta, the leading Bach authority of the day. Its elements certainly relate back to the sectional structures of the second period, although by now the working is so natural that the question of a specific Bachian background seems irrelevant. The particular feature of the recurring question 'Warum?' has been likened to the recurring 'Siehe' in Schein's motet *Siehe nach Trost war mir sehr bange*, although it seems very unlikely that Brahms knew it.[6] Background influence can better be suggested in the second section, which, as mentioned, draws on the four-part Benedictus from the *Canonic Mass* a work whose primary stimulus appears to have been Palestrina. Less commented upon, but more tangible is the style of the third section, where the upper line 'siehe, wir preisen selig, die erduldet haben' whose whole atmosphere seems in a moment to recall Schütz, perhaps the most apposite comparison coming from the setting of *Selig sind die Toten* from the *Geistliche Chormusik of 1648*, if not through textual stimulus, then certainly through style.

Yet, a purely historical view of these works misses their character, in which freedom and individuality, even current preoccupations in other, broader spheres, are also crucial. The arresting nature of the opening, for example, reflects the openings of the *Tragic* Overture and the finale of the F major String Quintet, though here in a manner less referable to tradition

Ex. 54 (i) Brahms: 'Siehe, wir preisen selig' from motet *Warum?*, op. 74 no. 1
(ii) Schütz: Motet *Selig sind die Toten* (*Geistliche Chormusik*)

than in these instances. Even the following fugue is constructed freely, with answers in fifths – D – A – E – B – rather than the conventional alternation of the previous fugues, choral and instrumental: the imitative writing of the second section is regularly directed to cadences whose harmonic focus is completely modern, as at 'und kommt nicht' at its two appearances, whilst the prevailing harmony of this passage is extremely rich in its chromatic alteration in the service of tonal mobility. A comparison of this passage with the relatively plain harmony of the canonic second section makes the point clear. Moreover, the variation of the fugue subject by augmentation and change of metre at the last entry section reflects current instrumental methods and is very uncharacteristic of Brahms's contrapuntal manner; this variation is not one of strict counterpoint as in the op. 29 motets but of expressive transformation, here at the service of text – 'And wherefore is this given the man from whom the way is hidden'. Most interesting of all, however, is the harmonisation of the concluding chorale. Here the preoccupation is again with the simulation of the Dorian mode, untransposed, as in 'Vergangen ist mir Glück und Heil', though not 'O Heiland reiss die Himmel auf'. However, Brahms goes beyond the mere substitution of major chords on IV or avoidance of C sharps to create both a synthesis with the past, and also a reflection of features of his own

Ex. 55   (i) Brahms: 'Mit Fried und Freud ich fahr dahin'

modally inclined harmony, a fascinating sequel to that of 'Es ist das Heil uns kommen her'.

Brahms's long inclination towards Bach in the evolution of his choral style seems to come to a conclusion in the motet *Warum?* With the three motets op. 110 and the 'Fest- und Gedenksprüche' op. 109, both published twelve years later in 1890, he draws yet more distant influences into his work, yet in a manner which seems even more natural, reflective of even broader aspects of his language. The texts of the three Motets continue to reflect the pessimism so characteristic of his choices in choral settings. Two are in strophic verse form, the third the well-known chorale *Wenn wir in höchsten Nöten sein* (Paul Eber, c. 1550), the second, *Ach, armer Welt*, by an anonymous poet. The first draws on two texts: Psalm 69, v. 30, divided by lines from Exodus, Ch. 34, vv. 6 & 7.

(ii) Bach: 'Mit Fried und Freud ich fahr dahin'

It is in the second setting that fusion is at its most obvious. As has been shown, Brahms draws on the striking harmonic character of the chorale melody 'Es ist genug', whose great interest to him is apparent in his coupling of two settings for a Gesellschaft concert in 1873, one by Bach, one by J. R. Ahle. As has been shown, however, Brahms's approach is not as adventurous as Bach's. It can be seen as mediating between Bach and Ahle, in the context of his own language. The stylistic source of this flowing, 6/4 chorale belongs, indeed, outside the chorale tradition, for it relates much more closely to such an example as the *Liebeslieder* waltz, 'Ein dunkeler Schacht ist Liebe', notably the second phrase. Thus the conflation of backgrounds.

Ex. 56 (i) Motet *Ach armer Welt*, op. 110 no. 2
        (ii) 'Ein dunkeler Schacht ist Liebe' (*Liebeslieder*, no. 16)

In the third setting, Brahms creates for the first line of text a 'chorale' melody which, bearing some relation to the shape of the previous example, and keeping the common metre of the original melody, exceeds the model in vocal range. From this phrase, he produces a variation which is used for the third line, and motivic variants, used in both original and inverted forms to provide the material of the alternate lines, the effect of the whole greatly enhanced by the use of double choirs, though sparingly employed in the choral scoring. This material is finely extended at its return for verse 3. Verses 2 and 4 bring us nearer to Brahms's background in the use of double choirs in the powerful use of homophonic writing for both choirs and concertante effects between them, though here the modern hand is still apparent in the subtle borrowing of earlier material for the extension of the opening idea. The historical links are most clear in the first setting, the most subtle and integrated of the three. Here the old love of Gabrieli and Schütz seems to have been reawakened through the recent appearance of the Schütz edition, edited by Spitta, in which Brahms took keen interest. Thus, after a setting of the opening lines 'Ich aber bin elend, und mir ist wehe', in which the tonality of E minor is coloured by suggestions of the Phrygian mode (through juxtapositions with chords of D and F and the incorporation of F within cadential progressions to A and E chords), he recalls the choral recitative style of Gabrieli, Monteverdi and Schütz in the passage beginning with antiphonal chords at 'Herr, Gott'. This opening continues to provide a varied response in Choir II, the material furnishing the basis of the closing passage. The skill with which Brahms integrates the triadic progressions and dissonance treatments of the old style with his own language is even more remarkable here than in the previous motet, op. 74. Its nature could provide the subject of a complete study in itself.

Brahms valued the Festival and Commemoration Sentences much less highly, having produced them for a definite occasion, the conferring upon him of the freedom of the city of Hamburg. His texts are suitably expressive of national and civic pride, the first, beginning 'Unsere Väter hofften auf dich' drawing on three psalm verses (Ps. 22: vv. 5, 6; 29: v. 11), the second, 'Wenn ein starker Gewappneter seinen Palast bewahret', on St Luke (Ch. 11: vv. 21, 17) and St Matthew (Ch. 12: v. 25), the third, 'Wo ist ein so herrlich Volk' . . . Amen' on Deut., Ch. 4: v. 9. Here the 'Venetian' style is at its most apparent with powerful alternations of material between two four-part choirs developed successively from fig. A in no. 1, a method providing the starting point for no. 2. But the working processes of Brahms are equally apparent as well. No. 1 opens with an extension of the process of the varied repetition of a simple progression apparent at 'Herr, Gott' in the first motet, though here the process is even more notable through the inversion of the opening idea at its repetition in bar 4. Such passages as the retransition to the opening material of no. 2 at bars 55–57, the syncopations of no. 1, bar 16 or the sudden focus on the diminished seventh chord at 'das wird wüsste' in no. 2, bar 37, and the whole sense of tonal direction point to the 'romantic' Brahms. In the last piece, the idioms appear more reflectively, not least at the close where Brahms recalls the opening material and writes a pedal passage that looks straight back to his youth in its expressive character.

Unaccompanied secular works

The close relation noted between the texts of the solo songs with piano and secular choral songs of the second period continues in the third, the ten settings of op. 93a and op. 104 reflecting the interest in German and translated folksongs, as well as romantic and classical poets. The only new name is Arnim, whilst Rückert achieves more of a focus than elsewhere in three settings. The single German folk text stimulates yet another Brahmsian folksong. A comparison with no. 36 of the 1894 collection shows Brahms retaining the metre and rhythm of 'The Hump-Backed Fiddler' whilst adding a new melodic line, extending cadences by one beat to 5/4 and providing a contrasted melody for verse 3, procedures directly analogous to the solo settings outlined.

The setting of Kapper's translation of 'Das Mädchen', though duplicating the solo setting op. 95 no. 1, suggests itself as the original through the effectiveness of the alteration of soloist and chorus, which much better suits the text than the solo version. In the other Kapper translation, 'Der Falke', the idiom absorbs the rhythmic distinctiveness of the other settings into a more Brahmsian form, with triplet against duplet rhythm and variation by imitation of the melody. The remaining pieces of op. 93a comprise canonic, homophonic and freer types. 'Beherzigung' ('Stout-hearted') unites Brahms's love of canon to a stiff moralising Goethe text 'No idle thinking, no timid shrinking . . .'.[7] Though it begins like a canon at the octave between the upper and lower voices, the leading pair gradually develop independence, a feature which characterises the second half in the major mode. In contrast, the setting of Rückert's 'Fahr wohl' (sung by the Musikverein chorus during Brahms's funeral procession) is a gentle 6/8 movement which merges a feeling of folk simplicity with the Mendelssohnian tradition in this metre, to great effect, not least at the very end, where the opening is suddenly recalled and dies away. Arnim's 'O süsser Mai' receives the most individual setting, with subtle harmonic colouring.

The five settings in the last set of secular songs, op. 104, offer the final synthesis of Brahms's unaccompanied choral style in pieces for four, five and six voices. An immediate link is through the device of canon, another canon in D minor now appearing in a fuller, five-part context in a much less 'learned' setting of a Wenzig folk translation 'Verlorene Jugend'. Here the canon is between the upper two parts with the answer harmonised throughout. As in the preceding canon, however, there is a contrast, though here to a purely homophonic and very romantic setting of the lines 'Jugend, teuer Jugend, flohest mir dahin . . .' The other four pieces give some of the composer's most autumnal expressions, reflecting both the contemporary motets and the more reflective of the earlier six-part settings. Most obviously, the four-part setting of Groth's poem 'Im Herbst' recalls the lyrical chorale character already noted in the second of the op. 110 motets, a broad minor movement in 6/4, though here more restrained and extended reflecting similar thoughts through the imagery of the seasons, 'Ernst ist der Herbst, und wenn die Blätter fallen sinkt auch das Herz'. The breadth of treatment enables a striking harmonic transformation at the third verse reflecting the text 'sanft wird das Mensch, er sieht die Sonne sinken . . .' Elsewhere, six parts permit even fuller textural expression. The link to the first of the op. 42 settings is particularly strong in the setting of Kalbeck's 'Letztes Gluck', another text to use the imagery of falling leaves. The two openings are virtually identical in their gentle reiteration of the first, minor chord between upper and lower three voices. Yet, the expression of the latter setting is much more intense, not an evocation of a far-off romantic world through the atmospheric contrast of voices but a personal expression; thus the music proceeds with much more direction, building to expressive climaxes with subtle harmonic colouring. In contrast, the two six-part Rückert settings titled 'Nachtwache I and II' exploit the double-choir potential much more: the first, 'Leise Töne der Brust', has a very atmospheric opening progression, so characteristically stressing the plagal progression from the tonic, the second, in complete contrast, boldly repeating the opening call of the watchman in canon in the lower parts against strident upper parts, a really descriptive opening which soon resolves, however, to subtler harmonies as the symbol of the call is reflected in personal thoughts in the text.

As in the other periods, canonic composition remained a Brahmsian constant. Published in this period are two canons, to which three others, grouped with them in the Complete Edition (vol. 21) can be added, all presumably of earlier date since they are for female voices, save for the setting of Fallersleben's 'Spruch' which is for voice (alto) and viola. Only one is simple – that of Goethe's 'Grausam erweiset sich Amor'. Daumer's 'O wie sanft' is a canon in four parts by inversion, Uhland's 'Wann?' a riddle canon in two parts at the fifth below and 'Mir lächelt kein Frühling' (no attribution given) a canon at successive descending minor seconds on a chromatic subject. Such pieces provide immense contrast to other compositions of a convivial nature, the settings of Eichendorff's 'Tafellied' and Keller's 'Kleine Hochzeitskantate', for mixed voices with piano, the latter yet another Brahmsian 'minuet'.

8

Chamber Music

The balance between the quality and output of chamber and orchestral music achieved enables very clear, common, phases of work to be discerned, phases which show a marked extension of the composer's expressive range. With the completion of the First Symphony, a very marked lyric phase is to be discerned whose main representations are the Second Symphony, the Violin Concerto and the G major Violin Sonata. Although this lyricism remains throughout the period as a deep spring of expressive significance, from 1880 there is a move toward a more heroic, and serious style, involving a new openness, a new almost symbolic kind of main idea. This is naturally most immediately apparent in the orchestral sphere. The *Tragic* Overture and the Third Symphony both seem deeply programmatic in effect and this quality is also present to a lesser degree in the first movement of the Second Piano Concerto, and, in its special way, the *Academic Festival* Overture. These patterns are partially reflected in the chamber music through some important links to the orchestral music, chiefly in the F major Cello Sonata. The Fourth Symphony and F major Quintet are of a more abstract and clearly historical inclination, whilst the final works of both genres – the Double Concerto and the G major String Quintet – refer back to the earlier preoccupations with the gipsy manner.

Whilst the chamber works are in no sense less important than the orchestral works, reflecting a wide range of characters and formal and technical devices, the orchestral works come into fuller focus against their background, though not in the fundamental sense of the second period. Thus, the first, most overtly lyrical group comprises first the G major Violin Sonata with its companion, the A major Sonata which, though written eight years later, shares much of its quality. The third, D minor Violin Sonata, with the second, F major Cello Sonata, comprise a later more rhetorical treatment of the duo medium, one which comes into fullest expression with the two mature piano trios in C major and C minor, to which can be added the revised version of the early B major Trio. The String Quintets in F major and G major complete the period, leaving one work – the Third String Quartet in B flat, published in the year of the First Symphony – as a very important link from second to third period in its special and new mode of expression. In considering the orchestral music subsequently, the style groupings outlined may be followed, with the exception that three works which do not follow Brahmsian precedent and pose special questions of medium and structure may be considered separately: namely, the B flat Piano Concerto, the Double Concerto in A minor and the *Academic Festival Overture*.

String Quartet in B flat

If any further evidence were required for the view that Brahms's chief problem in facing the string quartet lay at root in matching ideas to expression, it might well be found in the character of the Third String Quartet in B flat. For its outer movements set aside the striving or expansively lyrical qualities of the preceding quartets in favour of the most overtly 'classical' idiom since the first cello sonata, a signal example in the unfolding relationship with past manners and forms. Indeed, the texture and the very metrical and thematic idiom have drawn parallels to the *Hunt* Quartet of Mozart, whose key it shares in common with several other works of 'classical' associations – the First Sextet, *St Antoni* Variations and *Handel* Variations. Indeed, it throws an obvious link back to the *St Antoni* Variations in its structural nature – the first theme reappearing at the close of the work and revealing an inherent relation to what has preceded. Yet if the outer movements suggest the eighteenth century, the inner are decidedly nearer Brahms's time, if still at a distance. The second strongly suggests a Mendelssohn romance, whilst the third is a longing viola song most clearly traceable to the second movement of Schubert's G major Quartet. Thus, Brahms again unites a striking range of styles in one work. Indeed, the sharpness of the inherent contrast is such that he might be seen as attempting a conscious experiment in juxtaposition. This view can be supported by reference to the remarkable freedom – improvisatory elan – with which he plays with his ideas. In each movement there is a freedom in moving away, harmonically, rhythmically and texturally from the model, which is quite new in the chamber music, though certainly hinted at in earlier works, notably in the first movement of the A minor String Quartet. But the relationship is not merely of freedom. Brahms seems, especially in the first movement, to maintain a stylistic distance from his model, almost to comment on it through romantic eyes in a way which differs from preceding compositions which reflect the past, and can be seen as anticipating an important aspect of subsequent music, especially associated with certain neo-classical works of Stravinsky.[1]

Considered first in its structural outline, the work is notable for the function and nature of its variation finale, which brings together two of the composer's main preoccupations in earlier works: the role of the finale as the goal of a composition, and the interest in variation form. In placing his variations last rather than as middle movements he extends his own

Ex. 57 (i) Mozart: String Quartet in B flat K458, first movement, bars 1–16
         (ii) Brahms: String Quartet in B flat, op. 67, first movement, bars 1–23

methods, reflecting in the process an obvious classical precedent – Mozart's
Clarinet Quintet. But he also exceeds his own conventions in other ways.
Within the 'classical' expression, Brahms now creates a subtly irregular
structure, as clear in harmonic direction as the preceding works, yet
constructed in two unequal parts, the first of four, the second of six bars;
the second is achieved through the reduction of the middle section, the
whole ending quicker than one expects. Moreover, the harmonic scheme
brings to the fore, as part of the model itself, a tendency only apparent
once in the *St Antoni* Variations, and never in the *Handel* Variations: the
stress on the mediant, D major. This only appears at the first cadence in
the earlier work, stressing rather the submediant at the main division. The
harmonic pattern is balanced by a conclusion on the submediant. The
harmonic scheme is used rather more flexibly than previously, with moves
to the flat mediant, D flat, for variation 5 and the flat submediant, G flat,
for the sixth, via the minor tonic in variation 4. In the progress of the
variations also Brahms changes his preceding bias. Thus he moves very
gradually away from his theme through very obvious and traditional decoration and reduction in vars 1–3, setting up the motivic head of the more
distant variation 4 in tonic minor, which is then inverted over a pivoted
harmony in B flat's relative major. The more distant tonal point of G flat,
'molto dolce' masks the gradual reintroduction of the theme 'pizzicato', a
mood suddenly dispelled by the abrupt recall of the work's opening at
double its original speed. Yet this is no mere culminatory reprise, as in the
St Antoni Variations. Brahms brings his opening into the harmonic and
phrase scheme of the variations, following it with a similar treatment of the
first movement's second subject. Only at bar 150 does he work freely,
achieving a remarkable fusion of the ideas of both movements and

concluding with the re-introductory flourish. Thus the harmonic and thematic pattern achieves a new fluidity within firm bounds.

The intimate relationship achieved between the outer movements inevitably suggests that they were conceived together – the one as a variant of the other. Brahms certainly seeks to treat his first idea with a similar sense of growth away. Within its conventional schematic outline – repeated exposition, regular recapitulation, clear subject groups, etc., Brahms reaches stages of considerable contrast both thematically and, especially metrically and in rhythmic character. Indeed, rhythmic play and contrast becomes almost obsessional in the special character of this movement. A direct comparison with the *Hunt* Quartet is very instructional in showing the freedom of Brahms's phrasing and rhythmic evolution – indeed it might be extended to hypothesise the movement's background model: compare not only the openings, but also subsequent material.

Thus, Mozart phrases regularly, proceeding from one period to another, whereas Brahms persists with his first thought, playing with the contrast of 3/4 and 6/8 as a Brahmsian commentary on the original. The second group further redefines the original metre by establishing duple time as simple 2/4, though at first still alternating and re-establishing the compound duple at the close of the exposition. This contrast of metres dominates the development, a contrast also pursued actively in purely thematic terms, establishing an entirely new kind of development section which can be seen as bridge to his later treatments of the form. Thus, the development begins with a wholly fresh idea, scalic and in thirds, alternating with the fragmentary motive of the opening, a passage which returns to round out the section. It makes a striking contrast with the thoroughgoing development of the second subject which appears from bar 161. The metrical integration and variation here already sets up the expectation of rhythmic play which Brahms will recall with the return of the opening in the finale.

After such resource, the Mendelssohnian ease of the slow movement is very marked in effect. Although Brahms held Mendelssohn in high regard, his later influence seems limited in comparison with that of Schumann, the two being more balanced in the earliest works. Not only the chamber music, but even the manner of the choral style seem invoked in the first paragraph (bars 3–26) even despite the characteristically Brahmsian triplets and broadening of the harmony at the return from bar 19. But this is only one element in the movement. From bar 29, the now familiar agitated, almost gipsy manner established in the slow movement of the A minor Quartet and A major Piano Quartet appears, leading to a very improvisatory passage notated in 5/4, returning to 4/4, the retransition handled with the utmost finesse.

In the third movement, the lyric character appears in a much more intense context. The 'molto passionato' belongs to the class of instrumental songs – a viola song not unlike 'Verzagen' – though its rhythm relates to the waltzes. Brahms exploits the textural possibilities, giving a delicate quaver counterpoint to the first violin at the theme's return at bar 89. Yet the squareness implied by the dance background and by the phrasing of the opening provides a point of departure rather than a framework, for not only is the first period extended from 8 to 12 by internal augmentation, but the continuation leads at bar 57 to a capricious variation and subsequently a long dominant preparation for the return – improvisational, gestural tendencies which come most fully to the surface in the viola, bars 106–9.

Violin Sonata in G major

No such stylistic juxtaposition is present in the first Violin Sonata, op. 78, or indeed, its successor. Here Brahms speaks, or rather sings with a consistency of mood in the outer movements, subtly related by other means to the slow movement. Whereas the lyricism of op. 67 is passionate, almost overbearing, this is calm, unfolding easily and building gradually in the expansive outer movements. In compositional terms, it is far more straightforward in concept, though no less effective as a result.

Here the lyric character goes beyond mere idiom into the substance of Brahms's own songs, the first subject of the finale borrowing a song and its accompaniment, a source which inspires a related, though purely instrumental idea for the first movement. Since the Second Sonata in A major also explores the relationship with song, both have the special status of studies in the integration of song and instrumental music. Thus, Brahms draws on yet another established tradition for his work. Although it has been observed of the G major Sonata that it 'picked up the thread where Beethoven's last G major Sonata had dropped it',[2] it is not to Beethoven but rather to Schubert and Schumann that the essential link should be made. Schubert integrated his own songs into string quartets, either by their use as variation sources, as in the D minor Quartet's use of 'Death and the Maiden', or the borrowing of an opening, to be continued with new, generated material, as in the A minor Quartet, the relation of whose slow movement to the song 'Die Götter Griechenlands' is well established. Schumann, in his characteristic way, includes many references to song fragments, aspects readily reflected by Brahms, as will be shown in relation to the original version of the B major Trio. But Brahms far exceeds these models by the extent and implication of his treatment. For he constructs a full rondo movement from a song, building a complementary first movement to it and integrating the whole in a way never conceived by his predecessors. Thus he makes his slow movement part of the rondo structure of the finale, an example of quotation with no exact parallel in his work. But this thematic linking is underpinned by more profound tonal relationships. For when Brahms introduces the tonality of E flat into the finale in G minor, he is merely composing again a relationship established in the first movement. The clear G major with which the work begins is undisturbed in the exposition, save for some chromatic inflexion which is the source of harmonic colour in the coda. But the development soon modulates to the flat side, to the Neapolitan relationship of A flat, and when the close of the development is heralded at bar 134, the music is clearly in G minor where it stays for 17 bars prior to the restoration of the major tonic. Indeed, Brahms juxtaposes G minor and E flat harmony in a way which anticipates the relationship between the movement's close and the beginning of the slow movement.

The source of Brahms's lyric finale is his own setting of Klaus Groth's poem 'Regenlied'. It was a symbol both of his close friendship with this fellow north German and his obvious love of the song, of which two related, but separately worked, settings exist, as shown.

The first setting is an extensive A B A structure with a middle section of strongly contrasted material and metre and key, reached by modulation from the tonic, F sharp, to A as dominant of the contrast key D major. The second setting, of a much shorter text reflecting on the first, also maintains a ternary form, but without any material contrast. Brahms's sonata movement draws on the first five bars of the two settings only, generating a new continuation which creates in turn its own evolution, though retaining the original pictorial 'rain' motive of the accompaniment. A comparison of both with the sonata is revealing:

(i)

A comparison of later bars in the sonata shows the even closer relationship with the song material.

Although Brahms constructs two distinct sonata subjects from his song to sustain a sonata exposition, he retains the open quality of the model, so that the rondo structure which emerges with a strong tonal and thematic contrast in its central section seems entirely appropriate. In the first movement he set himself a more demanding task: that of conceiving a related and complementary movement which would facilitate a lyric quality within a sonata form structure, with its demands for development and more organic transition processes. This he achieves, partly by extending the scope of the main themes, both structurally and in range, and partly by his choice of sonata plan. Drawing on his skill in integrating a variation aspect into sonata form, he recalls the first subject, in the absence of an exposition repeat, in the tonic, proceeding directly to development.

But he proceeds anew in recalling, though very subtly and without preparation, the theme again after development, thus actually writing a rondo

Ex. 58   (i) 'Regenlied', op. 59 no. 3
       (ii) 'Nachklang', op. 59 no. 4

(iii) Violin Sonata in G major, op. 78, finale, bars 1–11

scheme for a first movement, though a sonata movement in spirit. Within this mould, he builds out from the opening of the finale's theme a more wide-ranging and evolutionary idea of 10 bars' length, a lyrical span which predicts the nature of the articulation of phrasing. Quotations from the piano accompaniment of 'Regenlied' serve to lead to the second theme, another instrumental lyric theme, vocally based, but exceeding vocal range. The norm of the lyrical paragraph is continued with the appearance of another theme at bar 60, sharply contrasted around the mediant, B major, which serves to effect the retransition to the return of the opening idea. It is in this development that Brahms has to confront the relationship between distinct thematic sections and the traditional processes of this section.

The central episode of the finale completely obscures the introspective original character of the slow movement, simplifying its complex phrasing and in the process revealing the subtlety of Brahms's art in this regard. The movement begins almost as though it were an intermezzo for piano, the violin singing an independent melody at its entry in a manner akin to the pattern of the slow movement of the Horn Trio, also set in E flat, though minor. But the reflective phrase structure, achieved through motivic development of the idea, belongs entirely to the mature master. Thus, what may reasonably be predicted from its first phrase as a basic structure of eight bars can be seen as extended to nine by the augmentation of the phrasing of the third bar, though Brahms also introduces other subtleties to create an entirely natural and characteristic theme:

Ex. 59 Violin Sonata in G major, op. 78, second movement
　　　　(i) Hypothetical version of 8 bars
　　　　(ii) Actual composition

Violin Sonata in A major

Although the G major Sonata is a remarkable achievement, it is essentially much simpler in conception than its successor which, whilst also achieving a balance in the characters of its outer movements integrates much fuller material, not least in the central movement which combines the functions and characters of a slow and quick movement: the alternating scheme relates back to the pattern of the third movement of the A minor String Quartet, as to the Second Symphony, although here the slow movement is entirely dispensed with to achieve a new level of integration. Brahms offers us a later and even more satisfying expression of the meeting of the world of song and of sonata composition. For here, the first movement is not cast

(i)

in a rondo-influenced sonata structure, but one of more conventional design and it is into this, as the second subject, that Brahms integrates a song, rather than as the first subject of a rondo structure. Brahms's variation of 'Wie Melodien zieht es mir' is even more subtle than of 'Regenlied', for here is not only the first phrase only taken from the song, but the rhythm is significantly changed within a new metre – 3/4 instead of 4/4, as follows.

The passage is completed as a sentence comprising a total of 16 bars structured in an antecedent-consequent relationship. This structure mirrors the first subject, similarly built on a four-bar model, although the suggestion that its opening phrase derives from Walter's 'Preislied' from *Die Meisters-*

Ex. 60 (i) 'Wie Melodien zieht es mir', op. 105, no. 1
(ii) Violin Sonata in A major, op. 100, first movement, bars 50–9

inger seems wilful[3] – the structure is quite different, Wagner being almost more Brahmsian than Brahms in the natural development of his lyric idea. Brahms's first theme has, however, far greater capacity for truncation, and it is striking that he completely ignores the more self-contained lyricism of the second subject in the development. Here, with no double bar or closing group to the exposition – his abruptness in A major is also characteristic of the A major Piano Quartet – he proceeds to work entirely with the first subject which, beginning in the dominant, is subjected to a progressive rhythmic treatment which gradually displaces the main beat, facilitating a new idea which grows directly from it, and which, as a striking example of his changing methods in development, becomes the subject of a character variation section which restores the lyricism of the second subject without restoring its identity. Further rhythmic play brings the development to another abrupt close, on the mediant major – another direct link to the A major Piano Quartet – from which the recapitulation proceeds directly and conventionally. Thus Brahms highlights the lyricism of the second subject by restricting its role to exposition only, just as he had done in the G major Sonata.

The rondo finale is finely matched to the first movement by use of a theme of comparable style and harmonic character. Thus, a twelve-bar melody with an extended consequent moves unusually to C sharp minor as late as bar 9. This balances the unusual movement of the sonata's opening through the submediant, F sharp and flat seventh, G, intensified even further in its repetition to move through the Neapolitan, B flat. Moreover, the special quality of the first movement is matched in the resigned mood of this finale, which is more gentle and less rondo-like in spirit than any previous movements of the kind in Brahms. Much of the quality arises from the recollection of the musing gipsy element first explored in the op. 26 Piano Quartet and here drawn into the more active context of a finale. Indeed, the second subject which follows the transition is also close to that work – to the scalic motivic figure which expresses the 'Scherzo' character. The breadth of the outer movements is contrasted in the inner movement, which unites the characters of a scherzo and slow movement, in an alternating form which extends the principles of the minuet of op. 51 no. 2 to the following scheme:

Bar	1	16	72	94	150	162
Subject	A (Andante)	B (Vivace)	A (var.) (Andante)	B (var.) (vivace di più)	A (var.) (Andante)	B (var.) (vivace)
Key	I	vi	VI	vi	VI–I	I

The tonal scheme obviously draws from the 'Lydian' movement in Beethoven's String Quartet op. 132.

Violin Sonata in D minor

The Violin Sonatas in G major and A major appeared as the products of Brahms's maturity – richly lyrical works in which form and content seem indissoluble in the context of a very sophisticated musical language, qualities which, though hard won, are repeatedly apparent in this period. But the earliest works had shown that the genre was also associated in his mind with works of a tougher and more demanding stamp. The Sonatensatz in C minor is a driving scherzo and we may well conjecture that the 'Sonata in D minor' to which reference is made in the correspondence was a work of similar quality. Whether elements of this work formed any part of the D minor Violin Sonata which appeared in 1889 as op. 108 is a matter for conjecture. Its finale could certainly derive from earlier times, since it recalls just that scherzo mood and the relatively crude duo texture which stands in such contrast to the achievements of the works just discussed. Moreover it makes very overt use of one of the F A E variants, that in its first theme and draws on a chorale-like theme which also relates to the earlier trio idioms. Like the Double Concerto, it may well contain a message to Joachim. Whatever its provenance, the sonata demonstrates how Brahms could use the medium for the expression of more intense ideas, a feature demonstrated even more clearly in the Cello Sonata in F major.

Despite the terseness of expression of the outer movements, Brahms achieves something of a broader sense of structure by the use of four rather than three movements. He includes a slow, song-like movement and an animated 'un poco presto e con sentimento' in the minor, prophetic of the mood of later piano music, notably the little Capriccio in E minor, op. 119 no. 2. Yet these, though offering greater sense of contrast, are also very pointed, lacking the genuine middle section of other scherzo and slow movement types; Brahms is here content with the simplest of strokes in effecting the retransitions. The median minor contrast of the slow movement is reflected significantly in the tonal structure of the first, arising in turn from its special character, and other parallels of working subtly underpin its totality.

As with so many minor key works, the first movement's emotional intensity creates special features which have consequence for the whole, even in a genre which clearly attempts much less in dramatic structural terms than the concerted chamber music. Here the mature absorption in the integration of variation passages into the traditional 'development' section leads Brahms to perhaps his most radical example. The contemporary preoccupations with Baroque forms – notably the ground of the Fourth Symphony – stimulate the incorporation of the device of pedal into the first movement's development, which is based entirely on the dominant. It is the most extensive example aside from the pedal fugue of the *Requiem* and shows Brahms's remarkable skill in this device very fully. In its turn it has profound consequences for the movement, since the normal tonal exploration of the section has to take place in the recapitulation. Thus, after restatement of the first theme, the section assumes the character of a development with a sudden shift to F sharp minor for sequential working of the original transition material. Indeed, the entire span of this recapitulation assumes the outline of the modified development-recapitulation schemes found in, for example, the finale of the First Symphony, with second subject following development. The reappearance of the pedal for a considerable part of the coda, which reflects even more on the opening idea, brings into a sonata-form context a device hitherto associated with the reflective conclusions of slow movements, such as those of the variations to the B flat and G major Sextets. Thus, overall, Brahms achieves another integration of sonata form with rondo, though of a very special character.

Developmental variation is taken up again in the structure of the finale, a more obvious sonata rondo, whose central section achieves a balance of the two characters by conventional 'development' of the first subject, but also contrast through its variation to a new, reflective character – 'espress' and 'sempre piano'. As in the First Symphony, Brahms builds a weighty movement on a scherzo rhythm, though here much closer to its source through the marking 'presto agitato'. Thus the form is not a rondo, but rather another special type of sonata form in which the first subject reappears as though a rondo after exposition, to lead to development after which the second subject is recalled with the rest of the original material. Recapitulation is resumed at bar 218 with the second subject, the transition material having been recalled in the preceding bars over a dominant. Yet, when the second subject arrives it is not in the expected key of the tonic – since its exposition had not been in the expected dominant or relative major. This chorale-like idea appears in the key of C major, via a sudden, almost Schubertian shift from the expected resolution to A minor, this key arising later as a more animated IIb of rhythmic interest. In the recapitulation, the relation F major – D minor mirrors C major – A minor to complete the movement's tonal plan. Brahms uses character variation not as a central, contrasted event, but rather as the first, reflective part of the development, from which the working-out of the original spirit of the theme resumes after a climax. Thus, just as the tonal character of the whole work reflects the special tonal character of the first movement, so the finale also looks back – here to the special roving qualities of the first subject whose modal tendencies lead it through F major and C major within the tonality of D minor prior to the conclusion on the goal dominant. Even the notable chromatic inflexion of the chorale melody at bar 42 finds its source here.

Short though they are, these movements project strong characters. The slow movement, whose thematic evolution is much less overtly based on internal variation, introduces a violin passage in suave thirds at bar 21 which immediately recalls the gipsy idiom, rhetorically repeated in the reprise with an intensity not seen since the slow movement of the A major Piano Quartet, which makes just such an event of the element, though within an infinitely broader pattern. Suggestions of the scherzo of that work also influence the third movement which creates a new character from the pizzicato manner of the middle movement of the A major Violin Sonata.

Cello Sonata in F major, Piano Trios in C, C minor and B

In the F major Cello Sonata the demands on the medium point even more specifically towards the orchestra. Indeed there are tangible links to the Third Symphony, only just completed as op. 90 in 1883, four years earlier.

The sonata's scherzo reworks the basic idea of the symphony's finale, providing a rare and fascinating glimpse into a process which may have influenced much of his creation. The tense emotional mood of the first movement gradually unveils even more tangible relations than those of the two openings. Both expositions close in a similar mood, with driving chords which lead into distant tonal regions for the development. In turn, both retransitions to the recapitulation are broadly planned, again with strident chords over pedal building to the recall of the opening. Moreover, the expositions are both united by the mediant span, F major – A major.

But if the elements are related, the wholes are quite distinct. Brahms could hardly have reproduced the special emotional pattern of the symphony with equal effect in the duo medium. Instead, he places much more weight on the inner movements, both substantial, leaving a finale which might perhaps be heard as insufficiently powerful to complete the scheme. Its mood and form are very close to the finale of the C major Trio op. 87, which concludes with less-demanding inner movements. Nevertheless, the work is strongly unified, not least in the finale. Brahms lays as much stress on tonal linking as in such works as the F minor Piano Quintet and C minor String Quartet. Here the stress is to the Neapolitan relationship, either directly, or through the mediant major, A. The first movement exploits this relationship in its development, whilst the finale recalls the rondo for the third time, in G flat major. Most strikingly, however, the second movement is boldly placed in F sharp major – the strongest tonal contrast in all the instrumental music, though one prepared and with consequence.

It is a measure of Brahms's mastery of the duo medium by this stage that he could write a first movement whose great intensity of piano writing does not create undue textural problems, as he here allows himself a more powerful manner than in any chamber works with piano since the Piano Quartet in G minor and the Piano Quintet. Indeed, the broad opening progression of the piano part, whose semiquaver articulation seems so closely to anticipate the opening of the String Quintet in G, permits a fragmentary theme in the cello, to whose advanced nature Schoenberg drew attention. Writing in 1931, in connection with his own orchestral variations and as a means of making them more accessible to a general audience, he says

> Younger listeners will probably be unaware that at the time of Brahms's death this sonata was still very unpopular and was considered indigestible. . . . At that time the unusual rhythm within this 3/4 time, the syncopations which give the impression that the third phrase is in 4/4 . . . and the unusual intervals . . . the ninths contained in this phrase . . . made it difficult to grasp. I felt all this myself, so I know how seriously it must be taken![4]

Schoenberg's lack of reference to the unifying power of the harmony deeply reflects his outlook and its narrowness. It was the developing thematicism, the sense of seamless continuity, of a prose-like structure, which so appealed to him. Like the earlier Sonata for Cello in E minor, the transition is hardly apparent – indeed, less so, and the second subject arises with no formal preparation, including in its course successive variation which recalls with less formality the method of the parallel section of the Piano Trio in C minor.

This flexibility enables, quite unlike the Symphony in F major, an improvisatory, almost fantasy-like development section which appears after the formal opening transition (bars 66–74). Brahms seems to bring in an element almost more characteristic of central sections of slow movements than of sonata movements before the symphonic parallels of the broad retransition. And similar variational qualities permeate the rondo finale along with the tonal parallels. The central episode is an almost slavic variation of the theme in B flat minor whilst the coda presents the theme in a comparably overt augmentation for broad expressive and culminatory purposes. Such variation assumes a more rhetorical character in the two powerful inner movements. Of these, the scherzo is the most clearly related to tradition, an 'allegro passionato' in the key of C minor and 6/8, which recalls the associations of this key and metre, though with a fleetness which relates to the later scherzo types. In terms of its expansiveness and developmental quality, it relates to the scherzo of the Piano Quintet – 128 bars in which the main idea comes three times in varied forms, the main section comprising three distinct elements and the central section roving widely tonally. The conclusion presents the basic idea in a rhetorical augmentation in the piano against the cello (bars 109–13) which is another reflection of the quality of overt transformation so common in the period. As in the earlier scherzo, the contrast is to a broad C major melody (compare also that of the Piano Trio in C major), likewise straightforward in its first part, though roving further after the double bar, during which it works in references to the prominent rhythmic motive just mentioned. Yet it is the slow movement which may be seen as carrying the main emotional weight of the work, for it not only appears in striking tonal relationship in F sharp major, but is very memorable for its main idea, a progression for the piano which can be seen as varying that which opens the F major Symphony in its expressive prolongation of the tonic chord, made more impressive by the use of the cello 'pizzicato', to provide a walking bass.

When the cello takes over the melodic role from bar 5, it is to herald a very fluid phrase structure in the section up to the third theme at bar 12, involving the very bold, though completely effective use of motivic augmentation in the line – bar 9 augmented to two bars in bars 10–11 over variation in the piano. The central section (whose keyboard sixths anticipate the scherzo) leads to a reprise which makes even more of the opening, recalling first over a chromatically inflected F sharp minor before a varied reprise from bar 44.

The Violin Sonatas and Cello Sonata in F show Brahms exploring widely differing characters and textures as a fully mature artist during the period 1878–86. The Piano Trios in C major, C minor and, in revised form, B reveal the slightly later preoccupation with a genre with which he had longer familiarity and certainly a special affinity. The Trio in B major was the only one of the many chamber works planned in youth to be released in the period and although the revision is an improvement, when set in relation to the later trios, Brahms still regarded the original as justified in its own terms, as has already been stressed. Such is the balance of compositional quality and textural command in 1854 that one might well argue for the piano trio as the most natural vehicle for Brahms's most intense expression – perhaps as occupying in his world the position given to the string quartet in the music of Beethoven, or to the single string quintet in that of Schubert. Certainly, the three mature trios which appeared between 1882 and 1890 offer his most subtle integration of piano and strings, and his most profound and radical treatment of the form with which he was so preoccupied – sonata first movement form. Both are very different in character. The contrast of tonalities inspires movements of different character which, in turn, prompt works of different proportions and moods. Thus the C major Trio concludes with a leisurely rondo movement much in the manner of that of the F major Cello Sonata, enclosing a full set of variations as slow movement and a scherzo, whereas the C minor Trio concludes with a terse scherzo-like sonata structure enclosing much more individual inner movements: like the D minor Violin Sonata, a very personal little 2/4 movement in the minor, and a song-like slow movement, though here with a definite middle section. The sense of the whole is even more instinctive, less rationally tangible than in earlier works. As with the thematic relationships of the F major Cello Sonata, these are very elusive, built on recurring shapes between successive movements rather than obvious quotation.

Something of the confidence and economy with which he handled his ideas is apparent in the revision of the B major Trio, which provides a natural introduction, despite its later date, to the language of the mature Trios in C major and C minor. The characteristic humour of Brahms's reference to his revision – 'I did not provide it with a wig, but just combed and arranged its hair a little' [5] – obscures its comprehensive nature. Though not radical in the sense of the C minor Piano Quartet or the D minor Concerto – none of the movements is actually replaced, and the whole retains its original outline – the change to the contents is comprehensive, affecting not merely the powerful outer movements but also the inner movements. Even the fine scherzo, the simplest in structure and most unified in idiom, receives significant modifications, as does the ternary slow movement.

The guiding principle of the major revisions of the outer movements is to give a greater sense of direction to the broadly conceived structures, bearing in mind that they retain their essential characters through the continued function of the expansive first subjects. Both movements modify the original transition sections and substitute entirely new second subject groups which drastically reduce the exposition in content and in length. The second group of the first movement originally included very different ideas, the first a scalic unison idea for piano leading directly into a theme for left hand clearly suggestive of a Bach fugue subject and recalling such an example as the Fugue in A flat minor for organ in its abstract quality. The repetition of these elements leads in turn to a Schumannesque figure, harmonised in four parts, 'poco scherzando', and thus to the closing figures of the exposition in the unusual key of G sharp minor, completing a total of 162 bars. The Schumannesque material provides a contrast, still in E major, to the sequential treatment of the first subject, which creates, with some fresh derivations, the substance of the development concluding with only a suggestion of the second subject's opening idea. This omission is never made good, for the second subject of the recapitulation is given to the fugue-like idea, now fully worked between strings and piano before the return of a modified continuation based on the transition and first subject, both of which are even more forcefully presented in the quicker coda, which even works in the fugue subject as a counterpoint, 312 bars of recapitulation and coda resulting. Brahms's approach to the form may therefore be seen as reflecting that of Schumann, especially in the tireless use of sequence in development, with his own desire to include as much contrast and to integrate by contrapuntal device and thematic combination to a much more ingenious degree. The revision reduces material drastically, by abbreviating the transition and employing only one second theme – a terse mirror idea whose only connection with the original is its unison presentation by the piano, continuing in harmony. The tight variation and repetition of the ideas serves to conclude the section, with further transition material, in a mere 118 bars. The development deals only with the transition ideas and first subject, creating from the latter another character variation, though closely integrated into the whole continuity from bar 137. Brahms's mature pianism, as evidenced, for example, in the syncopations of his figurations, expands the idioms of the exposition with remarkable ease and a subtle reintroduction of the first subject proper leads naturally into the recapitulation. Variation of detail makes no difference to the sequence of the recapitulation and a new coda completes the movement to a mere 290 bars.

Contrast was even more marked in the original finale, with direct quotations from Schubert's song 'Am Meer' and Beethoven's cycle 'An die ferne Geliebte', prominently given to cello, and reflecting Schumann's manner – and presumably its personal significance in relation to Clara – as the second subject group. The revision substitutes from the point of transition a new and simpler idea, removing the consequences in development and reducing the recapitulation and coda as a result. The allegro 'doppio movimento' section of the slow movement is also replaced by less contrasted material in the revision, whilst the scherzo is provided with a new coda; the original 'un poco piu lento' is replaced by a section of equal length in which the original static piano part, against pizzicato motives in the strings, is now transformed into figurations drawn from the previous bars, bringing the movement to a much more continuous and effective close.

Even with such significant revisions, the expansive quality of Brahms's ideas ensured that the essential character of the original conception remained. No greater contrast could be imagined than with the manner and length of the two mature trios, the more intense of which, the C minor, runs for barely a third of the length of the revised B major. Direct comparison of the first movements of the later works is very rewarding in showing Brahms's two most advanced treatments of sonata form and how they arise from their remarkably fluid first subjects, hitherto unparalleled in their asymmetrical motivic evolution.

Brahms's exploration of the potential of sonata form had fallen into two main channels, both arising from the desire to omit the repeat of the exposition – a tendency early apparent and consequent upon his love of varied repetition. In both, development and recapitulation are integrated through the reprise of the first subject in the tonic prior to development, after which the second and completion of recapitulation follow. Such is the form of such broadly conceived schemes as the finales of the Piano Quintet and later symphonic works. A more complex type shows the division of the first subject into elements which are separated in their recapitulation, the first prior to development, the second subsequently. This is the form of the experimental first movement of the G minor Piano Quartet – made possible by two very distinct subjects – and of the finale of the C minor String Quartet, a much tighter structure, though still divisible through its introductory gesture. The link is strongest to the C minor movement where the recapitulation of 1a is subtly divided between bar 81 and bars 134–140, 1c effectively recalled in the tonic at bar 199. The same principles of the economical re-shuffling of elements operates with more freedom in the first movement of op. 87, to give the following related but independent schemes:

			EXPOSITION					/DEVELOPMENT. RECAP.				
op. 101:	1	5	11	20	38	73	81	87	134		150	192	
Bar	1a –	1b –	1c –	tr.	2a –	C.G. –	1a –	dev –	1b –	tr (new) –	2a –	Coda	(1c–1a)
Subject	i	i	(III)	i	III	III	i		i		I	i	VI–i
Key													

op. 87:	1	13	21	33	57	80	102	129		189		235	258	293
Bar	1a –	1b –	1c –	tr. –	2a –	2b–	C.G.	1a –	dev –	1b –	(Ia)	2a –	2b –	Coda
Subject	I	I	I	I	V		V	I		I	I	I	I	I
Key														

The very different characters of these two main subjects determine sonata-form variants of very different kinds, the first broad and expansive in effect, the second terse, abrupt in gesture and handling. The strongly variational aspect of the first subject of the C major Trio predicts that variation will play a significant role throughout. Thus the transition at bar 33 achieves a synthesis of the opening statements, the strings retaining Ia in unison, the piano working from their variant at bar 13. In turn the development statement of the opening at bar 129 offers a new countersubject for cello as well as a new piano figure, the original semitonal inflexion now leading the material quickly to G minor for an intensive working of a figure derived by diminution from bar 80. The final, recapitulatory statement of 1a makes even further modifications to the subject. Yet all these developing variants fall into a different perspective in relation to the very bold transformation of the theme which appears in the development at bar 165, an augmented form which is much closer to the character of a waltz than to a sonata movement. This is resumed even more fully in the coda. The development may therefore be seen as incorporating the new feature of an overtly trans-formed version of the first subject into the context of a tightly worked section of great motivic economy – the contrast of two extremes drawn from the same root idea. In the process it sharply marks off the two ideas of the first subject – the opening, with its associated variants, and Ib, from bar 21; the first part of the development is therefore concerned with the first idea, the second, after the augmented variant, with the second, from bar 189, the recapitulation resuming from 1b at bar 189. In this context, the very stable character of the first part of the second subject stands out in both exposition and, especially recapitulation, a feature also determined by the lengthy pedal G at bar 115, which serves as a retransition in this scheme rather than a development, which is how it is first heard.

The principle of the variation of a complex first group and retention of a stable second group appears in quite a different context in the first move-ment of the C minor Trio. Here the same basic tendency of the first idea – to move from i to V for a contrast of material is accomplished very quickly, in only four bars. Yet in this case the following eight, all built on the dominant, G, serve to effect the transition to the second idea, a dotted figure which begins in E flat to lead back to the tonic for the transition. This naturally avoids the original progression, moving quickly to B flat, as dominant of the second subject, the entire twelve-bar passage (with one bar extended from 3/4 to 4/4) built on variation of a two-bar model (26–27). Thus Brahms can be seen to incorporate into another part of the sonata structure – the transition – a principle previously explored in relation to a subject group, the second subject group of op. 60. The second subject stands in great contrast to the first, a broad and expansive sixteen-bar period repeated in variation to lead to a closing group not unlike that of the companion movement in thematic outline. But it is much shorter, only seven bars, and is immediately displaced by the returning first subject, an augmented variant of the transition, as in the companion work, yet restoring the pattern of the opening by moving to the dominant, whence a further motivic variant leads into the variational element of the development, a capricious version of the derived motive, though it is quickly contrasted with a darker variant at bar 102. Thus it changes the pattern of the parallel movement by dispensing with any initial working of exposition material. This rather returns at bar 115, applied to Ib and leading to a dovetailed recall of the exposition from the dominant chord at bar 4. But the expected dotted figure, having been extensively treated previously, is now omitted, the new material which appears in its place at bar 141 creating great structural effect and leading directly to the second theme, whence the progression continues as before. The expectation that the dotted figure will be recapitulated is fulfilled in the coda, a lengthy section comparable in proportion with the parallel movement, yet not resuming the character variation of the development.

The two finales with which Brahms balances these movements reflect their differing characters very closely. Thus, that of the C major Trio is a rondo finale of an open quality in which variation of the returning theme is very conspicuous. Moreover the coda is very extensive and transforms its subject in the manner of the first movement, creating a natural balance between them. The rondo effect is enhanced by the very animated piano writing. In contrast, the finale of the C minor Trio is a sonata structure, rhythmically intense and insistent, but it seems the more effective since Brahms places it in the tonic to create a conventional tonal resolution and since it crowns a work of great terseness. In contrast, the finale of the C major Trio seems not quite powerful enough, even despite the craft and sheer compositional verve, especially in the coda, where Brahms recalls the theme in leisurely augmentation before a powerful and harmonically bold conclusion in the original tempo. It makes a fascinating comparison with the B flat Piano Concerto of the same period, another work whose conclusion seems not quite to balance fully out, and perhaps for the same reason – the relative weight of the first two movements. Indeed, like the Concerto, the fullness of the second movement seems to provide the focus of balance, here through a set of variations.

Brahms jokingly referred to the variations as justifying an extra fee, the public having 'come to expect them from him'.[6] Yet whilst these variations follow the outward pattern of the variations of the two string sextets – five variations, with a major contrast towards the end and a coda – they differ in two important respects: character and the phrase proportions of the model. Much of the impressive character of the subject can be ascribed to its transformation of a Brahms basic shape, here in a form which stands between the earlier types and those prominent in the last period, especially recalling the *Requiem* and the first of the *Serious Songs*. The guise is that of a passionate gipsy melody, not least through the octave writing for the cello and violin, a folk-quality Clara immediately recognised on first sight.[7] The gipsy quality accounts in turn for the long and freely evolving second part, almost a variation in itself, which produces the very unusual proportions of the two, unrepeated parts of 8/19, with no formal reprise. The unfolding of the variations reflects the later tendency to gradual evolution from simple variation, though it draws very precisely on an earlier method – the inversion of parts for the first variation, as in the variations of the G major Sextet.

The complementary scherzo movement also looks back to the past, here unusually to the scherzo types of Mendelssohn, Brahms's movement coming the closest he managed to the 'fairy' type of Mendelssohn – a rapid 6/8 of fleeting motives and piano semiquavers at 'allegro', throwing links also to the nimble quality of the third movement of the Violin Sonata in D minor. Like that movement, it seems to concentrate earlier tendencies. It seems able to integrate the earlier feeling for expansive development in the scherzo, as in op. 34, op. 26, op. 25, within a much tighter frame, notably omitting any formal reprise and rather moving easily into the Trio in the tonic major. Again the Trio looks back, here to the broad singing types last employed in the Piano Quintet and the Horn Trio, especially in the Quintet whose tonal pattern it mirrors, again reducing scale by economical treatment based on the first idea, the reprise not literal, but recomposed with notably effective cross rhythms.

It is fascinating to compare these types with those of the later C minor Trio, both appearing much later and more individual in essential character and working. Thus the 'scherzo' of the C minor work – marked 'presto non assai' also draws on the folk-archetype, though now reduced to a terse fragment 1 – 2 – 3 – 2 – 1 predicting a very tightly expressed movement which incorporates its contrast idea as an integral section rather than a Trio. Thus the scheme:

Bar	1	4	17	27	30	43	63	89	95	111	121	125
Subject	Intro –	1a –	1b –	1a –	2a –	2b –	2a –	retr.	1a –	1b –	1a –	Coda
Key	i	i	(i)	i	iv	(iv)	iv		i	i	i	i

In rhythmic type it is a very concentrated version of the 2/4 movements of the G major Sextet and the First Symphony, though the expression relates rather to an example such as the third movement of the Violin Sonata in D minor.

The slow movement is even more independent, a simple ternary form in which Brahms seems to draw on his love of the irregular metres of Serbian folksong as demonstrated in the backgrounds to his songs 'Das Mädchen' (op. 95 no. 1) or 'Mädchenlied' (op. 85 no. 3).

The setting of the folk-like melody for the cello and violin, especially in the recapitulation, suggests immediately the Double Concerto, notably its slow movement. However, the middle section looks back rather than forward to the later chorale passage. The quick move into 6/8 draws on the first section of the alternating form of the Horn Trio, though here Brahms's play with phrasing, extending freely, reveals the later hand.

String quintets in F major and G major

Of the many chamber genres explored by Brahms, only one remained to be essayed by the 1880s – that of the string quintet. Yet Brahms did not return to the genre which he had planned with the original version of the F minor Quintet for strings. The two later quintets both restore the form as used most significantly by Mozart: that with two violas rather than two cellos. Moreover, the very demanding and sometimes percussive writing of the earlier work yields to a style generally very naturally suited to strings, as are the string sextets, though also making much more expressive use of solo instruments. The contrast with the idiom of the piano trios is therefore quite considerable, especially in the first movement of the F major Quintet, contemporary with the C major Trio. The new instrumentation changes the opportunities for solo writing, removing the possibility of melodies on first cello, whilst giving them to viola, which is richly exploited in both works, and extends tendencies already apparent in Mozart's scoring in the late Quintets in G minor, C major and E flat major.

Yet in both style and form these works are very different. The F major possesses a distinctly historical character through its classically inclined fugal finale which stands in succession to the finale of E minor Cello Sonata and thus to a long tradition. Indeed, like the earlier work, the relationship is very direct, seeming to recreate the finale of the C major *Rasoumovsky* Quartet in not only form but also material and reflecting Brahms's intimate knowledge of the movement which he played in a piano transcription from early years. Though not obvious through its reworking, the main theme of the slow movement derives from a Sarabande, conceived as part of the Bachian Suites in 1855. The first movement, though of no such origin, also makes great play of traditional counterpoint. Thus the work offers something of a parallel to the Fourth Symphony which followed after only three years in integrating and recreating earlier models in full maturity.

In contrast, the G major Quintet lives in another world – the world of the dance and gipsy music. Its finale concludes with the most overt example of this manner since the Gipsy Rondo of the G minor Piano Quartet and its main part is of a very vernacular idiom, Brahms readily accorded with Kalbeck when he suggested it be titled 'Brahms in the Prater'[8]. The other movements also combine a slavic feeling with German moods, a contrast also sensed by Kalbeck though with reference to Italianate 'grave' and Magyar temperaments. Yet the difference is not just of mood. This, the last chamber work intended by Brahms, exhibits a sophistication of harmonic and thematic writing and phrasing which relates more closely to the Clarinet Quintet which followed in only two years.

The F major Quintet is perhaps the least well known of Brahms chamber works, setting aside, that is, the rather special case of the C minor Piano Quartet. This may perhaps be explained by the degree of the stylistic contrast. Joachim, in fact, remained unconvinced by the nature of the finale for some time, though he later accepted it. But, given that Brahms exposes these contrasted characters as points of reference at all, he achieves a remarkable integration of structure. Tonal relationships underpin the whole very strongly. Thus, to the now customary contrast of F major with its mediant major, A, he adds the contrast with the submediant, notated as C sharp, to link, again to A major. The outer movements, like those of the F major Cello Sonata and Third Symphony use A major for the second subjects, whilst the slow movement employs C sharp minor, with a contrast to A for the animated alternate section. Moreover, there is a unity of contrasts, both outer movements introducing distinct thematic and metrical contrast, which relates to that of the slow movement. Finally, pervasive variation often involving contrapuntal methods is characteristic of the whole.

As examples of recomposition – or, in the case of the Finale, recreation – the second and third movements relate obviously to earlier works, specifically the Finale of the E minor Cello Sonata and the 'Scherzo' of the G major String Sextet. Of these, the Sarabande represents the most radical transformation, not only because Brahms's movement was already a romantic reinterpretation of a baroque type demonstrated in Bach's *English Suites*, but because of the more extensive nature of its treatment. Whereas the scherzo of op. 36 takes the opening two bars of the Gavotte only and then works very freely, the model exerting no influence on the whole as such, Brahms used the whole of the Sarabande – though not in its original form – to impose a definite character on the later version. Thus, whilst retaining the opening eight-bar section he suddenly moves away through sequence for an equal period before restoring the opening in varied form, the first section concluding after 31 bars with a harmonically unusual prolongation of the tonic chord. It is only after the alternate section, marked 'allegro vivace' in contrast to 'grave e appassionato' and in the key of A, and the further statement of both characters, that the second part of the model appears – not in its original context, but after the varied recall of the first part at bar 189, its harmony revealing the source of the closing progressions of the first part. Although the formal pattern can obviously be traced back to the 'quasi minuetto' of op. 51, the archaism is here much more profound. Brahms seems to draw on the pattern of the Lydian movement of Beethoven's String Quartet in A minor op. 132, with its alternating variations, contrasts of speed and material, and of key (Brahms adopts the same relationship), yet to make his own, characteristic kind of historical reference; the Sarabande contrasts with a dance-like section which also turns out to derive from 1854–5, since its varied repetition is identical to the Gavotte II which appears to have been paired with the forementioned Gavotte in A minor, and to be drawn from it.

If Brahms could accommodate the Baroque character of the sarabande into his chamber style through the mediation of a piano work which reflects both romantic and earlier idioms, the fugue which concludes the Quintet does little to obscure its Beethovenian origins. Like the finale of the Cello Sonata in E minor the background is clear: the finale of the *Rasoumovsky* Quartet in C. The running semiquaver subject and strict fugal exposition united in a sonata structure are his inspiration, though he adds the abrupt chords recalling the opening of Beethoven's companion Quartet in E minor for good measure, perhaps revealing the source of the chords which similarly open the *Tragic* Overture. Yet Brahms's approach is much more relaxed than Beethoven's – and infinitely more than in his sonata finale. For Brahms

treats his fugal material as the basis for transformation rather than extension, or as an inspiration for fresh contrapuntal working. Unlike the sonata
finale, the exposition ends to inaugurate an essentially homophonic transition in which its basic idea is freely worked to lead to a lyrical second
subject which combines the original theme with a new idea, the two existing
in equal relationship: the former in the lower parts, the latter as a lyric
surface for first violin. In turn the development offers variation of the
original opening – a singing transformation of the fugal exposition, complete
with its chords, in terms of the second subject's triplet variant. When fugal
working returns at bar 81 it is of a playful, referential nature rather than
structural. Recapitulation offers further variation – the opening in harmonised terms which again transform the model until the return of the second
group. The coda transforms material more radically than that of any other
chamber work, coming closer to the methods in the concerto finales in its
metrical change, and in which the second idea is varied in a texture reminiscent of the close of the G major Sextet. To a greater extent than the Cello
Sonata in E minor, the broad and confident first 'allegro' – a movement of
direct and relaxed mastery – can be seen as composed to accommodate
both the other movements – for the finale must surely also have been long
in his mind. Thus, the second subject mirrors that of the finale in its tonal
relation F major – A major and its triplet contrast, the development drawing
strongly on the contrapuntal character, yet with the same lyrical asides.
Indeed, the F – A relationship is stamped on the music from the outset,
the second cadence, at bar 8 moving to A major, and opening up D major
as the contrast key of the subject, yet another mediant reference.

In Kalbeck's opinion, the very powerful opening of the G major Quintet
was intended for a symphony[9] – one of two which are believed to have
been worked on after the completion of the Fourth Symphony. It certainly
possesses a symphonic richness, with its main theme – uniquely in the
chamber music for strings alone, for cello, which has to produce a mighty
tone to match the fullness of the upper strings in semiquavers. It considerably exceeds the tremolando passage which opens the String Quartet in C
minor in its symphonic manner. The passage certainly strained the medium
and caused its first performers considerable problems, though, when played
to the highest standard, Brahms's original markings – which he retained
despite advice from Joachim to the contrary – produce one of his most
vibrant and rich textures. Indeed, as a work of super chamber aspirations,
it throws yet more links back to Schubert's quartet in the same key: the
massive alternation of major and minor chords which herald the transition
seem strikingly like the opening of the Schubert work – as does the '*pp*
tremolando' which opens the development to the passage which continues
Schubert's opening. This in turn takes us back to the G major Sextet, for
no work is as rich in pure sound as is that. Comparison enables the remarkable change in Brahms's handling of the medium to be observed. This is
not merely a matter of the different ensemble. Brahms handles his instru-

(i)

(ii)

Grave ed appassionato

Ex. 61 (i) Sarabande in A major, bars 1–11
(ii) String Quintet in F major, op. 88, second movement, bars 1–12

ments with much greater mobility. The kind of equality which was at its greatest in overtly contrapuntal contexts – fugal finales, contrapuntal developments and the like – here appears in an entirely free context. One notes especially the role of the cello, exchanging improvisatory figures with the upper parts in the slow movement as well as the first very openly, to say nothing of the apportioning of the first subject to this instrument.

Although Brahms intended this to be his last chamber work, its advanced language looks forward in several crucial respects, as well as reflecting old preoccupations. Indeed, the structure of the first subject is quite without precedent in his work, a continuously evolving structure of sixteen bars which, however, roves assertively through clear regions of the base tonality, of which E minor, F sharp minor (with several implicit meanings) and C major are notable.

Such a self-contained and powerful idea might seem to predict a movement of great lyric expansiveness. Yet Brahms responds to it with extreme economy of means, restricting his phrasing in the short transition to initiate a second subject group with two ideas, both built on single-bar motives which, though they generate the themes thereafter, also restrict them, in both cases to a mere four bars; after this they are respectively repeated in variation in fuller scoring with extension, that of the latter setting up a syncopated pattern which quite deceives the ear in the fluidity of its phrasing (bars 46–56), making an interesting parallel with the comparable passage in the Clarinet Quintet. As in all the later development sections, Brahms introduces strong contrast, though here again, to a very striking degree. Thus after the Schubertian transition after the double bar and the following contrapuntal working from bar 69 to bar 83, a sudden textural and thematic change accompanies the marking '*p* dolce' as Brahms transforms a preceding motive to create seemingly new material of a reflective nature, to which the return of the previous working offers yet another contrast at bar 93, leading quickly to a dovetailed recapitulation. This quieter material is destined in turn to dominate the coda growing naturally out of the closing group and sustained through subtle variations to take no less than 23 bars of a movement of 181 before the return of the powerful opening to conclude the movement.

This fluency and spontaneity of working characterises all the other movements. Although the finale brings Brahms closer to the undisguised gipsy spirit of the 'Rondo alla zingarese' of the G minor Piano Quartet than any other work, the rondo is now very cleverly worked, a sonata, rather than simple rondo, devious in harmonic method where the earlier work is blatant. Thus, Brahms begins in a subdued mood in the mediant minor, B minor, coming to a first cadence on its dominant, F sharp, before an abrupt transition back through B minor to the tonic and a forceful dance tune, with repetitions in variation. The establishment of the dominant for the contrasting subject is leisurely, its own dominant operative for no less than a sixteen-bar period, giving weight to a contrasting key which will not serve

Ex. 62 String Quintet in G major, op. 111, first movement, bars 1–16

to lead directly to the rondo return, in the tonic, but, recalling the opening, the introductory quality of the first idea in B minor. The immediate goal of this passage becomes a structural focus for Brahms, for it is to this degree that the driving development section leads at bar 163, expanding the original retransition to recall the second idea in varied form in the tonic. In turn, F sharp is the goal of the gently varied reprise, reached with great emphasis through a unison semiquaver run. The tonic now follows directly for the animated coda which creates a free variant of the omitted dance theme Ib, startling in effect because unprepared by the usual progression. Fluid as these outer movements appear, however, they do not reach the interest of the slow movement, immediately noted by Joachim for its harmonic individuality. For the opening theme, leaning towards the dominant of D minor makes an immediate move to the chord of C major through lowering of C sharp to move through E major back to the dominant to close the first paragraph. Although the movement falls into a broad A B A structure with an impassioned central section, the first section is proportionally lengthy as the composer explores the possible consequences of such an adventurous harmonic juxtaposition in the third bar only. Thus, after another, complementary theme, the opening returns intact, the alternate idea now leading to the original theme in G minor and initiating a progression which leads through modal progressions very reminiscent of Beethoven's Lydian movement to the central part which roves from an implied G minor widely before restoring the opening. The retransition is striking for its adapting of the parallel viola passage in the B flat String Quartet, to a much more overt formal context.

9

Orchestral Music

Violin Concerto

In the clear patterns of relationship which exist within the chamber and orchestral works of the third period, no two works stand as close in time and character as the Second Symphony and the Violin Concerto, produced within a year in 1877 and 1878 respectively. In the common moods of their first movements, symbolised by shared key, metre, triadic shape of opening themes and orchestral colour – warm lyricism coexisting with a rhetorical manner which results in identical rhythmic figures at one point – (compare bars 118 and 78 of the respective movements) they complement each other as different expressions of this aspect of Brahms's mature language. Yet they occupy rather different positions in his output. Unlike the Second, and to an even greater extent than the First Symphony, the Violin Concerto stands in a distinct tradition: that of the violin concerto as exemplified by Beethoven. The link reflects not only Brahms's interest in that work, but also the interest of the work's dedicatee, Joachim. Indeed, as a concerto conceived in terms of Joachim's playing and background, it represented a very clear challenge to the direction of concerto composition in Mendelssohn, and a gesture of faith in the greater musical resources of the classical form for the expression of the most profound ideas and their consequences. The relationship is, not unnaturally, most notable in the first movement, traditionally the most complex. In the finale Brahms acknowledges the friendship in a more direct manner, by writing a rondo 'alla zingarese', as Joachim had himself done in his Concerto 'in the Hungarian Manner'. Only the slow movement seems entirely personal to Brahms, cast in a form prophetic of the Second Piano Concerto, in which the soloist responds to a long, song-inspired melody, here given first by the oboe.

Whereas the influence of Beethoven on the First Piano Concerto had been that of a blueprint for most of the finale, Beethoven's influence on the Violin Concerto's first movement is very much broader, that of a general background of form and proportions which is especially clear at the main points of articulation. Thus Brahms also employs a full orchestral exposition with two main themes and a lengthy introduction to the solo exposition, which then deals with the first theme, finding further parallels in the retransition and the resolution of the cadenza, whence the first theme is restated. Indeed, the effect of these two outer passages is remarkably similar in figuration as well as context, reflecting Brahms's intimate acquaintance with Joachim's idiom, since the cadenza normal for the Beethoven Concerto was his own. However, Brahms builds in a highly individual way on the inherited foundation. As a work for violin, it is much more demanding in its figurations, and the musical line appears more full, more capricious and expansive as a result. It is particularly interesting to compare the two entries of the soloist, Beethoven building up from the dominant, Brahms moving directly into the tonic minor in a manner strikingly akin to the parallel passage of the Schumann Violin Concerto, also conceived in terms of Joachim's playing. But the most powerful difference is in language. Brahms conceived his work in a more symphonic manner, as is clear from the nature of his development which includes no episodic material, even such as he had included in the First Piano Concerto, but is close to the contrapuntal idiom and thematic preoccupations of the Second Symphony. In terms of harmony and phrase, Brahms's language is entirely his own. The very opening, for example, effects a quick and adventurous tonal contrast between the tonic and the flattened seventh degree, C major established clearly for four bars after the first period of 8 bars, through the lowering of the third of the dominant chord, A, after which the relationship is reversed to restore the tonal progress. At bar 190 another mediant contrast, here from F sharp minor to D major heralds five-beat phrasing within the triple metre five bars containing three phrases, further varied by Brahms's markings – 5, 4, 3, (3).

Similar relationships exist in the finale which reveals, additionally, links to Joachim's *Hungarian Concerto* and the Schumann Violin Concerto. Thus, Brahms does not establish a distinct self contained theme as the central episode, but plays very subtly with a cadence-derived figure at bar 120, maintaining the sense of development and restoring the second theme before the first to redistribute the normal pattern. Moreover, he places immense emphasis on the coda – thematically derived by variation in quicker tempo, after the manner of the traditional concerto finale, the most direct link being through the Piano Concerto in C minor of Beethoven, and intensifying the gipsy manner with uninhibited writing for the soloist. It is interesting to compare the manner of this finale with both that of Joachim's gipsy finale and the final 'alle zingarese' of Brahms's own Piano Quartet in G minor – his only previous such finale. The finale of the Piano Quartet offers Brahms's squarest sonata rondo structure, symmetrical to a remarkable degree, though, like the rondo of the D minor Piano Concerto, growing much more expansive towards the close. The finale of the Violin Concerto can hardly be designated even a rondo, since the rondo-like return yields to development after which the second subject returns. It is therefore to be related equally to the symphonic tradition, though the manner of the central section reconciles traditional development with improvisation. In fact, the pattern can be seen as mediating between the two concertos aforementioned, significant models in their personal association with Joachim's playing. For the sonata-rondo of the Schumann work is developmental in its central section – if uninspired in its nature – whilst the Joachim finale is much more sectional: indeed, the treatment of the central part includes a very clear episodic idea after which, as part of a very free continuation which only restates the main theme in considerable variation in the coda, the second subject reappears; a significant precedent.

If the outer movements lean fruitfully on tradition, it is in the slow movement that the deepest essence of Brahmsian expression is perhaps to be found. As in the previous D minor Piano Concerto, the soloist works most characteristic variations on the long opening orchestral paragraph. However, the idea is now given to a solo instrument and furthermore draws on an entirely Brahmsian archetype, the melodic shape already identified in the setting of Hans Schmidt's Sapphic Ode. Indeed, the movement can well be seen as representing a further stage in the process of instrumental treatment of a song-source more obviously to be traced in the two Violin Sonatas in G and A, as shown. In this case the reworking is much freer and more far-reaching, consistent with its function as the first section of a ternary form. Direct comparison is most appropriate with the second subject of the Violin Sonata in A, which also draws on a twelve-bar vocal model. But whereas Brahms simply varies the metre to create a simple variation of the original, he here works a much longer melody from two short, though very potent, phrases – the opening phrase, only the first three notes being retained, though a little more of the rhythm, and the descending phrase at bars 8–9, which he intensifies chromatically at bar 11 of the instrumental theme. Thus from 12 bars are created 31 in the pattern 2/8/4/9/2, which are supported by an entirely individual harmonic scheme – a new model. From this model the soloist then begins new variation, adopting figurations around the outline given fragmentarily in the orchestra and subsequently building to an impassioned central section following the pattern of the earlier concerto with varied recall. Not only is the model transformed formally, but so is its very character: an essentially alto song in vocal form, becoming an equally essential oboe melody in its instrumental realisation.

One of the most notable features of this movement in terms of Brahms's orchestral development is the richness of the wind scoring. The first theme is given entirely to wind chorus, with flutes, clarinets, bassoons and horns supporting the oboe melody to create an independence of scoring not heard as prominently before in Brahms's work. The manner of its integration with. the soloist, as for example in such passages as bars 38–44, or the return at bar 78, is highly individual. Moreover, this type of sound permeates the first movement. The second period of the first subject – that already noted for its placement on the flattened seventh C, contrasts the string subject of the opening with the lead of the oboe and oboe remains a prominent colour, especially in relationship with the horn, throughout recalling the Second Symphony.

Ex. 63 Violin Concerto, op. 77, slow movement, bars 1–10

Second Symphony

In providing such a powerful link between the two works, the sound-world and shared moods also serve to highlight the greater individuality of the Symphony in relation both to its predecessor and to the symphonic tradition in general. Symphonic first movements in the major mode in triple time were rare when Brahms wrote this work: only that of Mozart's Symphony in E flat approaches it, but has little affinity with the very relaxed atmosphere which Brahms creates for his opening. For in its mood he demonstrates that his love of popular idioms of the dance was not restricted to the small forms of piano music, but could as well provide the starting point for a great movement, as had the dramatic spirit of Beethoven inspired its predecessor. For the Second Symphony opens in the world of the symphonic waltz, as made familiar in Vienna by Johann Strauss Junior. Brahms had immense admiration for Strauss, reflecting the respect in which he has always been held in Austria as an artist, rather than merely as a writer of dances. He already seems to pay a tribute in No. 10 of the *Liebeslieder-walzer*, where his music for 'Am Donau Strande, da steht ein Haus' bears obvious relation to Strauss's most famous symphonic waltz, 'An der schönen blauen Donau' in its statement and response pattern between soloists and piano in major mode, recalling the horn figure and wind response of the Strauss. Moreover, the shape of Brahms's vocal line, with its stress on the semitone E – D sharp – E sets up the basic recurrent interval of the symphony's opening. And Wagner was not slow to observe this Strauss-relationship and pillory Brahms as a result.[1] Just what Brahms made of the dance-inspired character, though of no interest to Wagner, is of remarkable interest for students of the symphonic tradition. For nothing could be less like the mood of the First Symphony. Brahms's Second has been called his 'Pastoral', but the parallel is far less apposite than that between the First Symphony and Beethoven's heroic symphonic and keyboard works. Beethoven associates the pastoral mood with common time and relative homogeneity of expression, whereas Brahms brings his triple metre major mood into very powerful rhythmic contrasts and rich harmonic relations, including a characteristic stress on the minor submediant – G minor as part of D major – which projects a much more intense feeling of nature, a world of overtly romantic symbols. For if the horn sonority functions as a romantic symbol, not material for development, in the finale of the First Symphony, it shares in the very essence of the first movement of the Second.

However, the difference is not just one of mood. The protracted history of the First Symphony makes the traditional view of the two works as constituting a Brahmsian pair quite misleading. Only the middle movements of the earlier work approach the sophistication of language which Brahms reveals in maturity, and the Second seems by comparison much more spontaneous, improvisatory, in both its large and small aspects. Such is Brahms's resource, however, that these qualities can easily obscure the inevitable relations to the past – both Brahms's past and that of the symphony generally. The character of the third movement – an 'allegretto grazioso' (quasi allegretto) gives a clue to the Brahmsian background, for it recalls the Menuetto I of the D major Serenade and with it the very classical associations of that key, not explored orchestrally since the earlier work. Indeed, if the first two movements seem more fully romantic in mood, the finale can be placed in the symphonic tradition of D major, as restored in the Serenade, much more clearly. There is a bucolic and witty quality to the handling of the ideas of this sonata rondo movement which, Brahmsian textures apart, seems to illustrate his admiration for Haydn. Furthermore, there exists a notable parallel between the memorable rhythm of the finale's main theme and that of a Clementi piano sonata – the first theme of the Sonata in B flat major op. 8, reflecting Brahms's intimate knowledge of this composer, perhaps. Moreover, the work is replete with contrapuntal working of a more overt and integral nature than that of its predecessors. The development of the first movement, central section of the second and development of the finale all adopt a contrapuntal manner which is intended to be heard, rather than existing as part of the substructure. Indeed, even behind the surface of the first movement, the links of metre and triadic subject reveal Beethoven parallels in the contrapuntal/motivic working, as can be shown in the comparison of bars 186–206 with bars 395–402 of the *Eroica* and Brahms first movements.

To this background, Brahms brings much that is characteristic of the achievements in chamber music which followed the relative formal relaxation of the Serenade. Like the two Sextets and Piano Quartets of the early 1860s, Brahms produces not only a distinctly lyrical second subject, but a complex of ideas of considerable breadth, reflecting their Schubertian background in a two-stage tonal movement to the closing group by mediants – F sharp minor linking to the dominant, A major. Comparison with the second subject of the First Symphony, which has far less definition than the closing group, confirms the quite different stylistic stimuli of the two works. Moreover, allied to this chamber background is the texture of the later work. Much of the First Symphony already reveals this quality – most notably the source-complex and structure of the first subject – but in the Second Symphony it is much more pervasive, influencing not only the passages of contrapuntal working, but also the texture of the main ideas, whether in relaxed or in assertive contexts, as the main ideas of the outer movements show. No work could provide better evidence for Abraham's[2] assertion that Brahms created a 'super chamber medium', in terms of both orchestration and compositional texture. The association of counterpoint with instrumental colour is especially striking in the slow movement, whose transitional fugato builds on the parallel passage for horn and violin and piano in the slow movement of the Horn Trio. The deeply introspective symphonic slow movement draws on the earlier work in producing this characteristic intensification of the spirit of a Schumann symphonic slow movement, for it is even more powerful than that of the First Symphony.

Viewed overall, the Second Symphony might appear almost too rich in ideas and texture, to which sound – with trombones now integral rather than additional – adds another dimension. Yet Brahms was equally aware of the need for control and balance – indeed one might summarise the work's essential quality in this interaction of freedom and fullness with the sense of discipline, which is apparent in broad gesture and smallest detail: the heart of Brahms's language, yet here apparent in a very special way. As with the First Symphony, tonal organisation is very strong, mediant patterns again providing the background. However, the tonal contrast is not here as great, the progression of movements D major – B major – G major – D major not rivalling the contrast C minor – E – A flat major – C minor. Equally, however, that within the first and third movements is more complex, not only the two-stage exposition of the second subject, in which the idea therefore appears transformed in mode at its second statement, (D major – F sharp minor – A major), but in the third movement, which resumes the emphasis on F sharp to recall the main theme in this key rather than in the expected G at bar 194, before restoration at bar 219. The sense of formal balance complements the tonal relations. Since his finale does not follow the dramatic pattern of its predecessor, Brahms had no comparable need to compress the inner movements, which here unfold as fully as the outer movements, creating a more equal contour for the work as a whole. But every special formal feature is balanced in the overall scheme. This is especially notable in the first movement, where Brahms adapts his preference for the incorporation of an introductory character to the first movement into the broad planning of the whole. The first subject is of no less than 43 bars, necessitating a new theme for the transition at bar 44, whose figuration offers a memorable parallel to that of the first Violin Sonata in G. The full recapitulation of this opening would have been impossible within the bounds of sonata style, and Brahms thus seeks to conflate the ideas of first subject and transition at the point of recapitulation. The contrapuntal relation is not, however, simply one of combination – after the model of the *Meistersinger* Overture, but rather the unveiling of an existing relationship, for the transition is simply a variation of the opening with its source suppressed. In turn, Brahms balances the opening section with a coda of comparably distinctive character and proportions, introduced by variants of the opening horn material and leading into a gentle pizzicato passage, presenting the material in a new light. And in addition to the large patterns, there exist many small links of colour and key, as for example, between the pizzicato conclusion to the first movement and parts of the third. But the most pervasive sense in which Brahms unites this work is in the use of a three-note motive which is apparent in many of the work's main themes.

Various commentators have observed the fertility of the very opening notes D–Csharp–D in not only the themes of the first movement, but other movements as well, even the third. The feature arises in the first movement as a consequence of its pervasive thematic development. From the very outset, the broad phrases of the horns are connected by the motive and its transpositions, almost in the manner of a motto: something which stands

First movement

Ex. 64 Second Symphony, op. 73, thematic links

out. With the subtle variation of the first subject with which Brahms introduces the transition at bar 44, the motive assumes a key role in the opening
notes of the first violin figure, and thereafter it is permeative in the section,
appearing in augmentation and diminution from bars 58 to 66. After the
contrast of the second subject, where the shape is appropriately liquidated
for the new context, it returns to dominate the closing group. Even the
subtle contrast of the movement's coda draws on it. The principle is the
same in the finale, with the motive initiating the first theme's long bass
statement. The finale links in turn to the third movement which clearly
relates to the derivation which creates the second subject.

Given such a network of related themes, Brahms can afford to extend his
scope in their treatment without fear of incoherence, not least in the fields
of phrase and rhythm. The first movement and finale both explore extended
phrases which deceive the listener's sense of accent for long stretches, a
quality built in to the slow movement from the start. But the most striking
freedom is in the rhythmic methods of the third movement. Here Brahms
constructs a variation section on the main theme by diminution and metrical
change, completely transforming its character, yet retaining its identity: the
listener hears a variation. In the process of retransition to the original
tempo also, the sheer dominance of rhythm over theme in the composer's
imagination can have few parallels in the nineteenth century, prior to the
era of Stravinsky.

Ex. 65 Second Symphony, third movement, rhythmic transformations

Tragic *Overture*

The contrast of mood between the Concerto and Symphony and the next
orchestral works – the *Tragic* Overture of 1880 and the Third Symphony of
1883 is very great. Indeed, it is not surprising to learn from Kalbeck of the

possible dramatic associations of both works, for they possess a markedly gestural quality. Kalbeck argues that the Overture and the middle movements of the Symphony were part of music intended for a production of *Faust*[3] at the Vienna Burgtheater which never came to fruition. Although, as he pointed out, Brahms actually denied that he had any specific tragedy in mind for the Overture, the dramatic association seems clear. It is interesting to recall that the sketches for the Overture go back over ten years, and were associated with those for the *Alto Rhapsody*, another work of very dramatic and Goethean associations. As regards the Symphony, even Joachim, not normally given to interpreting music programmatically strongly considered the finale suggests the story of Hero and Leander, the second subject recalling to him 'the picture of an intrepid swimmer fighting his way towards the promised goal in the face of wind and storm'.[4]

Yet, it is the Overture which perhaps points most clearly to a dramatic background, for two reasons: the character of its opening subject and the unusual and incongruous nature of the form. Like the *Alto Rhapsody* – and even more relevantly, the *Parzenlied*, also set in D minor and composed only shortly afterwards – the work opens in harmonic ambivalence, a characteristic which, whilst appropriate to those dramatic settings, is without parallel in the purely instrumental compositions. The arresting chords of the opening are left ambiguous by the omission of the third, C sharp, which would define the dominant of D minor, and the unison theme which follows stresses F, the repeated cadence maintaining the original ambiguity. Although familiarity with Brahms's modal language would suggest D minor, the passage has certainly encouraged more speculative interpretation, as by Schoenberg, who even suggests the possibility of the Phrygian mode on A.[5] In either case, the passage can be seen as a further example of Brahms's exploration of modal effects, here in a dramatic context:

Ex. 66 *Tragic* Overture, op. 81, bars 1–6

However, this subject is not destined to sustain a conventional sonata structure. For, relative not only to Brahms's norms but also the works which offer the obvious background – Beethoven's overtures for the productions of Goethe's *Egmont* or Collin's *Coriolanus*, the structure is relaxed. Indeed, the transition section almost gives the impression of space-filling, a long series of sequences from D minor to F which suggest descriptive or evocative purposes rather than the normal thematic processes. Although the passage is justified formally by the great thematic fullness of the second group and closing group – a sequence of five ideas growing in intensity – the effect is notable. With the development section, it becomes even more marked, for the return of the first subject in the tonic heralds not the redistribution of sonata elements in the ways so richly explored in the chamber works – or later in the symphonic works – but a central passage of a completely contrasted nature. It is not a conventional development, neither is it a character variation section. It takes the dotted figure from the first subject and works it in gentle imitation, building to a climax, and relaxing back, without destroying its self-sufficient character. The impressive retransition to the recall of the second subject and remaining material effects a complete change of mood. Unassailable as the work may be in its formal logic and balance, one gains the impression of some deeply programmatic ideas adapted to a sonata context and in uneasy relationship with features of that tradition.

Third Symphony

Any tension of form and content is entirely absent from the Third Symphony. Whatever the nature of its background, Brahms here creates a work of immediately impressive unity and direction – his shortest and most gestural symphony by far, whose assurance was immediately caught by Hanslick with reference to the first movement: 'it seems to have been created in the flush of an inspired hour'.[6] Yet its achievement is by no means straightforward. Brahms here integrates a wider range of stylistic elements than in any other mature orchestral work – even than the B flat String Quartet. For his deep lyric preoccupations emerge even more strikingly here for their contrast with ideas of a passionate intensity. Both the middle movements resort to styles associated with smaller forms, the slow movement's main theme a Brahmsian folksong, with the simplest harmonic support and simple echo at the end of the phrases, the third movement a longing cello melody which, though less forceful in manner, recalls the viola movement of the B flat String Quartet. Nor is the contrast restricted to the middle movements. The second subject of the first is another simple idea, though very subtly varied by motivic repetition, which characteristically displaces the accent of the opening. It creates high relief in relation to the force of the opening subject which returns in the closing group and dominates the transition to development and most of that section. Comparable intensity exists in the finale after the quiet introduction of the first theme. The second subject here is a driving idea which leads to very abrupt cross-rhythms. The balance of the outer movements – and indeed the pattern of the main part of the finale up to the coda, reflect the First Symphony.

This integration exists within the context of a work in which two features are particularly powerful, the colour and finish of the scoring and the structure of the whole, as regards thematic and harmonic recurrence and tonal planning. This symphony has often been regarded as Brahms's most well-finished, most carefully calculated orchestral work. In its scoring it comes closer to his chamber ideals than any other, with clear links to the Serenades. Thus, the second movement contrasts a wind chorus with strings in the first section, whilst the drone second subject of the first movement clearly recalls the texture of the Menuetto of the First Serenade. The third movement recalls the Horn Trio in giving solo horn the reprise of the main subject so lightly scored in its accompaniment as to suggest chamber music. But Brahms also employs the orchestral effect in a very distinctive way. The coda of the finale, for example, makes highly atmospheric use of muted and pizzicato strings in its transformation of earlier ideas, impressions which linger on in the work of successors, most immediately Humperdinck, who borrows the source progression C – A flat – C from the close of the slow movement directly for the end of the *Hansel and Gretel* Overture.[7] In structure the work is perhaps even more notable in his output, for, whereas in the earlier symphonies and their chamber forerunners he seemed concerned to unify in the infrastructure and leave the surface to present contrast, he here guides the listener by the use of a basic theme, so clear as to obscure the many more subtle links to between movements. Thus the first movement is literally articulated by the gestures of its basic idea reaching its fulfilment in the quiet recall and transformation to major of the work's close, in which the poignancy of the close of the Clarinet Quintet seems so clearly foreshadowed in theme and texture. So powerful is the impression of this motto that it led Kalbeck to see the work as a self-portrait – Brahms's *Eroica* Symphony. Whilst there is no ground for attributing to Brahms the verbal motto 'Frei aber Froh',[8] the nature and extent of the function of the shape F A flat F certainly provides the conditions which encouraged him to this view. For the motto which appears at the outset permeates the entire work. On its transition from the opening statement in the upper parts of the initial wind chords to the work's close, it provides the bass for the new countersubject which functions as the first subject proper and the means of achieving modulation through the first transition – two simple gestures which move the music from the sphere of F to A major through D flat. The very broadly planned retransition to the recapitulation similarly uses the progression to dramatic effect. Whilst the harmonic supports are not present in the slow and third movements, the thematic outline permeates the main theme of the second movement and also the progress of the finale. The process by which an idea generates a counterpoint which then plays a central role, already shown in the *Requiem*, and First Symphony is here revealed in a particularly poetic manner, the work's opening being marvellously recollected in tranquillity, and its harmony also recalled at the quiet close of the second movement.

Ex. 67 (i) Third Symphony, op. 90, opening
(ii) Finale bars 294–9

Other gestures are, however, pervasive. The second section of the slow movement, a series of ominous chords beneath a wind figure, clearly recurs in the solemn introduction to the finale at bar 19, used as a preparation for the build-up to the powerful transition and provides another subject for reflection in the coda, revealing, by its treatment, the possible origin of the finale's stepwise theme itself.

Kalbeck's desire to see a motto 'F A F' as a 'leitmotive of his life and art' may betray more than a hint of the desire to see his hero as the equal of the master Kalbeck spent so much time opposing – Wagner, and may well reflect the realisation of a Wagnerian element in the work. Wagner died in

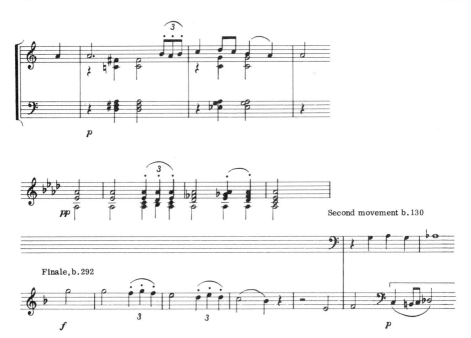

Ex. 68 Third Symphony, second movement, bars 41–2 and finale, bars 19–21

February 1883, and the work received its final form in the Summer of that year. Brahms admired Wagner and there seems no reason to suppose that the homage which he paid to earlier composers in his compositional methods should not also have been accorded to a contemporary. If he feared Wagner in the field of operatic composition, he knew that as a symphonist he was able to absorb such influences – here the principle of dramatic transformation – into his own language. If Hanslick's reaction was right, and this work was short in creation, if not perhaps in its sources, such an interpretation may not be unreasonable.

Yet this was surely not the only stimulus to the work. Like his most deeply experienced works – the *Requiem*, the First Symphony, the First Piano Concerto, it draws on symbolic ideas, in this case related to the worlds of Schubert and Schumann. In stressing the emotional association of the supposed motto 'Frei aber Froh', Kalbeck repeatedly refers to the Rhine as a symbol of the continuity of Brahms's work. This must reflect Kalbeck's realisation of the striking parallels with the *Rhenish* Symphony, not only the rhythm of which Brahms borrows (broadening the 3/4 metre to 6/4), but his first theme, drawn from bar 451 of Schumann's first movement – an idea which also appears impressively in the slow movement of the *Spring* Symphony, bar 72. That it had some special significance can surely not be dismissed. And the harmonic progression which forms its introduction is identical with the opening of the Schubert Quintet, Brahms realising through it the basic motto F – A flat – F. And just as Schubert's work reflects the implications of this colouring, so does Brahms explore the flat side of F as well as the sharp side related to the A natural of the first theme, to produce a wide, yet deeply organic, tonal scheme. Thus, the second subject appears in A, the same contrast as in the F major Quintet, naturally recapitulating in the parallel key of D major. The slow movement is in C major, the third in C minor. A flat appears as the tonality of the central section of the third movement and of the second idea of the finale, similarly relating to C minor. The final pages restore the opening before removing the ambivalence of the first subject in an unclouded F major. It is fascinating to compare such integration with the treatment of another Schubertian harmonic opening – that of the G major Sextet – which for all its richness draws no such consequences from its material.

Ex. 69   (i) Brahms: Third Symphony, opening subject, bar 3
       (ii) Schumann: *Rhenish* Symphony, bar 1
     (iii) Schumann: *Rhenish* Symphony, bar 451
     (iv) Brahms: Third Symphony, motto
      (v) Schubert: Quintet in C, opening

Fourth Symphony

To many listeners, the Third Symphony might have seemed like the natural goal of Brahms's development as a symphonist in its integration of the simple characters of folksong and romantic lied with an intense instrumental idiom and deep sense of coherence and overall structure, the whole resolving its tensions at the close in a manner increasingly characteristic of the expression of his most profound songs. Yet any such impression would soon have been dispelled by the symphony which followed shortly after in 1885, for here he recalls the wealth of ideas which characterise the Second Symphony and the earnestness and sense of structural culmination of the First Symphony. Yet here the drama is of a different kind; not the classic nineteenth-century struggle 'per ardua ad astra', from minor to major, in Brahms's case replete with romantic symbols in its final stages, but rather an abstract drama which reaches its climax through the sheer intellectual rigour and energy of its finale rather than through any conventional symbols; it ends securely in the key in which it began, E minor. And if the Third Symphony had gained something of the personal quality of its opening from the memories of Schubert and Schumann, this goes back to more austere memories of Beethoven and Bach. For, not only does the finale take Bach as its starting point, but the first movement takes Beethoven. As has been noted, the first subject clearly draws on the slow movement of the 'Hammerklavier' Sonata (bars 78–86) where an identical outline appears as a consequence of the evolving influence of the interval of the third. Yet it comes through an entirely Brahmsian mediation. The setting is very close to the sombre opening in which he was soon to place the first of the Motets op. 110, the same key and broad shape expressing the text 'Ich aber bin elend' – 'But Lord, I am wretched'. Yet the symphony's is a more animated, complex type of expression whose distinctive two-note phrasing actually finds its closest parallel in a piece in total stylistic contrast to the motet – the Waltz in D minor, op. 39 no. 9. From this very personal stylistic chemistry, Brahms builds a movement and a work whose lofty style is closest to the *Tragic* Overture, a greater example of the 'sublime style' noted in the great choral works with orchestra. And from them it takes much of its orchestral character, especially the fullness of Brahms's scoring, and the telling use of the flute, especially at bar 128 of the finale – surely a Grecian symbol.

  In viewing the work as a whole, its background again provides a key to its special nature and sense of direction. Indeed, it may well reveal the reverse case to that of the First Symphony, for whereas it seems clear that it was the resolution of the first movement's implications which provided the compositional problem of the earlier work, it appears likely that the finale was here the starting point and thus determinant of the work's structural nature. And even if other ideas existed at this earlier stage, the special nature of the finale provided the dominant focus for their working and shape.

Although the precise date is not known, Brahms had shown interest in the chaconne bass of the finale of Bach's Cantata No. 150 *Nach Dir, Herr verlanget mich* some time before the symphony's appearance. The conductor Siegfried Ochs recalls him demonstrating to Hans von Bülow the structure of the Bach movement, to which von Bülow responded coolly, arguing that it needed more than voices. Brahms agreed, commenting 'What would you say to a symphonic movement written on this theme one day? But it is too lumpish, too straightforward. It would have to be chromatically altered in some way.'[9] Just how the alteration was effected is clear from the work, where Brahms extends the model from its five-bar length to eight bars, substituting equal dotted minims for its minim-crotchet pattern and creating a climax in the chromatic alteration of A sharp, now appearing as leading note to the dominant, B. But how the work as a whole stood in his mind at this earlier stage is not clear. That he was aware of the possibility of a variation finale can be assumed from the model of Beethoven, and the *St Antoni* Variations had already presented a basso ostinato variation finale. Yet the precise nature of a finale which reflected both stimuli – that of a symphonic design in a harmonically restricted form – must have occupied him for long before a solution became clear.

In considering the problems, Brahms drew on a considerable knowledge of the form of the chaconne and passacaglia, as has earlier been shown. In the actual period of the work's completion, he acknowledged special interest in the Organ Passacaglia in G minor by Georg Muffat, describing it to Elizabeth von Herzogenberg in 1883 as very fine and acknowledging possession of a copy.[10] His work on the Couperin Edition for Chrysander would also have given him an acquaintance with an example from the very different tradition of the French clavecinists through the form of the Rondeau Passacaille. But the movement for which he had the deepest feeling was the Bach Chaconne for unaccompanied violin. He wrote to Clara, to whom the arrangement for the piano, left hand, was dedicated, in the following terms.

> For me the Chaconne is one of the most incredible pieces of music. Using a single system for a little instrument, the man writes a whole world of the deepest and most powerful expression. If I ask myself if I had written this piece – been able to conceive it – I know for certain the emotions excited would have driven me mad. If one does not have a great violinist at hand, the most exquisite of joys is surely simply to let the Chaconne ring in one's mind. But the piece certainly entices one to occupy oneself with it somehow.[11]

From this he concludes that the only comparable experience is to play it with the parallel restrictions of left hand alone. It seems interesting that in referring to the other ways of imagining the work recreated he mentions the orchestra. It is not difficult to see the manner and structure of this Chaconne, which he knew so intimately, fusing with his transformation of the Bach cantata bass to provide the foundations of a movement through which both vocal and instrumental limitations are transcended in his most powerful variation structure.

Seen against the background of Brahms's earlier variations, this movement is unique in its observation of a clear A B A – Coda form. The contrast
is provided by changes in dynamics, frequently in mode, and partly in
metre; the return of the opening introduces variation both thematically and
in the scope of harmonic movement within the tight restriction of the model,
taken even further in the coda. All the previous variations are continuous,
though the contrast of mode to major is established from the Variation on
an Original Theme. The Bach Chaconne therefore assumes great interest in
its adoption of a ternary outline through contrast of mode, in its variation
of harmony at the reprise (though the theme is not recalled) and in its
length – both movements building to thirty variations from an eight-bar
model. The form of the Chaconne is also crucial to understanding Brahms's
harmonic methods, for, although elements of passacaglia are used in this
movement – that is, of a repeated ground bass ostinato – the chief spirit of
the movement is that of harmonic retention, from which the composer can
dramatically move for effect. The model is compounded of Bach's bass in
modified form as upper part with a Brahmsian bass in which descending
thirds are prominent. This provides the model for the first four variations
and the background to the reprise, with its increasingly free harmonic
working until Brahms breaks completely away from the previous patterns
in the coda, loosening the original phrasing. The intervening harmony is
built either on the ground (variations 4–11, 14–16), or on pedal variants, as
in the central part, variations 12–13. Thus, as in earlier variation movements,
there are two harmonic models with other freer types, though it is the first,
with the theme in the upper part, which has the role of articulating the
large structure.

This represents, therefore, a considerably more complex form than its
immediate predecessor, the ostinato variations of the *St Antoni* Variations.

Ex. 70 Fourth Symphony, op. 98, harmonic models of the finale

Indeed, Brahms brings to fulfilment the inherent influence of the chaconne, noted as early as the variations of the B flat Sextet though with the added aspect of the passacaglia reflected in the Second Serenade and the *St Antoni* Variations, together with the outline of sonata form. It is the latter aspect which creates the variation of the reprise, since development cannot be used in the subdued central section.

Clearly, such a distinctive structure could not have provided the symphonic climax without intimate relations with the other movements. Schoenberg's observation[12] of the contrapuntal connection between the descending thirds of variation 30 and the first subject of the first movement is only one of many which could be made, for this work is perhaps more subtly and comprehensively integrated than any other. Not only are thirds omnipresent in the work's thematic material – as in the bass of the model – but many other links exist, including the anticipation of the ground in the first subject (bars 9–15). Most impressive, however, is the special harmonic language of the work which is drawn from the harmony of the model. Both plagal and Phrygian progressions contribute further to the deeply archaic quality of much of the music. For example, the first subject is built on plagal progressions and the movement ends with a very impressive plagal cadence enhanced by pedal. The harmonic language of the second movement is even more special in its modal associations, as will be shown. All these features serve to underpin the more obvious surface function of variation. For the principle of successive variation which dominates the finale also permeates the work as a whole.

The links are clearest in the first movement for two principal reasons; the structure of the movement as a whole and, directly related to it, the nature of the first subject. Brahms's tendency to recall the opening material after the recapitulation where no repeat is incorporated finds a particularly plain expression in this movement, which brings an approach associated with finales – those of the First and Third Symphonies and of the Piano Quintet into the context of a symphonic first movement. Yet the method is here different, for this is no conflated development/recapitulation structure, but rather a modification of the conventional scheme, since the recapitulation follows the third tonic statement of the idea at bar 246. The special form arises from the special nature of the main subject itself, a lyric paragraph whose essential sixteen bar structure is extended by internal variation to create a sectional impression – the sense of a model which demands repetition in a way quite unlike the main subjects of the other symphonies. Thus the movement assumes a variation-aspect at two levels. Viewed most broadly, it falls into three sections, closely related by their presentation of the same passage. Although the third statement is made more elusive by the recall of its opening phrases in augmentation, linked by figuration in the strings, the overall effect is clear when the theme resumes at bar 246. As far as the sections themselves are concerned, they also appear strongly variational through the immediate repetition of the first theme, that of the development offering an alternative to that of the exposition, bars 145–152 comparing with bars 1–7. Thus Brahms draws on his earlier tendency to construct the transition by variation of the first subject (compare with the Second Symphony) into a much broader context; for, as well as the sections of passing variation which have become so characteristic, although never with the clarity and deep thematicism of, for example, bars 80–6 or 95–8, the development draws so often on variation that it directly recalls the finale. Thus, after the varied repeat of the opening of the development, bars 169–84 present another section of clear variational identity, here through motivic variation of the preceding bars treated in a stretto which quickly removes the sense of accentual identity, offering yet a further example of how Brahms learned from Beethoven the art of displacing the beat through the relentless repetition of a simple figure. This passage is complemented at bar 192 by a more direct variation of the opening subject, the section again alternating with the marcato figure of the transition which serves to direct and articulate the music's progress. At bar 119, the finale is even more clearly foreshadowed, mediating between the variation and the work's first subject, which it clearly outlines, drawing particularly on the original flute parts to ensure connection. In turn, the following passage from bar 237 varies the following bars, focusing on a one-bar figure, whilst recalling the colour-contrast of the variations which lead to the reprise of the finale. It is inherent in such a structure that radical alterations of the recapitulation would have disturbed the variational relationship of the first three parts. Rather, as in the finale, it is the coda which exhibits the most developmental quality with the most rapid modulations and intense treatment of ideas. Yet variation remains the chief model, the powerful statement of the first subject at bar 394 is remarkable in its transformation, the theme appearing in canon between the outer parts, actually retaining its identity for far longer than the ear might suggest (14 bars in all) before a bridge to an intense treatment of the transition idea of bar 414, the remarkable intensity achieved through a use of stretto in which Brahms seems to press to extremes the possible relationship between the harmonies permissible in his style and the logic of the contrapuntal movement, a quality which he shared to a remarkable degree with Mozart. In a period which includes some of Brahms's most powerful first-movement codas, this is surely the most impressive in its nature and its structural function.

Of the impressive central movements with which Brahms completes his overall scheme, the second relates most clearly to the principles outlined. Indeed, its leisurely first section from bar 5 parallels that of the first in its relation to earlier works, an eight-bar theme of the simplest phrasing, which returns after a nine-bar digression to complete an exposition in simple A B A form. The following transition proceeds again by simple variation to establish, through ideas which relate to the parallel part of the first movement, the dominant of B for the second subject, after which there is a further variation of the first theme with descending wind figures reflecting the first subject of the work and strings employing pizzicato. Bar 74 initiates an imitative development very much in the spirit of that of the finale of op. 18, after which the second subject completes the conflated scheme: 1 – tr – 2 – 1 – dev – 2 – coda. Yet its straightforwardness comes into a completely different perspective when set in its harmonic context.

It can be seen as perhaps the boldest and most far-reaching of Brahms's experiments with modal effects. For, the opening partly suggests a tonic C; despite the preceding cadence, one interprets the unison opening as rooted in the lower mediant of E minor. Yet at the end of the phrase, Brahms turns the closing E into the tonic of a modified sonata movement which makes a conventional contrast (though now unusual for Brahms) with the dominant, B, for its second subject. Such an opening must, however, have a consequence in a Brahmsian movement and the key of C returns in the closing bars as an alternate harmonisation of the opening theme in succession to the chromatic harmonisation of the theme in E. Thus Brahms juxtaposes the keys of E and C through a common theme. The 'framing' effect of the C tonality and its final resolution can be shown as in example 71.

Ex. 71 Fourth Symphony, second movement, bars 1–3 and 113–15

Whilst this passage can be seen as simply one of effect, the suggestion of a Phrygian tonality, it may also be seen in more far-reaching terms. For, unlike the other authentic modes, the dominant of the Phrygian is not on B, but on C, since it cannot form a perfect fifth from B to F sharp. Thus,

though Brahms may well begin with a mere 'effect', the harmonic implications are readily grasped and he, though very briefly, actually contrives
to close with a Phrygian aspect. The Austrian theorist Heinrich Schenker
once stated that the capacity to write in the modes lay even beyond a genius
like Beethoven,[13] that the Lydian movement of op. 132 simply used modern
tonality to suggest a mode through the omission of any B flat and other
means. Is it not possible that Brahms's deep interest in the issue led him
to go a little further in the attempt to unite modern tonality and the principles of modality in one movement?

   After such tonal stress the key of the third movement appears inevitable.
Yet in its manner the movement stands in strong contrast to the parallel
movements of the later works. As is often pointed out, Brahms avoids the
scherzo-substitutes of his maturity for a scherzo of an individual nature –
not a 6/8, but a driving 2/4 movement. Yet its character is surely not without
precedent. Just as Brahms had drawn on the 'Hammerklavier' Sonata as
the starting point for a reinterpretation of a powerful idea, so the deep
historical background to this work leads him to draw on the second movement
of the late Piano Sonata in A flat op. 110 whose thematic outline complements its metrical character in providing his basis. Yet in no other sense
does the form relate to tradition, for Brahms constructs a continuous movement, sustained by variation in which the Trio contrast is limited to a very
brief passage from bar 178 to bar 198 which simply transforms the character
of the opening, to play a part in the broader scheme.

Academic Festival *Overture*

Of the three works which stand outside the tradition with which Brahms
was centrally preoccupied, the *Academic Festival* Overture is the shortest but
by no means the least interesting. For, in view of his reputation in the
'progressive' quarters of the day, it is revealing to observe his response to
the challenge of producing a work to acknowledge the award of a Doctorate
from the University of Breslau in 1879. A more predictable piece might well
have been its companion, the *Tragic* Overture, if not so titled, or a work
demonstrating Brahms's 'academic' skills. But he knew how to honour the
occasion without undue earnestness, for the work offers many surprises in
both its scoring and, more especially, its form and context. In scoring it
adopts a more popular vein than is normal, with prominent use of trumpets
in chorus (see bar 64), celebratory orchestral tuttis with triangle, bass drum,
cymbals and piccolo, and unison melody with full dress demisemiquaver
scales for the violins in a manner much closer to Grand Opera than to
Brahms's orchestral background to complete the movement. Of the form,
Brahms once jokingly referred to the work as 'a merry potpourri of student
songs à la Suppé' – an obvious reference to Suppé's overture *Flotte Bursche*,
which also includes several student songs, one of them used by Brahms,

'Gaudeamus Igitur'.[14] Comparison shows something of Brahms's achievement. The Suppé work simply strings four songs together in contrasting sections, the first beginning 'Maestoso' in C time, the second 'vivace' 2/4, the third Maestoso 3/4 and the last 'allegro con brio', 3/4. Brahms's only concession to this likely inspiration written in 1863 is the figure he employs over dominant harmony from bar 84 to bar 87 to initiate the first subject proper, drawing on bar 2 of the Suppé work. This apart, however, Brahms's student songs appear in a very different context – that of a sonata movement of very unusual design. The section up to that forementioned is not expositional, but introductory, a feature which confused his friends, though its function is clear if the minor tonality and use of its opening motive is seen against the following 'un poco maestoso', which transforms it. The passage in question is preceded by the first song, 'Wir hatten gebauet ein stattisches Haus'. The transition continues with variation leading to a second theme in E major, the first of a two-stage exposition which will present the song 'Fuchsliedes' ('Was kommt dort von der Höh') in the dominant at bar 157, serving then as closing group and unveiling its influence on the opening as the development proceeds. The recapitulation is almost completely obscured at bar 277 in order to shift the focus after considerable variation of earlier material, to the coda at bar 379, where appears 'Gaudeamus Igitur' to crown the work which, incidentally, recalls the close of Schumann's *Spring* Symphony in B flat in its final chord with triangle.

Piano Concerto in B flat

While, by its nature, the *Academic Festival* Overture had no precedent in Brahms's orchestral output, the two final concertos belong quite clearly to a tradition which they significantly extend. The B flat Piano Concerto has only one precedent in terms of its pianism – his own D minor Concerto, which itself reconciles symphonic and concerto elements from Beethoven. Yet Brahms expanded his original concept to include a fourth, scherzo movement and thus place the work outside the traditions he acknowledged – although Liszt had employed a scherzo, of a very different kind, in his First Concerto of 1848. The Double Concerto also extends tradition in the use of two soloists and orchestra. Yet in the form of its first movement it relates very closely to its predecessor which established a pattern for the entry of the soloists and the main points of articulation, whilst the more distant relation of Beethoven's Triple Concerto offers clear parallels for the handling of the string soloists. Of the two works, the Piano Concerto is in every sense the more broadly laid out. Its most notable feature is the relationship of the soloists in the first movement, which draws on Beethoven's example, the opening of the *Emperor* Concerto rather than the Fourth or even the Mendelssohn or Schumann Concertos, in giving the soloist a powerful and extensive rhetorical introduction. But Brahms handles this plan in his own way, creating not a Beethovenian call to arms, but a Brahmsian world of romanticism, symbolised in the presentation of the first subject by a solo horn to which the pianist responds.

Of the two powerful background models, it is the Beethoven work which offers Brahms his model for concerto writing, since, unlike the D minor Concerto, though like the Violin Concerto, Brahms follows tradition in giving the soloist the role of commentator on the orchestral material of the tutti exposition rather than making the part inseparable from the ongoing musical argument. This gave him the opportunity to exploit fully the soloist's capacity to vary the orchestral material in a way which was limited by the scope of the violin and his knowledge of it. The deepening maturity of Brahmsian pianism as shown in the *Klavierstücke* op. 76 is here explored to the very full to create writing which was without precedent in its difficulty, and has always been regarded as representing the summit of orchestral pianism. Two factors underpin the character of the first movement: the pervading influence of the opening three notes of the first subject – B flat – C – D – first given, and the ease, yet extreme subtlety, of the pianistic variation. The orchestral exposition is built very economically, the three-note figure pointing the passages of greatest emphasis, such as the closing group from bar 61, which is taken up by the piano at its following re-entry at bar 68 and, though less overtly because of its harmonic context, at the transition to the second subject at bar 42; indeed, this idea frames the second subject, providing its closing bar, prior to the assertive closing group at bar 56. Though very powerful, this exposition is compact and clearly articulated and provides the basis of a much broader and relaxed treatment of its material, the opening piano cadenza at bar 68 resuming the grand manner of the opening and resuming quietly the first subject at bar 73, from which it builds back into the rhetoric of the exposition, with the three-note figure prominent in directing the flow. The flexibility with which Brahms unites literal figurative variation with symphonic extension and growth is especially clear in bars 98 – 118, where two-bar and later one-bar orchestral phrases are repeated in direct variation and, from bar 107 with extension, to make more effective transition to the next orchestral idea at bar 118. Finally, this figurative decoration concluded, the expected return of the orchestral closing group comes in through a powerful transformation of the second subject, its reflective lyricism now rendered passionately assertive through its wide choral realisation in the minor, leading an intense passage to the closing paragraph which recalls the three-note figure with double trills which bring into this more suave symphonic context the rigour of pianism already seen in the D minor Concerto. The much greater formal subtleties of the later concerto reflect those of the Violin Concerto. Here Brahms makes a particularly effective retransition to the recapitulation through dovetailing of the horn entry over the piano figuration, and alternating passages between piano and orchestra. Similar qualities characterise the rondo finale, whose clear rondo pattern in the exposition and alternation between soloist and orchestra recall the formal clarity of the First Concerto. Yet both overall structure and themes are handled with much greater refinement – indeed, such qualities would have undermined the assertive mood of the earlier finale. Brahms draws on a Beethoven example in the harmonic setting which makes the rondo theme so memorable – its opening not in the tonic, but in the subdominant region, E flat, the tonic only appearing at the theme's close at bar 8. With the reappearance of the second group at bar 65, the gipsy-inclined melody (which takes up from the suave rhythm of Nos 1 and 8 of the Hungarian Dances – and provides, in turn, the idea of Dohnányi's variation 4 in his Variations for Piano and Orchestra), appears not in the dominant, which is only established at bar 81 (again with the initial stress on the subdominant), but in A minor, the mediant of F: this relation is recalled in the recapitulation, A – F balanced naturally by D minor – B flat. From the close of the exposition, the formal pattern recalls that of the Violin Concerto in the fluidity of the central section of the rondo structure, with the suggestion of a distinct thematic contrast, though one which actually arises through the natural and capricious treatment of the original ideas. Indeed comparison with the parallel passage of the Double Concerto is illuminating since it similarly makes pointed use of a forceful dotted rhythm. Yet, whereas the latter passage is in total contrast to the preceding material, this grows naturally from the original ideas and is worked into a rhapsodic section led by the soloist concluding on the dominant from which the first theme returns in its original form at bar 251. Like the earlier concertos, variation provides the contrasted mood of the coda, preceded by gentle suggestions of the theme's opening, with a motivic directness which recalls the function of the opening notes of the first movement. Further links to the Violin Concerto appear in the slow movement; here it is the cello which provides an instrumental theme – again drawn from song as shown, on which the soloist improvises, employing initial figuration which again recalls the distinctive feature of the earlier piano concerto (compare bar 29 of the D minor with bar 25 of the B flat Concerto). A broad A B A structure with developmental central section again serves, though here it is significantly varied by the false return of the opening in F sharp minor at bar 71. Moreover a very atmospheric passage for piano with clarinets precedes this, almost as a concession to pure sound; the obvious link to Liszt's E flat Concerto suggests some special significance for the passage.

Had Brahms completed this work in three movements as he may well have intended, it would – assuming the material in question was that which we know – have consisted of three movements in the same key, for the slow movement retains the overall tonic. The scherzo introduces the mediant minor contrast; this may have been the intended Scherzo, for the Violin Concerto, as a tonic minor contrast, prior to a mediant major slow movement. Although the manner of the movement is clearly imaginable on the violin, it is by no means clear why Brahms conceived a four-movement scheme in either case, for it raises problems of balance and structure in the Concerto as we know it. Brahms cannot have intended to produce a symphony in concerto form by the addition of the scherzo, since the material of the finale is not really weighty enough – at least in terms of his normal capacity to achieve balance and resolution. In practical terms, the hypothetical three-movement scheme needed tonal contrast, and it may be that Brahms wished to retain the existing elements for his second work in the form. In this case he needed another movement, and a scherzo was an obvious form in this context. However, its character and form would perhaps have better suited the Violin Concerto because of the clearer relation to the manner of the finale, especially its drive and gipsy element. The stylistic relation of the present finale to that which precedes it raises problems, despite the excellence of the music as such. Unlike the other concerto finales, Brahms here produces a much more relaxed conception – a dancing subject not dissimilar to the figuration of the Capriccio in B minor from op. 76, to which it bears some relationship in ideas (compare bars 19–20 of the Concerto's finale with bars 15–20 of the Capriccio). The breadth with which the movement is planned in relation to the total pattern indicates that there is no failure of structural sense. Brahms clearly conceived the whole in a much more relaxed and broad pattern than the other concertos and the finale offers a good balance to the breadth of the character of the work's opening with solo horn and piano. In the breadth with which the finale is planned – and it employs an extensive coda to which, though resorting to variation in quicker tempo as does that of the Violin Concerto, as well as a broadly spanned middle section, it is clearly matched. The problem concerns its character and contrasts. It lacks overall sufficient force and internal character to balance the rhetorical force of the first movement – especially its dramatic structure. Moreover, its gipsy idioms such as the singing second subject are insufficiently powerful to match the scherzo. The insertion of this scherzo with its immense force tends to divide the work into two halves – the first and second much more powerfully scaled than the third and fourth, creating a pattern which only a more impressive and dramatic finale could have balanced.

Much of the effect of the scherzo lies in its form, the interest of which falls into better perspective when placed beside the scherzo from which it draws its character – that of the First Serenade. The concerto movement brings the suppressed intensity of the earlier scherzo to full realisation in a theme which begins identically in outline as in key. Yet, whilst the earlier movement is set in a conventional context, the basis is a Scherzo in A B A form to which is contrasted a Trio in B flat. This movement is continuous in form, the repeated first section containing a theme in marked contrast leading to a development into which is integrated a trio-like contrast passage for orchestra, though one immediately subjected to pianistic variation of a very contrasted nature. This integration of the forms and characters of the scherzo/trio and sonata form reflects Brahms's approach to the scherzo form in maturity and makes interesting comparison with the scherzos of the C minor Piano Quartet and Fourth Symphony.

Double Concerto

Viewed very broadly, the Double Concerto may be seen as uniting the dominant features of the two previous concertos with the much greater concentration of material and yet compositional elan of the later music. Indeed, links of working to the String Quintet in G major are made even clearer by the sharp inclination to the gipsy manner, especially in the outer movements. Although Kalbeck stressed the influence of Bach's multi concertos on the work, it seems clear that Beethoven was the chief background. As in the Violin Concerto, Joachim's technique certainly reflects the study of Bach – especially the Chaconne, but the character of the whole relates rather to the Triple Concerto, in which the keyboard so often assumes an accompanimental, orchestral role, and the writing for the two stringed instruments throws many links to the Brahms's work. As the Violin Concerto leans on the framework of Beethoven's concerto, so does the Double Concerto on the Triple Concerto, though with much greater individuality. In so doing, Brahms made an important contribution to the repertory of the cello. Although Brahms's admiring reference to the Dvorak Concerto is often quoted – 'had I known . . . I could have tried to compose one myself'[15] – this work makes great strides to the establishment of a full concerto form involving the cello, one neglected since the Schumann Concerto, which was never played after its composition in 1848 until the pioneering work of Casals in the early twentieth century. Furthermore, as Brahms's second concerto with string soloist, it was also intimately associated with Joachim. In the years following the completion of the Violin Concerto Brahms had grown progressively distant from his friend, through siding with Joachim's wife in his divorce. Clara was of the opinion that this was a work of reconciliation and she noted in her diary[16] 'Joachim and Brahms have at last spoken to each other after many years'. In this connection, Kalbeck points out that the second subject is drawn from the first movement of Viotti's Violin Concerto in A minor[17] from which Brahms retains the rhythm, though evolving a new theme and harmony. However other links can surely be added. The predictable F A E variant may be found in the entry of the violin in the answering phrase of the first subject of the solo exposition bar 116, as well as in the rondo finale, the reiterated figure at bars 3–4 being aurally memorable. The gipsy association may well have thrown another memory back to the earliest years – the main theme of the second movement seems to recall the fourth variation of the Variations on a Hungarian Song in key and shape, if not rhythm.

In the powerful and expansive first movement, Brahms brings together two principles from major works of the period, the preceding Piano

Concerto in B flat major and the following final chamber work, the String Quintet in G major. From the Concerto he drew the expansive introduction for soloist, here greatly extended in scope to present both main themes by cellist and violinist respectively, both within a context of introductory improvisation leading to an assertive scalic drive to the dominant: and in the first subject of the orchestral exposition we find a parallel to the first subject of the Quintet in the forceful evolution of ideas in which tonal mobility is very clear in moving through several regions of G in a continuous passage of much greater length, essentially in bars 57–77, points of thematic connection being minimised harmonically. Moreover, this mature character also reflects an older tendency in themes in the minor mode, that of establishing a mediant relationship, here very quickly to C through its dominant G permitted by the modal inflexion of the main theme – A – G – E. These two characters – the driving and evolutionary thematic principle and the reflective and improvisatory – provide the movement's main contrasts. In broad formal terms, the fullness of the introduction predicts an even greater degree of variation of basic ideas than in the first movement of the preceding concerto. Thus, the appearance of the soloists from bar 112 presents a clear variation by extension of the first bar through three more bars of improvisation for cello, the violin following with the same treatment of the second bar of the theme, leading to further, diminished variants in rhetorical style in which contrary motion is especially characteristic. The same principle of improvisatory extension appears in the second subject, given first to cello from bar 153, from which follows new material leading to recall of the tutti at bar 198, resuming the original material of bar 79. With the development Brahms returns to the introduction in both material and tonality. However, the original harmonic ambiguity which arises from the unison presentation of the first theme starting on E (E – D – B, C – B – E), which might be a modal structure on E (by analogy with the opening of the *Tragic* Overture beginning modally on A) rather than the actual modal dominant of A minor, is now partly resolved through harmonisation implying E minor, which quickly leads to the dominant of G major. The improvisatory relationship to the introduction inspires a playful development with much use of sequence which leads to a retransition of the greatest subtlety in the free play of the two instruments. In both the remaining major points of articulation – the return of the tutti at bar 290 and the commencement of the coda at bar 416, harmonic effect suggestive of modality is prominent. Thus, the approach to the recapitulation is through the dominant of G major in the progression G – E7th – A minor, reflecting the relationship in the following tutti bars which proceed A minor – (D minor – F major) G major. At the coda, the tonic is regained through its subdominant, D minor, the preceding cadence presenting the tonic major as dominant of D minor with a characteristically archaic progression, the whole passage from bar 410 to bar 415 reading in essence: C – F major – G major minor – A major. The following progression is equally striking D minor – G major – C major – A minor prolonged to the final cadence from bar 420 to bar 427.

To a much greater extent than in the earlier concertos the last two movements of the Double Concerto serve to balance the first rather than in ternary (as in op. 15 and op. 77) or binary (as in op. 83) relationship. Any problem concerning the relationship of the finale to the first movement is completely solved in this work by the character of the Finale, which reflects the gipsy qualities of the passionate string writing in an overtly gipsy finale in a manner obviously analogous to the Quintet. Thus one notes particularly the tonal character of the rondo theme whose progression resumes the preoccupations of the first movement – A minor – C – (E minor) – D minor – A minor, with the strong move at bar 21 to C. However, the rondo is not now of conventional sonata type but a fusion of this with the central contrast characteristic of single rondos, with a sonata exposition yet a quite distinct middle section, stressing the Hungarian character in its dotted rhythms and its modal enrichments, as at bars 119–22, which recall the first movement. Unlike the other concerto finales, however, the pervasive variation does not determine a coda in quicker tempo; rather Brahms recalls the first theme in the reflective manner noted at the close of the Third Symphony before the abrupt recall of the opening. The slow movement is comparably tight in structure and expression. Again it differs significantly from precedent in outer plan, with no introductory section, either for orchestra or orchestral soloist, rather beginning directly with the two soloists in unison presenting a theme of great simplicity with direct orchestral repetitions. The move to the central section is also direct, the cadence in D leading directly to the contrast of F for the chorale-like second section in which the soloists elaborate with figurations strongly akin to those of the slow movements of the piano concertos, already observed.

Part Four

10

The Final Period

The two works with which Brahms was occupied during the Ischl Summer of 1890, the String Quintet in G major and the revision of the Piano Trio in B major, symbolise the transition towards retirement from composition which Brahms planned from the following year, the year in which he also drew up his will. He offered the four-handed version of the Quintet in December of that year with the remark: 'The time has come for you to say goodbye to any further compositions of mine.'[1] Henceforth, he seems to have nothing other than the revision for publication of existing items, most obviously those of his most cherished project – the collection of 49 German Folksongs for solo voice and piano. That the two other collections – the Eleven Chorale Preludes for Organ and the Thirteen Canons for Female Voices also derived in part from earlier years seems very likely from their style and resources. Canons had been a lifelong preoccupation, and the setting for female voices points to the possibility of much earlier origin of the contents, if not the conception of the collection. Similarly, Brahms had no obvious motive for writing for organ at this stage, and grounds were long ago advanced for the view of the origin of some of the material in the period of the earliest organ music. Thus, the traditional view of Brahms turning to religious music on his deathbed may well not be true – for even the *Serious Songs* seem in part of earlier provenance in conception. That he was preoccupied with death from 1890 was observed by Kalbeck, and there is a profoundly resigned quality to much of the music. But there seems no special reason to assume that he knew of his approaching end.

Whether Brahms's output would have remained in this form without outside stimulus is a matter of conjecture. That the playing of the Meiningen clarinettist Richard Mühlfeld inspired him to write extensively for an instrument not hitherto conspicuous in his sound world is well known. But it seems very difficult to believe that such rich piano music as appeared between 1892 and 1893 was dependent for its creation upon this prompt. Rather it seems to reflect his observation to Clara in 1894 to the effect that he no longer wrote for the public, but only for himself.[2] Although this period can rightly be termed 'autumnal', not least because of the deep colouring of the clarinet works, especially with strings, resignation is not their only quality. The assertive, rhetorical aspect is there to the last, as in the Rhapsody op. 119 no. 4 in E flat major, the Scherzo of the Clarinet Sonata in this key, or even the last of the *Serious Songs*. The 'autumnal' character arises more deeply from the remarkable synthesis of elements which reveal the composer in his technical and expressive essence. Even such a distinctive element as the gipsy idiom is expressed in new ways as part of the language, as in the slow movement of the Clarinet Quintet – or, even more subtly, the first subject, whose turning shape like that of the Intermezzo in E flat minor op. 118 no. 6 can be traced back to the improvisatory shapes of the Hungarian Dances. Yet, the final concentration of Brahms's language was not to be without its consequence. If deeply retrospective in terms of the composer's musical symbols and mode of expression, the ultimate concentration of means – a thematic process so pervasive that it can be taken as read, new forms of thematic economy, thematicism determining harmony, new degrees of dissonance – had significant influence on some of the younger generation, if not in manner, certainly in working process.

Folksong settings and canons

The depth of Brahms's feeling for his favourite folksong sources confirms that the emphasis he placed on the 1894 collection was entirely genuine. Despite its characteristic exaggeration – 'this is the first time I look back with any tenderness on what I have produced'[3] – these settings ideally represent certain basic aspects of Brahms's art. Since many earlier solo settings had not been published, their release was therefore a proud moment for him, the presentation of the distillation of a lifetime's work, embodying values which were deeply held. Indeed, the recent publication in 1893 of F. M. Böhme's *Deutscher Liederhort*, against which Brahms intended to write a polemic, gave his collection an added personal significance in embodying the finest examples of popular song rather than the 'sweepings of the highroads', as he described the vast and unselected

(i)
Ruhig und erzählend

Voice

1. Ma - ri - a ging aus wan-dern, so fern ins frem-de Land,
2. Sie hat ihn schon ge - fun - den wohl vor des He - ro - des Haus,
3. Das Kreuz das musst er - tra - gen nach Je-ru-sa-lem wohl vor die Stadt,

Piano

Ex. 72 Folksong settings
   (i) 'Maria ging aus wandern' 1858
   (ii) 'Maria ging aus wandern' 1894
   (iii) 'Es ging ein Maidlein zarte' 1858
   (iv) 'Es ging ein Maidlein zarte' 1894

collections of the folksong researchers. Brahms's were not the songs 'which workmen sing at street corners'.[4] And although he seems to have acknowledged from time to time that his values were aesthetic rather than scholarly – hardly surprising, since Erk's *Deutscher Liederhort* came out as early as 1856 – aesthetic values remained central. With very few exceptions his source remained Kretzschmer-Zuccalmaglio, others from Arnold, one source remaining unidentified – that of 'Erlaube mir', no. 2. With the passage of time, he grew ever closer to the perfect realisation of his melodies. A comparison of the 15 settings which were earlier harmonised in the 1858 collection shows this clearly. In both harmony and the aptness of figuration, the later settings are vastly more subtle, as a familiar example confirms (Example 72).

In making these settings into *his* songs – 'Those who hear and see them . . . declare that they are mine and very like my work'[5] – he clothed melodies which he might have written himself, with harmony, counterpoint and piano textures that were entirely his own. It was necessary to change the melodies to a remarkably small degree. Apart from three instances, the changes amount merely to tiny rhythmic details in declamation or the octave transposition of an upbeat. The exceptions are interesting in showing the removal of the commonplace from melodies whose qualities appealed. The highly characteristic and influential 'Maria ging aus wandern' (no. 14) is the result of a radical repositioning of original material, enabling one of his most effective and resourceful settings.[6] 'Es ging ein Maidlein zarte' (no. 21) transforms a melody originally written in the Phrygian mode by Nicolai in the attempt to ridicule the folksong movement. Brahms harmonisation in the 1858 collection (no. 23) is necessarily clumsy, despite its triadic archaisms, and the later version converts it to E minor in a striking setting using pedal and chromatic inner parts. And 'Verstohlen geht der Mond auf' is actually significantly different in structure and cadential pattern than the earlier form, Brahms retaining for this, the last of the settings with Vorsänger and Chorus (nos 43–49), the original intact.

These apart Brahms follows certain procedures with great variety. Some settings are strophic, some add varied accompaniments for alternate verses, some – the most dramatic – employ successive and more expressive accompaniment. Of the total, five are for solo voice and choral response though several are performed as dialogue songs. Few have any introduction worth the name, notably nos 28 and 41. Brahms's harmonic treatment is at its most subtle in the minor settings where he refines the love of modal effect through his contrapuntal sense, most notably in no. 14, a feature which gave him a remarkable affinity with Zuccalmaglio's own melodies, apparently nos 12, 36 and 38.

Such was the love of folksong that it also permeated Brahms's 11 Canons for Female Voices op. 113 of which nos 3–5 draw on melodies set in the *Volkskinderlieder* of 1858 (nos 2, 11 and 5 respectively). Indeed, their striking simplicity characterises most of the collection, of which another seven are simple canons to proverbial texts of the kinds already associated with the genre, two each by Goethe, Eichendorff and Rückert. Only two recall the strictness which characterises the earlier canons, no. 6 a canon by inversion on a text by Fallersleben and no. 9 a double canon of a text by Rückert. But the last piece achieves a balance – a four-part canon on the last touching song of *Die Winterreise*, 'Der Leiermann', accompanied by another canon between two altos, to Rückert's text 'Einförmig ist der Liebe Gram'.

Chorale preludes

It seems quite natural that, having completed his extensive collection of folksongs, which represented an ideal of melodic style for him, he should have also given expression to his love of chorale melodies. The art of chorale harmonisation had already been well represented in the motets. In turning to the form of organ prelude on the chorale Brahms was returning to a form of his youth, for the early works include a prelude and fugue upon a chorale, 'O Traurigkeit, O Herzeleid'. Kalbeck's assertion that they are drawn from a wide period seems therefore perfectly reasonable,[7] and can be supported on grounds of style and formal relationship to the early works. Whether, however, Brahms wished to emulate Bach in the structure of his collection – Kalbeck argues for a parallel with Bach's *Orgelbüchlein* or third part of the *Clavierübung* on the hypothesis that he was planning a longer series – is open to question. As with the parallel cases of the motets, Brahms's response is to the aesthetic character of the works, including their spiritual associations, rather than to any functional purpose or imitation. As far as is known, Brahms never played the organ in his later years. In its turn, the effect of this recreation of Bachian forms and development of new exercised profound influence on the German organ school of the early twentieth century represented chiefly by the work of Reger and Karg Elert.

In proposing a broad chronology for these preludes, relations to Bach and his tradition and to the forms employed in the early motets provide the obvious criteria. Thus, the chorale fugue, 'Mein Jesu, der du mich' is an obvious example of earlier composition, with its cantus firmus entries in the bass preceded by imitation in diminution as in the fugue on 'O Traurigkeit' and the motet fugue on 'Es ist das Heil', whose inversions, diminutions and stretti it mirrors. Though having no earlier models, the two figurative chorales, 'Schmücke dich O liebe Seele' (no. 5) and 'O wie selig seid ihr doch, ihr frommen' (no. 6) both reproduce the Bachian approach, the former with remarkable stylistic affinity, the latter relating very closely to the figuration and harmonic language of the earlier chorale prelude 'O Traurigkeit'. Other preludes evoke Bach with greater freedom. Herzliebster Jesu (no. 2) suggests in its distinctively articulated pedal part the manner of Bach's preludes on 'Durch Adams Fall' and 'In dich hab' ich gehoffet, Herr' from the *Orgelbüchlein*. In 'Es ist ein Ros entsprungen', however, we meet an entirely different mood, a prelude whose complete obscuring of its melody through decoration belongs entirely to Brahms's time. Indeed, in both its character and the way in which the melody is alternated in the tenor register, we observe rather Brahms the pianist, for the idiom suggests the 'tenor thumb' with which Brahms would bring out inner melodies, rather than genuine organ writing, in which context this passage is less effective.

Ex. 73 Chorale prelude 'Es ist ein Ros entsprungen' for organ, op. 122

In other pieces, this essentially romantic expression seems to reach back into the traditional forms to offer more Brahmsian recreations of past styles. Thus, the second setting of 'O Welt, ich muss dich lassen', uses the same kind of expressive decoration to clothe its double echo effects after each chorale phrase, whilst a similar idiom is present in the pre-imitation of the melody in 'O Gott, du frommer Gott' (no. 7), which stands in striking contrast to the formality of the first prelude which uses the same principle. The introduction to 'Herzlich tut mich erfreuen' (no. 4) applies initial derivation much more freely, with figurations which, like those of the early Preludes in G minor and A minor, reflect the pianistic background in their outline of larger internal lines, though here with more idiomatic cross-rhythms. In the second setting of 'Herzlich tut mich verlangen', the historical link is again reinterpreted with great individuality, the pedal solo melody surrounded by characteristic harmonic progression after a texture which may well find an historical source. Finally, the first version of 'O Welt ich muss dich lassen' seems to draw together a range of expressive models – the opening of the final movement of the *Requiem* in the shape of the opening with its firm two-note phrasing in the key of F major.

Clarinet Quintet

By the time of Brahms's intended retirement, the range of instruments which he had employed was limited by comparison with the predecessors on whose work he had built. As a composer of the romantic era with a wide range of interests, his work is conspicuously lacking in the miniatures for wind explored by Schumann or others, to say nothing of the resources of the classical composers. His focus had been to the conventional media of the violin and cello sonata, apart from the Horn Trio or Songs with Viola. If one instrument does suggest itself as the agent of enrichment in this sphere, it is the oboe, which plays such a prominent role in the Brahmsian orchestral sound, not least in the context of choral and solo setting, as in parts of *Rinaldo*, the Alto Rhapsody and, supremely, the soprano solo of the *Requiem*. However, the oboe could not have offered the range which Brahms needed for his favoured genres of sonata and it was to the clarinet that this opportunity was offered through the medium of the playing of the Meiningen court principal clarinet, Richard Mühlfeld. Mühlfeld was noted for the warmth and expressiveness of his playing – Brahms used to call him 'Fräulein Klarinette' a quality enhanced by his instrument: he played Baermanns with a particularly mellifluous tone.

Accordingly Brahms did not write in the virtuoso manner of many earlier clarinet works, but explored the instrument for its expressive potentialities, although extreme difficulties do arise for the player in the process, as in the passage from bar 85 to bar 86 of the slow movement. Of particular note is the integration of the instrument into the general texture, playing purely harmonic supportive roles as often as a leading one. Brahms first heard Mühlfeld in 1890 and produced the Quintet and Trio in the following Summer at Ischl. The Sonatas belong to a later phase, 1894, postdating the piano works and were thus his final chamber works, followed only by the *Serious Songs* in 1896 and the posthumously published organ preludes. The greater popularity of the Quintet may well rest on its stronger relation to the past, for its string writing and advanced phrase structure draw directly from the G major Quintet of the previous year; and its outer form, concluding with variations relating to the first movement, as in the B flat Quartet, is particularly clear and powerful in emotional terms. The gipsy section of the slow movement and the variations by rhythmic diminution also recall the earlier works. The Trio is much more individual in form, whilst the Sonatas have no significant historical precedents.

Although the first movement of the Clarinet Quintet can be easily related to earlier chamber works in its handling of the major points of articulation – compare the transition to development with the Piano Quintet, the variation section of the development with the Piano Trio in C, the powerful coda with the G major Sextet, for example, – there is a crucial difference in the character of this piece in terms of tradition: for its opening subject possesses a reflective, improvisatory quality which is unusual in the chamber works and confirms the tendency to be found rather in the piano works of the period. Indeed, the turning figure with which the work begins relates as a type more closely to the beginning of the Intermezzo in E flat minor of op. 118 than to the other clarinet works, to say nothing of the earlier chamber works. Brahms enhances this quality by following it with another theme, beginning differently, not in the tonic B minor but in D major, of which the opening idea becomes a part, giving the latter the impression of an introduction to a movement in D, which is only challenged when the transition idea appears in B minor at bar 14. The flexibility of phrasing which arises in the transition through augmentation from bar 27 completely obscures the sense of a downbeat, which is only restored through the clear phrasing of the second subject at bar 38, but is ever-present thereafter. The 'quasi sostenuto' variation of the transition at bar 98 in the development further suggests a gipsy background, which comes to clearest focus in the intense passage of the coda from bar 188, the movement closing quietly. This close is to be memorably recalled in the finale, with the striking variation of a penultimate chord, *'forte'*, a passage which is approached through a recall of the opening material of the first movement. This, in turn, emerges from a set of variations of regular structure which gradually move from their lyrical model until the appearance of a variation in 3/8 which re-establishes the opening quaver movement and leads entirely naturally into the memorable recall of the opening. Whilst the function of the variations is analogous to those of the finale of the B flat String Quartet, the mood of the variation theme is different: no longer a classically inclined type, matching its parallel first movement, but a folk-like melody which is capable of relating to more intense, gipsy-oriented ideas. Indeed there is a striking parallel between the theme's opening and that of the folksong 'Dornröschen' (set in the 1858 collection), which also extends to the harmony, offering a parallel, if less obvious, example of 'the snake biting its own tail' – his familiar comment on the use of the folksong 'Verstohlen steht der Mond auf' in the 1894 collection as well as the Sonata in C major of 1853. From the common opening, Brahms evolves a much more resourceful theme and powerful model for variation, by extension, repetition and development.

Within his simple framework of two sections of 16/16, both parts repeated, Brahms gives both structural and character variation of the most natural kind. Thus, in variation 1 he changes the function of the third chord, substituting for the dominant, F sharp major, its own dominant chord, C sharp major, to give more emphasis to the F sharp chord of bar 5, a method continued throughout to subtly redefine the model's structure. In the second variation the harmony is handled more freely in the creation of a gipsy manner. The third variation sets up the quaver diminution which is to be resumed after the major variation no. 4 in the 3/8 retransition to the opening. Stylistically, the movement subtly reflects the strongly contrasted characters of the middle movements. The major variation parallels the

Ex. 74 Clarinet Quintet in B minor, op. 115, finale, with folksong 'Dornröschen'

opening section of the slow movement in its major mode of the tonic, rich inner parts and imitations of the singing upper part by the first violin, though greatly intensified by the slow tempo. Similarly, the highly atmospheric gipsy improvisations of the central 'piu lento' section are reflected in the character of variation 2. The third movement lies closer to the finale in both the shape of its main theme – which could well be a variant of the finale theme – and in the figuration of its 'presto non assai' second section, which itself contains a considerable degree of internal variation clearly setting up the terms of the finale.

Clarinet Trio

Only in the character of the opening of its slow movement does the Clarinet Trio significantly relate to the Quintet, offering the last, and one of the most interesting, examples of Brahms's independence of approach to two works written in close proximity, and posing similar compositional demands. The opening subject, whose descending, reflective outline seems so apt an expression of the clarinet's nature, draws on the same stylistic idiom as the parallel 'Adagio' of the Quintet, a relationship strengthened by the gentle imitation of the accompaniment, anticipated in diminution in the case of the Trio. But the subsequent pattern of the Trio movement is much more concentrated and formally obscure than the expansive and highly atmospheric ternary form of the Quintet. The form gives the impression of a sonata structure, with a clear transition to a second subject in the dominant. Yet, as in the slow movement of the Violin Sonata in D minor, the form reveals itself as a broad A B with a retransition to the tonic rather than development. The tonic return presents the first subject in a simplified variant, which seems to reveal its essence – another stage from the theme/accompaniment of the opening, and which offers the possible rhythmic and intervallic source of the finale. This is not, however, the true reprise, and it leads to a broadening and intensification of these ideas in the manner of a development, which then returns to the thematic substance of the opening, only now in the subdominant, G major, to commence a subdominant recapitulation which literally recalls the original material of exposition though significantly varied in scoring and with a short coda, to close in the tonic. Thus Brahms throws links back to the experiments of the C minor Piano Quartet, though in a completely new context, in the service of yet further and consummate formal flexibility. The quality characterises the work's outer movements which, unlike those of the Quintet are much shorter and more concentrated, a quality especially clear from the much more abstract and constructivist working. The third movement, like the second, is broad, taking a proportionally large amount of the whole. Cast in a ternary structure, it looks backwards, like the parallel movement of the Quintet, though here to a more obvious dance source, the waltz. Here again, however, variation permeates, with the second subject a skeletal variant of the first.

Formal interest is at its most overt in the first movement. Although Brahms does not recall his most radical reintegrations of sonata elements, he returns to the preoccupation with the presentation of contrasted material in the first group, a preoccupation seen so strongly in minor key works such as the op. 25 Piano Quartet, Piano Quintet and C minor String Quartet. Here the pattern seems to fuse both, for, as well as giving a contrasted idea – bars 14–18 (though in the tonic), it offers variation of the original, though not through rhetorical diminution: rather, formal, sectional variation, which turns out to serve as the transition, from which there is very quick move to the second group, in C major. Unlike earlier works, this mediant relationship is not retained: it is only the first stage of a two-stage movement to the minor tonality on the fifth degree, an expansion already established in the second period – the first movement of the Sextet in B flat – and used in the third – the first movement of the Second Symphony. The special quality of the first group serves again to predict an unusual handling of the recapitulation, for Brahms again obscures the identity of recapitulation by recalling the second element, Ib, in a form integrated into the close of the development, the first following in not only varied form, but so handled as to direct attention rather to the return of the second subject. Its focus, on F major, enables another literal recall of the tonal pattern of the exposition, C major – E minor returning as F major – A minor. The obscuring of the recall of the first group reflects its greater significance elsewhere. After a conventional sequential movement away from the end of the exposition, Brahms becomes preoccupied with the second idea of the first group – Ib – presenting it now with harmonic intensification, now in varied augmentation as the support for atmospheric runs by the 'cello and clarinet in mirror. Its 'recapitulatory' recall in the tonic at bar 126, still seems like developmental material, hence its alternation with other related material. The expressive power of this material demands its recall at the movement's close, where Ib further unmasks itself as a symbolic gesture – the chorale shape which is to occur even later with its tangible identity as text/music relation in the first of the *Serious Songs*. The movement is balanced with the most concentrated rondo finale in Brahms, showing constructivist links in the similar setting of the second subject as a canon by inversion. Variation again permeates, revealing its special character in the closing bars, whose rhetorical augmentation is so similar to that of the Scherzo of op. 99.

Clarinet sonatas

In bringing the clarinet into the world of the duo-sonata Brahms effectively created a new chamber form, for there are no comparable works before them but many in the tradition he establishes. It is interesting to note Brahms's preference for the medium to that with strings,[8] finding a better blend from the combination with piano than with strings, a feature which especially commends these works, for they are amongst the most consistently admired of compositions for the instrument. Mühlfeld's playing, taken with Brahms's own ripe maturity, enables him to create works which are even more resourceful in their balance and exploitation of the distinctive characters of both instruments. There seems no rein on Brahms's natural expression as a pianist – as in the passionate scherzo of the E flat sonata or forceful development of the F minor, yet the clarinet is always scored appropriately and the economy of piano writing elsewhere is comparable to that of the G major Violin Sonata in its delicate balances. In composing the work for viola as well, Brahms took the opportunity to express his love for this instrument, previously only employed in a solo role in the Alto Songs op. 91, though very prominent in his orchestral language. His contribution to the viola repertory was therefore even more significant historically than to the clarinet, for the instrument was even less used.

The two works explore the very different potentials of the instruments. The first, in F minor, is the final work in the tradition of this key which Brahms associated with passionate, rhetorical expression and formal adventure, as in the Sonata op. 5, the Piano Quintet and in aspects of the Cello Sonata op. 99. Indeed, the opening subject draws, through the mediation of the Quintet, on a basic melodic type, whilst its powerful development and false reprise in F sharp minor recall the preoccupations of the Quintet and the Cello Sonata, avoiding the variational methods of the development of the Cello Sonata, which shares features in its enriched F major tonality. The E flat Sonata, by comparison, could be termed 'classical' for its directness of lyrical expression, a quality certainly intensified if one knows an earlier and more intense form in the climax of the song 'Nachtigall', op. 97 no. 1.

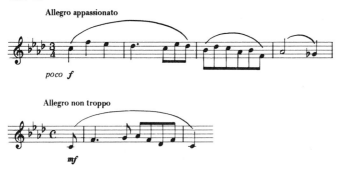

Ex. 75 Clarinet Sonata in F minor, op. 120, no. 1 and Piano Quintet, op. 34

If the mood in which the F minor Sonata opens reflects the Quintet, however, its working bespeaks a different period, for its ideas are both more economical and smaller scaled, yet treated with greater economy as well, with variation by decoration a central factor, as in the repetition (functionally the transition) of the first subject and the derivation of the second subject from it, the instruments sharing the material in a way characteristic of the later style. Like the earlier work, however, Brahms's prefer-

Ex. 76 (i) Clarinet Sonata in E flat, op. 120 no. 2
       (ii) 'Nachtigall', op. 97 no. 1

ence for a more extensive second subject group is apparent, with a very distinctive IIb, not dissimilar in effect from the closing group of the first allegro of the First Symphony, yet an entirely new closing paragraph to conclude the unrepeated exposition with a double-line bar. The development compresses power of expression parallel to that of the Quintet into a small space – forty bars against ninety-nine in the exposition (the Quintet relates eighty to ninety-five) – to reach its climax in a recall of the first subject in F sharp minor, subsequently shifting to a varied and significantly truncated recapitulation in the tonic. The subtlety with which Brahms constructs the first part of the development from the second subject, though completely loosening its rhythmic identity, lends power as well as means to the 'marcato' treatment which follows. The seemingly free coda 'sostenuto ed espressivo' is another product of the variation process, growing from and returning to the concluding bars of the recapitulation which give the opening in an even more bleak form, anticipating the first of the *Serious Songs* in effect. The 'Vivace' finale banishes both this mood and any suggestion of the finale of the Quintet in its directness of expression and formal character, that of a very economical rondo structure, though with an omitted third statement:

A tr B retr A tr C B A

The need of some introductory material is here accommodated within an opening eight-bar flourish – a call to attention – built round the repeated tonic note, to which the first theme is contrasted 'grazioso'. Predictably, the feature has a deeper function, serving as the pedal bass for the second theme which falls into triplet movement, and it is the aural guide through the roving passage which prepares the final statement of the rondo at bar 174. This statement presents the theme in a style of variation characteristic rather of formal variations – with the entire section reworked over the same thematic/harmonic foundation. It finds a freer complement in the internal variation of the second theme, where bars 50–53 are repeated in rhythmic diminution from triplet crotchets to quavers. The repeated minim also seems to offer a gentle link to the third movement, another waltz idea like that of the Trio whose second part is built on pedal, a feature employed at the beginning of the trio section, where the 'grazioso' mood changes to a more intimate 'molto dolce' in F minor. Like the parallel movement of the C minor String Quartet, the tonal scheme is more complex than it seems, the opening as though on the dominant, though actually on the dominant of the dominant, thus moving a stage further at its conclusion in the eighth bar. The slow movement, similarly placed in A flat major, also avoids tonal confirmation. This movement, in strong contrast to the third through its reflective, improvisatory character can be seen to fuse the rhapsodic aspect of the clarinet idiom with the pianism of the late pieces, its decorative line complementing a harmonic progression which reveals its affinity with the Intermezzo in B minor op. 119 no. 1 at bar 49.

Though completely different in mood, the first movement of the E flat Sonata follows a similar formal pattern to the F minor, with a contained first subject whose varied repetition for transition leads quickly to the second group, again comprising two distinct ideas. However, the formal progress is now much more fluid with no indication of the exposition's close. The returning first subject over varied harmony at bar 52 seems like a closing group, though it functions as the start of development only passing through the tonic at bar 56. This fluidity of form is more fully exploited in the development, where, after initial treatment of exposition material in the forceful manner of the earlier work, Brahms effects a beautiful transition to a lengthy passage exploring a simple cadential figure from bar 97, which generates in its turn very characteristic piano spacings in the motivic play from bar 93 to bar 99. This focus on the latter part of the development had inevitable consequences later, for it forms through subtle harmonic shifts at the end of the recapitulation, the material of the coda, now marked 'tranquillo'. The very atmospheric quality of this passage – the apparent enjoyment of sound – clarinet triplets against piano duplets – purely for its own sake is rare in Brahms and, taken with the parallel focus in the first movement of the Trio, as well as other examples in the later orchestral music, serves to reveal a changing emphasis in the late Brahms, complemented in the almost 'impressionistic' quality of parts of the piano music.

The classical mood is further apparent in the variation finale, though the third movement, which preserves the tonic, only contrasting in mode, like the other E flat work (the Horn Trio), explores a totally different mood. Though its broad Trio immediately recalls that of the B major Piano Trio, the character of the 'allegro appassionato' itself is new, its one-in-a-bar movement and very taxing piano part having no precedent in the scherzos. As well as recalling the past, the Trio may also be seen as revealing the source of the frequent tonal contrast E flat minor – B major by recalling Beethoven's very progression in the connection of the second and third movements of the E flat Piano Concerto; B major – B flat unison – E flat though here treated through C flat. The passionate mood is, however, absorbed into the finale, variation 5 recalling E flat minor for another fiery treatment for the piano with energetic cross rhythms which (like those of the first movement of the F minor Sonata bars 184–6) seem the very quintessence of the rhythmic Brahms. In its passionate reinterpretation of the model, this variation, which lacks the normal repeats, stands at the most distant point of a structure which unfolds very naturally in Brahmsian terms and concludes with a coda which unites its two characters – the reflective and the impassioned, the latter making the final gestures.

Piano music

In the late piano pieces op. 116–119 which appeared in 1892–3, the basic types of capriccio and intermezzo explored in op. 76 are characterised even more individually, though the tendency is towards the latter, no capriccio appearing after op. 116. Additionally, older types also appear – one ballade and one rhapsody, larger in scope, yet still very economical in structure, whilst the influence of song is further revealed in the single Romance op. 118. Although we do not know the precise chronology of the pieces, they seem the products of these late years, with the growing introspection of the intermezzos, the new impressionism of textural and harmonic effect, remarkable economy yet richness. Even pieces whose characters seem to relate to the past – the C major Intermezzo of op. 119, or the G minor Ballade of op. 118 – are handled with a mastery which suggests a different period from their soul mates in op. 76 – the B minor Capriccio, and the G minor Rhapsody of op. 79. As with the chamber music of this period, the late style exists in the context of very marked symbols, chiefly the recollections of the Fourth Symphony and the presence of the 'chorale shape'. But the expression is not merely one of refinement and concentration. The very character of harmonic device is strikingly progressive.

Of the four sets of piano pieces of the late period, only the first can really be regarded as a planned structural whole in the way of op. 76.[9] Indeed, its unity is very much clearer because of overt tonal and thematic links. The first and last pieces are both powerful capriccios in D minor and preoccupied with descending patterns of thirds in different forms. These thirds also dominate the central Capriccio no. 3 in G minor and can be found as less prominent counterpoints in the Intermezzi nos 4 and 5, creating a strong sense of cohesion.

Different aspects of variation, all found in the Fourth Symphony, can be found in the Capriccios. The first D minor piece uses octave displacement and anticipation in the left hand to create a very forceful character which becomes the basis of successive variation which draws its intensity from the Capriccio in C sharp minor of op. 76, though its special pattern also relates more broadly to the experiments in sonata form in which the first subject initiates the development. Here, however, the second subject does not return in the tonic, requiring a strong tonal shift at the coda to restore the true dominant. The variation of the opening is by invertible counterpoint, leading through a transition to a second theme in V of F major, and the thirds dominate the bass part until they also appear in the upper part as part of a cadence in contrary motion. The re-exposition of the first subject then leads to a character variation, *piano*, with a modified theme closely presented between the hands, repeated and developed more distantly from the fifth to sharp seventh degree, C sharp, followed by an inversion of II with the same descending thirds in the left hand. The final return of the first idea as a coda intensifies the continuation by rhythmic reduction and generates yet another version by rising sixths as inversion of the falling thirds in canon between the voices.

In the final D minor Capriccio the falling third is accommodated within the beat in 2/4 time, left hand mirroring right in rapid semiquavers and both relating to a larger two-voice outer framework. In contrast to the first piece, variation is here by rhythm – a syncopation of the upper line similar to that noted in op. 76 no. 1 and the Scherzo of the B flat Concerto. In this case the form is simple ternary with a powerful retransition to the reprise and a coda presenting a chordal version – a simultaneity – of the first

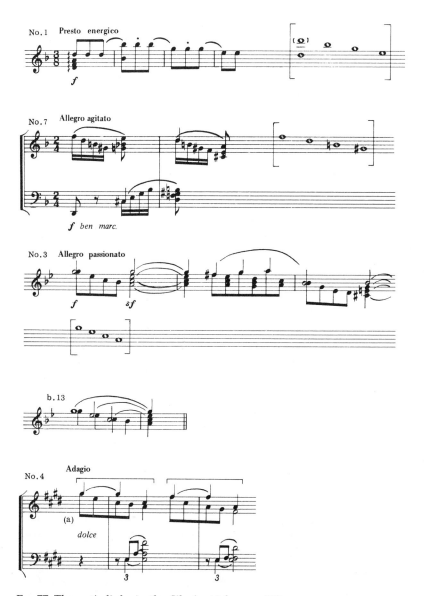

Ex. 77 Thematic links in the *Klavierstücke*, op. 116

subject. The middle section changes the metre to 6/8 with a syncopated
middle voice drawn from the original melodic outline and accompanied by
a version of the thirds. The rich sixths of the final cadence of this section
recall the manner of the piano waltzes. The Capriccio in G minor, no. 3
also incorporates the falling third beneath the upper line, though here the
rhetorical manner creates augmentation and double augmentation after the
manner of the Scherzo of the F major Cello Sonata. The final cadence is

particularly powerful in presenting two complementary versions of the idea in augmentation from upper to lower voice to great effect. The middle section creates a complete contrast, set in the submediant, E flat, and incorporating the triplets generated at the previous cadence.

The falling thirds function in an analogous fashion, but in a subsidiary role in the Intermezzo in E, no. 4, where they serve to create variation of the repeated first idea. This subject itself has aspects of the Fourth Symphony's opening in its falling intervals across the bar, but the harmonic setting is very individual, hovering between the E major implied by the upbeat left hand and the C sharp minor resolved downbeat, on which the composer plays. Formally this is also a very subtle structure involving progressive variation on the broad A B A B pattern with the consequences of the tonal

(i)   Andante con grazia ed intimissimo sentimento

ambiguity being pursued through the piece. Thus, the first section closes at bar 36 with a resolution of the first idea to G sharp minor, a chord related to both possible tonics. There follows a passage 'dolce, una corda' in which Brahms's 'bravura' style, with octaves enclosing thirds in the right hand and running figuration in the left, seem to be recollected in tranquillity, stabilising E as tonic, from which the original progression now leads to C sharp major, intensifying the possible tonic, C sharp minor. A harmonically enriched recall of the falling thirds variant of the first idea recalls the original progression to cadence on to E major, through A, closely associated previously, for a return of the middle material and subsequently a stabilisation of the triplet passage. This complex piece thus reveals several types of growth and variation within its reflective exterior.

In the Intermezzo in E, no. 6, the falling thirds appear again beneath a more prominent singing upper line, here to form the middle part of a simple A B A form. However, the mood of the piece is very different. The gentle homophonic movement of the opening 'andantino teneramente' provides yet another example of Brahms's feeling for inner melodies, though here the character is unusual in its stress on accented notes in the line. The reprise of this simple form is notable for the intensification of the Neapolitan passage and the fuller harmonisation of the middle section, its final cadence suspension being entirely characteristic of the late pieces.

Harmonic features are even more notable in the Intermezzi nos 5 and 2 in E minor and A minor. The former is perhaps the most 'progressive' of the late pieces in terms of its appearance in the score. The strictly mirror appearance of the hands in the outer parts and extreme consistency of figuration in the middle section suggests the Webern of the Piano Variations. Thus there exists a connection between the instinct for contrary

Ex. 78 (i) Intermezzo in E minor, op. 116 no. 5
(ii) Webern: Model of the Piano Variations, op. 27

motion of outer parts so strong from the earliest Brahms, to the strict symmetries of the twentieth century. So strong is the feature that it seems of itself to generate the harmony, creating unusual dissonances, as at bars 6–10. Though by a different means, no. 2 does similarly.

Brahms's love for the character of the lullaby, which appears increasingly in the transformations of these pieces, is most openly demonstrated in the first of the Intermezzos op. 117. As in the early Ballade in D minor ('Edward') and the slow movement of the F minor Sonata, he gives a clue to its inspiration here in a quotation from Herder's folksongs: 'Schlaf sanft mein Kind, schlaf sanft und schön!/Mich dauert's sehr, dich weinen sehn' which likewise fits his melody, as does its conclusion. The middle section also retains the simple phrasing of the opening, whilst the return of the opening reveals another example of the prophetic nature of the late pieces in its transformation of the surface through octave transposition, the concluding bars' imitation and cross rhythm offering a fine example of the richness of Brahms's late cadences. The lullaby model also underlies the third piece, whose textual source Kalbeck has identified, reflecting Brahms's comment on the piece as 'the lullaby of all my griefs' – perhaps pointing more significantly to the shape which underlies it. Again the design is simple ternary, though with more variational interest. It retains the simple phrasing of no. 1 with internal variation of the first eight-bar sentence, followed by an arpeggiac contrast idea. The whole passage is then repeated in a harmonised form which stresses IV – F sharp minor – as bass with the theme in the inner parts, the concluding codetta being harmonically astringent through the force of the pedal tonic; the middle section is built in two clearly related parts, the range now greatly expanded by octave transposition. The retransition from bar 78 is a consummate example of his art: he seems at first to recall the Ruckblick of the F minor Sonata with its falling thirds and to establish the dominant of his home key. Yet this is quickly clouded through a cadence on B leading to sequential repetition which concludes not on C sharp but its 'dominant', though actually a minor chord, betraying its function: as the effective dominant at four removes (A sharp – D sharp – G sharp – C sharp). The coda built on dominant pedal, brings this fundamental feature of his language to one of its richest expressions, deeply reflective. Unlike the other pieces, no. 2 in B flat minor has a continuous structure in its first part, permitting the appearance of a clear second subject. The finesse of the transitional process noted in no. 3 is here intensified in the reprise, and the coda makes equally telling use of pedal. The exposition takes its figurative idea through a wide range of keys which the second subject in D flat major stabilises initially. The progressive feature of this development is the simultaneous statement of the motivic content of the opening bar. The role of the pedal in the coda, and the expressiveness of the closing cadence, match those of the following piece.

Although Brahms returns to a broader grouping for the Six Pieces op. 118, the emotional pattern of the set is now very different from that of op.

116. The forceful manner of the pieces in D minor and G minor is recalled in only one piece – the Ballade in G minor, no. 3; whilst the improvisatory quality of the opening piece relates clearly to the outer pieces of op. 76 in the role of a short scalic outline above pervasive quaver figuration, the closing piece is now deeply introspective. Yet it may also be seen as culminatory if the quaver figuration is traced through the set as means of connection much less obvious than the descending thirds of op. 116. That the descending shape of the first piece is also a recurrent feature, perhaps relating to the overall tonal progression A minor/A major/G minor/F minor/F major/E flat minor is also not impossible in terms of Brahms's structural preoccupations, as shown earlier. Although no capriccios appear in the set, intermezzos being the only type save the ballade and the romanze, the range of its possible expression has become much broader, absorbing the more forceful and animated qualities of the genre. The parallels between the first Intermezzo in A minor and the outer Capriccios of op. 76 reveals this clearly, whilst even the last, E flat minor piece rises to an intensity not previously found, as does the latter part of the fourth, in F minor.

Like the outer pieces of op. 76, Brahms is immediately concerned to show both original and inverted forms of his scalic segment and to use it in augmented form for intensification at the cadence. Yet within this much shorter piece – a mere 43 bars, though he indicates repeats – his tonal planning is much more adventurous. All the tendencies towards harmonic ambiguity at the beginning of a composition seem to come to a focus in this impassioned first number. As in the Trio in A minor, the natural axis of A minor is with F major, though here it is stated directly, the opening seeming to lie clearly in this key, though past experience of Brahms's use of sequence at the outset of a piece predicts that the goal will lie elsewhere (as most notably in the Rhapsody in G minor). The cadence to the first repeated part at bar 10 is to C major, the closest common degree to A minor and F. Although the continuation touches on the true dominant, E, the sequence again leads the idea away, with the tonic only established in the last six-bar period of the second part, where it moves through F to the dominant. The following coda stresses not the dominant, but subdominant, D minor. The mood of the final piece does not admit such tonal elusiveness. The contrast of the tonic and its relative major, G flat, is absolutely clear in articulating the A B A structure. Indeed, it is notably free of the complexities of some of these pieces. Rather Brahms draws on another archetype of expression, and one much more pervasive in its association with introspection – the turning figure already noted in the Hungarian Dances which it simply varies by free inversion. It can well be observed that this single-line opening has soloistic quality, and, viewed additionally against a Hungarian background, it emerges as a highly original tone picture – a gipsy improvisation in the spirit of the slow movement of the Clarinet Quintet, with solo instrument and cimbalom accompaniment. Now though, this background is transformed by Brahms's characteristic late pianism and his formal control, the first part clearly successively varying its basic thought with thirds in the upper parts, close imitation through the exchange of hands and a stark octave doubling in the lower register, so characteristic of his treatment of such scalic ideas, most notably of the 'chorale-shape' in op. 114, the latter returning with great intensity to conclude the piece. The central section is essentially a pianistic response to this introversion, an equally pictorial passage of animated contrast, yet conceived in entirely pianistic terms.

Of the other Intermezzos, No. 2 in A relates much more closely to the past, recalling just the mood of the Intermezzo in the same key of op. 76, a parallel intensified in the middle section, whose upper line over triplet quaver figuration is very similar. The contrast in formal treatment points the essential difference between the sets; in the earlier piece the first section returns with no change. Here the return is the occasion for slight but most telling emphasis of the responding phrases of the simple opening, of bars 3–4 and 7–8. In harmony also, one observes the subtle individuality of the late composer, not moving widely through in the context of rhetorical pianism, but simply obscuring the full sense of the tonality even at the very opening, here by another example of the unusual use of inversion, the opening tonic chord followed not by D root but D 6/4, to intensify the effect of the cadence to the first phrase at bar 3. The Intermezzo in F minor is, by contrast, of an anxious, suppressed nature, a quality arising from its strict use of canon at the octave, though with a triplet, 'poco agitato' figure which implies more capricious working, as occurs in the continuation from bar 16 – 'delicamente'. In the central section this tension is temporarily eased through a very contained passage which employs the canon in chordal terms between the hands, but with the return of the opening material the music grows in intensity, free variation of the original material revealing the imitative principle even more powerfully. It is interesting to compare the close imitations of the sixth and seventh bars from the end with the parallel method in the much more reflective context of the close of the Intermezzo in E flat major of the previous set. The title Romanze for No. 5 in F major indicates a very different kind of mood, relating (if to anything) to the Intermezzo in A minor of the op. 76 set. The mood is one of utter simplicity through its gentle chordal movement, suggesting a lullaby, an association which grows stronger in the central 'allegretto grazioso' with its succession of 27 repetitions of a triadic ostinato over which the upper part weaves a succession of naïve diminutions, culminating in atmospheric trills before the move back from D to F for the return of the opening. (Perhaps Chopin's Berceuse was not far from his mind in this section.) Yet variation is still pervasive in this first part, whose four-bar idea is repeated in decoration, with the exchange of upper voices to give a new, intensified aspect to the progression, the passage which serves in the reprise for further intensification to conclude the simple ternary design. The lullaby effect provides an additional link back to the larger genre of the Rhapsody in the Ballade in G minor, by far the most powerful piece of the group. The association of G minor with a mood of energy and passion is clear from the Rhapsody op. 79 no. 2 as from the Capriccio op. 116 no. 3. But the sudden contrast with a 'una corda' *pp* central section, with strong use of pedal-based left-hand quavers, comes from the companion op. 79 piece, the Rhapsody in B minor, and Brahms again works material from the opening into it (here not the second, but the first subject) as a means of concluding the first part as a preparation for its repetition: in turn this passage serves as the retransition to G minor.

With the Four Pieces op. 119, Brahms brings to focus some of his most characteristic moods in three Intermezzos and one Rhapsody with an ultimate concentration of means and effect. The first Intermezzo in B minor draws on the Intermezzo in B flat minor, op. 117 no. 1 in its descending quaver figuration and contrasted second theme in the relative major, whose more direct character reveals close rhythmic parallels between the pieces. The Intermezzo in E minor recalls in its 'poco agitato' marking and repeated brief figures the mood of the Intermezzo in F minor from op. 118. Qualities of a capriccio underlie the third Intermezzo in C major, especially the quaver movement of the Capriccio in B minor from op. 76. Finally, the Rhapsody brings a dramatic figure from the sonata tradition into the context of the piano miniature to provide the basis of the most extensive composition of all, providing a fitting climax to this last phase of piano composition: the main theme is very close to the cadential gesture at bar 39 of the first movement of the Clarinet Sonata in E flat.

The greater concentration of the three Intermezzos arises from the intensified use of variation, and, especially in the first piece, of formal restraint, arising from the nature of the main idea. Where the Intermezzo in B flat minor unfolds freely, its central part evolving naturally from the second subject, the outer plan of the Intermezzo in B minor is clearer, though with subtle internal structure of its opening eight-bar periods. The second subject, marked off by double bar, is scarcely more complex, its fourteen bars determined by the extension of the passage from the fifth bar and free close. Its reworked repetition is notable for the unexpected character of the return to the opening material. The form arises organically from the idea, not a flowing andante but a reflective adagio, and one built on yet another manifestation of the falling third pattern, here handled, as it is to be in the song 'O Tod, wie bitter', op. 121 no. 3, to create harmonic astringency. And in addition to the harmonic interest of the chordal progression at the outset, chords of superimposed thirds, conceived surely from above, not below, the harmonic context is notable as another example of the avoidance of tonic confirmation at the beginning of a piece, which oscillates between suggestions of D major as well as B minor. The Intermezzo in E minor draws on the formal principle of the Intermezzo in F from op. 118, though now in the context of a much more agitated self-absorbed type of movement. The entire piece is in successive variation form. Thus the first idea is repeated in a triplet variant at bar 13, whilst it follows at bar 18 in a syncopated version beginning in F minor. The first section is concluded from bar 29 with yet another variant of the tonic version. In the central section the idea becomes in turn a gentle waltz 'Andantino grazioso', almost giving the impression of another lullaby, which recurs reflectively as a coda after the pattern of the Rhapsody in B minor op. 79. The Intermezzo in C brings the figurative type of the Capriccio in B minor into relation with both successive variation and with motivic variation within the main idea itself. Where the earlier theme simply fills space with its quaver patterns, this plays with a four-note figure which it displaces rhythmically in repetition in an entirely characteristic manner. This motivic preoccupation becomes the principle of the piece, appearing in syncopation, extension, augmentation and cross rhythm to point the music's continuous unfolding. Finally the Rhapsody in E flat brings variation into a much broader struc- ture, a large A B A form with coda, and enclosing smaller ternary designs. The reprise is so patterned to give a mirror effect to the whole before the powerful coda. Consistent with the scope of the piece, this variation is of a radical nature in transforming mood. Thus, the assertive opening idea 'allegro risoluto' reappears '*pp, ma ben marcato*', gradually broadening into the original transition through legato extension, whilst the second idea – yet another form of the chorale shape in clear relation to that of the Inter- mezzo in F minor from op. 118 – is completely changed into a 'grazioso' form with broken chords, intensifying the parallel figuration of the Intermezzo in A flat of op. 76 which key it shares.

Four Serious Songs

'Words such as these have long been in my mind and I did not think that worse news of your mother was to be expected – but deep in the heart something often whispers and stirs, quite unconsciously perhaps, which may in time ring out in the form of poetry or music.'[10] Thus wrote Brahms to Clara's daughter Marie after her death on 20 May 1896. Just how funda- mental were these latent ideas in Brahms's expression will already be apparent from the preceding discussions of text and music. The text gives an even more intense expression of that preoccupation with transience, of man going to dust, which, apparent in the early choral texts, comes to massive emphasis in the *Requiem* and is never far away thereafter, as in the 'Warum?' and later motets. From them also comes the power of the thought of death as a comfort, here made much more tangible through his most open expression of the philosophy of love as presented in St Paul's letter to the Corinthians – 'But now abideth faith, hope and love, but the greatest of these is love'. The strength of this last expression must owe much to the personal reality of the sentiments through the large number of close friends that Brahms lost in the last years of his life – von Bülow,

Billroth, Elizabeth von Herzogenberg, Hermine Spies, finally Clara. With
the text comes its musical association. The melodic line of the first song
'Denn es gehet dem Menschen wie dem Vieh' draws again on the chorale
source – itself a realisation of a deeper personal motive – which underlies
'Denn alles Fleisch, es ist wie Gras', to reveal an indissoluble association.

Ex. 79 (i) 'Denn es gehet dem Menschen wie dem Vieh', op. 121 no. 1
(ii) 'Denn alles Fleisch, es ist wie Gras' (*Requiem*, second movement)

Yet the closing text is no longer expressed through climactic fugue or
counterpoint or chorale. Brahms's love is that of his solo songs, and as has
been rightly pointed out, the musical language hymns *amor* rather than
caritas[11] recalling, for example, the ecstatic conclusion of the song 'Wie bist
du meine Königen' op. 32 no. 9, though the close of 'Auf dem Kirchhofe'
also shows its application to a mood of resignation, as shown.

It is not unnatural that difficulty be found in classifying the songs in
relation to tradition. If Geiringer's emphasis on the past – 'a continuation
of the Protestant Church Cantata . . . its language definitely Baroque and
archaic'[12] gives one source, it is the fusion which matters, one of the most
notable of Brahms's later years.

In achieving it, he treads new paths, however. For, whereas the free
Biblical verse of his selected sources was set in open forms in the *Requiem*
and the motets, he here accommodates them within the broad framework
of the lied – for all these songs have stronger links to this tradition than to
that of the oratorio. The relations are obviously closest in the song whose
text is closest to the strophic models of the earlier lieder. Though not
balanced as precisely as lied texts, that of no. 4 is nearest to this background
in the clear relationship of expression, parts 2 and 3 elaborating the thought
of part 1 with a framework of similar expression. Thus 'Wenn ich mit
Menschen und mit Engelszungen redete, und hätte der Liebe nicht, so
wär' ich ein tönend Erz, oder eine klingende Schelle' ('If I speak with the tongues
of men and angels yet have not love so am I nothing') . . . 'Und
wenn ich weissagen könnte . . . und hätte der Liebe nicht, so wäre ich
nichts' ('And though I understand all things, yet have not love, so am I
nothing') . . . 'Und wenn ich alle meine Habe den Armen gäbe . . . und
hätte der Liebe nicht so wäre ich nichts' ('And though I give to the poor all

I have . . . but have not love, so am I nothing'). This text structure provides
the basis for the first three clearly related and developing sections of the
setting. With the freer structure of the text's continuation, Brahms can work
more broadly introducing a new melody – Adagio, in B major for the section
'Wir sehen jetzt durch einen Spiegel in einem dunkeln Worte . . .' ('For
now we see as through a glass darkly . . .'), this material ending the song
after a brief recall of the opening idea for 'Nun aber bleibet . . .' which
restores the tonic E flat. To observe a close text/music relationship is not,
however, to make an aesthetic judgment of the relationship. It has often
been observed that music seems to fit this text with less of a sense of
inevitability than in the other settings and this must be attributed to the
origin of the music. Kalbeck points out that the material was drawn from
discarded songs, the opening from a setting of 'Traulied' by Rückert, the
calm close to the first section drawing on a setting of Keller's 'Nixe im
Grundquell' whose personal meaning has actually been related not to Clara
but to Elizabeth von Herzogenberg.[13]

In the other settings, text is treated much more freely. Not only does
Brahms employ his characteristic emphasised repetitions at the close of a
section with even greater scope, but such repetition is now employed
within the section to a very marked degree for both expressive and formal
purposes, growing in intensity as the concentration of expression increases
through the first three songs. Thus, the third and most freely declamatory
song is inconceivable without its repetitions. In all senses, the first three
songs reveal a growing intensity towards the resolution of the last, drawing
on the 'heathenish' texts to which Brahms so often inclined; Ecclesiasticus
Ch. 41: vv. 1–4 is preceded by Ecclesiastes Ch. 3: vv. 19–22 and 4: vv. 1–3,
the source of texts 1 and 2 with their bleak pessimism: 'Death cometh alike
to man and beast: as one dies, so all die, for man is no better than the
beasts'; 'And so I wandered and observed all the oppression which exists
under the sun . . .' In the third text the emotions are much more pointed:
'O Death how bitter art thou to a man who thinks on these things . . .' The
progression is clearly reflected in the music. Thus, the first song sets its
text in a musical form A B A B, contrasting 'andante' with 'allegro', the
chorale building to an expansive passage which recalls the baritone writing
of the *Requiem* in such a passage as the first section of the sixth movement,
the musical returns covering much less text. With the second text, Brahms
draws on the other great seeming musical symbol for stoic acceptance of
fate in the later years, the descending thirds of the Fourth Symphony, here
given a pointed meaning through their textual association and presented,
like the chorale, in a more basic, stable and impressive form than ever
before. With the song's unfolding, the thirds are progressively extended in
their harmonic potential. Thus at 'And then I praised the dead' they are
repeated literally to cadence on D major to be repeated more precisely to
cadence on A major, with a subsequent, interrupted progression from C
which mirrors the text. These tendencies are given strongest focus in the

third song through their harmonic treatment, the composer mirroring the bitterness of death through a false relation of C to C sharp as a consequence of the progression. Against this opening, the warmth of the transformation to major and the inversion of the falling third to rising sixth at 'O Death, how welcome art thou' is the more memorable.

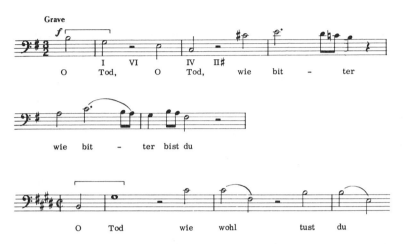

Ex. 80 *Four Serious Songs*, op. 121, no. 3, bars 1–5 and 19–21

After this, the last song tends to appear as a musical anticlimax: yet without it, we would be left with a false view of the composer's religious outlook. 'But the greatest of these is love' is its proper expression.

When Brahms died on 3 April 1897 at the age of almost sixty-four, three years before the turn of the century, it seemed to many like the end of an era, the end not of one period, but of an entire tradition. Indeed, the pioneering theorist of tonal music, Schenker, dedicated his study of Beethoven, written in 1912 – to 'Johannes Brahms, the last master of German composition'. With the passing of the Romantic Period in music this view became solidified, prompting the quite natural observation by Abraham with which this study began. Yet this 'conservative' view of Brahms must be kept in historical perspective, because the 'antithesis' between Brahms and Wagner was essentially the product of history. In the desire to observe patterns of development, the opposed yet complementary aspects of their languages created the view of them as figures of equal status in their day. Yet in the middle-class environment which dominated music making in the later nineteenth century, these two composers had quite different roles. Brahms was essentially an embodiment of that culture in music, but Wagner was something else, a new kind of artist who at best was regarded as the pioneer of a new aesthetic, at worst someone who existed outside the bounds of good taste through the enormity of his conceptions and immense expansion of permissible sound. Passionately as he evoked responses in his admirers, Wagner's music was heard and understood in the nineteenth century infinitely less well than that of Brahms, who wrote for a tradition in which everyone shared – and made his financial fortune from it in turn. And for those who related naturally to tradition, who had no sense of the need for 'progressiveness', it was Brahms not Wagner who was the modern master, because he so demonstrably extended a known tradition. There is no mention of 'conservatism' when we read the views of Reger (another misunderstood figure), or the strong English supporters of Brahms – Stanford, Parry, Abdy Williams or Tovey;[14] rather the stress is on the difficulty of Brahms's music. Thus Schoenberg's familiar words of 1947 appear as part of a broader tradition of criticism. What makes them especially important is not their sentiments – although they were certainly necessary by then – but their technical expression, a depth of understanding which goes much deeper into many areas than is to be found elsewhere. In essence, this was the capacity to distinguish 'style' from 'idea', surface manner from inner working processes, and this insight he passed to his students and listeners with a special sense of responsibility. Thus he was able to create a new language, drawing fruitfully on Brahms where others merely absorbed manner. Brahms could have had no closer soul mate than Schoenberg in matters technical, and Brahms deeply affected Schoenberg's philosophy, stimulating his natural inclination towards rigour, a work ethic symbolised in the belief in the dominant importance of a composer's 'responsibility to his materials'.[15] And if Brahms's harmonic methods, like those of Wagner, were destined to play little identifiable role in the evolution of his later music, the whole apparatus of thematic process and formal unity which he discerned in Brahms were to be pervasive in his development – a continuing link to his roots. For, as Wellesz points out in this context after outlining the various other early influences on Schoenberg, 'the composer who influenced him decisively throughout his life, and whom he rated highest among modern composers, was Brahms'.[16] And Schoenberg himself gives us an important clue to the pattern of that development in pointing out the Brahmsian quality of the phrasing in *Verklärte Nacht*; we might well supply a model in the shape and extensions of an example previously quoted.

As has emerged clearly, Brahms's thematic processes anticipate those of Schoenberg and assume especially prophetic forms in the intense concentration of means in the final period.

Yet, viewed outside this particular world of values, Schoenberg's Brahms appears a very narrow figure – an elitist, intellectual figure: Brahms in Schoenberg's own image. One would doubt from reading Schoenberg that Brahms could ever have communicated to a wide audience. Indeed, Schoenberg's discussion inevitably reflects his own nature. Setting aside the broad question of Brahms's historical relationships, his transformation of the archetypes of popular expression, Schoenberg's technical discussion is one-sided, notably omitting any analysis of Brahms's very advanced rhythmic

Ex. 81 (i) Schoenberg: *Verklärte Nacht*, op. 4, second subject
(ii) Brahms: Violin Sonata, op. 78, second movement

sense. Schoenberg says much about phrasing in the abstract – about the virtue of irregularity as a compositional feature, but he says little about rhythm as such. Although he clearly understood Brahms's importance – 'when Brahms demanded that one hand of the pianist played twos or fours while the other played threes . . . this was probably the start of the polyrhythmic structure of many contemporary scores'[17] – he never delved into the methods as he did with theme and its formal consequences.

For comparable interest in rhythm amongst Schoenberg's generation one has to look elsewhere. Indeed, only one composer rivals him in the advanced nature of his rhythmic thinking, and that is Stravinsky. And although it is customary to regard Stravinsky as belonging to an entirely different culture, and comparison as therefore irrelevant, there are many important parallels and links between them. One basic relationship exists in the roles of simple rhythmic motives in their music, and their comparable capacity for extension from a given impulse of the simplest nature with profound rhythmic consequences. Indeed, there are no other composers in whose music the discrepancy between sound and notated score is so great. Although Stravinsky's rhythmic instincts were, like those of Brahms, all his own, it is not impossible that he absorbed something of Brahms's technique in youth, since he probably learned a great deal of it through his uncle Ielachich. And in later years he certainly regarded Brahms as one of the classics to whom he could devote study for specific purposes.[18] But the parallel is a rare one. In general, the Brahmsian manner of expression has been almost symbolic of the textural and formal inhibitions from which twentieth century composers have sought to escape. Those who were unable to distinguish style from idea have found in him great fault and looked elsewhere for stimulus. An interesting example is provided by Benjamin Britten, who in many respects might be seen as reflecting similar interests – the love of folksong and its integration into his style, the interest in contrapuntal methods, in the music of the past, in the fruitful relationship between the performance of earlier music and composition. After early enthusiasm, Britten came to hate Brahms's music for its thickness of texture and self-consciousness of expression, his resort to complexities of working in order to offset the charge of sentimentality[19] an interesting parallel to Wagner's difficulties in following Brahms's themes, which he found contrived,[20] Britten's interest declining after the more direct youthful works such as the Piano Concerto in D minor. Mahler, whose compositional preoccupations relate clearly to Britten, as to Brahms, and whose material links are often very strong, reveals an interesting ambivalence also, respect alternating with distaste in the recollections of Bauer-Lechner.[21] Yet, attitudes change: the fate decreed for Brahms by many writers has not come to pass – on the contrary: links have already been drawn between Brahms's metrical processes and those of a composer who, if of Britten's generation, is hardly of his technical inclinations, Elliott Carter,[22] though I would comment that Brahms's methods need to be set in the much broader perspective of the tradition of rhythmic transformation from the Baroque variation suite. The work of many younger composers is now being described as expressing a 'new romanticism', though certainly not that announced by Schoenberg in the 1930s. Is it perhaps possible that after so long a period of rejection or idiosyncratic interpretation, the deep balance of immense compositional finesse, yet capacity for broad communication which allies his art to the greatest, may yet serve to stimulate afresh, in the way that he himself drew so richly and so naturally on the past?[23]

List of Works

In view of the long gestation period of Brahms's works, dates of composition are not suggested, save in cases where completion is known to have significantly pre-dated publication, here added in brackets before.

Piano Solos

Opus

1 Sonata in C major 1853
2 Sonata in F sharp minor 1854
4 Scherzo in E flat minor 1854
5 Sonata in F minor 1854
9 Variations on a Theme by Schumann 1854
10 Four Ballades (No. 1 in D minor; No. 2 in D major; No. 3 in B minor; No. 4 in B major) 1856
   Two Gigues (No. 1 in A minor; No. 2 in B minor) (1855) 1927
   Two Sarabandes (No. 1 in A major; No. 2 in B minor) (1855) 1917
   Two Gavottes (No. 1 in A minor; No. 2 in A major, incomplete, (1854, 1855) 1979
21 Variations: No. 1 on an Original Theme 1862; No. 2 on a Hungarian Theme 1862.
   Piano Piece in B flat major (1859–62) 1979
24 Variations and Fugue on a Theme by Handel 1862
35 Studies (Variations) on a Theme by Paganini (two sets) 1866
   Canon in F minor (1864) 1979
76 Eight Pieces 1879:
   Set 1: No. 1, Capriccio (F sharp minor); No. 2, Capriccio (B minor); No. 3, Intermezzo (A flat major); No. 4, Intermezzo (B flat major).
   Set 2: No. 5, Capriccio (C sharp minor); No. 6, Intermezzo (A major); No. 7, Intermezzo (A minor); No. 8, Capriccio (C major).
79 Two Rhapsodies (No. 1 in B minor, No. 2 in G minor) 1880.
116 Fantasias 1892
   Set 1: No. 1. Capriccio (D minor); No. 2, Intermezzo (A minor); No. 3, Capriccio (G minor).
   Set 2: No. 4, Intermezzo (E major); No. 5, Intermezzo (E minor); No. 6, Intermezzo (E major); No. 7, Capriccio (D minor).
117 Three Intermezzi (No. 1 in E flat major, No. 2 in B flat minor, No. 3 in C sharp minor) 1892

118 Six Pieces 1893
>   No. 1, Intermezzo (A minor); No. 2, Intermezzo (A major); No. 3, Ballade
>   (G minor); No. 4, Intermezzo (F minor); No. 5, Romanze (F major); No.
>   6, Intermezzo (E flat minor)

119 Four Pieces 1893
>   No. 1, Intermezzo (B minor); No. 2, Intermezzo (E minor); No. 3, Intermezzo
>   (C major); No. 4, Rhapsody (E flat major).

— Fifty-one Exercises 1893
Cadenzas:
— Piano Concerto in D minor (Bach) 1927
— Piano Concerto in G major (Mozart, K. 453) – two cadenzas 1927
— Piano Concerto in D minor (Mozart, K. 466) 1927
— Piano Concerto in C minor (Mozart, K. 491) 1927
— Piano Concerto in G major (Beethoven, Op. 58) – two cadenzas 1907

Arrangement for Piano Solo

— Theme and Variations in D minor (slow movement of Sextet, Op. 18) (1860)
  1927

Piano Duet

23 Variations on a Theme by Schumann (E flat major) 1863
39 Waltzes 1866
— Hungarian Dances, four sets:
>   Sets 1 and 2 1869
>   Sets 3 and 4 1880

52A *Liebeslieder-walzer* (see Vocal Quartets) 1874
65A *Neue Liebeslieder* (see Vocal Quartets) 1875
— 'Souvenir de la Russie', Fantasias on Russian and Bohemian Airs. ('G. W.
  Marks' – publisher's pseudonym) Before 1852

Two Pianos

34B Sonata in F minor (an earlier version of the Piano Quintet, Op. 34) 1871: See
  Chamber Works.
56B Variations on a Theme by Haydn (*St Antoni* Variations); (for the orchestral
  version see Orchestral Works) (1873)

Organ Works

— Two Preludes and Fugues:
>   No. 1, in A minor (1856) 1927
>   No. 2, in G minor (1857) 1927

— Fugue in A flat minor (1856) 1864
— Chorale Prelude and Fugue, *O Traurigkeit* (A minor) (1858) 1882

122 Eleven Chorale Preludes 1902
>No. 1, Mein Jesu, der du mich; No. 2, Herzliebster Jesu; No. 3, O Welt, ich muss dich lassen; No. 4, Herzlich tut mich erfreuen; No. 5, Schmücke dich, O liebe Seele; No. 6, O wie selig seid ihr doch; No. 7, O Gott, du frommer Gott; No. 8, Es ist ein Ros' entsprungen; Nos. 9 and 10, Herzlich tut mich verlangen; No. 11, O Welt, ich muss dich lassen.

Chamber Music

— Sonatensatz. Scherzo in C minor for violin and pianoforte, from a Sonata written jointly with Schumann and Dietrich (1853) 1906
  8 Trio in B major for violin, cello and pianoforte 1854 The same, revised 1891
18 Sextet in B flat major for 2 violins, 2 violas and 2 cellos 1862
25 Quartet in G minor for violin, viola, cello and pianoforte 1863
26 Quartet in A major for violin, viola, cello and pianoforte 1863
34 Quintet in F minor for 2 violins, viola, cello and pianoforte 1865
36 Sextet in G major for 2 violins, 2 violas and 2 cellos 1866
38 Sonata in E minor for cello and pianoforte 1866
40 Trio in E flat major for violin, horn (or cello or viola) and pianoforte 1866
51 Two Quartets for 2 violins, viola and cello: No. 1 in C minor: No. 2 in A minor 1873
60 Quartet in C minor for violin, viola, cello and pianoforte 1855–1875
67 Quartet in B flat major for 2 violins, viola and cello 1876
78 Sonata in G major for violin and pianoforte 1879
87 Trio in C major for violin, cello and pianoforte 1882
88 Quintet in F major for 2 violins, 2 violas and cello 1882
99 Sonata in F major for cello and pianoforte 1887
100 Sonata in A major for violin and pianoforte 1887
101 Trio in C minor for violin, cello and pianoforte 1887
108 Sonata in D minor for violin and pianoforte 1889
111 Quintet in G major for 2 violins, 2 violas and cello 1891
114 Trio in A minor for clarinet (or viola), cello and pianoforte 1892
115 Quintet in B minor for clarinet, 2 violins, viola and cello 1892
120 Two Sonatas for clarinet (or viola or violin) and pianoforte: No. 1 in F minor, No. 2 in E flat major 1895
— 'Hymn to the Veneration of the great Joachim': Waltzes for two violins and bass or 'cello (1853?) (1976)

Orchestral Works

11 Serenade in D major 1860
15 First pianoforte Concerto, in D minor 1861–74
16 Serenade in A major for small orchestra (without violins) 1860
56A Variations on a Theme by Haydn, in B flat major *St Antoni* Variations 1874
68 First Symphony, in C minor (1862–76) 1877
73 Second Symphony, in D major 1878
77 Violin Concerto in D major 1879
80 Academic Festival Overture 1881
81 Tragic Overture 1881
83 Second Pianoforte Concerto, in B flat major 1882

90 Third Symphony, in F major 1884
98 Fourth Symphony, in E minor 1886
102 Double Concerto in A minor for violin and cello 1888

Arrangements for Orchestra

— *Liebeslieder* – and *Neue Liebeslieder-Walzer*, op. 52, 65 (various), 1938; Hungarian
Dances, 1, 3, 10, 1874

Songs for Voice and Piano

Opus
  3 Six Songs 1853
      1 Liebestreu   Robert Reinick
      2 Liebe und Frühling, I   Hoffmann von
      3 Liebe und Frühling, II   Fallersleben
      4 Lied aus dem Gedicht 'Ivan' Bodenstedt
      5 In der Fremde   Eichendorff
      6 Lied   Eichendorff
  6 Six Songs 1853
      1 Spanisches Lied   Paul Heyse
      2 Der Frühling   J. B. Rousseau
      3 Nachwirkung   Alfred Meissner
      4 Juchhe!   Reinick
      5 Wie die Wolke nach der Sonne Hoffmann von Fallersleben
      6 Nachtigallen schwingen   Hoffmann von Fallersleben
— Die Müllerin (incomplete) (1853?) Chamisso 1984
  7 Six Songs 1854
      1 Treue Liebe   Ferrand
      2 Parole   Eichendorff
      3 Anklänge   Eichendorff
      4 Volkslied   Traditional
      5 Die Trauernde   Traditional
      6 Heimkehr   Uhland (1852)
— 'Mondnacht' 1854
14 Eight Songs and Romances 1861
      1 Vor dem Fenster   Traditional
      2 Vom verwundeten Knaben   Traditional
      3 Murrays Ermordung   Herder, from the Scottish
      4 Ein Sonett   13th Century
      5 Trennung   Traditional
      6 Gang zur Liebsten   Traditional
      7 Ständchen   Traditional
      8 Sehnsucht   Traditional
19 Five Poems 1862
      1 Der Kuss   Hölty
      2 Scheiden und Meiden   Uhland
      3 In der Ferne   Uhland
      4 Der Schmied   Uhland
      5 An eine Aeolsharfe   Eduard Mörike

32 Nine Songs 1865

SET I

1 Wie rafft' ich mich auf in der   August von Platen
   Nacht
2 Nicht mehr zu dir zu gehen   G. F. Daumer
3 Ich schleich' umher betrübt   Platen
   und stumm
4 Der Strom, der neben mir   Platen
   verrauschte

SET II

5 Wehe, so willst du mich   Platen
   wieder
6 Du sprichst, dass ich mich   Platen
   täuschte
7 Bitteres zu sagen   Daumer, after Hafiz
8 So stehn wir   Daumer, after Hafiz
9 Wie bist du, meine Königin   Daumer, after Hafiz

33 Fifteen Romances from   Ludwig Tieck
    'Magelone' 1865, 1869

SET I

1 Keinen hat es noch gereut
2 Traun! Bogen und Pfeil
3 Sind es Schmerzen

SET II

4 Liebe kam aus fernen
   Landen
5 So willst du des Armen
6 Wie soll ich die Freude

SET III

7 War es dir
8 Wir müssen uns trennen
9 Ruhe, Süssliebchen
10 Verzweiflung
11 Wie schnell verschwindet
12 Muss es eine Trennung geben

SET V

13 Sulima
14 Wie froh und frisch
15 Treue Liebe dauert lange

43 Four Songs 1868

1 Von ewiger Liebe   Joseph Wenzig
2 Die Mainacht   Hölty
3 Ich schell' mein Horn   Old German
4 Das Lied vom Herrn von   Uhland, from 'Volkslieder'
   Falkenstein

46 Four Songs 1868

1 Die Kränze   Daumer, from 'Polydora'
2 Magyarisch   Daumer, from 'Polydora'
3 Die Schale der Vergessenheit   Hölty
4 An die Nachtigall   Hölty

47 Five Songs 1868
    1 Botschaft   Daumer, after Hafiz
    2 Liebesglut   Daumer, after Hafiz
    3 Sonntag   Uhland, from 'Volkslieder'
    4 O liebliche Wangen   Paul Flemming
    5 Die Liebende schreibt   Goethe

48 Seven Songs 1868
    1 Der Gang zum Liebchen   From the Czech
    2 Der Ueberläufer   From 'Des Knaben Wunderhorn'
    3 Liebesklage des Mädchens   From 'Des Knaben Wunderhorn'
    4 Gold überwiegt die Liebe   From the Czech
    5 Trost in Tränen   Goethe
    6 Vergangen ist mir Glück und Old German
      Heil
    7 Herbstgefühl   A. F. von Schack

49 Five Songs 1868
    1 Am Sonntag Morgen   Heyse, from 'Italienisches
                               Liederbuch'
    2 An ein Veilchen   Hölty
    3 Sehnsucht   From the Czech
    4 Wiegenlied (to 'B. F.' in   G. Scherer
      Vienna)
    5 Abenddämmerung   Schack

57 Eight Songs 1871   G. F. Daumer

             SET I
    1 Von waldbekränzter Höhe
    2 Wenn du nur zuweilen lächelst
    3 Es träumte mir
    4 Ach, wende diesen Blick

            SET II
    5 In meiner Nächte Sehnen
    6 Strahlt zuweilen
    7 Die Schnur, die Perl' an Perle
    8 Unbewegte laue Luft

58 Eight Songs 1871

            SET I
    1 Blinde Kuh   August Kopisch, from the Italian
    2 Während des Regens   Kopisch
    3 Die Spröde   Kopisch, from the Calabrian
    4 O komme, holde   M. Grohe
      Sommernacht

            SET II
    5 Schwermut   Carl Candidus
    6 In der Gasse   Friedrich Hebbel
    7 Vorüber   Hebbel
    8 Serenade   Schack

59 Eight Songs 1873
            SET I
    1 Dämm'rung senkte sich von Goethe
      oben
    2 Auf dem See   Carl Simrock
    3 Regenlied   Klaus Groth

4 Nachklang   Groth

SET II

5 Agnes   Mörike
6 Eine gute, gute Nacht   Daumer
7 Mein wundes Herz   Groth
8 Dein blaues Auge   Groth
— Five Songs of Ophelia from 'Hamlet' Shakespeare
 (1873) 1935
 1 Wie erkenn' ich dein Treulieb
 2 Sein Leichenhemd weiß wie Schnee zu seh'n
 3 Auf morgen ist Sankt Valentin's Tag
 4 Sie trugen ihn auf der Bahre bloss
 5 Und kommt er nicht mehr zurück?
 German Version by Schlegel und Tieck
63 Nine Songs 1874

SET I

 1 Frühlingstrost   Max von Schenkendorf
 2 Erinnerung   Schenkendorf
 3 An ein Bild   Schenkendorf
 4 An die Tauben   Schenkendorf

SET II

 5 Junge Lieder, I ('Meine Liebe Felix Schumann
  ist grün')
 6 Junge Lieder, II ('Wenn um   Felix Schumann
  den Hollunder')
 7 Heimweh, I ('Wie traulich   Groth
  war')
 8 Heimweh, II ('O wüsst ich   Groth
  doch')
 9 Heimweh, III ('Ich sah als   Groth
  Knabe')
69 Nine Songs 1877

SET I

 1 Klage, I   Joseph Wenzig, from the Czech
 2 Klage, II   Wenzig, from the Slovak
 3 Abschied   Wenzig, from the Czech
 4 Des Liebsten Schwur   Wenzig, from the Czech
 5 Tambourliedchen   Carl Candidus

SET II

 6 Vom Strande   Eichendorff, from the Spanish
            Carl Lemcke
 7 Über die See   Gottfried Keller
 8 Salome   Kapper, from the Serbian
 9 Mädchenfluch
70 Four Songs 1877
 1 Im Garten am Seegestade   Lemcke
 2 Lerchengesang   Candidus
 3 Serenate   Goethe
 4 Abendregen   Keller
71 Five Songs 1877
 1 Es liebt sich so lieblich   Heine
 2 An den Mond   Simrock

3 Geheimnis   Candidus
4 Willst du, dass ich geh'   Lemcke
5 Minnelied   Hölty

72 Five Songs 1877
    1 Alte Liebe   Candidus
    2 Sommerfäden   Candidus
    3 O kühler Wald   C. Brentano
    4 Verzagen   Lemcke
    5 Unüberwindlich   Goethe

84 Five Songs and Romances (*see also* Vocal Duets) 1882
    1 Sommerabend   Hans Schmidt
    2 Der Kranz   Schmidt
    3 In den Beeren   Schmidt
    4 Vergebliches Ständchen   Traditional
      (Lower Rhenish)
    5 Spannung (Lower Rhenish)   Traditional

85 Six Songs 1882
    1 Sommerabend   Heine
    2 Mondenschein   Heine
    3 Mädchenlied   Siegfried Kapper, from the
                                               Serbian
    4 Ade!   Kapper, from the Czech
    5 Frühlingslied   Geibel
    6 In Waldeseinsamkeit   Lemcke

86 Six Songs (1882)
    1 Therese   Keller
    2 Feldeinsamkeit   Hermann Allmers
    3 Nachtwandler   Max Kalbeck
    4 Über die Haide   Theodor Storm
    5 Versunken   Felix Schumann
    6 Todessehnen   Schenkendorf

91 Two Songs for contralto with viola *obbligato* 1884
    1 Gestillte Sehnsucht   Rückert
    2 Geistliches Wiegenlied   Geibel, after Lope de Vega

94 Five Songs 1884
    1 Mit vierzig Jahren   Rückert
    2 Steig auf, geliebter Schatten   Friedrich Halm
    3 Mein Herz ist schwer   Geibel
    4 Sapphische Ode   Schmidt
    5 Kein Haus, keine Heimat   Halm, from a drama

95 Seven Songs 1884
    1 Das Mädchen   Kapper, from the Serbian
    2 Bei dir sind meine Gedanken   Halm
    3 Beim Abschied (2 versions)   Halm
    4 Der Jäger   Halm
    5 Vorschneller Schwur   Kapper, from the Serbian
    6 Mädchenlied   Heyse, from the Italian
    7 Schön war, das ich dir weihte   Daumer

96 Four Songs 1886
    1 Der Tod, das ist die kühle   Heine
      Nacht
    2 Wir wandelten   Daumer
    3 Es schauen die Blumen   Heine
    4 Meerfahrt   Heine

97 Six Songs (1886)
    1 Nachtigall   C. Reinhold

97 Six Songs (1886)	
1 Nachtigall	C. Reinhold
2 Auf dem Schiffe	Reinhold
3 Entführung	Willibald Alexis
4 Dort in den Weiden (Lower Rhenish)	Traditional
5 Komm bald	Groth
6 Trennung (Swabian)	Traditional
105 Five Songs 1888	
1 Wie Melodien zieht es	Groth
2 Immer leiser wird mein Schlummer	Hermann Lingg
3 Klage (Lower Rhenish)	Traditional
4 Auf dem Kirchhofe	Detlev von Liliencron
5 Verrat	Lemcke
106 Five Songs 1888	
1 Ständchen	Franz Kugler
2 Auf dem See	Reinhold
3 Es hing der Reif	Groth
4 Meine Lieder	Adolf Frey
5 Ein Wanderer	Reinhold
107 Five Songs 1888	
1 An die Stolze	Flemming
2 Salamander	Lemcke
3 Das Mädchen spricht	O. F. Gruppe
4 Maienkätzchen	Liliencron
5 Mädchenlied	Heyse
121 'Vier ernste Gesänge' 1896	Biblical
1 Denn es gehet dem Menschen	
2 Ich wandte mich und sahe	
3 O Tod, wie bitter	
4 Wenn ich mit Menschen-und mit Engelzungen	
— 'Regenlied' (1872) 1908	Groth

Arrangement for Voice and Piano

103 Eight *Zigeunerlieder* (from the Vocal Quartets) 1888

Vocal Duets

20 Three Duets for soprano and contralto 1862	
1 Weg der Liebe, I	Herder, from 'Stimmen der Völker'
2 Weg der Liebe, II	
3 Die Meere	'From the Italian'
28 Four Duets for contralto and baritone 1863	
1 Die Nonne und der Ritter	Eichendorff
2 Vor der Tür	Old German
3 Es rauschet das Wasser	Goethe
4 Der Jäger und sein Liebchen	Hoffmann von Fallersleben

61 Four Duets for soprano and contralto 1874
    1 Die Schwestern   Mörike
    2 Klosterfräulein   Justinus Kerner
    3 Phänomen   Goethe
    4 Die Boten der Liebe   Wenzig, from the Czech
66 Five Duets for soprano and contralto 1875
    1 Klänge, I   Groth
    2 Klänge, II   Groth
    3 Am Strande   Hölty
    4 Jägerlied   Candidus
    5 Hüt' du dich   From 'Des Knaben Wunderhorn'
75 Four Ballads and Romances (1878)
    1 Edward (contralto and tenor)   From Herder's 'Volkslieder'
    2 Guter Rat (soprano and   From 'Des Knaben Wunderhorn'
      contralto   Wenzig, from the Czech
    3 So lass uns wandern (soprano
      and contralto)   Willibald Alexis
    4 Walpurgisnacht (2 sopranos)
84 Songs and Romances, for 1 or 2 voices (*see* Songs) 1882

Vocal Trio

— 'Dar geit en Bek' (see op. 44/9) 1952   Groth

Vocal Quartets[1]

31 Three Quartets, with pianoforte 1864
    1 Wechsellied zum Tanze   Goethe
    2 Neckereien (Moravian)   Traditional
    3 Der Gang zum Liebchen   Traditional
      (Czech)
52 *Liebeslieder-walzer*, for pianoforte   Daumer
    duet with voices *ad lib* 1869

64 Three Quartets, with pianoforte 1874
    1 An die Heimat   C. O. Sternau
    2 Der Abend   Schiller
    3 Fragen   Daumer
65 *Neue Liebeslieder-walzer, with*   Daumer (final number Goethe)
    pianoforte duet 1875

92 Four Quartets with pianoforte 1874–84:
    1 O schöne Nacht   Daumer
    2 Spätherbst   Allmers
    3 Abendlied   Hebbel
    4 Warum?   Goethe
103 'Zigeunerlieder',
    with pianoforte 1888:   From the Hungarian tr. H.
                         Conrat

---

[1] All for soprano, contralto, tenor and bass.

       1 He, Zigeuner
       2 Hochgetürmte Rimaflut
       3 Wisst ihr, wann mein Kindchen
       4 Lieber Gott, du weisst
       5 Brauner Bursche
       6 Röslein dreie
       7 Kommt dir manchmal in den Sinn
       8 Horch, der Wind klagt
       9 Weit und breit
      10 Mond verhüllt sein Angesicht
      11 Rote Abendwolken ziehn
112 Six Quartets with pianoforte 1891:
       1 Sehnsucht   F. Kugler
       2 Nächtens   Kugler
       3 Himmel strahlt so helle
       4 Rote Rosenknospen   'Zigeunerlieder' (H. Conrat)
       5 Brennessel stehtam
          Wegestrand
       6 Liebe Schwalbe

Choral Works (Accompanied)

— Kyrie for 4-part mixed choir with continuo (1856) 1984
 12 Ave Maria for female voices,   Liturgical
     orchestra or organ 1861
 13 Funeral Hymn for mixed voices and
     wind band 1861
 17 Partsongs for female voices, 2 horns
     and harp 1861
  1 Es tönt ein voller Harfenklang   Ruperti
  2 Song from 'Twelfth Night'   Shakespeare
  3 Der Gärtner   Eichendorff
  4 Gesang aus Fingal   Ossian
 27 Psalm XIII for female voices and   Biblical
     organ (or pianoforte) 1864
 30 Geistliches Lied 'Lass dich nur nichts   Paul Flemming
     dauern' for mixed voices and
     organ (or pianoforte) 1864
 44 (With pianoforte ad lib., see Choral
     Works (Unaccompanied))
 45 Ein deutsches Requiem for soprano   From Luther's translation of the Bible
     and baritone solo, chorus and
     orchestra 1869
 50 Cantata Rinaldo for tenor, male   Goethe
     chorus and orchestra 1869
 53 Rhapsodie (fragment from   Goethe
     'Harzreise im Winter') for
     contralto solo, male chorus and
     orchestra 1870
 54 Schicksalslied for chorus and   Hölderlin
     orchestra 1871

55 *Triumphlied* for chorus and orchestra   Revelation of St John
    1872
— 'Kleine Hochzeitskantate' for 4-part   Gottfried Keller
    chorus and pianoforte 1927
82 *Nänie* for chorus and orchestra   Schiller
    (1881)
89 *Gesang der Parzen* (from 'Iphigenie   Goethe
    auf Tauris') for chorus and
    orchestra 1883
93ʙ *Tafellied* ('Dank der Damen'),
    drinking/glee for 6-part chorus
    and pianoforte 1885

Choral Works (Unaccompanied)

Mass movements for 4- and 6-part mixed choir: Sanctus, Hosanna, Benedictus,
Agnus Dei, Dona Nobis Pacem (1856) 1984
22 'Marienlieder' for 4-part mixed voices. Traditional 1862
    1 Der englische Gruss
    2 Marias Kirchgang
    3 Marias Wallfahrt
    4 Der Jäger
    5 Ruf zur Maria
    6 Magdalena
    7 Marias Lob
29 Two Motets for 5-part mixed voices 1864
    1 Es ist das Heil   Paul Speratus
    2 Schaffe in mir, Gott   Psalm LI
37 Three Sacred Choruses for female voices   Liturgical
    1865
    1 O bone Jesu
    2 Adoramus te
    3 Regina coeli
41 Five Partsongs for male voices 1867
    1 Ich schwing mein Horn ins   Old German
        Jammertal
    2 Freiwillige her!   Carl Lemcke
    3 Geleit   Lemcke
    4 Marschieren   Lemcke
    5 Gebt Acht!   Lemcke
42 Three Partsongs for 6-part mixed voices 1869
    1 Abendständchen   Clemens Brentano
    2 Vineta   Wilhelm Müller
    3 Darthulas Grabesgesang   Ossian, translator Herder
44 Twelve Songs and Romances for female voices (with pianoforte *ad lib.*) 1866
                PART I
    1 Minnelied   J. H. Voss
    2 Der Bräutigam   Eichendorff
    3 Barcarole   Traditional Italian
    4 Fragen   Traditional Slav
    5 Die Müllerin   Adalbert von Chamisso
    6 Die Nonne   Uhland

PART II

1 Nun stehn die Rosen
2 Die Berge sind spitz
3 Am Wildbach die Weiden   From Paul Heyse's 'Jungbrunnen'
4 Und gehst du über den
    Kirchhof   Müller
5 Die Braut   Uhland
6 Märznacht

62 Seven Partsongs for mixed voices 1874
1 Rosmarin   From 'Des Knaben Wunderhorn'
2 Von alten Liebesliedern
3 Waldesnacht   From Heyse's 'Jungbrunnen'
4 Dein Herzlein mild
5 All' meine Herzgedanken
6 Es geht ein Wehen
7 Vergangen ist mir Glück und   Old German
    Heil

74 Two Motets for mixed chorus 1878
1 Warum ist das Licht gegeben?   Luther
2 O Heiland, reiss die Himmel   Anon.
    auf (1863–)

93A Six Songs and Romances for mixed chorus 1884
1 Der bucklichte Fiedler   Rhenish Folksong
2 Das Mädchen   Siegfried Kapper (Serbian)
3 O süsser Mai   L. Achim von Arnim
4 Fahr wohl   Rückert
5 Der Falke   Kapper (Serbian)
6 Beherzigung   Goethe

104 Five Partsongs for mixed chorus 1888
1 Nachtwache: 'Leise Töne der   Rückert
    Brust'
2 Nachtwache: 'Ruhn sie?'   Rückert
3 Letztes Glück   Max Kalbeck
4 Verlorene Jugend   J. Wenzig, from the Czech
5 Im Herbst   Klaus Groth

109 'Fest und Gedenksprüche' 1890   Biblical
1 Unsere Väter hofften auf dich
2 Wenn ein starker Gewappneter
3 Wo ist ein so herrlich Volk

110 Three Motets for 4- and 8-part mixed chorus 1890
1 Ich aber bin elend   Biblical
2 Ach, arme Welt   Anon.
3 Wenn wir in höchsten Nöten   Paul Eber
    sind

— Dem Dunkeln Schoss der Heil'gen   Schiller ('Lied von der Glocke')
    Erde (for four-part chorus)
    1927

— Dein Herzlein mild, (4-part female chorus), Heyse, 1938

Folksong Arrangements for Solo Voice and Pianoforte

Volks-Kinderlieder (1858) 1926
  1 Dornröschen
  2 Die Nachtigall
  3 Die Henne
  4 Sandmännchen
  5 Der Mann
  6 Heidenröslein
  7 Das Schlaraffenland
  8A Beim Ritt auf dem Knie ('Ull Mann wull riden')
  8B Beim Ritt auf dem Knie ('Alt Mann wollt reiten')
  9 Der Jäger im Walde
  10 Das Mädchen und die Hasel
  11 Wiegenlied
  12 Weihnachten
  13 Marienwürmchen
  14 Dem Schutzengel

Twenty-eight *Deutsche Volkslieder* (1858) 1928
  1 Die Schnürbrust
  2 Der Jäger
  3 Drei Vögelein
  4 Auf, gebet uns das Pfingstei
  5 Des Markgrafen Töchterlein
  6 Der Reiter
  7 Die heilige Elisabeth an ihrem Hochzeitsfeste
  8 Der englische Gruss
  9 Ich stund an einem Morgen
  10 Gunhilde
  11 Der tote Gast
  12 Tageweis von einer schönen Frauen
  13 Schifferlied
  14 Nachtgesang
  15 Die beiden Königskinder
  16 Scheiden
  17 Altes Minnelied
  18A Der getreue Eckart
  18B Der getreue Eckart
  19 Die Versuchung
  20 Der Tochter Wunsch
  21 Schnitter Tod
  22 Marias Wallfahrt
  23 Das Mädchen und der Tod
  24 Es ritt ein Ritter wohl durch das Ried
  25 Liebeslied
  26 Guten Abend, mein tausiger Schatz
  27 Der Wollust in den Maien
  28 Es reit' ein Herr und auch sein Knecht

Forty-nine *Deutsche Volkslieder* (various dates): 1894

BOOK I
  1 Sagt mir, o schönste Schäf'rin mein
  2 Erlaube mir, feins Mädchen
  3 Gar lieblich hat sich gesellet
  4 Guten Abend, mein tausiger Schatz

5 Die Sonne scheint nicht mehr
6 Da unten im Tale
7 Gunhilde lebt gar stille und fromm

BOOK II

8 Ach, englische Schäferin
9 Es war eine schöne Jüdin
10 Es ritt ein Ritter
11 Jungfräulein, soll ich mit euch gehn
12 Feinsliebchen, du sollst mir nicht barfuss gehn
13 Wach auf, mein Hort
14 Maria ging aus wandern

BOOK III

15 Schwesterlein, Schwesterlein
16 Wach auf, mein Herzensschöne
17 Ach Gott, wie weh tut scheiden
18 So wünsch ich ihr ein gute Nacht
19 Nur ein Gesicht auf Erden lebt
20 Schönster Schatz, mein Engel
21 Es ging ein Maidlein zarte

BOOK IV

22 Wo gehst du hin, du Stolze?
23 Der Reiter spreitet seinen Mantel aus
24 Mir ist ein schöns brauns Maidelein
25 Mein Mädel hat einen Rosenmund
26 Ach könnt ich diesen Abend
27 Ich stand auf hohem Berge
28 Es reit' ein Herr und auch sein Knecht

BOOK V

29 Es war ein Markgrai überm Rhein
30 All mein Gedanken
31 Dort in den Weiden steht ein Haus
32 So will ich frisch und fröhlich sein
33 Och Moder, ich well en Ding han!
34 Wie komm ich denn zur Tür herein?
35 Soll sich der Mond nicht heller scheinen

BOOK VI

36 Es wohnt ein Fiedler
37 Du mein einzig Licht
38 Des Abends kann ich nicht schlafen gehn
39 Schöner Augen, schöne Strahlen
40 Ich weiss mir'n Maidlein hübsch und fein
41 Es steht ein Lind
42 In stiller Nacht, zur ersten Wacht

BOOK VII (with 4-part chorus *ad lib.*)

43 Es stunden drei Rosen
44 Dem Himmel will ich klagen
45 Es sass ein schneeweiss Vögelein
46 Es war einmal ein Zimmergesell
47 Es ging sich unsre Fraue
48 Nachtigall, sag, was für Grüss
49 Verstohlen geht der Mond auf

Thirty-Two New Folksongs (Nos. 1–28 solo with piano, 29–32 for four-part mixed choir), ed. Friedlander, Deütscher Brahms, Gesellschaft, (various dates), 1926.

1 Verstohlen geht der Mond auf	18 Die beiden Königskinder
2 Der Ritter und die Feine	19 Scheiden
3 Die Schnürbrust	20 Altes Minnelied
4 Der Jäger	21a Der getreue Eckart
5 Der Zimmergesell	21b Der getreue Eckart
6 Drei Vögelein	22 Die Versuchung
7 Auf, gebet uns das Pfingstei	23 Der Tochter Wunsch
8 Des Markgrafen Töchterlein	24 Schnitter Tod
9 Der Reiter	25 Marias Wallfahrt
10 Die heilige Elisabeth	26 Das Mädchen und der Tod
11 Der englische Gruß	27 Es ritt ein Ritter
12 Ich stund an einem Morgen	28 Altdeutsches Kampflied
13 Gunhilde	29 Liebeslied
14 Der tote Gast	30 Guten Abend
15 Tageweis' von einer schönen Frauen	31 Die Wollust in den Maien
16 Schifferlied	32 Es reit' ein Herr und auch sein
17 Nachtgesang	Knecht

(Only nos. 3, 7, 10, 11, 12, 18, 21a, 21b, 28 are not duplicated elsewhere.)

Canons

113 Thirteen Canons for female voices:
      No. 1, Göttlicher Morpheus (Goethe); No. 2, Grausam erweiset sich Amor (Goethe); No. 3, Sitzt a schöns Vögerl aufm Dannabaum; No. 4, Schlaf, Kindlein, schlaf (Traditional); No. 5, Wille wille will (Traditional); No. 6, So lange Schönheit wird bestehn (Hoffmann von Fallersleben); No. 7, Wenn die Klänge nahn und fliehen (Eichendorff); No. 8, Ein Gems auf dem Stein (Eichendorff); No. 9, Ans Auge des Liebsten (Rückert); No. 10, Leise Töne der Brust (Rückert); No. 11, Ich weiss nicht, was im Hain die Taube girret (Rückert); No. 12, Wenn Kummer hätte zu töten Macht (Rückert); No. 13, Einförmig ist der lieber Gram (Rückert).
— Canons for 4 female voices: No. 1, Mir lächelt kein Frühling (? words); No. 2, Grausam erweiset sich Amor (Goethe); No. 3, O wie sanft (Daumer) 1908
— Canon for soprano and alto: Wann (Uhland) 1885
— Canons for 4 mixed voices: No. 1, Töne, lindernder Klang (? words); No. 2, Zu Rauch (Rückert). 1927
— Canon for voice and viola: Spruch (Hoffmann von Fallersleben)

Folksong Arrangements for 4-part Chorus Unaccompanied

Fourteen *Deutsche Volkslieder* 1864

BOOK I

    1 Von edler Art
    2 Mit Lust tät ich ausreiten
    3 Bei nächtlicher Weil
    4 Vom heiligen Märtyrer, Emmerano, Bischoffen zu Regenspurt
    5 Täublein weiss

6 Ach lieber Herre Jesu Christ
7 Sankt Raphael
8 In stiller Nacht
9 Abschiedslied
10 Der tote Knabe
11 Die Wollust in den Mayen
12 Morgengesang
13 Schnitter Tod
14 Der englische Jäger
Additional Numbers (? 1863–1864) 1927
15 Scheiden
16 Wach auf!
17 Erlaube mir
18 Der Fiedler
19 Da unten im Tale
20 Des Abends
21 Wach auf!
22 Dort in den Weiden
23 Altes Volkslied ('Verstohlen geht der Mond auf')
24 Der Ritter und die Feine
25 Der Zimmergesell
26 Altdeutsches Kampflied ('Wir stehen hier zur Schlacht bereit'). *See also* '49 Deutsche Volkslieder,' Book VII, *above.*

Folksong Arrangements For 4-part Chorus Unaccompanied

(Various Modern Collections). Seven Folksongs, ed. Drinker, University of Pennsylvania, 1940 (from the part-books of the Hamburg Women's Choir)
Altes Lied (Minnelied)
Der todte Gast
Ich hab' die Nacht geträumet
Altes Liebeslied
Es waren zwei Königskinder
Spannung
Mit Lust thät ich ausreiten

Thirteen Folksongs, ed. Kross, *Der Chorsänger*, Bärenreiter, 1965
Bärenreiter, 1965
Ich hab die Nacht getrnümet
Schwesterlein, Schwesterlein
Ich hörte ein Sichlein rauschen
Ich stand auf hohem Berge
Die Versuchung
Altes Minnelied
Da unten im Tale
Der Jäger
Scheiden
Zu Straßburg auf der Schanz
Minuelied
Wach auf, mein Hart
Ständchen

Twenty-six Folksongs (with canon 'Göttlicher Morpheus' and 'Benedictus') ed.
Gotwals and Keppler, Smith College 1968
    1 Auf, auf, auf! Schätzelein
    2 Der Holdseligen sonder Wank
    3 Des Abends kann ich nicht schlafen
    4 Dort in den Weiden
    5 Erlaube mir, feins Mädchen
    6 Es glänzt der Mond nieder
    7 Es ist ein Schnitter
    8 Es reiten drei Reiter
    9 Es stehen drei Sterne
   10 Es steht ein Baum im Odenwald
   11 Es war ein Markgraf
   12 Es war eine stolze Jüdin
   13 Es war einmal ein Zimmergesell
   14 Gar lieblich hat sich gesellet
   15 Ich schwing mein Horn
   16 Kein Feuer, keine Kohle
   17 Mein Herzlein thut mir gar zu weh!
   18 Mein Schatz, ich hab es erfahren
   19 Mein Schatz ist auf die Wanderschaft
   20 Mein Schatz ist nicht da
   21 Morgen muss ich fort von hier
   22 Sind wir geschieden
   23 So hab ich doch die ganze Woche
   24 Soll sich der Mond
   25 Verstohlen geht der Mond auf
   26 Wenn ich ein Vöglein wär
Twenty-seven Folksongs ed. Helms, Bärenreiter, 1970
    1 Die Entführung
    2 Minnelied
    3 Gang zur Liebsten
    4 Erlaube mir, feins Mädchen
    5 Der Gang zum Liebchen
    6 Liebeslied
    7 Dauernde Liebe
    8 Heimliche Liebe
    9 Altes Liebeslied
   10 Während der Trennung
   11 Sehnsucht
   12 Scheiden
   13 Morgen muß ich fort von hier
   14 Sonntag
   15 Vor dem Fenster
   16 Ständchen
   17 Spannung
   18 Mit Lust tät ich ausreiten
   19 Der Zimmergesell
   20 Die stolze Jüdin
   21 Der Baum im Odenwald
   22 Der eifersüchtige Knabe
   23 Des Markgrafen Töchterlein
   24 Die Bernauerin

25 Schifferlied
26 Schnitter Tod
27 Wenn ich ein Vöglein wär
For further arrangements (for mixed voices) see:
S. Kross, 'Brahmsiana, Der Nachlass der Schwestern Völkers', *Die Musikforschung*, vol. 17, no. 2, pp. 137–151.

Editions of Works by Other Composers

C. P. E. Bach. Six Concerti for Clavier with two violins, viola, cello
(Hamburg, Cranz, 1862)
W. F. Bach. Sonata for two Claviers by W. F. Bach (Sonata in F) (later printed as a first edition of a work by J. S. Bach in vol. 43 of the Bach Gesellschaft Edition), but restituted.   1864
Chopin *Friedrich Chopins Werke, Erste kritisch durchgesehene Gesamtausgabe*, ed. Brahms, Liszt, and others. 14 vols, Breitkopf & Hartel. Vol. 8 Sonata in B flat minor, op. 35, Sonata in B minor, op. 58   1878
Vol. 10 Fantasia in F minor, op. 49, Barcarolle in F sharp minor op. 60   1879
Vol. 3 Mazurkas   1880
Vol. 13 Sonata in C minor op 4   1880
(Brahms also advised Bargiel in the editing of the Polonaises (vol. 5) and Nocturnes (vol. 4))
Couperin *Denkmäler der Tonkunst (ed. F Chrysander) Vol. 4* Fr. Couperin, Pièces de Clavecin, Livre 1, 11 (Paris, 1713 and 1716–17) published as *Clavierstücke*.   1871
Mozart *Wolfgang Amadeus Mozart, Kritisch durchgesehene Gesamtausgabe* (Breitkopf & Härtel) Series 24, *Requiem* K. 626.   1877
Schubert *Three Piano Pieces by F. Schubert* (Impromptus in E flat minor, E flat major and C major) Rieter-Biedermann.   1868 1869
Schubert Twelve Ländler for Piano op. 171, Spina   1864
Schubert Twenty Ländler for Piano (posthumous), Gotthard,   1869
Schubert Twenty Ländler for piano duet (posthumous), Gotthard,   1869
Schubert *Franz Schuberts Werke, Kritisch durchgesehene Gesamtausgabe* Series 1. Symphonies 1–4, 5–8 Vols Breitkopf & Härtel   1884–5
Schubert Quartet-movement in C minor for two violins, viola and 'cello, Senff 1870
Schubert Song: 'Der Strom', Stadler, for voice and piano, Fritsch,   1877
Schumann *Scherzo and Presto Passionato for Piano* (from Schumann's posthumous works) Rieter-Biedermann   1866
Schumann *Etudes Symphoniques en Forme de Variations* for Piano. Third Edition, including five discarded variations. Simrock (First published 1861)   1873
Schumann *Robert Schumanns Werke, herausgegeben von Clara Schumann* Breitkopf & Härtel,   1893
Series 14. Nine posthumous Works ed. with preface by Brahms. 1 Andante and Variations for two Pianos, two Cellos and Horn
2–4 Songs for solo voice and piano.
5 Song for two voices and piano
6 Symphonic Studies – see above
7 Scherzo for Piano
8 Presto for Piano
9 Theme in E flat for Piano.
Schumann 'Vom Pagen und der Konigstöchter' for solo voices, choir and orchestra, op. 140. Rieter-Biedermann   1857

Arrangements of Works by Other Composers

For Piano, 2 hands

Studies for Piano, Senff,

Etude after Chopin (Etude in F minor, op. 25)	1869
Rondo after Weber (Sonata op. 24 in C, Finale)	
Presto after J. S. Bach. (Violin Sonata in G, Presto)	1878
The same, version 2	
Chaconne by J. S. Bach. (Chaconne for Violin solo) for left hand	

Gluck *Gavotte in A* (from Iphigénie en Aulide – originally composed for Paride e
Elena), Senff,   1871(?)

Schumann. Scherzo from Piano Quintet in E flat, op. 44, Breitkopf and Härtel
(Wiesbaden) (1854)   1983

For Piano, 4 hands

For two pianos

Joachim *Overture to Shakespeare's 'Henry the Fourth'* op. 7 Simrock (1855)   1902

For one piano, four hands

Schumann Piano Quartet in E flat op. 47, Fürstner (1855)   1887

Continuo realisation

Handel *Georg Friedrich Handels Werke,* ed. F. Chrysander, Breitkopf and Härtel,
Vol. 32 (13) Duets and (2) Trios for Solo Voices   1870
Vol. 32 (6 Duets for Soprano and alto)   1880

Violin and piano

C. P. E. Bach Sonata in B minor and C minor (Wotquenne 76, 78), Rieter-
Biedermann,   1864

Choral

J. R. Ahle Chorale from Cantata 'Es ist genug', Bosse,   1933
J. S. Bach Chorale from Cantata 'O Ewigkeit, du Donnerwort', Bosse,   1933
J. S. Bach Chorale 'Ach Gott, wie manches Herzeleid' from Cantata 'Sie werden
euch in die Bann tun'
Mozart Offertorium 'Venite Populi' for double four-part chorus and organ K 260
(now 248a), Gotthard,   1873
Schubert Mass in E flat, Rieter-Biedermann   1865
Schubert Ellens Second Song from Scott's *Lady of the Lake* arranged for soprano
solo, three-part female chorus horns and bassoons, Deutsche Brahms
Gesellschaft,   1906
Eccard 'Marienlied' (Übers Gebirg Maria geht') University of Pennsylvania,   1943

Vocal and orchestral

Schubert 'Tartarus' arranged with orchestral accompaniment   1937
'Memnon', 'An Schwager Kronos', 'Geheimnis', 'Griesengesang', arranged with
orchestral accompaniment, Oxford University Press,   1933

For details of further, joint editorial activity see K. Hofmann, *Die Erstdrücke von Johannes Brahms*, Tutzing, Schneider, 1975, pp. 378 et seq.

Literary Work

Des Jungen Kreislers Schatzkästlein ('The Treasure Chest of the Young Kreisler') ed. C. Krebs, Deutsche Brahms Gesellschaft	1909

Theoretical Work

Oktaven und Quinten u. A., ed. H Schenker (Facsimile of Brahms's autograph transcriptions from the works of various composers), Universal	1933

Dubious Works

Trio in A major for Piano, Violin and Cello, Breitkopf and Härtel	1938
Trumpet Studies, Leichssenring	1920
Cadenza for Mozart's Piano Concerto K. 466, ed. Badura-Skoda, Doblinger	1980
Arrangement of the Violin Sonata in G major, op. 78 for 'cello, ed Starker, International	1975
Arrangement of Schubert's Impromptu in E flat major for left hand, Breitkopf and Härtel	1927

Calendar

This calendar emphasises Brahms's activities as a performer in relation to the outer pattern of his life and includes first and other early performances of his works, including some in England.

It is selective, both of the contents of his programmes – to reflect their range, and some recurrent preferences – and of first performances, omitting individual short pieces which are hard to trace consistently. For a full treatment of first performances the reader is referred to:

R. and K. Hofmann, *Johannes Brahms. Zeittafel zu Leben und Werk*, Tutzing, Schneider, 1983

First reference to a Brahms's work, with opus number, is to its first public performance, insofar as this can be established.

Successive locations do not necessarily imply successive movement. Brahms travelled frequently: Until the summer of 1862 his base was Hamburg, thereafter Vienna. Bracketed locations are to performances other than by Brahms.

Abbreviations

VPO   Vienna Philharmonic Orchestra
HPO   Hamburg Philharmonic Orchestra
LGO   Leipzig Gewandhaus Orchestra
RPS   Royal Philharmonic Society
CPO   Crystal Palace Orchestra
HCO   Hanover Court Orchestra
HFC   Hamburg Frauenchor
GdM   Gesellschaft der Musikfreunde in Wien.

Chamber, other than named, groups are indicated by the leader's name, e.g. Deichmann group. Chamber works with piano give the violinist first and pianist last.

Life		*Performances*
1833		
May 7	Born in Hamburg, son of Johann Jacob Brahms and Christiane Nissen	
1835	Birth of brother, Friedrich	
Mar 26	(Fritz)	
1839	Father teaches him the elements of music with the aim of making him an orchestral player	
1840	Takes lessons from Otto Cossell (pupil of Marxsen)	
1842	Rapid progress at the piano	
1843	Some lessons from Marxsen	Private subscription concert for funds for his future education by Brahms, his father and local musicians: includes Beethoven's Wind Quintet op. 16, a Mozart piano quartet and an Etude by Henri Herz
1845	Becomes entirely Marxsen's pupil	
1846		Plays at bars in dockside Hamburg
1847	Invited for long summer at Winsen, near Hamburg, where composes male-choir pieces (unpublished)	
Nov 20	Hamburg	First public concert. Plays Thalberg's Fantasia on Themes from Bellini's *Norma*
1848		
Spring	Winsen	
Sep 21	Hamburg	*First solo concert.* Plays Adagio and Rondo from Rosenhain's Concerto in A major, Döhler's Fantasia on Themes from Rossini's *Wilhelm Tell*, a J. S. Bach Fugue, Marxsen's Serenade for left hand, a Herz Etude
	Hamburg First visit to the opera to see Mozart, *The Marriage of Figaro*	
1849		
Apr 10th	Hamburg	*Second public concert* – better advertised. Programme includes Beethoven, *Waldstein* Sonata, Brahms, Fantasia on a favourite waltz, Thalberg Fantasia on Themes from Don Juan. Mayer, *'Air italien'*
1850		
Aug 14	Meets Eduard Reményi and becomes acquainted with his	

	'Hungarian' music	
	Continues piano and composition studies with Marxsen. The Schumanns visit Hamburg: Brahms sends manuscripts, but they are returned unopened.	
Feb	Plays Scherzo in E flat minor (op. 4) to Henry Litolff	
1851	His friend Louise Japha leaves Hamburg to study with the Schumanns at Düsseldorf, but	
1852	Brahms continues his studies and writes the Sonata in F sharp minor (op. 2) [Bach Gesellschaft Edition begins]	
1853		
Apr	Reményi returns to Hamburg. Brahms begins concert tour with him. Winsen, Celle, Luneberg	Programmes include Vieuxtemps, Concerto in E major; Beethoven, Violin Sonata in C minor, which Brahms transposes at sight to C sharp minor because of the low-pitched piano at the Celle concert
Apr	Meets Joachim at Hanover with Reményi	Gives private performance of Scherzo in E flat minor (op. 4) to court audience
Jun 8	Hanover. Court Concert	Scherzo in E flat minor, (op.4)
Jun 12	Meets Liszt at Weimar, also Cornelius and Raff	Plays them the Scherzo in E flat minor. Liszt plays his new Sonata in B minor
	Brahms and Reményi separate. Brahms visits Joachim at Göttingen	
Summer	Walking tour through Rhine Valley alone. Visits Cologne. Meets Hiller, Reinecke	
Sep 30	Düsseldorf. Meets the Schumanns and their circle, including Schumann's pupil Albert Dietrich, who becomes a lifelong friend	Plays them the Sonata in F sharp minor, Scherzo in E flat minor, as well as Trio Fantasy for String Quartet, String Quartet, and Violin Sonata
Oct 28	Leipzig. Schumann's article 'New Paths' appears in his *Neue Zeitschrift fur Musik*	
Nov 17	Arrives in Leipzig and is quickly introduced to the musical circle including J. Rietz, F. David, Moscheles, Friedrich and Marie Wieck. Begins his long friendship with Julius Otto Grimm.	
Dec 4	Meets Berlioz and Liszt in Leipzig	

Dec 17	Brahms's first public performance in Leipzig.	Sonata in C major (op. 1) Scherzo in E flat minor
1854		
Jan	Travels to Hanover to stay with Joachim, where he meets von Bülow	
Feb 27	Schumann attempts suicide in the Rhine and is taken to a clinic at Endenich	
Mar	Brahms hurries to Düsseldorf, as do Joachim and Dietrich	
Mar 1	(Hamburg. Von Bülow gives first public performance of a Brahms work other than by Brahms himself, at Liszt's prompting)	Sonata in C major (first mvt)
Jun	Clara's seventh child born (named Felix), Brahms takes the individual variations on a Schumann theme (op. 9) to Clara as they are composed	
Oct 23	(Leipzig. Gewandhaus Concert)	Sonata in F minor (op. 5) (mvts 2, 3. C. Schumann)
Nov 27	Schumann writes to Brahms about the op. 9 variations favourably, recognising their messages	
Dec (beginning)	(Magdeburg)	Sonata in F minor (complete) C. Schumann
1855		
	Brahms remains in Düsseldorf to help run Schumann's affairs	
May 27–9	Düsseldorf. Lower Rhine Music Festival. Meets Hanslick. Private study. Free use of Schumann's library	
Nov 20	Bremen. Brahms's first piano performance with orchestra	Beethoven, Piano Concerto in E flat major
Nov 27	(New York. First Brahms performance in America)	Piano Trio in B major (op. 8) (Thomas, Bergmann, Mason)
1856		
Jan 10	Leipzig	Beethoven, Piano Concerto in G major (LGO/Brahms)
Jan 26	Mozart Festival in Hamburg (Otten Concert)	Mozart, Piano Concerto in D minor (Brahms)
Feb	Concerts in Kiel and Altona	Programmes include: Beethoven, Sonata in E flat major op. 27; Variations in C minor; J. S. Bach. Organ Toccata in F major transcribed for piano; Beethoven, *Eroica* Variations
Feb 24	Begins contrapuntal studies with Joachim	

May 11–13	Dusseldorf. Lower Rhine Festival. Meets Julius Stockhausen and Klaus Groth	
Jun 17	(London. Hanover Square Rooms. C. Schumann Concert. First Brahms performance in England)	Sarabande and Gavotte in the style of Bach (C. Schumann)
Summer	Rhineland Concerts with Stockhausen in Cologne and Bonn	Brahms solos include: Bach, Chromatic Fantasia and Fugue and the Beethoven Variations in E flat major and C minor
Jul 27	Visits Endenich for Schumann's birthday	
Jul 29	Schumann dies. Brahms stays with Clara	
Oct (25)	Brahms returns to Hamburg	Performs Beethoven, Piano Concerto in G major
Nov	Visits Detmold	
1857		
	Hamburg. Quiet study.	
May	Visits Detmold (after contact through Clara)	Performs Beethoven's Piano Sonata in C sharp minor
Autumn	Detmold, first season	
1858		
March	Hanover	Private rehearsal of Piano Concerto in D minor
Summer	Göttingen with Clara and Joachim Meets Agathe von Siebold (expectations of engagement, but he withdraws)	Folksong arrangements for Clara's children
Autumn	Detmold (second season)	
Oct	Hanover	Joachim rehearses the Piano Concerto in D minor with the Court Orchestra
1859		
Jan 22	Hanover	Piano Concerto in D minor (op. 15) (HCO/Joachim/Brahms. Badly received)
Jan 27	Leipzig	Piano Concerto in D minor (LGO/Joachim/Brahms. Likewise)
Mar 24	Hamburg	Piano Concerto in D minor (HPO/J. Rietz/Brahms). Better reception
Mar 28	Hamburg (Wörner Hall) Concert by Brahms, Joachim, Stockhausen	Serenade in D major, (op. 11) advertised as 'Serenade for string and wind instruments' (Joachim)
Jun	Forms Ladies Choir in Hamburg further to successful performances of his choral works by *ad hoc* group	
Autumn	Detmold (third season)	
Sep 19	Hamburg. St Peter's Church	Psalm 13 (op. 27) (HFC/Brahms)

Dec 2	Hamburg. Grädener-Academy	Ave Maria (op. 12): (with orchestra) Funeral Hymn (op. 13): (HFC/ Brahms)
1860		
Jan	Leaves Detmold and returns to Hamburg	
Feb 10	Hamburg	Serenade in A major (op. 16) (HPO/Brahms)
Mar 3	Hanover	Serenade in D major (op. 11) 'for full orchestra' (HCO/Joachim)
Mar 21	(Vienna)	Ballades for Piano (op. 10 nos 2, 3.) (C. Schumann)
June	Remains at Bonn till August with Joachim.	
May 6	'Manifesto' published prematurely by Berlin Music Journal, *Echo*	
Oct 20	Hanover	String Sextet in B flat major (op. 18) (Joachim Quartet)
Nov 26	Leipzig	Serenade in D major for full orchestra, second performance/ LGO/Brahms). Badly received
1861		
Jan 15	Hamburg	Songs with Horns and Harp (op. 17) (HFC/Brahms)
Jan	Hamburg. Frequent visits from Clara, Stockhausen, Dietrich	
Mar 8	Hamburg	Beethoven, Triple Concerto (HPO, David, Davidoff/Brahms)
Summer	at Hamm, quiet suburb of Hamburg	
Nov 4	Hamburg	*Handel* Variations (op. 24) (Brahms)
Nov 16	Hamburg	Piano Quartet in G minor (op. 25) (Böie group/C. Schumann)
Dec 3	Hamburg	Piano Concerto in D minor (HPO/C. Schumann/Brahms)
Dec 7	Hamburg	*Handel* Variations (C. Schumann)
1862		
Jan 19	Munster am Stein Joachim Concert	Schumann Piano Concerto (Brahms)
Mar 14	Oldenburg. Hofkonzert	Beethoven Piano Concerto in G major J. S. Bach Chromatic Fantasia and Fugue
Spring	(Paris/Salle Erard) Brahms hopes for the directorship of the Hamburg Philharmonic, which goes to Stockhausen a year later)	Clara Schumann includes no Brahms in her programmes
Sep 8	Leaves Hamburg for Vienna In Vienna meets prominent	

	musicians including Hellmesberger, Julius Epstein, Gänsbacher, Goldmark, Grädener	
Nov 16	Vienna GdM Brahms's first public performance in Vienna. Hellmesberger Concert	Piano Quartet in G minor (Hellmesberger Quartet Brahms)
Nov 29	Vienna. Brahms's first solo appearance in Vienna	*Handel* Variations; Schumann, Fantasia in C major; J. S. Bach, Toccata in F major for organ transcribed for piano; Piano Quartet in A major (op. 26) (Hellmesberger Quartet/Brahms)
1863		
Jan 6	Vienna	Second solo performance includes Sonata in F minor complete
Mar	Wagner visits Vienna to perform parts of *Die Meistersinger*. Brahms helps to copy parts and converses, with other young composers, with Wagner (aged 50, Brahms aged 30). Meets Tausig. Meets the publisher Spina who allows him access to many Schubert manuscripts. Appointed conductor of the Wiener Singakademie	
Oct	Hamburg	*Schumann* Variations for piano duet (op. 23) (Fritz Brahms, S. Smith)
Nov 15		First Singakademie Concert Programme includes: J. S. Bach, Cantata 'Ich hatte viel Bekümmernis'; Schumann, *Requiem fur Mignon*; Pieces by Isaak
1864		
Jan 6	Singakademie Concert	Includes pieces by Eccard, Schütz, Gabrieli, Rovetta; J. S. Bach, Motet 'Liebster Gott';
Mar 20	Singakademie Concert	Bach, *Christmas Oratorio*.
May 10	Singakademie Concert	Includes English madrigals by Morley and Bennet
Apr 17	Vienna. Singakademie Concert	includes Sonata in F minor for two pianos (op. 34) (Brahms/Tausig) Motet (op. 29 no. 1) (Singakademie/Brahms)
	Resigns from Singakademie Returns to Hamburg	

Summer	Visits Baden-Baden. Meets Clara's circle which includes	
1865	Turgenev, Levi, Viardot-Garcia	
Feb 2	Hamburg. Death of Brahms's mother	
Jul 2	Chemnitz. St James' Church	*Geistliches Lied* (op. 30)
Jul 6	(London. Hanover Square Rooms. First Brahms public chamber music performance in England)	Piano Quartet in A major (L. Straus group/Agnes Zimmermann)
Summer	Lichtental, nr Baden Baden, close to C. Schumann	
Oct 31	Frankfurt am Main	Variations on an Original Theme for Piano op. 21 no. 1 (C. Schumann)
Nov	Concert Tour (Carlsruhe, Basle, Zurich, Winterthur, Mannheim)	
Nov 3	Carlsruhe	Piano Concerto in D minor, now well received (Brahms)
Nov 25	Zürich	*Paganini* Variations (op. 35)/ (Brahms)
Nov 28	Zürich	Horn Trio (op. 40) (Hegar/Gläss/ Brahms)
Dec 12	Cologne	Beethoven, Piano Concerto in E flat major
(later Dec)	Cologne. Musikverein	Programme includes J. S. Bach, Organ Prelude and Fugue in A minor
1866		
Jan	Oldenburg Hof Konzert	Schumann, Variations in B flat for piano duo, with Dietrich
	Tour of Switzerland with Joachim	
Apr/May	Winterthur (work on the *Requiem*)	
Jun 22	Leipzig (Conservatoire Concert)	Piano Quintet (op. 34) (?)
Summer	Zürich. Meets Billroth and the Wesendoncks	
Aug	Winterthur	
Oct 11	(Boston)	String Sextet in G major (op. 36) (Mendelssohn Quintet augmented/Schultze)
Nov 23	Oldenburg Hofkonzert	Waltzes (op. 39), for piano duet (C. Schumann/A. Dietrich)
	Return to Vienna	
Christmas	Oldenburg, with Dietrich	
1867		
	During this year meets the Neo-classical painter Anselm Feuerbach, whom he admires. (Feuerbach moves to Vienna in 1873)	

Feb 3	Vienna	String Sextet in G major (Hellmesberger Quartet, augmented)
Feb 25	(London, St James's Hall. First prestigious Brahms performance in England)	String Sextet in B flat major (Joachim group. Not well received)
Mar 17	Vienna.	Concert with Joachim. Brahms includes his transcription of Beethoven's String Quartet (op. 59 no. 3) – last movement
	Tour of Austrian provinces with Joachim	
Apr 7	Vienna	Concert: Programme includes Beethoven, Sonata in E (op. 109); Pieces by Scarlatti, Schubert; Arrangement of movement from the Schubert Octet.
Summer	Walking tour with father and Gänsbacher in Upper Austria	
Nov 9	Concert tour of Vienna, Budapest and provinces with Joachim	
Nov 23	Vienna	Ballades for piano (op. 10 nos 1, 4) (Brahms)
Dec 1	Vienna. GdM	*Ein deutsches Requiem* (op. 45) First performance of movements 1–3 GdM/Herbeck, Pänzer (baritone)
1868		
Feb/Mar	Tour with Stockhausen in Germany. Hamburg (expectation of the Hamburg Directorship on resignation of Stockhausen) Tour to Kiel and Copenhagen with Stockhausen	includes Schumann: Symphonic Variations with unpublished variations and Schubert songs
Mar 24	(Paris. Salle Erard. First important Brahms performance in France)	Piano Quintet in F minor Erard group/Louise Japha – now Dr Langhans-Japha)
Apr 10 (Good Friday)	Bremen Cathedral	*Ein deutsches Requiem* (op. 45) First performance, of movements 1–4, 6–7 Bremen Court Orchestra/ Brahms, J. Stockhausen, baritone
May 31–Jun 2	Cologne. Lower Rhine Festival Meets Max Bruch	
Jun/July	Bonn, with Hermann Deiters	
Nov	Oldenburg, Bremen, Hamburg Concerts with C. Schumann and Stockhausen	
1869		
Feb/Mar	Tour with Stockhausen. Vienna, GdM	*Rinaldo*, (op. 50) (Brahms, Walter)
Feb 28	Leipzig	*Ein deutsches Requiem*

Feb 28		First performance of final, seven-movement work. (LGO/C. Reinecke, E. Bellingrath-Wagner, soprano, Dr Krückel, baritone)
Summer	Lichtenthal Tour to Budapest with Stockhausen	
1870		
Mar 3	Jena Akademie-Gesangverein	Alto Rhapsody (op. 53) (Viardot-Garcia/Naumann) – later frequently by Amalie Joachim
Jul 14	Munich Attends performance of Wagner's *Die Walküre*	
Jul 17	Munich Attends a performance of Wagner's *Das Rheingold*	
1871		
Jan 14	Leipzig	Cello Sonata in E minor (op. 38) (Hegar/Reinecke)
Mar 5	Vienna GdM. First time in Vienna	*Ein deutsches Requiem* (M. Wilt, soprano, E. Kraus, baritone, Brahms)
Apr 7 (Good Friday)	Bremen Cathedral	*Requiem* and first part of the *Triumphlied* (in memory of the victims of the Franco-Prussian War (1870–1871) (Brahms)
Summer	Lichtenthal	
Oct 18	Karlsruhe	*Schicksalslied* (op. 54) (Brahms) Programme includes parts of Schumann's *Faust* (Levi)
Dec	Settles in final Viennese lodgings at 4, Carlsgasse, close to the Karlskirche and within sight of the Musikverein	
1872		
Feb 11	Death of Brahms's father	
Mar 9	(London/Crystal Palace First concerto performance by English performers)	Piano Concerto in D minor (op. 15) (CPO/Manns/Baglehole)
Jun 5	Karlsruhe H. Levi's farewell concert	*Triumphlied* (op. 55) (Court Orchestra/Levi)
Summer	Baden-Baden	Vacation includes performance of Schumann Piano Concerto and he conducts his Serenade in A major (op. 16)
	(Meets Nietzsche, whose enthusiasm for the *Triumphlied* further alienates Wagner) Vienna. Appointed to the Directorship of the Gesellschaft concerts in succession to Anton Rubinstein	
Nov 10	Vienna	First Gesellschaft concert includes Handel *Te Deum* (Dettinger)

		Schubert 'Symphony in C' (Grand Duo/orchestrated Joachim)
Nov 27	(London/St George's Hall)	Sextet in G major (op. 36)
Dec 8		Second Gesellschaft concert: Includes Brahms, *Triumphlied* (second performance); Handel, Organ Concerto; Bach, Prelude and Fugue in E flat for organ
1873		
Jan 5	Vienna	Gesellschaft Concert: Hiller, Concert Overture in D; Schumann, *Des Sängers Fluch*; Mendelssohn, *Die Erste Walpurgisnacht*
Feb 28	Vienna	Gesellschaft Concert: Handel, *Saul*
Mar 23	Vienna	Gesellschaft Concert includes Bach, Cantata 'Christ lag in Todesbanden'; Brahms, Folksong arrangements; Schubert, *Ellens zweiter Gesang*
Apr 2	(London/St James's Hall. First time in England)	*Ein deutsches Requiem* (RPS/Cusins, S. Ferrari, soprano, G. Santley)
Apr 6	Vienna	Gesellschaft Concert includes Bach, Cantata 'Liebster Gott'; Cherubini *Requiem* in C minor
May 22	Oxford	Piano Quartet in G minor (W. Parratt group)
Summer	Tutzing	
Aug 17–19	Bonn. Visits the Schumann Festival	
	Lichtenthal (with Clara)	
Autumn	Visits Vienna World Exhibition.	
Oct 18	Berlin	String Quartet in A minor (op. 51 no. 2) (Joachim Quartet)
Nov 2	Vienna GdM	*St Antoni* Variations (op. 56a) (VPO/Brahms)
Nov 29	Hamburg	String Quartet in C minor (op. 51 no. 1) (Schradieck group)
Nov 12	(London/Crystal Palace. First performance of a major solo work by an English performer)	*Handel* Variations (Florence May)
Dec 7	Vienna	Gesellschaft Concert: includes Schubert, Overture to *Fierrabras*; Schubert, Tenor aria written for Herold's *Zauberglocken*; Volkmann, Concertstuck for piano and orchestra; Ahle and Bach chorale settings; Bach, Cantata 'Nun ist das Heil'; Gallus, Motet 'Ecce quomodo';
Dec 10	Munich	*St Antoni* Variations (Levi)
1874		
Jan 1	Awarded the Order of	

	Maximilian by Ludwig of Bavaria (as is Wagner who nearly refuses it in protest) Visits Leipzig and Munich Meets the Herzogenbergs and Spitta	
Jan 25	Vienna. GdM	Gesellschaft Concert includes: Mozart, Cantata 'Davidde Penitente', Rheinberger, Prelude to opera *The Seven Ravens*; Goldmark, *Frühlingshymne*
Mar 2		Gesellschaft Concert: Schubert, Kyrie and Credo from Mass in B flat (unpublished); Schumann, *Manfred* music
Mar 25	(London/Crystal Palace)	Variations on a Hungarian Theme op. 21 no. 2 (Florence May)
Mar 31		Gesellschaft Concert; Handel, *Solomon*
Apr 19	Vienna	Gesellschaft Concert includes: Dietrich, Violin Concerto; Rietz, Arioso for violin; Bach, Pastoral from *Christmas Oratorio*
Summer	Nidelbad, above Ruschlikon, Lake Zürich Many visitors, but forms an especially strong friendship with J. V. Widmann, pastor and theologian, with whom he travels often in subsequent years.	
Nov 8	Vienna	Gesellschaft Concert includes: Beethoven: Piano Concerto in E flat. (Brahms); Brahms, Choral Pieces, op. 62; Berlioz, *Harold in Italy*
Dec 6	Vienna	Gesellschaft Concert:
Dec 11	Meets Georg Henschel (Oxford)	Beethoven, *Missa Solemnis* String Quartet in C minor (Deichmann group)
1875		
Jan 10	Vienna	Gesellschaft Concerto includes Joachim, *Hungarian* Concerto; Brahms, Alto Rhapsody (Amalie Joachim); Schumann, Fantasia for violin (Joachim); Bach, Cantata 'O ewiges Feuer'
Feb 28	Vienna	Gesellschaft concert: includes Bach, Prelude and Fugue in E flat arr. for orchestra B. Scholz; Brahms, *Requiem*

Mar 23	Vienna	Gesellschaft Concert: Bach, *St Matthew Passion*
Apr 18	Vienna	Gesellschaft Concert: Bruch, *Odysseus*
	Resigns from Gesellschaft.	
May 8	Karlsruhe	*Neue Liebeslieder-walzer* (op. 65) (L. Walter/J. Schwarz/B. Kurner/J. Hauser/Brahms/Dessoff)
	Becomes member of the Music Committee for the award of grants from the Austrian Government. Awards to Dvorak, in whose music he takes a very strong interest.	
Summer	Nidelbad nr. Ruschlikon (Lake Zürich)	
Nov 18	Vienna	Piano Quartet in C minor (op. 60) (Members of the Hellmesberger Quartet/Brahms)
1876		
Jan 17	Visit to Holland (meets Theodor Engelmann)	Conducts *St Antoni* Variations and plays Concerto in D minor
Feb 3	Visits to Munster am Stein, Mannheim, Wiesbaden, Coblenz	
	Offered Doctorate by University of Cambridge through Stanford and Macfarren (refuses for fear of lionization)	
Summer	Sassnitz (Isle of Rügen) with Henschel	
Autumn	Baden-Baden. Beginning of estrangement from Levi.	
Oct 30	Berlin	String Quartet in B flat major (op. 67) (Joachim Quartet)
Nov 4	Karlsruhe	Symphony in C minor (op. 68) (Karlsruhe Orchestra/ Dessoff)
Nov 15	Munich	Symphony in C minor (Munich Orchestra/Brahms)
1877	(Mozart Edition begins)	
Mar 8	Carlsruhe	Symphony in C minor (Carlsruhe Orchestra/Brahms)
Mar 8	Cambridge	Symphony in C minor (Cambridge Orchestra/Joachim)
Summer	Pörtschach Lichtenthal	
Dec 30	Vienna GdM	Symphony in D major (op. 73) (VPO/Richter)
1878		
Jan 10	Leipzig	Symphony in D major (LGO/ Brahms)

Feb 4	Amsterdam	Symphony in D major (Brahms)
Feb 6	The Hague	ditto
	Holiday in Italy.	
	Venice/Florence/Rome/Naples	
Summer	Pörtschach	
Sep 28	Hamburg	Symphony in D major (HPO/ Brahms)
Nov	New enthusiasm of Bülow, who makes his famous alliteration 'Bach, Beethoven, Brahms'	
Dec 8	Vienna GdM	Motet (op. 74 no. 1); (Singverein/ Kremser)
1879		
Jan 1	Leipzig	Violin Concerto (op. 77) (LGO, Joachim/Brahms)
14	Vienna GdM	Violin Concerto (Joachim/Brahms)
Mar	Honorary Doctorate by Breslau University	
Summer	Pörtschach	
Autumn	Concert tour with Joachim in Hungary and Transylvania	
Oct 29	Berlin	Piano Pieces (op. 76) (Bülow)
Nov 8	Bonn	Violin Sonata in G major (op. 78) (R. Heckmann/M. Heckmann-Hertig)
Dec 12	Berlin	*Schumann* Variations for piano (op. 9) (von Bülow)
c. 1879	Hugo Wolf seeks Brahms's support; Brahms recommends him to study counterpoint with Nottebohm	
1880		
Jan 20	Hamburg	Piano Pieces (op. 79) (Brahms)
Jan 30	Concert tour of the Rhine includes visit to Crefeld	Motet (op. 74 no. 2) (Cäcilians-verein/J. Spengel)
Feb 22	Cambridge	Violin Sonata in G major (op. 78) (Von Bülow/Norman-Neruda)
	Attends opening of the Schumann Memorial at Bonn	
Summer	First year lodging in Ischl in Salzkammergut (Summer residence of the Emperor and fashionable Viennese society) Meets Johann Strauss and Ignaz Brüll	
Dec 26	Vienna	*Tragic* Overture (op. 81) (VPO/ Richter)
1881		
Jan 4	Breslau	*Academic Festival Overture* (op. 80) (Brahms)
		Tragic Overture (Brahms)
Jan/Feb	Tour of Holland	
Feb	Tour of Hungary. Meets Liszt	

	who is also attending a concert by von Bülow	
Apr/May	Italian trip with Billroth Rome, Naples, Messina, Palermo, Siena, Florence, Pisa	
Summer	Pressbaum (Vienna suburb)	
Nov 9	Budapest	Piano Concerto in B flat major (op. 83) (Budapest Philharmonic/Erkel/ Brahms) Frequently repeated in Germany and Holland by Brahms
	New intimacy with von Bülow, who henceforth devotes himself and his excellent ducal orchestra to Brahms's music	
Dec 6	Zürich	*Nänie* (op. 82) (Zürich Tonhalle Gesellschaft/Brahms)
1882		
Feb 2	Vienna	Piano Sonata in F sharp minor (op. 2) (von Bülow)
Apr 7	Hamburg. First performance in his native city.	*Ein deutsches Requiem* (HPO/Brahms)
Summer	Ischl	
Aug 25	Altaussee	Piano Trio in C major (op. 87) (L. Straus/R. Lutz/Brahms) String Quintet in F major (op. 88) (L. Straus group)
Sep	Italy with Billroth, Brüll, Simrock	
Sep 14	(London/Crystal Palace)	Piano Concerto in B flat major (CPO/Manns/Beringer)
Dec 8	Basle	*Parzens-Gesang* (op. 89) (Allgemeine-Musik-Gesellschaft/ Brahms)
1883		
Apr 3	Celebration of his fiftieth birthday with Billroth, Hanslick, Faber for bachelor supper	
May	Cologne Festival	
May 14	Cologne	Piano Concerto in B flat (op. 83) (Cologne Orchestra/Brahms)
Summer	Wiesbaden. Close emotional relationship with Hermine Spies (mezzo-soprano)	
Dec 2	Vienna	Third Symphony (op. 90) (Richter/ VPO) (who coins title 'Brahms's Eroica')
1884		
	Schütz Edition begins under Spitta. Brahms very interested. Directly involved in Schubert Edition which begins in this year.	

Spring	Italy (Lake Como) with Rudolf von der Leyen Summer Mürzzuschlag (with Hanslick)	
Winter	Hamburg, Bremen, Oldenburg Crefeld.	Performs songs with Spies
1885		
	Vienna (settles into his later pattern of life. Socialising with Wiener Tonkünstler-Verein and walks with friends on Sundays The artist Max Klinger begins his series of forty-one engravings, etchings and lithographs which he designated 'Brahms-Phantasie', inspired by Brahms's works (1885–1894)	
Jan 30	Crefeld	Two Songs for alto and viola (op. 91) (A. Hohenschild/Brahms.)
Summer	Mürzzuschlag	
October 25	Meiningen	Fourth Symphony (op. 98) Meiningen (Orchestra/Brahms)
	Tour of Holland with Fourth Symphony with Meiningen orchestra and von Bülow	
1886		
Jan 17	Vienna (first time in Vienna)	Fourth Symphony (VPO/Richter)
Feb 18	Leipzig	Fourth Symphony (LGO/Brahms
Apr 9	Hamburg	Fourth Symphony (Hamburg Cäciliens-Verein/Brahms)
Summer	Hofstetten nr. Thun, Switzerland with Widmann Visits by H. Spies, K. Groth (Honorary President, Wiener Tonkünsler-Verein)	
Oct	Meiningen Hears Richard Strauss's Symphony in F minor. Advises the young composer, but does not warm to his subsequent music	
Nov 24	Vienna	Cello Sonata in F major (op. 99) (Hausmann/Brahms)
Dec 2	Vienna	Violin Sonata in A major (op. 100) (Hellmesberger/Brahms)
Dec 20	Budapest	Piano Trio in C minor (op. 101) (Hubay/Popper/Brahms)
	Frau Truxa becomes his housekeeper for rest of his life	
1887	During this year meets twenty-five-year-old Debussy	
Feb 26	Vienna	Piano Trio in C minor (Members of the Heckmann Quartet/Brahms)
Spring	Italy (Simrock, Kirchner)	

Summer	Thun (ditto)	
Oct 18	Cologne	Double Concerto in A minor (op. 102) (Joachim/Hausmann/Brahms)
Nov	Marxsen dies	
1888		
Jan 2	Meets Tchaikovsky and Grieg	
May	Italy with Widmann, Verona, Bologna, Rimini, Ancona, Loretto, Rome, Turin	
Summer	Thun	
Oct 31	Berlin	*Zigeunerlieder* (op. 103) (Singakademie)
Nov 26	London	*Zigeunerlieder* (Henschel Group/F. Davies)
Dec 21	Budapest	Violin Sonata in D minor (op. 108) Hubay/Brahms)
Dec 23	Vienna (first in Vienna)	Double Concerto (VPO/Joachim, Hausmann/Brahms)
1889		
Jan 18	Vienna	*Zigeunerlieder* (Walter group/ Brahms)
Feb 13	Vienna	Violin Sonata in D minor (Joachim/ Brahms)
Summer	Ischl	
May 23	Awarded the Freedom of Hamburg (rare honour – also awarded to Bismarck)	
June 6	Awarded the Order of Leopold	
Sep 9	Hamburg	*Fest u. Gedenksprüche* (op. 109); (Cäciliens-Verein/J. Spengel) (written in response to the Freedom of the city of Hamburg)
1890		
Jan 10	Budapest	Piano Trio in B major (op. 8 – second version – first performance) (Hubay/Popper/Brahms)
Jan 15	Hamburg	Motet (op. 103 no. 3) (Cäciliens-verein/Spengel)
Feb	Cologne	Motets (op. 110 no. 1, 2) Cäciliens-verein/Wüllner
Spring	Italy with Widmann. Parma, Cremona, Brescia, Vicenza	
Summer	Ischl Vienna Meets Alice Barbi (mezzo soprano)	
Autumn	Plans his will	
Nov 11	Vienna	String Quintet in G major (op. 111) (Rosé Quartet with Hausmann)
Dec 25	Meiningen to hear Mühlfeld	

	play Weber, Concertino	
1891	Christmas with Fellingers	
	Denkmäler deutscher Tonkunst series begins with Scheidt's keyboard music 'Tabulatura Nova' Brahms highly enthusiastic	
Spring	Berlin	
May	Ischl. Writes his Will, the 'Ischl Testament'	
Summer	Ischl	
Dec	Prague Attends Mahler's performance of *Don Giovanni* and is highly impressed	
Dec 12	Berlin	Clarinet Trio, in A minor (op. 114) (Mühlfeld/Hausmann/Brahms) Clarinet Quintet in B minor (op. 115) (Joachim Quartet, Mühlfeld)
	Vienna	Clarinet Trio (Syrinek, Hellmesberger/Brahms)
1892		
Jan 2	Leipzig. Death of Elizabeth von Herzogenberg	
Jan 21	Vienna	Clarinet Quintet in B minor (Rosé Quartet/Steiner)
Spring	Italian trip (with Widmann, Hegar and R. Freund)	
Apr 5	Friendship with Alice Barbi begins after concert in which she performs his songs	
May	Vienna, Honorary member Tonkünstler-Verein	
Jun	Death of Brahms's sister Elise	
1893		
Feb 6	Vienna. Billroth dies	
Feb 10	Vienna. von Bülow dies Vienna. Hermine Spies dies (aged 36) Works on Schumann edition	
April	Italy	
Summer	Ischl	
Dec 21	Vienna Alice Barbi's farewell concert	
1894	(*Denkmäler der Tonkünst in Österreich* Series)	
Mar 7	(London. St James's Hall)	Piano Pieces (op. 118) (Ilona Eibenschütz) (Piano Pieces (op. 119) (Ilona Eibenschütz)
Summer	Ischl	
1895		
Jan 8	Vienna	Clarinet Sonata in E flat major (op. 120 no. 2) (Mühlfeld/Brahms)

Jan 11	Vienna	Clarinet Sonata in F minor (op. 120 no. 1) (Mühlfeld/Brahms)
Mar 18	Vienna. Last Viennese appearance as conductor, in concert by students of Vienna Conservatoire	Conducts *Academic Festival* Overture
Summer	Ischl Meiningen	
1896		
Jan 10	Berlin Last public appearance as conductor	Piano Concertos in D minor and B flat major (BPO, Brahms/ D'Albert)
May 20	Frankfurt Clara dies	
Summer	Ischl	
Autumn	Vienna. Brahms ordered to Karlsbad for a cure (palliative gesture by doctor) Steady decline in health and appearance	
Nov 9	Vienna	The *Four Serious Songs* (op. 121) (A. Sistermans/ A. Ruckauf)
1897		
Mar 7	Vienna. Last public appearance at a concert including his Fourth Symphony Rapid decline	
Apr 3	Dies of cancer of the liver, as did his father	
1902		
Apr 24	Berlin	Chorale Preludes (op. 122) (H. Reimann)

Notes

1 An introduction to Brahms and his early music

1 G. Abraham, *A Hundred Years of Music*, 3rd edn, London, Duckworth, 1964, p. 172–3.
2 M. Kalbeck, *Johannes Brahms*, Berlin, Deutsche Brahms Gesellschaft, 1904–16, vol. 3, p. 409 (hereafter Kalbeck)
3 In 'Brahms the Progressive', a 'fully reformulated' version of his centenary broadcast of 1933 (1947, published 1950). See A. Schoenberg, *Style and Idea*, ed. L. Stein, London, Faber & Faber, 1975, pp. 401 and 532.
4 Abraham, op. cit., p. 283.
5 Schoenberg, op. cit., p. 439.
6 Kalbeck, vol. 4, p. 345.
7 J. V. Widmann, *Johannes Brahms in Erinnerungen von Josef Viktor Widmann*, ed. W. Reich, Basel, Amerback, 1947, pp. 36–7.
8 Kalbeck, vol. 2, p. 154.
9 A Holde, 'Suppressed Passages in the Brahms-Joachim correspondence published for the first time', The *Musical Quarterly*, vol. 45, 1959, p. 312/324.
10 For a recent discussion of Brahms's cultural interests see M. Musgrave, 'The Cultural World of Brahms', in R. Pascall (ed.), *Brahms: Biographical, Documentary and Analytical Studies*, Cambridge, Cambridge University Press, 1983, (Hereafter *Studies*) p. 1.
11 See K. Hofmann, *Die Bibliothek von Johannes Brahms*, Schriftenreihe zur Musik, Hamburg, Wagner, 1974.
12 Widmann, op. cit., pp. 28, 77.
13 C. Goldmark, *Erinnerungen aus meinem Leben*, Vienna, Rikola, 1922, p. 85.
14 C. V. Stanford, *Studies and Memories*, London, Constable, 1908, p. 132.
15 Kalbeck, vol. 2, pp. 314–15.
16 Kalbeck, vol. 4, p. 275.
17 G. Henschel, *Personal Recollections of Johannes Brahms*, Boston, Badger, 1907, p. 39.
18 R. Schumann, *On Music and Musicians*, ed. K. Wolff, London, Duckworth, 1946, pp. 252–3.
19 *Brahms Briefwechsel*, Berlin, Deutsche Brahms-Gesellschaft, 1908–22, (hereafter Bw), vol. 12, p. 151.
20 B. Litzmann, *Clara Schumann Ein Künstlerleben*, Leipzig, Breitkopf & Härtel, 1906–9, (hereafter Litzmann), vol. 3, pp. 111–12.
21 Muzio Clementi, *Original-Sonaten fur das Pianoforte solo in 60 Heften*, ed. Jul. Knorr, Wolfenbuttel, L. Holle. [1855?]
22 The compositions which appeared under the title 'G. W. Marks' by the publisher Cranz are discussed by O. E. Deutsch in 'The First Editions of Brahms', *Music Review*, vol. 2, 1940, pp. 276–8.

23 F. May, *The Life of Brahms*, London, Reeves, 1905 (hereafter May), vol. 1, p. 145.
24 C. Krebs (ed.) *Des Jungen Kreislers Schatzkästlein*, Berlin, 1909. See also K. Geiringer, 'Brahms zweites Schatzkästlein des Jungen Kreisler', *Zeitschrift für Musik*, vol. 100, 1933, pp. 443–6.
25 Kalbeck, vol. 1, pp. 81–2.
26 Schoenberg states that 'in the succession of motive-forms, . . . there is something that can be compared to development, to growth' (in contrast to 'local variants' which have 'little or no influence on the continuation'). See *Fundamentals of Musical Composition*, ed. G. Strang, London, Faber, 1967 (hereafter *Fundamentals*), pp. 8–9.
27 See *Zeitschrift für Musikwissenschaft*, vol. 2, p. 225; Kalbeck, vol. 1, p. 190.
28 See C. Floros, *Brahms and Bruckner, Studien zur musikalien Exegetik*, Wiesbaden, Breitkopf & Härtel, 1980, pp. 115–43. Further suggestions have been added, and fundamental thematic principles of Brahms and Schumann compared by O. W. Neighbour. See 'Brahms and Schumann: Two Opus Nines and Beyond', *19thC Music*, vol. 7 no. 3, 1984, pp. 266–70.
29 Clara Schumann, 'Variationen über ein Thema von Robert Schumann', op. 20, in *Romantische Klaviermusik*, ed. F. Goebels, Heidelberg, Müller, 1967, vol. 1, pp. 16–25.
30 In the Brahms Collection of the Gesellschaft der Musikfreunde, Vienna.
31 Litzmann, op. cit., vol. 2, p. 320.

Chapter 2   Songs and piano music

1 B. Litzmann (ed.), *Clara Schumann-Johannes Brahms Briefe aus den Jahren 1853–1896*, Leipzig, Breitkopf & Härtel, 1927 (hereafter *Schumann-Brahms Briefe*) vol 1, p. 294.
2 A. Einstein, *Music in the Romantic Era*, London, Dent, 1947, p. 40.
3 *Bw*, 16, p. 102.
4 See Werner Mörik, Booklet to recording of *Johannes Brahms Volkslieder*, DGG 2563 432–4.
5 G. Jenner, *Johannes Brahms als Mensch, Lehrer und Künstler*, 2nd edn, Marburg, Elwert, 1930, p. 31. A. Schoenberg, *Style and Idea*, p. 418.
6 G. Henschel, *Musings and Memories of a Musician*, London, Macmillan, 1918, p. 113.
7 M. Friedländer, *Brahms's Lieder*, tr. C. L. Leese, London, Oxford University Press, 1928, p. 33.
8 Ibid., p. 32.
9 Not least interestingly, the fragment of Goethe's 'Harzreise im Winter' which begins 'Ach, wer heilet' set by Brahms in the Alto Rhapsody: op. cit., p. 73.
10 Henschel, op. cit., p. 87.
11 Ludwig Christoph Heinrich Hölty, *Werke und Briefe*, Berlin/Weimar, 1966, pp. 139–40.
12 *Bw*, 5, p. 146.
13 *Bw*, 1, p. 8.
14 Jenner, op. cit., pp. 48–9.
15 Geiringer, op. cit., p. 213.
16 Kalbeck, vol. 1, p. 460.
17 Kalbeck, vol. 2, p. 117.
18 Schoenberg, *Fundamentals*, p. 169.
19 'not the stupid tunes, but the interesting rhythms'; see: R. H. Schauffler, *The Unknown Brahms*, 1933, repr. Westport Conn., Greenwood, 1972, p. 176. But

Brahms's quoted reference to 'ragtime' seems unlikely in view of its premature date – 1895? See also Kalbeck, vol. 4, pp. 383–4, who merely refers to a song and dance with banjo accompaniment.

20 Geiringer published the theme in its original setting in 1932. See *Divertimento from Feld-Partita für 8-stimmige Bläserchor* (Hoboken no. 11/46), ed K. Geiringer, Leipzig, F. Schuberth, 1932.

Chapter 3   Choral music

1 See: S. Kross (ed.), *Johannes Brahms Volkslieder fur Frauenstimme* (Der Chorsinger), Bärenreiter, 1965; V. Gotwals and P. Keppler (eds), *Folksongs for Women's Voices*, Smith College, 1968; S. Helms (ed.), *Volksliedbearbeitungen für Frauenchor* (The Nineteenth-Century), Bärenreiter, 1970.

2 *Bw*, 9, p. 23.

3 *Bw*, 4, p. 79.

4 Heinrich Reimann, *Johannes Brahms*, Berlin, Harmonie, 1919, p. 32. Kalbeck suggests that bars 232–6 of the first movement of the First Symphony quote 'Ermuntre dich, mein schwacher Geist'. See vol. 3, p. 99.

5 *Schumann-Brahms Briefe*, vol. 1, p. 73.

6 *Bw*, 6, p. 137.

7 *Bw*, 6, p. 148.
The 'Kyrie' and 'Mass' movements were acquired by the Gesellschaft der Musikfreunde in 1982 and published together as *Messe*, ed. O. Biba, Vienna, Doblinger, 1984 with added continuo part to the latter. Namely Kyrie (SATB) with continuo bass (fugal); Sanctus (SSATB), Hosanna (SSAT), Benedictus (SSAT), Agnus Dei (SSATB) and Dona Nobis Pacem (SSATB). The surviving music furnishes further evidence of Brahms's re-use of material and length of preparation, for the Agnus Dei and Dona Nobis Pacem complement the known Benedictus in providing sources for the 'Warum?' Motet, op. 74 no. 1 – the shape of the first idea ('Agnus Dei') and the later passage at 'Siehe wir preisen selig' ('Dona Nobis Pacem'). The latter passage is also interesting in view of its possible stylistic links with Schütz, to be discussed later, perhaps strengthening the view that Brahms already knew some of his music before the *Requiem*, notably 'Selig sind die Toten' (*Geistliche Chormusik*). But the most telling feature of the later work – the recurring question 'Warum?' with which it opens is not anticipated in the earlier work.
For full documentation of the 'Mass', including a Credo of 1861 which does not survive, see: S. Kross, *Die Chorwerke von Johannes Brahms*, Berlin – Hallensee u. Wunsiedel/Ofr., Hesse, 1963, pp. 514–24.

8 See Virginia L. Hancock, *Brahms's Choral Compositions and his Library of Early Music*, Ann Arbor, U.M.I. Research Press, 1984, p. 189. This study includes a full discussion of the many manuscript copies which Brahms made from early printed editions and surveys all the sources of his study. See also Hancock, 'The growth of Brahms's interest in early choral music and its effect on his own choral compositions' in Pascall, *Studies*, pp. 27–40.

9 Hancock, op. cit., p. 117.

10 Richard Heuberger *Erinnerungen an Johannes Brahms*, ed. K. Hofmann, Tutzing, Schneider, 1976, p. 49.

11 Widmann, op. cit., p. 29.

12 See Michael Musgrave, 'The Cultural World of Brahms' in R Pascall (ed.), *Studies*, pp. 14–16, for an outline of the play and Brahms's operatic interests.

13 *Lazarus oder die Feier der Auferstehung*, oratorio 3 movements, only Act 1 and part of Act 2 complete 1820. Vocal score by J. Herbeck, Vienna, Spina, 1866. Complete score in the *Schubert Works*, vol. 17, 1892.

14 Kalbeck, vol. 1, p. 220.

15 Geiringer, op. cit., pp. 354–5 and Kalbeck, vol. 2, p. 8.

16 Albert Dietrich, *Erinnerungen an Johannes Brahms*, Leipzig, Wigand, 1898, p. 47.

17 A. Einstein, *Schubert*, tr. D. Ascoli, London, Cassell, 1951, pp. 204–5.

18 *Bw*, 3, p. 7.

19 Ibid., p. 10.

20 See Richard Specht, *Johannes Brahms*, tr. E Blom, London Dent, 1930, p. 185.

21 *Schumann-Brahms, Briefe*, vol. 1, p. 505.

22 Dietrich, op. cit., p. 45.

23 Kalbeck, vol. 2, p. 232.

24 For a fuller discussion of the background, see Michael Musgrave, 'Historical Influences in the Growth of Brahms's Requiem', *Music and Letters*, vol. 53 no. i, January 1972, pp. 3–17.

25 *Schumann-Brahms Briefe*, vol. 1, p. 505.

26 Floros, op. cit., p. 43.

27 For Brahms's knowledge of Schütz see Hancock, *Brahms's Choral Music*.

28 Klaus Blum, *Hundert Jahre Ein deutsches Requiem von Johannes Brahms*, Tutzing, Schneider, 1971, pp. 101–2.

29 See 'On Poetry and Composition' in *Richard Wagner's Prose Works*, tr. W. A. Ellis, London, Kegan Paul, Trench & Trübner, 1897, vol. 6, pp. 143–4.

30 *Bw*, 7, p. 120.

Chapter 4   Chamber music

1 Wagner referred to Brahms as a 'street minstrel and Jewish tuner-up of Czardas' in the same passage that he attacked his 'Halleluia perruque'. See *Richard Wagner's Prose Works*, vol. 6., pp. 143–4.

2 See J. Webster, 'Schubert's Sonata Form and Brahms's First Maturity', *19thC Music*, vol. 3, no. 1, p. 61. However, Beethoven may also be in the background. Brahms's shape is actually more closely outlined in the slow movement of his Serenade in D major, bars 184–5, a passage whose string figuration and register are closely akin to those of the slow movement of the *Pastoral Symphony*, bar 5 et seq.

3 As in the case of *Lazarus*, Spina published the newly appeared Quintet (in 1853 as op. 163).

4 *Schumann-Brahms Briefe*, vol. 1, p. 75.

5 See Robert Pascall, (ed.) *Kleine Stücke fur Klavier*, Diletto Musicale, No 819, Vienna, Doblinger, 1979, p. 3. The Gavottes are discussed more fully in 'Unknown Gavottes by Brahms', *Music and Letters*, vol. 57, no. 4, p. 404.

6 *Arnold Schoenberg Letters*, ed. E. Stein, London, Faber, & Faber 1964, pp. 207–8.

7 *Schumann-Brahms Briefe*, vol. I, p. 370.

8 Indeed, Brahms's pupil Florence May devotes a very long footnote to it. See May, op. cit., vol. 1, p. 289.

9 E. Hanslick, *Music Criticisms, 1846–99*, ed. H. Pleasants, Harmondsworth, Penguin, 1950, p. 84.

10 For an attempt to reconstruct the work as a Quintet with two cellos, see Sebastian H. Brown, Brahms: *String Quintet in F minor*, London, Stainer & Bell, 1947.

11 D. F. Tovey, *Essays in Musical Analysis*, London, Oxford, 1935, vol. 1, pp. 217–18.

12 P. Latham, 'Johannes Brahms' (Hereafter *Essays*) in *Chamber Music*, ed. A. Robertson, Harmondsworth, Penguin, 1960, p. 194.
13 W. Altmann, 'Bach-Zitate in der Violoncello-Sonate op. 38 von Brahms', *Die Musik*, vol. 45, no. 1, 1912, pp. 84–5.
14 The recent re-issue of Aubrey Brain's recording of 1926 (Opal 805) using French-type valve horn in F at least gives an indication of the sound with which Brahms would early have been familiar, for example from Schumann's pioneering works for the instrument of the late 1840s.
15 Kalbeck, vol. 2, p. 183.
16 Schoenberg, *Style and Idea*, p. 402.
17 Latham, op. cit., p. 193.
18 William G. Hill, 'Brahms's op. 51: A Diptych', *Music Review*, vol. 13, 1952 pp. 110–24.
19 Schoenberg, *Style and Idea*, p. 430.
20 See Edward T. Cone, 'Stravinsky: The Progress of a Method' in *Perspectives on Schoenberg and Stravinsky*, ed. B. Boretz and E. Cone, New York, Norton, 1972, p. 156.
21 J. Webster, 'The C sharp minor version of Brahms's op. 60', *Musical Times*, vol. 121, pp. 89–93.
22 M. Kalbeck (ed.), 'Fragebogen fur Herrn Hofkappelmeister Albert Dietrich', in: *Hans Schneider, Katalog 100 – Johannes Brahms*, Schneider, Tutzing, 1964, p. 12.
23 Kalbeck, vol. 3, p. 12.

Chapter 5   Orchestral music

1 Kalbeck, vol. 3, p. 92.
2 *Schumann-Brahms Briefe*, vol. 1, p. 211.
3 *Letters to and from Joseph Joachim*, selected and translated by N. Bickley, London, Macmillan, 1914, p. 66. The editor suggests, however, that the letter may belong to the following month, April.
4 *Bw*, 5, p. 43.
5 *Schumann-Brahms Briefe*, vol. 1, p. 69.
6 Geiringer, op. cit., p. 248. However, Bachian influences are certainly present in the movement. See, for example, the remarks of Tovey to the effect that the soloist's opening subject could be an arioso from the *St Matthew Passion* in its particular movement and phrasing, *Essays*, vol. 3, p. 116.
7 Tovey, *Essays*, vol. 3, p. 118.
8 Kalbeck, vol. 1, p. 139 and p. 297. Tovey dismisses the idea that the work could have had choral origin, even though he underlays the first violin part with the inscription. See Tovey, op. cit., vol. 3, p. 118.
9 Published by Spina as op. 166 in 1853.
10 Geiringer, op. cit., p. 252.
11 Kalbeck, vol. 1, p. 165.
12 Ibid., vol. 3/i, p. 109.
13 Litzmann, vol. 3, p. 123.
14 *Schumann-Brahms Briefe*, vol. 1, p. 597.
15 M. Kalbeck (ed.), 'Fragebogen fur Herrn Hofkappelmeister Albert Dietrich', pp. 15–16. This source reprints 'd moll' for 'c moll', although the relevance to the C minor work is clear from comparison with his *Reminiscences*, Leipzig, 1898, p. 46.
16 E. Hanslick, op. cit., p. 126.
17 W. Mellers, *Man and His Music. The Story of Musical Experience in the West*, London, Barrie & Rockliff, 1962, vol. 3, p. 697.

18 *Bw*, 16, p. 146 and Litzmann, op. cit., vol. 3, p. 343. For a discussion of the earlier version of the slow movement given at the Vienna premiere and in Cambridge see R. Pascall, 'Brahms's First Symphony Slow Movement: the Initial Performing Version', *Musical Times*, vol. 122, 1981, pp. 664–7.
19 For more detailed discussion of this subject see Michael Musgrave, 'Brahms's First Symphony: Thematic coherence and its secret origin', *Music Analysis*, vol. 2 no. 2, pp. 117–33.
20 See: E. Sams, 'Brahms and his Clara themes', *Musical Times*, vol. 112. May, 1971, pp. 432–4.
21 *Schumann-Brahms Briefe*, vol. 1, p. 371 and p. 279.
22 Kross has recently suggested that this inscription refers not to Schumann, nor to Clara, as suggested by Geiringer (op. cit., or Flores (op. cit., pp. 144–6) but to the Kreisler identity rooted in the writings of Hoffmann. See S. Kross, 'Brahms and E. T. A. Hoffmann', *19thC Music*, vol. 5, no. 3, 1982, pp. 193–200.
23 *Schumann-Brahms Briefe*, vol. 1, p. 198.
24 Kalbeck, vol. 3, pp. 95–6.

Chapter 6   Songs and piano music

1 This term, generally translated 'basic shape', seems to have had very wide meaning for Schoenberg, partly a product of his projection of the concepts of unity fundamental to serialism back to the music of the past. For further exploration of the idea, including its application to Brahms, see D. Epstein, *Beyond Orpheus: Studies in Musical Structure*, Cambridge, Mass., MIT Press, 1979.
2 Kalbeck, vol. 3, p. 141.
3 Friedländer, op. cit., p. 144, 161.
4 Ibid., pp. 161–2.
5 According to Friedländer, who was well placed to know, Brahms found the Sonata in the anonymously edited *Sämtliche Werke für das Pianoforte von Dominic [sic] Scarlatti* [ed. and rev. C Czerny], Vienna, Haslinger, 1840, where it appears as no. 133. See Friedländer, op. cit., p. 132.
6 A. Clarkson, 'Brahms's Song op. 105 no. 1: A Literary-Historical Approach' in: *Readings in Schenker Analysis and Other Approaches*, ed. M. Yeston, New Haven, Yale University Press, 1977, p. 233.
7 A. Schoenberg, *Style and Idea*, p. 421.
8 Schmidt adopts the metre associated with the Greek poetess Sappho. Three lines of 11, 11, 16 syllables.
9 Kalbeck, vol. 4, p. 476.

Chapter 7   Choral music

1 English translation: *Nenia* (Latin, Naenia, Exequiae). Funeral Song of ancient Rome in praise of a dead person, analogous to the Greek *threnody*.
2 In the anonymous introduction to the Philharmonia Score No. 282.
3 Hermann Goetz (1840–1876) was very highly regarded in Germany, not least by Brahms. Although Geiringer (op. cit., p. 321) is entirely justified in placing this stress on the relationship, the remainder of the settings are very different, that of Goetz being pitched in F sharp throughout, much more sectional in

structure and interpreting the opening words in an anguished manner 'con moto appassionato' where Brahms achieves a lofty repose.

4 H. Barkan (ed.), *Theodor Billroth and Johannes Brahms: Letters from a Musical Friendship*, Oklahoma, University of Oklahoma Press, 1957, p. 122.

5 A. Webern, *The Path to the New Music*, tr. L. Black, Bryn Mawr/London, Presser/Universal, 1963, p. 46.

6 Geiringer, op. cit., p. 301.

7 Perhaps the canonic treatment of the opening shape reflects a familiarity with Bach's canonic setting for organ of 'Nun komm' der Heiden Heiland' as a Trio in the 'Eighteen Chorale Preludes', BWV 660.

Chapter 8 Chamber music

1 Of numerous examples, perhaps *Pulcinella* (1919) and *Dumbarton Oaks Concerto* (1938) make most apposite comparison.

2 P. H. Lang, *Music in Western Civilisation*, New York and London, Norton, 1941, p. 902.

3 This seems to have come from Kalbeck (vol. 4, p. 18) and reflects more the desire to relate them than the sensitivity to their musical languages. If Brahms must have a Prize Song, it is surely 'Minnelied' op. 71, no. 5.

4 Schoenberg, 'The Orchestral Variations, op. 31' (Radio Lecture, Frankfurt Radio, 1931) translated in *The Score*, no. 27, 1960, pp. 27–40.

5 *Bw*, 4, p. 150.

6 *Bw*, 10, p. 224.

7 *Schumann-Brahms Briefe*, vol. 2, p. 258.

8 Kalbeck, vol. 4., p. 211.

9 Kalbeck, vol. 4/1, pp. 207–8.

Chapter 9 Orchestral music

1 See Cosima Wagner, *Diaries*, ed. M. Gregor-Dellin and D. Mack, vol. 2, London, Collins, 1980, (hereafter C. Wagner, *Diaries*).

2 Abraham, op. cit., p. 162.

3 Kalbeck, vol. 3, p. 258.

4 *Bw*, 6, p. 197.

5 Schoenberg, *Style and Idea*, p. 140.

6 Hanslick, op. cit., p. 211.

7 Elgar had a particularly strong interest in Brahms. See, for example, his lecture on the Third Symphony in *A Future for English Music and other Lectures*, ed. P. M. Young, London, Dobson, 1968, pp. 99–110.

8 But rather to Kalbeck. See Michael Musgrave, 'Frei aber Froh: A Reconsideration', *19thC Music*, vol. 3, p. 251.

9 Specht, op. cit., p. 270.

10 *Bw*, 2, p. 14.

11 *Schumann-Brahms Briefe*, vol 2, p. 111.

12 Schoenberg, *Style and Idea*, p. 406.

13 H. Schenker, *Harmony*, tr E. M. Borgese, Cambridge, Mass, MIT, 1954, p. 61.

14 Kalbeck, vol. 3, p. 252.

15 May, op. cit., vol. 2, p. 663.

16 Litzmann, vol. 3, p. 496.

17 Kalbeck, vol. 4, p. 62.

Chapter 10   The final period

1 *Bw*, 12, p. 35.
2 F. Schumann, 'Brahms and Clara Schumann', tr. J. Mayer, *Musical Quarterly*, vol. 2, 1916, p. 515.
3 Bw 3, p. 126.
4 Friedländer, op cit., p. 206
5 Friedlander, op. cit., p. 207.
6 Friedlander, op. cit., p. 222.
7 Kalbeck, vol. 4, p. 469.
8 F. Schumann, op. cit., p. 508.
9 See J. Dunsby, 'The multi-piece in Brahms', Fantasien op. 116, in R. Pascall (ed.) Studies, p. 167, for a full exploration of the relationships.
10 Litzmann, op. cit., vol. 3, p. 609.
11 E. Sams. Brahms songs, London, BBC, 1972, p. 65.
12 Geiringer op. cit., p. 288.
13 Sams, op. cit., pp. 64–5.
14 Reger. See 'Degeneration und Regeneration in der Musik', *Neue Musik-Zeitung*, vol. 29, no. 3, 1907, p. 49. Stanford was well acquainted with the Brahms circle and corresponded with Brahms. He wrote his Clarinet Concerto for Mühlfeld, although Mühlfeld apparently never played it. See his analyses in *Musical Composition*, London, 1911. Parry was sufficiently enthusiastic to copy out the Serenade in A in its entirety, now in the possession of the Bodleian Library, Oxford. See his comments in *Style in Musical Art*, London, 1911. Abdy Williams was particularly sensitive to Brahms's rhythmic character which he discusses through reference to the Second Symphony in *The Rhythm of Modern Music*, London, 1909, pp. 210–36, and in numerous shorter examples. Tovey, as a friend of Joachim, gained unique insights into Brahms's music, which he understood in its historical context with great sensitivity.
15 See further: Michael Musgrave, *A Study of Schoenberg's Response to Brahms's Music as revealed in his didactic writings and selected early compositions*, Ph. D. thesis, London, 1980. Jonathan Dunsby, *Structural Ambiguity in Brahms. Analytical Approaches to Four Works*. Ann Arbor, UMI Research Press, 1981. Walter Frisch, *Brahms and the Principle of Developing Variation*, University of California Press (California Studies in 19thC Music), Los Angeles, 1983.
16 E. Wellesz, *The Origins of Schoenberg's Twelve Note System*, Washington D.C., U.S. Government Printing Office, p. 4.
17 Schoenberg, *Style and Idea*, p. 131.
18 For example he 'steeped himself in the variations of Beethoven and Brahms' in preparing before writing the last three movements of the Concerto for Three Pianos. See Eric Walter White, *Stravinsky: The Composer and his Works*, London and Boston, Faber & Faber, 1979, p. 390. Stravinsky's attitude to Beethoven and Brahms is further discussed in Roman Vlad, *Stravinsky*, tr, F. Fuller London, Oxford University Press, 1978, p. 148, where is also recorded his love, among others, of playing Couperin in the Brahms/Chrysander Edition in reply to Craft's question 'What music delights you most today'.
19 See Alan Blyth, *Remembering Britten*, London, Huchinson, 1981, p. 88. 'It's not bad Brahms I mind, it's good Brahms I can't stand.'
20 C. Wagner, *Diaries*, vol. 2, p. 362.
21 N. Bauer-Lechner, *Recollections of Gustav Mahler*, ed. P. Franklin, tr. D. Newlin, London, Faber & Faber, 1980.
22 B. Jacobson, *The Music of Johannes Brahms*, London, Tantivy Press, 1977, pp. 51–2.
23 As this book leaves for press the Trio for horn, violin and piano by Gyorgy Ligeti comes to notice, as does its subtitle 'Homage to Brahms'.

Bibliography

The extensive Brahms literature in English and German which appeared after his death and at the centenary of his birth in 1933 is now largely unavailable to the general reader. However, the starting point for virtually all work has remained the four-volume study of life and works by Max Kalbeck who was part of the Brahms circle. Despite many errors of detail and some poetic invention, it offers the most extensive general view for readers of the old German gothic print.

M. Kalbeck, *Johannes Brahms*, (2nd edn), Berlin, Deutsche Brahms-Gesellschaft, 1904–14, 4 vols (repr. Schneider, Tutzing, 1974–5).

Two important earlier English writings remain available. Florence May's life and works, and Edwin Evan's analytical coverage of the entire works. May's book includes much independent material as well as important personal recollections: F. May., *The Life of Brahms*, (2nd rev. edn), London, Reeves, n.d (1st edn, 1905). Evans's book covers the works in three volumes which still provide the most important traditional discussion of them. E. Evans, *Historical, Descriptive and Analytical Account of the Entire Works of Brahms*, London, Reeves, 1912–38, 4 vols.

The bulk of the Brahms correspondence was published by the Deutsche Brahms Gesellschaft during the period 1908–1921 in 16 volumes (repr. Schneider, Tutzing, 1974). *Brahms im Briefwechsel mit . . .* (various editors). The correspondence with Clara Schumann appeared separately: *Clara Schumann-Johannes Brahms Briefe, 1853–1896*, ed. B. Litzman, Leipzig, 1927 (repr. Olms, Hildesheim 1970). Other volumes have appeared variously since. A complete list is given in *The New Grove*, ed. S. Sadie, London, Macmillan, 1980, vol. 3, pp. 155–90. An important continuing source of primary biographical material and correspondence is the recent series *Brahms Studien*, ed. various, Hamburg, Hamburg Brahms Gesellschaft, 1975 –

Only three volumes of correspondence have appeared in English translation: *The Herzogenberg Correspondence* (translated H. Bryant from *Briefwechsel* I–II, ed. M. Kalbeck, 1909); reprinted edition with new introduction by W. Frisch, New York, Da Capo, 1987.

Letters of Clara Schumann and Johannes Brahms, a selection from the German edition, translated 1926 (anonymously) and reprinted in paperback 1973 by Vienna House.

Johannes Brahms and Theodor Billroth: Letters from a Musical Friendship, tr. H Barkan, Oklahoma, University of Oklahoma Press, 1957.

Works

Complete Edition: *Johannes Brahms: Sämtliche Werke*, ed. H. Gal and E.
  Mandyczewski, Leipzig, Breitkopf & Härtel, 1926–8, 26 vols. (Some of these,
  including the complete piano music, are reproduced at full size in paperback
  by Dover Publications.)
Catalogue of works M. McCorkle, *Brahms Thematisch-Bibliographisches Werk-
  verzeichnis*, Munich, Henle 1984. A Thematic catalogue listing all known
  manuscript locations and essential information on the history of each
  composition.
Catalogue of manuscripts in fascimile See D. Dedel, *Johannes Brahms. A Guide to his
  Autograph in Facsimile*, M.L.A. Index and Bibliography Series, No. 18, (Detroit
  Studies in Musicology), Detroit, 1978.
Of various subsequent additions, the most substantial are of the full score of the
  Violin Concerto (Library of Congress, 1979) and of the chamber works ops 18,
  34, 39, 40, 87 and piano works op. 39, op. 118 no. 1 and op. 119 no. 1 (Garland
  Press, 1984).
List of First Editions The only English source remains O. E. Deutsch, 'The First
  Editions of Brahms', *Music Review*, vol. 1, nos 1 and 2, 1940. It has been
  superseded by K. Hofmann, *Die Erstdrücke der Werke von Johannes Brahms*, Tutzing,
  Schneider, 1975. See also McCorkle.
Calendar of Brahms's Life R. Hofmann and K. Hofmann, *Johannes Brahms: Zeittafel
  zu Leben und Werk*, Tutzing, Schneider, 1983.
Complete Listing of Writings on Brahms S. Kross, *Brahms-Bibliographie*, Tutzing,
  Schneider, 1983.

Select Listing of Writings on Brahms

Abraham, G., *A Hundred Years of Music*, London, Duckworth, 1964.
Adler, G., 'Johannes Brahms: His achievement, his personality and his position',
  Musical Quarterly, vol. 19, no. 2, 1933, pp. 113–42.
Bell, A., *The Songs of Brahms*, Darley, Grian-Aig Press, 1979.
Bernstein, J. A., 'An autograph of the Brahms "Handel Variations" ', *Music Review*,
  vol. 34, 1973, pp. 272–81.
Blum, K., *Hundert Jahre Ein Deutsches Requiem von Johannes Brahms*, Tutzing,
  Schneider, 1971.
Boyd M., 'Brahms's *Requiem*: A note on thematic integration', *Musical Times*, vol.
  115, pp. 140–41.
Bozarth, G., 'The Lieder of Johannes Brahms, 1868–71', PhD thesis, Princeton,
  1978, unpublished.
Biba (ed), *Johannes Brahms in Wien* (Catalogue), Archiv der Gesellschaft der
  Musikfreunde in Wien, 19 April-30 June, 1983.
Clarkson, A., 'Brahms, Song Op. 105/1 A literary-historical Approach', in: M.
  Yeston (ed.), *Readings in Schenker Analysis and other Approaches*, New Haven and
  London, Yale University Press, 1977, pp. 230–53.
Callomon, F., 'Some unpublished Brahms correspondence', *Musical Quarterly*, vol.
  29, no. 1, 1943, pp. 32–44.
Dahlhaus, C., Johannes Brahms, *Klavierkonzert Nr 1 d moll, op. 15*, Munich, Finck
  (Meisterwerke der Musik), vol. 3, 1965.
Dunsby J., *Structural Ambiguity in Brahms: Analytical Approaches to Four Works*, Ann
  Arbor, UMI Research Press, 1981.

Dunsby, J., 'The multi-piece in Brahms's: *Fantasien* op. 116' in Pascall (ed.) *Studies*, pp. 167–89.

Einstein, A., *Music in the Romantic Era*, London, Dent, 1947.

Elgar, E., *A Future for English Music and other Lectures*, ed. P. M. Young, London, Dobson, 1968, pp. 99–110.

Epstein, D., *Beyond Orpheus: Studies in Musical Structure*, Cambridge, Mass, MIT Press, 1979.

Fellinger, I., 'Brahms's view of Mozart', in Pascall (ed.), *Studies*, pp. 41–57.

Fiske, R., 'Brahms and Scotland', *Musical Times*, vol. 109, 1968, p. 1106.

Floros, C., *Brahms und Bruckner, Studien zur musikalischen Exegetik*, Wiesbaden, Breitkopf & Härtel, 1980.

Forte, A., 'The Structural Origin of Exact Tempi in the Haydn Variations', in McCorkle, *Variations on a Theme of Haydn*, pp. 185–99.

Friedländer, M., *Brahms's Lieder*, tr. C. L. Leese, London, Oxford University Press, 1928.

Frisch, W., *Brahms and the Principle of Developing Variation*, Los Angeles, University of California Press, Berkeley, 1984.

Fuller-Maitland, J. A., *Brahms*, London, Methuen, 1911.

Gal, H., *Johannes Brahms. His work and Personality*, tr. J. Stein, London, Weidenfeld & Nicolson, 1963.

Geiringer, K., 'Brahms as Reader and Collector', *Musical Quarterly*, vol. 19, no. 2, 1933, pp. 158–68.

Geiringer, K., *Johannes Brahms. His Life and Work*, (3rd edn revised and enlarged), London, Allen & Unwin, 1982.

Geiringer, K. and Geiringer, I., 'The Brahms Library in the Gesellschaft der Musikfreunde in Wien', *Notes*, vol. 30, 1973, pp. 7–14.

Graf, M., *Composer and Critic, Two Hundred Years of Musical Criticism*, London, Chapman & Hall, 1947.

Hancock, V., *Brahms's Choral Compositions and his Library of Early Music*, Ann Arbor, UMI Research Press, 1983.

Hancock, V., 'The growth of Brahms's interest in early choral music and its effect on his own choral compositions', in Pascall (ed) *Studies*, pp. 27–40.

Hanslick, E., *Music Criticisms, 1846–1899*, rev and ed. H. Pleasants, Harmondsworth, Peregrine, 1963.

Harrison, M., *The Lieder of Brahms*, London, Hutchinson, 1972.

Hill, W. G., 'Brahms's op. 51: A Diptych', *Music Review*, vol. 13, 1952, pp. 110–24.

Hofmann, K., *Die Bibliothek von Johannes Brahms*, (Bücher und musikalien Verzeichnis, Hamburg), Hamburg, Wagner (Schriftenreihe zur Musik), 1974.

Holde, A., 'Suppressed passages in the Brahms-Joachim correspondence published for the first time', *Musical Quarterly*, vol. 45, no. 3, 1959, pp. 312–24.

Horton, J., *The Orchestral Music of Brahms*, London, BBC, 1968.

Heuberger, R., *Erinnerungen an Johannes Brahms* (2nd edn), ed. K Hofmann, Tutzing, Schneider, 1976.

Henschel, G., *Musings and Memories of a Musician*, London, Macmillan, 1918.

James, B., *Brahms. A Critical Study*, London, Dent, 1972.

Jacobson, B., *The Music of Johannes Brahms*, London, Tantivy Press, 1977.

Kalbeck, M., *Johannes Brahms*, Berlin, Deutsche Brahms-Gesellschaft, 1904–14.

Keys, I., *Brahms Chamber Music*, London, BBC, 1974.

Klenz, W., 'Brahms's op. 38; Piracy, pillage, plagiarism or parody', *Music Review*, vol. 34, 1973, pp. 39–50.

Kross, S., 'Brahms and E. T. A. Hoffman', *19thC Music*, vol. 5, no. 3, 1982, pp. 193–200.

Kross, S., 'Brahms und Schumann', *Brahms Studien*, vol. 4, Hamburg, 1981.

Kross, S., 'Brahms the Symphonist', in Pascall (ed.), *Studies*, pp. 125–46.

Latham, P., *Brahms: (The Master Musicians)*, London, Dent, revised edn, 1962.

Laufer, E., 'Brahms. Song, op. 105/1, A Schenkerian Approach', in M. Yeston (ed.), *Readings in Schenker Analysis and other approaches*, New Haven and London, Yale University Press, 1977.

Lewin, D., 'On Harmony and Meter in Brahms's op. 76, No. 8', *19th-Century Music*, vol. 4, no. 3, 1981, pp. 261–265.

McCorkle, D., *Johannes Brahms. Variations on a Theme of Haydn, for orchestra and for two pianos (with sketches and essays)*, New York, Norton, 1976.

McCorkle, D., 'Five fundamental Obstacles to Brahms Source Research' in *Acta Musicologica*, vol. 47, 1976, pp. 253–72.

McCorkle, M., *Brahms Thematisch-Bibliographisches Werkverzeichnis*, Munich, G. Henle Verlag, 1984.

McGuiness, R., 'Mahler und Brahms Gedanken zu "Reminiszenen" in Mahler's Sinfonien', *Melos/Neue Zeitschrift für Musik*, vol. 3, no. 77, 1977, pp. 215–224.

Mast, P. 'Brahms's Study, Octaven und Quinten und A' in *Music Forum*, vol. 5, New York, Columbia University Press, 1980, pp. 1–196.

Matthews, D., *Brahms Piano Music*, London, BBC 1978.

May, F., *The Life of Brahms* (2nd edn), 2 vols., London, William Reeves, n.d.

Musgrave, M., 'Historical Influences in the growth of Brahms's *Requiem, Music and Letters*, vol. 53, no. 1, 1972, pp. 3–17.

Musgrave, M., 'Frei aber Froh': A Reconsideration', *19thC Music*, vol. 3, 1980, pp. 251–8.

Musgrave, M., 'Schoenberg and Brahms: A Study of Schoenberg's response to Brahms's music as revealed in his didactic writings and selected early compositions', PhD thesis, London, 1980, unpublished.

Musgrave, M., 'The cultural world of Brahms', in Pascall (ed.), *Studies*, pp. 1–26.

Musgrave, M., 'Brahms's First Symphony: thematic coherence and its secret origin', *Music Analysis*, vol. 2, no. 2, 1983, pp. 117–34.

Newman, S. T. M., 'The Slow Movement of Brahms's First Symphony', *Music Review*, vol. 9, 1948, pp. 4–12.

Newman, W. S., 'A "Basic Motive" in Brahms's "German Requiem" ', *Music Review*, vol. 24, 1963, pp. 190–194.

Newbould, B., 'A new analysis of Brahms's Intermezzo in b op 119/1', *Music Review*, vol. 38, 1977, pp. 33–43.

Ophüls, G., *Brahms Texte*, Berlin, Simrock, 1898.

Osmond Smith, D., 'The retreat from dynamism: a study of Brahms's Fourth Symphony', in Pascall (ed.), *Studies*, pp. 147–66.

Pascall. R., 'Formal Principles in the Music of Brahms', Ph.D thesis, University of Oxford, 1972, unpublished.

Pascall, R., 'Some special uses of sonata form by Brahms', *Soundings*, vol. 4, 1974, pp. 58–63.

Pascall, R., 'Ruminations on Brahms's chamber music', *Musical Times*, vol. 116, 1975, pp. 697–9.

Pascall, R., 'Brahms First Symphony Slow Movement: The initial performing version', *Musical Times*, vol. 122, 1981, pp. 664–7.

Pascall, R., 'Brahms and the definitive text' in Pascall (ed.), *Studies*, pp. 59–76.

Pascall, R. (ed.), *Brahms: Biographical, Documentary and Analytical Studies*, Cambridge University Press, 1983, elsewhere referred to as *Studies*.

Rosen, C., 'Influence: 'Plagiarism and Inspiration', *19thC Music*, vol 4, no. 2, pp. 87–100.

Sams, E., 'Brahms and his Clara themes', *Musical Times*, vol. 112, 1971, pp. 432–4.

Sams, E., *Brahms Songs*, London, BBC, 1972.

Schumann, R., *On Music and Musicians*, London, Dobson, 1946.

Schumann, F., 'Brahms and Clara Schumann' tr. J. Mayer, *Musical Quarterly*, vol. 2, no. 4, 1916, pp. 507–15.

Schoenberg, A., 'Brahms the Progressive' in *Style and Idea*, ed. L. Stein, London, Faber & Faber, 1975.

Shaw, B., *Shaw on Music*, Harmondsworth, Penguin, 1962.

Specht, R., *Johannes Brahms*, tr. E Blom, London, Dent, 1930.

Tovey, D. F., Article 'Brahms' in *Cobbett's Cyclopaedic Survey of Chamber Music*, ed. C. Mason, 2 vols, 1963, vol. 1, pp. 158–85.

Tovey, D. F., *Essays in Musical Analysis*, 6 vols, London, Oxford University Press, 1935–9.

Thatcher, D. S., 'Nietzsche and Brahms: A forgotten relationship', *Music and Letters*, vol. 54, no. 3, 1973, pp. 261–80.

Truscott, H., 'Brahms and Sonata style', *Music Review*, vol. 25, 1964, pp. 186–201.

Wagner, C., *Diaries*, ed. M Gregor-Dellin and D. Mack, tr. G Skelton, 2 vols, London, Cassell, 1978, 1980.

Walker, A., 'Brahms and Serialism', *Musical Opinion*, vol. 81, 1958, pp. 17–21.

Walker, A., *An Anatomy of Musical Criticism*, London, Barrie & Rockliff 1966.

Walker, A., *A Study in Musical Analysis*, London, Barrie & Rockliff, 1962.

Webster, J., 'Schubert's Sonata Form and Brahms's First Maturity', *19thC Music*, vol. 2, no. 1, 1978, pp. 18–35 and vol. 3, no. 1, 1979, pp. 52–71.

Webster, J., 'The C sharp minor version of Brahms's op. 60', *Musical Times*, vol. 121, 1980, pp. 89–93.

Whittall, A., 'The *Vier ernste Gesänge*, op. 121: enrichment and uniformity', in Pascall (ed.), *Studies*, pp. 191–207.

Some Major Bibliographical Additions since 1983

Collections of Essays

Musgrave, M., (ed.), *Brahms 2. Biographical, Documentary and Analytical Studies*, Cambridge, Cambridge University Press, 1987.

Bozarth, G. (ed.), *Brahms Studies. Analytical and Historical Perspectives*, Oxford, Clarendon Press, 1990.

Frisch, W. (ed.), *Brahms and His World*, Princeton, Princeton University Press, 1990.

Comprehensive Bibliography

Quigley, T., *Johannes Brahms: An Annotated Bibliography of the Literature through 1982*, Metuchen, N.J., and London, Scarecrow, 1990.

Performance Studies

Pascall, R., *Playing Brahms: A Study of 19th-Century Performance Practice*, Papers in Musicology No. 1. Department of Music, Nottingham University, 1990.

Pascall, R., *Brahms's First Symphony Andante—the Initial Performing Version*: Commentary and Realization, Papers in Musicology No. 2. Department of Music, Nottingham University, 1990.

General Studies

Keys, I., *Johannes Brahms*, London, Christopher Helm, 1989.

MacDonald, M., *Brahms* (The Master Musicians), London, Dent, 1990.

Correspondence

Brahms Briefwechsel, Vol XVII (New Series): Muller, H., and Hofmann, R., *Brahms in Briefwechsel mit Herzog George II. von Sachsen-Meiningen und Helene Freifrau von Heldburg*, Tutzing, Schneider, 1991.

Index